W9-AZJ-172

# WORLD BOOM AHEAD

**Why Business and Consumers Will Prosper**

*With best wishes.*

*— Knight Kiplinger*

## Knight Kiplinger

Kiplinger Books, Washington, D.C.

**Published by**
**The Kiplinger Washington Editors, Inc.**
**1729 H Street, N.W.**
**Washington, DC 20006**

Kiplinger publishes books and videos on a wide variety of personal-finance and business-management subjects. Check our Web site (www.kiplinger.com) for a complete list of titles, additional information and excerpts. Or write:

Cindy Greene
Kiplinger Books & Tapes
1729 H Street, NW
Washington, DC 20006
email: cgreene@kiplinger.com

To order, call 800-280-7165; for information about volume discounts, call 202-887-6431

*Library of Congress Cataloging-in-Publication Data*

Kiplinger, Knight A.
    World boom ahead : why business and consumers will prosper /
Knight Kiplinger. -- [Rev. ed.]
        p.   cm.
    Includes index.
    ISBN 0-938721-70-4 (paperback)
    1. Economic forecasting.    2. Business forecasting.    3. Twenty
-first century--Forecasts.    I. Title.
HB3730.K517  1999
338.5'42--dc21                                                    99-27769
                                                                      CIP

This publication is intended to provide guidance in regard to the subject matter covered. It is sold with the understanding that the author and publisher are not herein engaged in rendering legal, accounting, tax or other professional services. If such services are required, professional assistance should be sought.

First edition. Printed in the United States of America.
9  8  7  6  5  4  3  2  1

# Acknowledgments

book of this breadth could not have been researched, reported and written by one author working alone. By the time I finished the last chapter, events would have overtaken the forecasts I had written a year or two earlier.

So, much of the reporting and analysis came from my colleagues at Kiplinger, who cover these subjects for our weekly and biweekly reports on the business outlook. Their input was the starting point for my writing, and near the end of the job, they critiqued, challenged and helped me refine my forecasts. My use of the first-person plural—the editorial "we"—is not an author's false modesty. It reflects the reality of our collegial reporting and forecasting process.

I tip my hat with great respect to the Kiplinger colleagues who assisted me on the first edition of *World Boom Ahead*: our longtime executive editor Jack Kiesner, who retired in mid '99; editorial manager and foreign affairs editor Gary Matthews, who has since returned to U.S. diplomatic service in Bosnia; chief of research Annemarie Albaugh; editors Gini Barazia, Peter Blank, Melissa Bristow, Marty Chase, Martha Craver, Ken Dalecki, Mike Doan, Bill Eby, John Fogarty, Jerry Idaszak, Steve Ivins, Elizabeth Kelleher, Joan Pryde, and Mark Sfiligoj; and research reporters Romaine Bostick, Greg Luberecki, Gerry Moore, Jenny Morrison, and Amy Roberts. I am especially indebted to David Koenig, a former Kiplinger editor, for his timely and diligent help in organizing the staff's work into some well-focused drafts.

Austin Kiplinger—my father, colleague and editor emeritus of our organization—provided astute judgment, inspiration and (most appreciated of all) editorial supervision of the weekly *Kiplinger Letter* during the final months of my writing and revision.

Every author needs a tough and caring editor, and I was very fortunate to have one in David Harrison, the director of Kiplinger Books. With candor and good humor, he kept the project on schedule, revived my spirits when they flagged, and made countless improvements in the content and presentation of my ideas. My executive assistant, Emily Melton, was the best scheduler, facilitator, gatekeeper and friend an author could have. Several other Kiplinger staffers contributed valuable assistance: Rosemary Beales Neff fine-tuned the manuscript; Daniel Kohan provided a clean design; Dianne Olsufka proofread the galleys; and Don Fragale smoothed the book's course through production and printing.

I reserve my deepest gratitude and affection for my family—my wife, Ann, my son, Brigham, my daughters, Sutton and Daphne—who gracefully endured Dad's preoccupation, distraction and occasional irascibility while he was working at home on "the book." (Although our beloved Kerry Blue terrier, Henry, cannot read this acknowledgment, I hope he can sense my gratitude for his comforting presence, lying nearby while I banged on the keyboard, paced back and forth and struggled for the right words.)

Finally, I want to acknowledge the contributions of our many editorial sources—the men and women in business, government, academe and research who give us the benefit of their judgment every week for our *Kiplinger Letters*. Some of our best sources are our subscribers, who suggest story ideas and contribute to our knowledge of their fields. It is they who are the real experts on what lies ahead. We journalists are simply the communicators of their knowledge, experience and foresight.

**K.A.K.**

# Introduction to the 1999 Edition

T he world is at the end of an amazing decade of political and economic turmoil, which is also the close of the most remarkable century in world history, which is also the end of a millennium. Democracy is on the ascendance. In most nations, accelerating economic openness is laying the groundwork for higher growth in the decades ahead. And the nation leading the way is the United States, a situation that was not assumed by most people a decade ago.

Now the big question is: Will these positive trends continue, or does the world face a very different future? That's the subject of this book, a revised edition of a work completed in the summer of 1998 and published that fall. It's a very broad treatment of many complex subjects. It is intended to give people in management a quick, easy distillation of what lies ahead in technology, population, world markets, government policy, business management, key industries and much more.

## CREDIBILITY IN FORECASTING

The plausibility of a long-range forecast is too often colored by ephemeral conditions of the present moment and recent past. Forecasts that don't square with the prevailing public mood, whether optimistic or pessimistic, tend to be met with scepticism.

At the Kiplinger organization, we have an uncanny knack for issuing forecasts that—however accurate they later turn out to be—are out of sync with public sentiment at the time they are published. We showed this knack once again in the fall of 1998, with the publication of the first edition of *World Boom Ahead*.

As it arrived at book stores, the U.S. stock market was in the throes of a sharp decline that would depress the Dow Jones Industrial Average by more than 19%, from a peak of 9337 in July to 7539 in September. A drop of this magnitude—twice the decline of a mere "correction"—is normally defined as a bear market. Amid panic selling, many market analysts predicted a lengthy bottom before prices recovered. Growing concern about the condition of overseas markets compounded public anxiety. Over the previous few months, the Russian economy had gone into a free-fall, and its government virtually defaulted on its debts. Then Brazil teetered on the edge of collapse. The rescue resources of the International Monetary Fund were being rapidly depleted. The ailing economies of Asia were showing few signs of recovery from the currency and stock collapses that began a year earlier. More than half the world was in recession.

While the U.S. economy continued to grow, America's struggling trade partners weren't able to buy as many U.S. exports as before. After more than a dozen years of double-digit growth, total U.S. exports of goods and services would register an annual decline of about 2%. There was talk of a U.S. recession in 1999, as weak global markets finally took their toll on our domestic economy.

All in all, this was not a propitious moment to release a book entitled *World Boom Ahead*. The book's jacket copy acknowledged that the thesis suffered from a credibility problem. "After seven years of economic expansion and soaring stock prices, some dark clouds are forming on the horizon. Do they presage a severe storm or just a passing shower?" My answer: "a passing shower," probably a brief period of slow global growth, followed by a long trend of robust expansion. But the public mood remained very wary. I was clearly on the defensive. At the start of an interview on a radio program, the host asked, only half in jest, "World *boom* ahead? Don't you mean world *doom* ahead?"

## FROM GLOOM TO EUPHORIA

But over the following 12 months, the pendulum of public opinion began a slow swing back toward a higher level of confidence in the future. The major U.S. stock indexes arrested their slide, and began a wild ride that took the Dow over 11,000 in the spring of '99, with stock prices racing far ahead of likely growth in corporate earnings. The American people—exhilarated by low unemployment and strong gains in personal income, stock prices and home values—maintained a spending spree fueled in part by heavy borrowing.

While the economies of emerging markets weren't improving very rapidly, neither were they getting worse. Crises in Russia and Brazil didn't spread worldwide and exhaust the resources of the IMF. Investors began to return cautiously to the stock markets of developing nations, bringing large gains to emerging-market equity indexes. All in all, it looked as if the U.S.—indeed, the whole world—had dodged the bullet of a broad economic collapse.

The odds are good that, early in the year 2000, the U.S. economy will set a record for the longest expansion in our nation's history— longer than the peacetime record of continuous growth between 1982 and 1990, and longer even than the expansion of '61 through '69, when high military spending, federal social spending and consumer demand combined into a powerful stimulus.

Once again there is talk of "The New Economy"—a perpetual-growth machine that defies traditional business cycles. This theory first surfaced in '97, went dormant during the emerging-market crises of '97-'98, and resurfaced during the euphoria of surging stock indexes, productivity gains and consumer spending in 1999.

But my colleagues and I at *The Kiplinger Letter* remain skeptical. Market excesses—labor shortages, capital crunches, euphoric specula-tion in tech stocks, excess capacity, import competition—will continue to cause occasional corrections and economic downturns. After a hot decade, the U.S. economy will need to catch its breath, as will Europe. Meanwhile, Japan and the rest of Asia will slowly get back on their feet and resume strong growth, They will once again help the U.S. bear the burden of stimulating global growth, and in the process, they will create better overseas markets for American goods and services.

The "world boom ahead" foreseen in this book is much more than the expansionary phase of any one nation or region. It will be a long, broad sweep of gradually accelerating global growth, stimulated by a convergence of new technology, growing political and economic free-dom, investment in less-developed nations, more-open trade, the rising status of women, slowing population growth and many other trends.

## FRESHENING THE FORECASTS

Writing a book of forecasts is like trying to hit a moving target. Parts of it will be outdated soon after publication as new developments occur. These new developments—in world affairs, technology, business conditions, whatever—can make the forecaster look either foresighted or foolish. In reviewing a first edition for possible revisions, the author is torn between two impulses: either changing nothing, to highlight both his earlier prescience and his (hopefully few) miscalls, or updating everything that has changed in the time since first publication.

I have chosen a middle ground, which I hope is useful to you the readers of this new edition of *World Boom Ahead*. I have tried to take note of significant new developments, but only if they materially affect the outlook in a certain area. I have not attempted to re-report every subject, which would be a Herculean effort in a book as broad as this is. As a result, some facts may be out of date, some predicted events may have already occurred as forecast, and some may have turned out differently.

Who knows what the future holds for us, what sudden crisis or startling scientific breakthrough will drastically change the course of history? Certainly not I. As this book goes to press in the middle of 1999, its thesis could be seriously undermined by any number of life-changing developments. I've tried to anticipate as many as possible and assess their likelihood, but forecasting is a fragile art, not a science.

### ASSESSING LIKELIHOOD

Subscribers to *The Kiplinger Letter* don't want wishy-washy analysis of all the things that might happen; they want our clear, informed judgment on the most likely outcome. This book is full of such judgments and, in most cases, the reasons why we reached those conclusions.

The Kiplinger mission is to help managers with their decision-making. The foundation of our method is a combination of current reporting and historical analysis. Current reporting helps us with the task of short-run predictions. Historical analysis helps us with the task of projecting long-term trends.

"Real-time" forecasting—based on constant, fresh interviews with management decisionmakers—gives us an earlier alert of what lies ahead than if we waited for the release of statistical reports and "leading indicators," which are actually snapshots of recently past events.

This is the way three generations of our staff have worked since our organization was founded in 1920 by my grandfather, W. M. Kiplinger, a former Associated Press reporter who specialized in the then-unfashionable beat of economics.

The Kiplinger publications, then and now, have always been a query service, helping our readers with their special information and forecasting needs. I look forward to hearing from you about any questions or comments you may have about the judgments in this book.

My best wishes to you for success and satisfaction in the exciting and challenging years ahead.

**Knight A. Kiplinger**
**July 28, 1999**

# CHAPTER 1

# The Big Picture

O n the eve of the 21st century, the world stands on the threshold of a long, strong surge in economic growth and living standards, unprecedented in world history. Over the next few decades, this boom will bring several billion more people—now toiling in marginal local economies—into a fully integrated world marketplace. They will constitute an immense new global middle class with vast purchasing power, and they will be both tough competitors and avid customers of the advanced nations.

This global expansion will be driven by technology—more specifically, by the dispersal of late-20th-century technology to the far corners of the earth, sharply lifting the productivity (output per hour worked) of the world's labor force. This, in turn, will boost the real incomes of hundreds of millions of workers, enabling them to afford more of the goods and services of their own country and other nations. These products will flow ever more freely as trade barriers gradually decline worldwide.

The bywords of the 21st century will be the 3 Ds: *dispersal* (of technology and production), *decentralization* (of leadership in world affairs and business) and *democratization* (of information, political authority and ownership of capital). The result will be a powerful convergence in economic performance worldwide. Economic success will be more broadly shared by more people in more nations than ever before.

The nations will be knitted together in near-seamless webs of telecommunications, trade in goods and services, and instant flows of capital. This is already happening, but by comparison with the vastly more open markets of 2020, today's world economy is a labyrinth of trade barriers, currency controls and restraints on foreign investment.

This entire process—technology dispersal, rising real incomes, freer world trade—will bring about more fundamental change in the way people live than has occurred in the previous several hundred years.

## GRADATIONS OF GAIN

The speed and degree of change will be most startling in today's less advanced nations. These nations will also be the greatest beneficiaries of the world boom ahead, experiencing a doubling of their share of annual world production over the next 20 years. The wealthiest nations, with only 15% of the world's population, will also enjoy rising incomes and living standards, even as their share of the world's output steadily declines from its dominating level of 80% today.

As a group, the wealthiest nations will see only modest improvement in their late-20th-century growth rates. Their scientists, entrepreneurs, giant transnational corporations and surplus capital will be the engines of growth in the world boom ahead. But their domestic economies—being so big and rich already—won't achieve rates of growth that anyone would mistake for a boom. The United States, as the most open, scientifically creative and economically free large nation, will set the pace for the advanced economies.

If the advanced nations won't be booming, who will be? The primary beneficiaries of the world boom ahead will be today's least affluent nations—in Asia, Latin America and Africa. But not all of them . . . only those whose leaders choose to create and maintain economic systems hospitable to both home-grown entrepreneurship and foreign investment. Their fortunate citizens will enjoy the greatest percentage rise in their living standards, albeit from very low levels today.

The citizens of the world's most advanced nations—the United States, Japan, the European Union and a few others—will have to cope with tough competition from low-wage workers in the less developed nations. This competition will intensify over time as workers benefit from modern education, declining trade barriers, and rising productivity from the dispersal of capital and manufacturing technology to all lands.

## MEETING THE CHALLENGE OF NEW COMPETITION

This would be bad news for the advanced nations were it not for the fact—often overlooked—that capable producers soon become capable consumers. Fierce competition from newly industrialized nations has not caused any decline in absolute living standards in the advanced world over the past two decades, and it won't in the future.

The labor forces of the richest nations will—out of sheer necessity—upgrade their education and skills, building on their big leads in science and technology to stay one step ahead of rivals overseas. As they always have, the advanced nations will continually create new, high-tech products and services to replace those that other nations can make at a lower cost.

Even though global competition will restrain income growth in many advanced nations, pay hikes will continue to exceed inflation over the long run, due to productivity gains. The purchasing power—and therefore living standards—of the advanced nations will get a boost from stable prices and improving quality of countless consumer goods, especially imports from low-wage nations. In many categories, especially apparel, electronic devices and some other consumer goods, prices will actually decline over time, either nominally, adjusted for inflation or both.

Today's wealthy nations will sustain their growth by aggressively seeking new, larger markets abroad. The United States will look far beyond its own, rich consumer market of 270 million people to the other 95% of the world's population—5.7 billion potential customers. Today the vast majority of these people are too poor to afford imported goods, and those who can are often denied the opportunity by trade barriers their governments erect to protect inefficient domestic industries. But this will change dramatically in the decades ahead.

## THE URGE TO MERGE

The world economy will be increasingly dominated by a new kind of business enterprise—the transnational corporation, combining several multinational firms of various national origins under one corporate umbrella. Multinationals already account for one-fifth of all global manufacturing, and their share will continually rise. Transnational giants will move into the power vacuum created by the waning ability of governments to control their economies—and their nations' futures—in a global economy. More of these companies will be "virtual corporations" that contract for most or all of their manufacturing from independent suppliers, while employing only a small cadre of executives and creative employees in the conception, design and marketing of new products. They will be increasingly free to do their manufacturing anywhere in the world, moving wherever suppliers offer them the best quality at the lowest price.

The role of small and medium-size enterprises will be to supply multinational companies with ideas, inventions, technology, raw materials, components, full assemblies and business services. Closely held companies will grow to a certain size, go public, catch the attention of bigger companies in their field, and then willingly submit to acquisition.

## TECHNOLOGY AT THE FOREFRONT

Advances in technology will be the driving force of this world economic boom, as they always have been. Human ingenuity will find new ways to make life more comfortable and interesting for its inhabitants. The technology of every field—whether in communications, energy, entertainment, agriculture, medicine, transportation or education—will rise in performance and decline in cost through mass production and worldwide dissemination.

The dominant technologies of the coming century will be microelectronics, biotechnology, telecommunications and information technology. The biological sciences will be the brightest stars. The payoff from years of scientific research and investment in genetics is almost here, and it will change everyday life just as much as—perhaps even more than—the revolutions in telecommunications and computers.

## UNBELIEVABLE PRIVATE FORTUNES

The first few decades of the coming century will be richer in opportunity for entrepreneurs than ever before. More enormous fortunes will be created by more entrepreneurs and financiers on every continent than at any time in world history. And most of these new fortunes of breathtaking magnitude will end up being used for human betterment, through charitable giving. The new generation of global philanthropists—modern-day Carnegies, Rockefellers and Fords—will make a deep impact on education, medical research, public health, the arts and humanities, and population control.

Due to pressure on wages worldwide, owners will fare better than employees, and millions of employees all over the world will recognize this. Whether by becoming their own bosses or by investing in the stock of their employers, more workers will begin to think and act like capitalists. Small-business start-ups and stock ownership by average citizens will soar on all continents. America's stock markets, led by powerful, U.S.-based transnational businesses, will continue to achieve their historical levels of total return, and probably a little more. Stock markets in many other nations, both developing and advanced, will generate higher average returns than the U.S. markets, but with much more volatility.

# The Meaning of a 'Boom'

The word "boom" usually refers to a relatively short period of brisk economic growth. A boom typically lasts a couple of years or less, and it's often followed by a bust—not just lower growth, but an actual contraction in output—because spikes of superheated growth usually sow the seeds of their own demise.

But that isn't how we're using the term "boom." The world boom that we foresee will be a long, strong but gradual expansion, in which the world's annual growth rate moves to a substantially higher, sustainable plateau. There will be periods in which output marks time, barely advancing, and even periods in which total output declines for a time. But we do not foresee any slump as deep or long-lasting as the Great Depression or the oil-induced global downturn of the '70s. In general, globalization of trade and capital flows will be a force for shorter, less severe global recessions.

"Boom" is a relative term. One nation's boom could be another's bad year, depending on what each is accustomed to. The United States, the world's largest economy, is used to growth averaging between 2% and 3% a year. So a growth spurt—say, 7% in calendar 1984 or 5% in the first quarter of 1998—could be considered a boom in this country. But that rate of growth would be an off year in a rapidly developing nation like Singapore or China, which have been routinely achieving double-digit or high-single-digit growth year after year.

Our forecast of a world boom means just that—accelerating growth worldwide. It doesn't mean that the advanced world will experience boom levels of growth for a long period of time, even by their own modest standards. In North America, Europe and Japan, absolute levels of productivity, labor-force participation, resource utilization and infrastructure development are already so high that there isn't room for a big jump on the order of two additional percentage points, which would be a near-doubling of the long-term growth trend.

Instead, these nations will see their long-term growth move only modestly higher than in the past 20 years. In the U.S., productivity gains from better education and higher automation will probably boost growth to an average level approaching 3%, a significant improvement over the mid 2% range of recent years. In the advanced nations, especially the U.S., the higher growth averages will likely be achieved by smoothing out the extreme highs and lows and beefing up the middle range, with longer expansions of moderate growth, interrupted by fewer severe recessions.

The less-developed nations will be growing at true boom levels, probably tripling their anemic rates of growth in this century. All of their elements of growth—labor supply, capital, natural resources, technology, education—will be trending sharply upward. Liberalization of world trade will create strong demand for their production. Most significantly, governmental conditions will be conducive to strong growth. Public sectors will be shrinking due to privatization, lower tax burdens, diminishing market regulation, and openness to foreign goods and capital.

# The 20th-Century Growth Record

The legacy of the 20th century is generally a good one in terms of economic growth and improvement in living standards—probably higher than in any previous century. But given the remarkable scientific inventions and technological developments that have occurred, economic growth could have been—*should* have been—much stronger.

Too often, human ingenuity was trumped by human folly. The benefits of science and free-market economics were often thwarted by governmental ineptitude, greed and hostility toward neighboring nations. Improvement in the material well-being of most of the world's people in this century has been tragically stunted by colonialism, communism, fascism, two devastating world wars, local dictatorships of the right and left, countless civil wars and regional conflicts, persistent barriers to the free flow of goods and capital, inadequate education, and the systematic wasting of the talents of more than half the world's population, its women.

Estimates of total world production are imprecise, given vast differences in the quality of statistics and methods of measuring output from nation to nation. And the further back you go in time, the harder it is to reconstruct what was really happening. But economic historians make educated guesses, and it's likely that output in this century has increased, on average, about 1% a year. The developed nations achieved about twice that rate, but the less-developed nations lagged far behind until the last 25 years, when their growth surpassed that of the advanced nations.

During a century of 1% average annual global growth were periods (such as the 1920s, '40s and '50s) when various nations and whole continents achieved boom levels of growth. But there were also periods (the '30s, '40s, '70s and early '80s) in which most of the world experienced a painful erosion of living standards. Over the past quarter-century, world growth trended up to about 2.5% a year on average, but there were sharp variations among continents and nations. The Soviet Union and its Eastern European satellites experienced an erosion of output and living standards. So did the highly populous region of sub-Saharan Africa, with its 700 million citizens.

## 21ST-CENTURY GROWTH WILL DOUBLE OR TRIPLE

If a boom can be reasonably defined as a doubling of growth, then our idea of a world economic boom would be a whole century of global growth averaging at least 2% a year, twice the growth of the century now coming to a close. The odds are quite good, however, that the record of the next century will be much better than this, building on the higher performance of the past quarter-century and hitting a stride of about 3% a year on average.

This is consistent with recent World Bank forecasts of a 3% average annual growth rate in the global economy between now and 2020, assuming a continuation of trade liberalization. World Bank economists project a continuation of recent growth trends (about 2.5%) for the highest-income nations and, for developing nations, average rates ranging from 4% per year for sub-Saharan Africa to 7% for Asia (excluding Japan). Among the high-income nations, we believe that only the United States will match the global average of 3%, while Western Europe and Japan will fall a little short.

A doubling or tripling of 20th-century growth is not a pie-in-the-sky fantasy. It's eminently doable because the political and economic ideologies that stunted growth through most of this century are discredited and in decline, freeing human creativity and ambition to accomplish remarkable things.

# How the U.S. Will Fare

The United States will retain its current position as the world's economic, technological and political leader throughout most of the next century. It will do this by maintaining its preeminence in scientific research, its flexible military might and its uniquely successful economic-development model, which will be emulated and adapted by more nations around the globe. It will also enjoy the highest rate of population growth among the advanced nations—slightly less than 1% a year, coming from a combination of fertility slightly above the population-replacement level and immigration of more than one million newcomers each year. These immigrants, like those before them, will ease U.S. labor shortages, in both unskilled and high-tech jobs, and contribute to the constant revitalizing of American society.

## FACING UP TO ITS PROBLEMS

The U.S. has done a good job of putting its economic house in order over the past 15 years, with deregulation of markets, declining government budget deficits, stable tax burdens and falling trade barriers. But still to be dealt with are looming problems in social security and medicare. Solutions are not difficult to craft in an economic sense, but they will require some straight talk and courage on the part of Congress.

As much progress as America has made economically, it has a lot of unfinished business in healing its social ills—crime, falling educational performance, divorce, teen pregnancy, out-of-wedlock births in all income levels and races, drug addiction, strained race relations, resistance to assimilation of immigrants, declining spiritual health of youths, and other issues. Fortunately, many of these problems appear to be in the early stages of turnaround, and there are reasons to believe that improvement will continue.

## CHANGING SHARES OF WORLD OUTPUT

Today the United States, with less than 5% of the world's population, accounts for an amazing 22% of its total annual output. That share will slowly but steadily diminish throughout the next century. This shouldn't cause any alarm, hand wringing or self-doubt, because in absolute terms—growth in real personal income and standard of living—the U.S. will keep making solid progress.

At the end of World War II, the United States was the only victorious nation whose territory wasn't part of the battleground, whose industrial infrastructure wasn't badly damaged, and whose ranks of future leaders weren't decimated. In the first few years after the war, with the economies of Europe and Japan in ruins, the U.S. accounted for a stunning 45% of total world production. It was inevitable and natural that this share would decline, as the rest of the world recovered, with great help from the U.S. But contrary to popular mythology, the long decline of America's world market share bottomed out some 35 years ago, in the early '60s, and there has been no significant decline since then. The U.S. share of aggregate world Gross Domestic Product (GDP) held firm even as Asia's production soared. Asia's rising world market share comes not at the expense of America's, but from the declining shares of Europe, the Soviet bloc and Latin America.

But now the U.S. is poised for a resumption, after 35 years, of a gradual decline in its world market share, in which it will be joined by the other advanced nations. And this decline, like the one after World War II, will be natural, inevitable and beneficial for the world and for the U.S., because it will result from an enlargement of the entire global economy. In total output, the United States will continue to be the world's largest economy for the next ten or 15 years. It will eventually be eclipsed in annual GDP (but not in wealth or per-capita output) by China, whose rate of growth will run triple that of the U.S. over most of the next few decades, before cooling off to a more moderate level at mid century.

## PROSPERITY AMID RELATIVE DECLINE

America's relative decline shouldn't be mistaken for an absolute decline in any measure of American success—the living standards and wealth of its citizens or the competitiveness and profitability of its businesses. All of these will continue to grow. The U.S. will experience the seeming paradox of rising real prosperity amid relative decline. America's increasing well-being will come about not despite the growing economic power of the poorer nations, but because of it. The U.S. is the most open and international nation, and it is also the world's leading exporter. So it has the most to gain from the soaring purchasing power of less-affluent nations. It will actually benefit from earning a progressively narrower slice of a vastly larger pie. That ever-skinnier slice—a shrinking percentage of surging world output—will be much bigger in actual size than America's fatter slice of today's world economy.

# Labeling the Century Ahead

We've never cared for the game of naming centuries after particular nations. While many people hasten to tag this century "the American Century," we prefer to call it "the Atlantic Century," recognizing the gradual passage of leadership from Europe to the U.S. But a better label would be "the Democracy Century," in honor of the triumph of self-determination over colonialism, fascism and communism. Better still, it could be called "the Technology Century," because it has seen more world-changing inventions than any previous 100-year span.

## ASCENDANT ASIA

Acknowledging the risk of labeling a century before it even begins, we will make a stab at anticipating how the next one will be known to historians 100 years from now, at the dawn of the year 2100. Those partial to regional labels shouldn't be surprised if the 21st century comes to be called "the Asian Century," reflecting the surging economic power of that continent.

It will take the nations of Asia a few years to recover fully from their current woes, but recover they will, and they will emerge more open, democratic and economically vital for having undergone the trauma of this shakeout. In fact, the ongoing slump has accelerated the long-delayed restructuring of Japan and South Korea. In a few years Asia will resume a high level of growth. The Asian continent, including India, will undoubtedly be the star region of the next century. If one nation's name had to be conferred, ill-advisedly, in advance, "the Chinese Century" would be the best bet, because China will be the world's largest economy in 15 years or so, as well as a political and military superpower.

But a better regional label for the next 100 years would be "the Pacific Century." Why? Because of the likelihood that one non-Asian, but thoroughly Pacific, nation will continue to be an extremely powerful force, economically, militarily and technologically. That nation is the United States, whose economy will increasingly be tied by trade and investment to the rapid growth of Asia.

### A CENTURY FOR ALL PEOPLES

But we continue to stand by our preference for labels that capture the essence of deep-seated, fundamental change in the worldwide human condition. The world boom ahead will be the product not of one nation or one continent, but of the talents of all peoples in all nations. So we believe—and hope—that historians in 2100 will see the appropriateness of labels like "the Century of Free Markets" or "the Age of Convergence." Such titles would reflect how the advanced and developing nations grew together in political and economic freedom, rates of growth, income, living standards and technological leadership. In the course of this book, we'll give you plenty of reasons why this will come to pass.

# 50 Years of Amazing Change

A few decades from now, our daily lives will be as fundamentally different from today as our present lifestyles are from the world of the late '40s and early '50s. But the changes will be gradual, building on technologies and social changes already under way.

Five decades ago, many of the aspects of our lives today would have seemed to most Americans like science fiction. Imagine the incredulity that would have met a prediction of cheap, powerful per-sonal computers in the home, or instant worldwide communication on the Internet, or pocket-size wireless telephones capable of calling any-where on earth. Or organ transplants and artificial hearts. Or in vitro fertilization of human eggs, with embryo transplantation to a surrogate mother. Or space research stations, supersonic jetliners and 160-mph bullet trains. Or a pill that prevents pregnancy. Or automated factories creating many different products on the same assembly line, with a single operator changing the mix. Or a choice of several hundred TV channels on large-screen color TV sets. Or low-cost, online trading of stocks from your own desk. Or the repair of genetic defects in plants, animals and humans. Or the ability to exactly replicate any living thing.

Back in 1950, only the richest 9% of American households, living in a few urban areas, owned a television set, on which they could receive three or four channels. A 12-inch, black-and-white model cost about 13% of the average family's entire income for the year—equivalent to about $5,200 today, on an average family income of about $40,000.

Imagine the disbelief you'd have encountered in 1950 if you had predicted that, by 1998, nearly 100% of all American households would own at least one color TV, priced at less than 1% of average annual income, on which they could watch hundreds of different programs, including events happening at this very moment anywhere in the world.

But even with all the changes we've seen in the past several decades, it's surprising how many things haven't changed much. Our cars still run on the same fuel that propelled them in the 1890s. Our homes are still built by workers on site, mostly out of pieces of wood. We still pay for a lot of daily expenses with paper money and paper checks given at the point of sale, and even if we charge our purchases, we pay the monthly bill with a paper check we send in the mail. Our children still learn by listening to a teacher explain things in a classroom. Most of us still go to work each day in offices, and the vast majority of our purchases are made in stores. We still get most of our health care—including routine monitoring—by visiting medical professionals at their place of business. We still use wired telephones for most of our com-munication.

But many of these daily activities, and countless others, will be changing in the years ahead, in more and varied ways than we can imagine today. A few decades from now, our children's children will pester us for stories of what the world was like when we carried paper money in leather wallets; steered our own cars on the highways (occa-sionally colliding with other cars); and had to drive to and from a "video store" (twice) to rent and return movies recorded on a grainy videotape. All these now-familiar activities will seem as peculiar to children in 2030 as rotary-dial phones, record players, black-and-white TVs and manual typewriters seem to our kids today.

# A Technology Sampler

In this book we'll tell you about a lot of remarkable changes in the decades ahead. Some you'll like the sound of, and others will trouble you. We'll try to present them without wishful thinking or judgment as to their desirability, but we will try to hint at the impact they will have on American life and business. Here's a brief sampling of some of the technological changes ahead:

**Medicine.** "Germline" gene therapy, with genetic changes in sperm and eggs that will pass to succeeding generations forever. "Designer animals," genetically engineered to have organs and tissues that can be transplanted to humans. Cancer therapies that will trick the cancerous cells into dying off fast. Therapies to slow the aging process, by tricking cells into decaying more slowly. Gene therapies that will prevent most inherited diseases, stimulate insulin production, and reduce the incidence of conditions like obesity and baldness. Vaccines for AIDS and herpes. Edible vaccines, designed into common foods, for malaria, hepatitis, cholera and other diseases. Patenting of genetic material, triggering an endless debate over "genetic colonialism" by biotech firms seeking to own unusual substances found in the plants and animals of developing nations.

**Agriculture.** Genetically engineered grains and produce, resistant to drought, cold, disease and pests, requiring less water and fertilizer. Biomass susbstituting for wood pulp in newsprint. Hydroponic (soilless) production of vegetables. A boom in low-fat, low-cholesterol, high-fiber foods.

**New materials.** Plastics that conduct electricity, for use in semiconductors and batteries. Plastic ball bearings, aircraft fuselages, car bodies, bridges, freeway pylons and rebar for reinforced concrete. Ceramic auto engines. Ceramics that conduct electricity, for use in generators. Plastics made from biomass rather than petrochemicals.

**Energy.** Fuel and fast-charging batteries for generating and storing electricity at home and in cars. Superconductivity, with stunning increases in the efficiency of electric-power generation and transmission. Photovoltaic panels that will be increasingly cheap, large and powerful. Broader use of gasolines blended with alcohol (from cheap biomass, not corn) and diesel fuels blended with vegetable oils.

**Transportation.** Low-polluting, high-efficiency (80 mpg) hybrid cars, typically running with both a small gasoline engine and an electric motor. High-speed conventional and magnetic-levitation trains. Super-wide-bodied jets carrying 600 passengers on trans-Pacific routes. New supersonic airliners. Smart highways and cars, with hands-free driving and collision-avoidance systems. Global positioning for navigating private cars to their destinations.

**Computers and software.** Faster chip speeds (but not increasing at the rate of recent years). Semiconductors whose digital switches are controlled by beams of light rather than electrons. Artificial intelligence approaching the speed and versatility of the human brain. The embedding of microprocessor controllers in virtually every mechanical device. Virtual-reality programs and graphics that simulate every imaginable human experience and sensation. "Knowbots" — intelligent personal-assistant software that will keep track of your activities, anticipate your needs and execute simple tasks of many kinds. Voice-recognition programs that will take dictation flawlessly and produce written transcriptions of rapid speech by any person in any accent. Simultaneous-translation software, coupled with synthetic-voice programs, enabling tourists and business people to converse in real time on the Internet with anyone in any land, verbally or in writing. PCs that are much easier to learn and use than today's. Devices to give new capabilities to disabled people.

**Telecommunications.** Totally global satellite telephones, enabling you to talk with anyone anywhere on earth, from the Sahara to Antarctica. Lightning-fast Internet access speed, via a variety of competing media—phone lines, cable-TV modems, broadcast TV, satellite, even the electric-power service to your home. "Instant-on" Internet connections, with graphically elaborate Web pages appearing faster than you can flip the pages of a magazine. Delivery of every kind of information and entertainment on whatever kind of "information appliance" you prefer, from a smart phone to your HDTV or PC. Flat, bright video screens the size of your living room wall. Vast databases from which, for a small fee, you can download and record, on reusable CDs, any music, literature, movie, art or TV program ever made, in any language.

Living in the United States, we can easily forget that our current lifestyles—with cell phones, infertility therapies, satellite dishes, personal computers and Internet shopping—seem unbelievably futuristic to most of the world's people. Their dreams are of a basic middle-class lifestyle that most Americans achieved a generation or two ago—good nutrition, education for their kids, homeownership, an inexpensive car, a few labor-saving appliances in the home. The economic challenge of the next century will be to make our comfortable lives of today the norm for the rest of the world. And this will happen.

# Alternative Scenarios

In arriving at our judgment of accelerating growth in the decades ahead, we carefully considered, analyzed and finally set aside a variety of alternative scenarios. There are elements of plausibility in all of them, so any of them could happen. But we believe that they are much less likely than the vision we present in this book. Here are summaries of a few of today's leading anxieties about the world's future:

**Severe overcapacity and deflation:** The growth in world manufacturing capacity will be so great, especially in the developing nations, that even rising consumer demand cannot possibly keep up. This will lead to aggressive dumping of exports, price cutting, the raising of trade barriers, general deflation, shrinking output worldwide and declining real wages, especially in the advanced nations.

**"Hot money" chaos:** Uncontrollable flows of capital will surge in and out of world economies, especially emerging markets, destabilizing currencies and causing wild swings in production and living standards. Currency and stock speculation will run amok. A series of serious national and regional recessions will infect the entire global economy, causing worldwide slumps of long duration. The rescue resources of the advanced nations, funneled through the International Monetary Fund, will not be sufficient to shore up all the economies in need of help at one time.

**Burdensome aging populations:** About 15 or 20 years from now, the advanced nations, with their low or negative population growth (including even China by then), will be groaning under the social-service expenses of their aging populations. A mass of retirees will have to be supported by a proportionately smaller group of workers, pushing taxes up and diverting economic resources from investment to consumption. What's more, stock markets will decline as seniors cash out to cover their living expenses.

**The Malthusian nightmare:** Soaring populations in today's "Third World" will outstrip the world economy's capacity to support them with food, water, fuel and jobs. This will lead inexorably to resource depletion and soaring prices, famine, out-of-control urbanization, environmental degradation and attempted mass migrations of poor people into advanced nations, where they will be unwanted but sometimes needed to fill labor shortages.

**Four Horsemen of the Apocalypse:** The biblical scourges—famine, plague, conquest and war—will recur as they have throughout history, but in more-virulent forms. Populations will be decimated and living standards compromised by antibiotic-resistant bacterial and viral infections, some of them trans-species infections like AIDS. Raging nationalism, ethnic and racial conflict will be as devastating to life and material well-being as communism and fascism were in this century. New kinds of tyrannies will subjugate large portions of the globe. Warfare will be made all the more terrible by the use of nuclear, chemical and biological weapons.

The personal nightmares that come to us in our sleep are frightening precisely because they grow out of real issues in our lives. Likewise, the scenarios above are troubling to us precisely because aspects of them have already occurred—the lethal spread of AIDS across Africa, economic chaos in markets from Asia to Russia to Latin America, overcapacity and deflation in some industries, and genocide in the Balkans.

But for a variety of reasons that we will discuss throughout this book, none of these gloomy scenarios is as plausible as our vision of a steadily improving human condition.

# Sneak Previews of the 21st Century

I f you're wondering what new directions the world will take in the next century, you don't have to wait for the year 2000 to find out. The millennium jumped the gun. It burst from the starting gate more than two years early, in the summer of 1997. And in the following 12 months, the world was treated to an amazing array of startling developments—in technology, world affairs and business. These developments—a dizzying mix of the heartening and the scary, the troubling and the exhilarating—foreshadow several major trends of the next century.

They came in a rush, in week after week of news headlines, symbolizing the quickening pace of global transformation. Consider these recent occurrences, which in an earlier time would have constituted a whole decade of change, but now are crammed into one year:

**Near-collapse of Asian economies,** followed by an expensive international rescue, amid growing concern that it would engulf the whole world in recession.

**Western corporate invasion of Japan and South Korea** by U.S. and European multinationals buying assets at distress prices.

**Indian and Pakistani nuclear testing** and mounting belligerence.

**Transnational megamergers** of gigantic European and U.S. corporations.

**Rebirth of U.S. antitrust policy,** with suits against Microsoft, Intel and Lockheed Martin, and challenges to many more mergers.

**New drugs for breast cancer, AIDS and impotence.**

**Disabling of telecommunications** across America by the malfunction of one satellite, Galaxy IV, taking out pagers, credit card verification computers, police and hospital radios, commercial TV and public radio broadcasts.

**Signs of revolution in U.S. education,** in the form of vouchers, charter schools and serious public-school reform.

**Communications marvels** including direct-from-satellite phoning, high-definition TV and accelerating Internet speed.

**A new for-profit venture to decipher and patent the human genetic code,** in competition with the federal government's Human Genome Project.

**The specter of cybersabotage,** with mounting evidence that the U.S. computer infrastructure—systems controlling military defenses, commercial air traffic and telecommunications—is highly vulnerable to being crippled by hackers and foreign agents.

More than just news events that would fade from memory in a few weeks, these events were telling glimpses of the century just ahead. They brought startling messages about a new world that will be very different—for better or worse—from the world we know today. The deepening Asian crisis, for example, was a splash of cold water in the face of "New Economy" theorists and cheerleaders, giddy over the globalization of investing and their certainty of smooth, never-ending global growth. The Galaxy IV satellite problem reminded us of the world's growing dependence on technology, and how the compression of more capacity into smaller devices increases the degree of disruption from the disabling of a single satellite or breaking of one high-capacity transoceanic fiber-optic cable. Tensions on the Indian subcontinent underscored the reality that the post-Cold War world will not necessarily be a safer place to live.

# A Millennium of Progress

As forecasting journalists, we at the Kiplinger organization try to be calm, hard-headed and realistic in weighing the prospects for change. But we admit to one bias born of our study of history and our 75 years of experience in reporting the world economy: We cannot help but be impressed by humankind's long record of adapting to changing circumstances, finding solutions to problems and inventing devices to make life easier. We view history as a long, gradual improvement in the material well-being of the human species, and based on the record, we believe this trend will continue.

Like other trends, this improvement hasn't moved in a straight line. There have been descents of great depth and duration, such as the centuries-long social and economic devastation of sub-Saharan Africa by European, African and Arabic slave traders, by subsequent colonization, and by the corruption and incompetence of postcolonial regimes. In this century, the scourge of communism in Russia and China, as well as tight government economic control in India, caused a half-century of stagnation in living standards for more than half of the world's people. And we should soberly note that the global trade and investment liberalization now under way has a precedent—the late-19th-century movement that collapsed with the start of World War I and remained on hold until late in this century.

Nor are we sanguine that the passage of time brings any discernible improvement in human nature. The greatest genocides in history have occurred in the present century, in which the technology of modern killing was harnessed to the will of evil individuals, misguided ideologies, and racial, religious and ethnic hatred.

But even accounting for horrors and follies, the world has seen a broad, jagged upward trend in the human condition—in health, longevity, income, comfort, education, political self-determination and personal self-fulfillment. Shortly before his death in 1998, economist and business professor Julian Simon wrote, "The progress that humanity has experienced in the last two centuries has no precedent. Since 1750, every trend in material human welfare has shown accelerating improvement, almost everywhere. It is our happy fate to live in the midst of this most amazing time."

We agree, and we are convinced that the most dramatic improvement in world living standards lies just ahead. Most of the world's people did not participate in the bounty of the 20th century to nearly the degree that those in a few advanced nations did. This is about to change, as the developing nations move to center stage.

The world will discover that economic growth is not a zero-sum game, with one nation's gains coming at the expense of others. In the world boom ahead, there will be only gradations of winners.

The Chinese have a wonderfully understated curse: "May you live in *interesting* times," meaning treacherous times as fraught with danger as they are rich in opportunity. This will describe very well the early decades of the 21st century. There will be unlimited opportunities for nations, companies and individuals who can see the changes coming—in technology, demographics, business organization and marketing, and social attitudes. For those who cannot or will not accept the inevitability of fundamental, rapid change, the dangers will be overpowering. But if you prepare for them and adapt your way of thinking, working and viewing the world, you will prosper mightily.

# CHAPTER 2

# Major Global Trends

S everal broad economic, geopolitical and social trends, many of them already well under way, will characterize the coming century and, 100 years from now, will define its place in world history. This chapter presents a brief overview of the major themes:

## HIGHER GROWTH, GREATER WEALTH

Worldwide economic growth will probably average about 3% a year for most of the 21st century, a rate that, if sustained, would be three times the average annual rate of the century now coming to a close.

This will create more new personal wealth, worldwide, than in any previous period of history, including the era of industrialization in the late 19th and early 20th centuries. So many new centimillionaires and billionaires are already being created every year that *Forbes* magazine has to continually raise the qualifying hurdle on its list of the world's richest plutocrats.

And it's not just the high-tech boom that will make people rich. Take, for example, the story of Pleasant Rowland, a former school teacher and reporter, who in 1986 created a line of high-priced dolls depicting girls who lived in various eras in American history, sold not in stores but by catalog. As her American Girl dolls and accessories approached $300 million sales in 1998, Ms. Rowland sold her closely held Pleasant Company to Mattel for $700 million.

## DECLINING NATIONAL SOVEREIGNTY

The power of governments to shape their nations' destinies will steadily decline in the years ahead. The forces of this erosion will be many and varied: globalization of markets, the rise of transnational corporations, international environmental treaties, adjudication of trade disputes by the World Trade Organization (WTO), antitrust action across national boundaries, and demands for structural economic change from the International Monetary Fund (IMF) as a condition for massive financial aid in times of crisis.

With foreign trade growing as a share of virtually every country's GDP, a nation's well-being will increasingly be determined by economic conditions outside its control—especially the economic health of its trading partners. Recession in the economy of one nation will diminish demand for the products of its trading partners. And it will also increase the flow of excess production to other, more prosperous nations. So governments will cajole each other to bring their economic policies more in line with the needs of other nations, by raising or lowering interest rates, stimulating or curtailing domestic consumption, easing trade barriers, etc. This is the sort of pressure that the U.S. and other nations were exerting on Japan in mid 1998, when stimulation of its economy was perceived to be crucial to avoiding a deepening and spreading of the Asian slump.

In Western Europe, nations joining the European Community and the new euro currency group will surrender (sometimes grudgingly) a good deal of their political and fiscal sovereignty, in the hopes of stronger economic growth in the entire region. But even in regions where formal integration never happens, markets will be reaching similar ends on a piecemeal basis.

More and more trade disputes will go for settlement to the World Trade Organization, whose verdicts will ruffle feathers and affect commercial interests everywhere, but generally level the playing field for all exporters. Occasionally its rulings will conflict with a nation's initiatives on nontrade issues like environmental control, human rights and food safety. For example, the WTO ruled in 1998 that the U.S. was guilty of imposing nontariff trade barriers on shrimp from Thailand, Pakistan and Malaysia that was caught with nets that don't conform to American standards for protection of the endangered green sea turtle. The WTO also nixed an eight-year-long European Union (EU) ban on imports of U.S. beef raised with hormones, calling it an illegal trade barrier to protect European cattle interests. Similarly, it ruled against the EU on a banana-import policy that favored produce from European colonies.

The erosion of sovereignty will be especially pronounced in developing nations that seek large amounts of foreign capital, because those investors will often demand market reforms in exchange for their financial commitments. And if things go badly wrong, and governments need a bail-out from the IMF, they will find themselves forced to surrender even more control over their nation's fiscal, monetary and business management practices.

## GOVERNMENTS AS FACILITATORS OF GROWTH

Throughout the world, many governments don't just *regulate* businesses, they *own and manage* businesses—and generally rather badly. But in the years just ahead, most government-owned enterprises in most nations—telephone systems, factories, power plants, airlines—will be sold to private, profit-making interests in their own country and abroad. In the process, the public sectors of most nations will drastically shrink, employing fewer people and passing less of the GDP through their budgets. But this trend will meet with great resistance in many developing nations, where government-owned enterprises are sources of vast embezzled wealth for ruling elites. ("In Nigeria, corruption isn't part of government; it's the *object* of government," a Nigerian political scientist told *The Washington Post* after the death of dictator Sani Abacha in 1998.)

This doesn't mean that governments will cease to regulate business in countless ways; in fact, there will generally be more, not less, regulation of workplaces, environmental conduct, health care, etc. But the new, emerging role of government in most nations will be as a facilitator of economic development.

At their best, governments at all levels—from municipalities to national capitals, even supergovernments like the European Union—will try to smooth out conflicting standards, shorten approval processes and remove bottlenecks. They will do this not out of compassion for businesses, but to make their cities, states, nations and regions more attractive to business investment and job growth for their citizens.

The most successful governments won't try to fine-tune national economies that are too diverse and fast-changing to be tuned at all. They will see their role to be clearing the way for entrepreneurs to organize human resources, technology and capital to create wealth for everyone. Governments will do this by creating and maintaining environments of economic openness and opportunity, while making sure—through quality education and job-training programs—that their citizens are able to compete in the global economy.

## EMERGENCE OF A GLOBAL MIDDLE CLASS

The chief socioeconomic phenomenon of the 20th century has been the creation of large, high-producing, high-consuming middle classes in North America, Western Europe, Japan and a few other nations. In these societies, the very rich and the very poor make up relatively small portions of the population, and most people live in a middle range with a level of material comfort once enjoyed only by a few.

Most of the world's people still live far below the Western standard of middle class, at or just above subsistence level. But this is beginning to change very rapidly, and the trend will accelerate in the first few decades of the new century. To be middle-class means different things in different nations, of course. The statistical middle range of living standards in many other nations, even relatively advanced nations, would strike many Americans as Spartan.

Nonetheless, thanks at least in part to the ubiquity of American pop culture, the rest of the world is increasingly familiar with the American model of middle-class life, and it is that model to which it aspires. It includes, at a minimum, the ability to afford a multi-room apartment or ideally your own home, a car, a phone, labor-saving appliances, home entertainment devices, occasional meals outside the home, and occasional travel in your own land or maybe abroad.

Middle classes are born of political rights, universal education, entrepreneurial opportunity, strong job creation, and governmental policies that foster open markets and proconsumer policies, rather than the protection of entrenched business elites. As these conditions spread worldwide, so will the new global middle class.

Today's middle classes, with their vast purchasing power, have been instrumental in stimulating economic growth throughout the world by their appetite for imported products made by the mass of lower-income people elsewhere. Their support (willing or not) of economic globalization—foreign investment, technology transfer, free trade—will lead to the emergence of a new, vastly larger, truly global middle class. It is estimated that the middle-class population of Asia alone will reach one billion people in a few decades.

This powerful new middle class will, in turn, fuel growth in the advanced nations through its purchases of the more sophisticated products and services of the mature economies.

## CONVERGENCE OF LIVING STANDARDS

Great disparities in national income and living standards, which have typified the 19th and 20th centuries, will flatten out. In the process, the enormous share of total world GDP now enjoyed by the developed nations will decline, and that of the less-developed ones will rise by the same percentage.

According to the World Bank, the less-advanced nations, with the vast majority of the world's population, now account for less than 20% of aggregate Gross Domestic Product (GDP) , while the 23 most-developed ones (the U.S., Japan, Canada, Australia, New Zealand and the countries of Western Europe) account for more than 80%. Within that four-fifths, the U.S. and the nations of the European Union each account for more than 20% of aggregate world GDP and Japan for less than 10%.

The World Bank estimates that by 2020 the developed nations' share of annual world GDP will decline to 67%. The so-called "newly industrializing" nations—Korea, Singapore, and Taiwan—will see their share rise from 2.3% in 1992 to 3.8%. The "developing" nations (including most of Asia, Latin America, the Middle East, Africa, Eastern Europe and Russia) will nearly double their present share to a projected 30%. The stars within this group will be what the World Bank calls the "Big 5" economies of the Third World—China, India, Brazil, Indonesia and Russia (and some of its former republics and satellites). The Big 5's share will double to 16%. Malaysia, Thailand and the Philippines will also more than double their world market share, to 2.4%, up from less than 1% in 1992.

The standout region in the next century will continue to be Asia. The burst bubble of the "Asian miracle," and the painful restructuring that followed, will lay the groundwork for a stronger Asian future.

The U.S. economy is so much larger than any other nation's that it will remain the largest national economy for another decade or so. But eventually it will be surpassed in total annual output (but not per capita product) by China, a nation with lots of land, resources and an enormous (but now slow-growing) population. It's simply a matter of growth arithmetic. The U.S. economy will be expanding at about 3% a year, and China will be growing at an average of two to three times that, from a much smaller base.

China has been averaging about 11% annual growth for the past 15 years, but that rate is already beginning to decline. It is not likely that even the most dynamic newly industrializing nations will be able to sustain double-digit, or even high-single-digit annual growth for long periods of time. In the early stages of industrialization, nations tend to build productive capacity before they do their infrastructures and the amenities of modern societies. These will soon require enormous financial commitments. While such investments are essential foundations of future economic development in any nation, for a time they will divert capital from the creation of additional manufacturing capacity and will moderate the boomy growth rates of early industrialization.

## EMULATION OF THE AMERICAN GROWTH MODEL

Key elements of the American development model are private ownership of business; public stock markets; decentralized economic decision making; a relatively small regulatory role for government; low taxation; borders that are relatively open to the flow of goods, capital and even people (immigrants); and a pro-consumer, rather than pro-producer, bias in economic policy.

Since the end of World War II, the American economic model had two main rivals competing for the allegiance of both developed and less-developed nations: the socialist model (either democratic or communist) of state-owned and -directed business; and the Japanese capitalist model of privately owned businesses engaged in cooperative planning with the government and among themselves. Both have been discredited by their inability to adapt quickly to changing world circumstances, sustain growth and achieve high personal income without high consumer costs.

So the American model of decentralized markets and individual freedom—accompanied by constant and jarring restructuring to adapt to rapid change—is catching on worldwide, and it will continue to be ascendant in the early decades of the 21st century. Emulation of the American model will be a major force in opening markets, stimulating the flow of goods and capital among nations, transferring technology and production, and creating markets for broad public stock ownership.

It is tempting to equate the modernization of the world with the "Americanization" of the world, but that's too simple. The American model will be creatively modified and localized to reflect the richly varied cultural, religious and economic histories of each nation.

In Asia, for example, there will be a persistent feeling that the Western political and economic tradition puts too much emphasis on individual rights and privileges, rather than the citizen's obligation to society. The Asian emphasis on community interests and values as superior to individual rights will temper American-style capitalism from Japan to Singapore to China. In the Arab world, Muslim clerics will play a role in the economies of Middle Eastern nations, limiting the intrusion of American-style popular culture, defining the role of women, and choosing trading partners on political and religious grounds as much as market considerations.

## MORE POLITICAL FREEDOM AND DEMOCRACY

The past economic progress of autocracies such as China, Singapore and formerly white-ruled South Africa have shown that rapid economic modernization does not require a high degree of political freedom. But in the long run, political repression is almost as devastating to economic enterprise as wars are. Fortunately, it is not possible for repressive governments to maintain their political grip very long after they have uncorked the genie of economic freedom.

Centrally controlled economies can achieve *faster* development in the short run than democracies, and this will still be attractive to some foreign investors. But in the long run, societies that adopt more-participatory systems for both economic and political decision making are likely to achieve steadier and ultimately higher levels of development, with less political turmoil.

Some people dispute that democracy is a necessary precondition for economic development, and in fact argue the opposite—that messy self-governance can't achieve modernization as efficiently as an authoritarian regime can. This notion was widespread in global investment circles in the mid '90s, as far more capital poured into such authoritarian societies as China, Indonesia, Nigeria and Vietnam (and only slightly less repressive regimes such as Singapore and Malaysia) than into established democracies such as India or the chaotic new democracies of Russia and other former Soviet republics. For example, China attracted some $44 billion of capital inflow in 1996, helping it achieve a stunning 10% rate of growth. Indonesia pulled in some $18 billion. But India's economy, considered to be an Asian growth laggard at 6.8%, received far less.

This hard-nosed capitalist preference for investing in centrally controlled economies was expressed with blunt eloquence in the spring of 1996 by a noted Asia investor, Philip Tose, speaking at a gathering of Harvard Business School alumni in Hong Kong. According to a *Wall Street Journal* report on his remarks, Tose specifically cited democracy as the reason that nations such as India would forever lag the economic development of an Indonesia or China.

At the time of his unabashedly elitist remarks, Tose was flying high as founding chairman of Hong Kong's Peregrine Securities Group, one of the world's biggest investors in Asia's emerging markets, especially one of his favorite repressive regimes, Suharto's Indonesia. Within nine months of his remarks, Peregrine was bankrupt, a victim of the bursting Asian bubble, and within a year thereafter, Suharto was deposed and Indonesia was plunging into economic chaos.

## NO BROADLY CONQUERING NEW TYRANNIES

Another factor in stronger economic growth in the next century will be the absence of any new, lengthy and geographically broad subjugations of large numbers of people by global or regional tyrannies, akin to 20th-century communism in Russia and China, which depressed living standards in those nations for decades. Similar restraints on living standards were caused by dictatorships of the left and right in certain nations of Latin America, Africa and Asia, and by well-intentioned democratic socialism and central planning in parts of Western Europe.

But democracy is fragile, and there will be occasional regression to tyranny in many nations, in response to political and economic instability or ethnic and religious conflict. These tyrannies won't last as long as they have in the past, when societies could be closed off to the outer world. In addition to police enforcement, tyranny requires ways to keep its people in ignorance of the outer world, to control the society's economic resources, and to tax its businesses to support the government. A global society, with a freer flow of information, goods and capital, makes all of these conditions hard to sustain.

## FEWER WORLD-CHANGING NEW INVENTIONS

Some 100 years ago, a U.S. government official named Charles Duell opined, "Everything that *can* be invented *has* been invented." Duell's myopia would be easier to understand had he not been the head of the U.S. Patent Commission.

We don't wish to associate ourselves in any way with this sentiment. Inventiveness will be just as robust in the next century as it has been in this one. However, the new inventions, by and large, will be improvements and refinements of current technologies. It will be well-nigh impossible for coming generations to top the 20th century's record in the breathtaking magnitude of its two greatest achievements: breaking free from Earth's gravitational pull through powered flight, progressing from a vertical distance of a few feet in 1903 to thousands of miles into space by the 1960s; and unlocking the fundamental secrets of life through the unraveling of the DNA code, which led to the ability to clone existing species and create custom-designed plants and animals.

Comparable achievements this century include the wireless transmission of sound, pictures and data; tiny electronic devices that do elaborate calculations and simulate human thinking; drugs that kill bacterial infections in humans and animals; effective birth control; in vitro fertilization and embryo transplants in humans; the splitting of the atom; and organ transplants and artificial organs.

But the geniuses of the 20th century have left a lot of unfinished business. New mountains to climb include: achieving nuclear fusion, to create a virtually limitless supply of energy; conquering the aging process; discovering life elsewhere in our universe (or another one); achieving superconductivity, virtually eliminating resistance in electrical generation and transmission; improving artificial intelligence to the point that robots can truly mimic human reasoning and choices; and perfecting cryogenics—the ability to suspend life and revive it at any later date.

While there will not be as many world-changing inventions and discoveries in the coming century, the benefits of science that until now have been narrowly enjoyed by a few wealthy nations will be dispersed throughout the world.

## INTEGRATION OF ALL PEOPLES INTO ONE GLOBAL MARKET

The volume and diversity of world trade in both manufactured goods and services will rise at an accelerating pace in the 21st century, picking up the torrid pace at the end of this century. Between 1987 and 1997, the total value of world trade *doubled*, growing at a rate of 7% per year, far faster than world economic activity in general.

Continued accelerating growth in world trade will come from the gradual acceptance of empirical evidence that everyone prospers when each nation makes what it can most efficiently and then acquires from other nations the goods and services it makes less efficiently.

### *Ceaseless domestic efforts to thwart globalization*

Despite the clear superiority of open markets, the trend of globalization will not advance in a straight line. It will progress in fits and starts for decades, forcefully resisted in every nation, highly developed or less so. When citizens whose jobs are threatened by foreign competition clamor for help, their governments will be tempted to respond with protectionist measures. The larger constituencies on the other side of the issue—consumers whose cost of living would be raised by the protective measures, or the growing corps of workers whose jobs depend on free-flowing trade—will be harder to mobilize.

### *Free-flowing capital*

The free flow of investment capital, the lifeblood of economic expansion, will accelerate. The wealthy nations proved very willing suppliers of capital in the '90s, with several years of double-digit increases in capital flows to the developing nations—a surge of 20% in 1996 alone. This money—largely from private sources, as opposed to the governmental aid programs so common in previous decades—

went into building new factories, and purchasing privatized government assets, corporate stocks, government bonds, etc.

That 1996 surge looked suspiciously unsustainable at the time, and it turned out to be. Much of it was lavished on speculative investments in Asia—including office towers and shopping malls—contributing to the overheated conditions that led to the Asian financial shakeout the following year.

In addition to the prospect of a high rate of return, foreign investors demand other conditions to justify taking a risk. Their ideal investment site has political stability and a respect for private property, with little danger that assets will be expropriated; relatively low inflation, so that the value of their assets won't be eroded by soaring prices; and a liquid securities market and easy currency trading, so they can sell their assets and bring their capital home, even on short notice.

Until recently, few less-developed nations met these conditions. That has changed greatly in the past decade, and the trend will continue. So there will be hot global competition for investment capital, with nations vying for it through incessant improvement of their investment climates—lower taxation, improved market liquidity, generally pro-business regulatory conditions. The U.S. will meet the competition by continuing to combine a superb business environment with unmatched political stability.

### *Capital flows as a barometer of national health*
The global liquidity boom, with stock markets flourishing everywhere, has emboldened owners of capital to invest it in once-shunned corners of the globe. But as the nations of Asia discovered in 1997-1998, foreign capital is a stern master. If it perceives financial trouble ahead in a wildly boomy economy, it will flee as swiftly as it arrived, sending the local currency into a tailspin and robbing the economy of fuel for future growth.

In the early stages of the Asian financial crisis, some Asian government leaders blamed their woes on fickle or cynical foreign-currency traders and institutional investors. They failed to see that they can't have it both ways—attracting foreign capital when they want rapid growth but also limiting the ability of that capital to withdraw when it wants.

Daily flows of capital, as reflected in currency values, are an instant, continuous referendum on the perceived dynamism, stability and future prospects of every nation. The capital markets aren't always right in the long run, but they have a good sense of what the near future holds. Investors who have fled will return to a foreign market when they see that its government and business leaders have taken steps to correct imbalances.

### The spread of individual stock ownership

Nothing gives people a sense of attachment—to their economy's success, to their employer, to their nation—like ownership of stock, especially in the enterprises where they work. So the American concept of broadly fragmented private ownership through individual stock-holdings, mutual funds, pension funds and other institutional investors will spread worldwide.

During the '90s, new public stock markets were established in some 50 nations—from formerly communist Eastern Europe to Africa to the South Pacific—that previously had no mechanism for daily pricing and transactions in securities issued by corporations in their countries.

Not surprisingly, many of these new stock markets are rife with accounting problems, trading irregularities and illiquidity, problems typical of small, thinly traded markets. But in a decade or two, investors and speculators in any nation will be able to buy and sell, with ease and safety, the foreign currencies, stocks and bonds of virtually any nation or corporation. And Western concepts of accounting "transparency" will make such investing much less risky than it is today.

### Relentless spread of manufacturing

The geographic dispersal of manufacturing capacity has been going on since the dawn the industrial revolution. Technological knowledge and the resulting manufacturing capacity have moved gradually but relentlessly from high- to lower-cost production centers. Low-cost production centers are not just low-wage locales, but places where total production costs—including wages, capital, land, transportation, taxes and regulatory burdens—are lower than elsewhere.

In the 19th century, America was the new, low-cost manufacturing center feared by British manufacturers, even as it was favored by British financiers, who sent their capital to this fast-growing, less-developed land. Subsequently, American manufacturers sought out lower-cost production centers, too, and today U.S. multinational companies manufacture their goods all over the world.

In the 21st century, regions of the world never before heavily engaged in manufacturing, including parts of Africa and Latin America, will be called into global production. This will boost living standards dramatically in those countries, while restraining labor costs in more-developed nations. Heavy capital investment in the Third World will move these nations into higher levels of manufacturing, as is already happening in electronics, automobiles, printing and pharmaceuticals.

The broad adoption of manufacturing technology in the poorer nations could reasonably be expected to lead to declining living standards in the more-developed nations. But the world's richer nations will, by and large, continue to excel in leading-edge technologies that will keep them one step ahead of the developing nations in creating new products and services that haven't yet been replicated and transferred overseas.

Manufacturing will *not* atrophy in the developed world. The U.S., Japan and Europe will continue to be the centers of high-value manufacturing, especially the sophisticated capital goods with which the rest of the world will make less-expensive consumer products. The U.S. will continue to be a world leader in the manufacture of aircraft, aerospace equipment, microprocessors, scientific-research equipment, medical devices and pharmaceuticals derived from genetic engineering.

## BOOMING TRADE IN SERVICES

The newest battleground in world trade won't be manufactured goods, farm products or fuel, but something you can't even see or touch—services.

As manufacturing, both low- and high-tech, moves to the less-developed nations, the growth of service exports will be the best opportunity for many mature economies to grow, prosper and maintain world economic leadership. This will be especially true of the United States, which is already the world's low-cost, high-productivity exporter of services—finance, telecommunications, architecture, health care, education, tourism, transportation, engineering and law, among others—and is poised to broaden its lead over the competition.

### More global competition in services

While the U.S. has a strong trade surplus in services, other nations are enviously eyeing the growth of world trade in services, and they're getting in on the act.

Using low-cost international phone lines, any lower-wage English-speaking nation (Jamaica, Ireland, India and Australia, for example) can provide the U.S. market with teleservices, word processing and data entry, with the data telecommunicated back to the U.S. Computer programming is booming in India. Engineers and mechanical draftsmen in India and Eastern Europe, using computer-assisted design (CAD) software, do drafting for General Electric that was once done in

GE's midwestern U.S. factories. Every airline in the world is competing hard for the same business travelers. International engineering and construction management pits strong U.S. firms such as Bechtel and Fluor against competitors from South Korea and Europe. And the world's biggest banks are all seeking access to each other's turf.

## NO GLOBAL DEPRESSION, BUT PLENTY OF REGIONAL SLUMPS

Entire regions will continue to be susceptible to business cycles, and rapid movements of capital in an integrated global economy will accentuate volatility. These boom-and-bust episodes will result from the overenthusiasm of world investors for a particular region that they deem to be the next hot place, a sure-fire success that knows no limits of growth. And there will be occasional worldwide slumps caused by geopolitical situations, such as a war accompanied by curtailing of production of the world's most commonly used commodity, petroleum.

The Asian financial crisis wasn't the first of these regional shake-outs, just the biggest so far. The first one was the Latin American debt crisis of the 1970s, followed by the Mexican banking crisis of 1994-1995. In an increasingly interconnected global economy, a broad and deep regional recession will depress demand throughout the world, heightening competition among all exporters, driving down prices for a period of time and raising calls for protection of domestic producers. And as we have seen several times before, a deep plunge in the stock markets of one region or another will often trigger drops in others, until traders refocus on the unique fundamentals of each market and look for buying opportunity, thereby stabilizing prices.

Will heightened globalization make it more likely that severe regional recessions will spiral into global recession or even depression? It's possible, but not likely. In the last global depression, in the 1930s, nations foolishly thought they could insulate their populations from the effects of global competition and falling prices by closing their borders to imports. This is less likely to be repeated, because the world has learned from past protectionist follies and because the world is vastly more interrelated. Exports account for so much more of most large corporations' total sales that they will resist government efforts, often on behalf of organized labor, to push over the first domino and start a chain reaction of contracting world trade.

The International Monetary Fund is another force that will minimize the risk of regional recessions' expanding into global depressions. With its emergency war chest of contributions from the advanced nations, the IMF can inject capital into a sick economy on short notice and—most significantly—demand deep structural reforms as a condition for the aid. The fund's resources are not limitless, of course, and its coffers could be overwhelmed by simultaneous crises around the globe—as nearly occured in 1998, with massive assistance to Southeast Asia, Russia and other trouble spots. The system depends on the willingness of the wealthy nations to replenish the IMF bailout funds, and as Congress showed in 1998, there will be considerable resistance to continuously bailing out nations that don't seem to be helping themselves enough. The best argument for such aid will continue to be the risk of letting a major economy collapse, dragging down many others.

### *Globalization a force for long-term stability*

Some people fear that a knitting together of world financial markets—with rapid, electronic movement of capital in and out of equity markets, corporate and government bonds and national currencies—will aggravate economic instability.

Volatility will increase, but slumps will be briefer. Recoveries will start almost immediately, as capital rushes opportunistically into nations where inflated prices have been brought back down to earth—if governments take corrective actions fast to win back the trust of foreign capital. Those Asian governments that moved quickly to restore confidence in their economies through market liberalization recovered soonest. Those that refused simply prolonged the pain.

## BIGGER AND BIGGER ENTERPRISES

Merger and acquisition activity will boom both within nations and between nations, as seen in the combining of Daimler-Benz with Chrysler and Bertelsmann with Random House in 1998. Many of the resulting giants will be *transnational* corporations, distinctly different in their structure and management style from the traditional multinationals that have grown over the last 40 years. In corporate culture, breadth of stock ownership and global political power, they will be truly global citizens, belonging and beholden to no single nation, only to their global shareholders.

The growth of transnationals will be just one aspect of a worldwide trend toward bigness in business that will see an explosion of consolidations in virtually every industry, from steelmaking and autos to retailing and telecommunications.

Some mergers, combining firms in separate but related fields, will have the potential to either heighten or reduce competition, and the outcome won't be clear for some time thereafter. For example, the $48 billion merger of AT&T, the largest long-distance phone company, with Tele-Communication, Inc., the second-largest U.S. cable-TV company, combined two potential rivals for the Internet access market in homes. But it may enable AT&T/TCI to compete with the Baby Bells for local phone service, where the promise of competition has been woefully unfulfilled since telephone deregulation. The new company will be positioned to offer the long-anticipated "one-wire" integration of local calling, long-distance service, cable TV and Internet on one monthly bill.

## GLOBALIZING OF ANTITRUST POLICY

Antitrust officials in the advanced nations will get more involved in pursuing anticompetitive mergers and behavior by companies not residing in those nations.

There will generally be more consultation and coordination to avoid duplicative investigations and differing recommendations. In 1998, for example, antitrust officials in the U.S. and the European Union made a pact to coordinate a variety of antitrust activities, especially in price fixing.

But they pointedly declined to include joint review and approval of transnational mergers, leaving the U.S. and EU to go their separate ways. In theory, this continues to give each side veto power over enormous corporate combinations on each continent, because access to each market is essential to the combined firm. But a lot of backstage dickering will usually result in agreement among the various antitrust agencies in different countries.

EU trustbusters balked at giving their blessing to the $15 billion merger of Boeing and McDonnell Douglas, a deal that passed muster with the U.S. Federal Trade Commission, because of a fear that the combined U.S. manufacturers would hamper the sales of Europe's Airbus consortium. The U.S. threatened trade reprisals if the EU didn't back down, and the Europeans eventually did. Similarly, the EU considered withholding approval of the MCI-WorldCom deal, unless the merged firms sold not only MCI's Internet business but WorldCom's UUNet as well. But the EU eventually let the merger go forward.

## ECONOMIC SANCTIONS WILL WANE

One of the most common forms of international punishment of rogue states and repressive regimes in the late 20th century has been the economic boycott, which the United States has made into an art not appreciated even by its allies.

The U.S., with its tradition of moralism rather than pragmatism in world affairs, has long been partial to using economic boycotts, embargoes and other trade sanctions to effect political change. It's increasingly evident that such boycotts have a dubious record of accomplishing the desired results, in large part because rival nations rush in to fill the trade vacuum, hurting U.S. companies.

The high-water mark for this American impulse to use trade as an instrument for social change in foreign lands has probably been reached with the Helms-Burton Act, which punishes foreign firms that acquire Cuban assets once expropriated from U.S. corporations. In the next century, this American moralism will yield to a less judgmental approach, under pressure from allies and American corporations seeking a level playing field with their multinational competitors.

Sanctions don't have a very good record of deterring negative behavior or forcing errant regimes back into the fold after they have strayed. What they do achieve is the imposition of enormous hardship on the citizens of the targeted nation, who in most cases (as in Saddam Hussein's Iraq) are so oppressed that they are unable to effect real change. Sanctions also seem to harden the resolve of the rogue regime, enabling it to whip up an "us against them" mentality toward the U.S.

The immediate imposition of U.S. sanctions on India after its nuclear testing in 1998 did not deter its neighbor, Pakistan, from undertaking similar testing soon thereafter, even though both nations could ill afford the cutoff of international aid and loan guarantees that followed. And the U.S. sanctions left many American corporations in limbo on large infrastructure projects that could not go forward without U.S. loan guarantees, opening the door for competing corporations to take over the ventures. With Pakistan, there is the added concern that a desperately poor government, weakened further by international sanctions, might become a rogue state desperate to generate revenue by selling its nuclear technology to other Islamic governments.

Over time, economic sanctions will fade as a tool of international order. The United States will move toward embracing the concept of "constructive engagement," in which active trade and open channels of discussion are used to influence outcomes and keep nations in line. In the near future, U.S. sanctions will even be eased against Iran, Cuba and Iraq, under pressure from U.S. allies that want to do business there.

## LOW WORLD INFLATION

Inflation is far from dead in the world economy, and periods of high global economic growth will be accompanied by rising costs for fuel, labor, capital and resources. But high inflation will be confined largely to domestic markets. It will be caused by these factors: rising service-sector prices (in health care, for example) in local and national sectors not susceptible to international competition; rising wages from labor shortages (especially of skilled workers); and, mostly in developing nations, monetary policies that are overly loose.

But there won't be long, broad rises in world commodity prices caused by widespread shortages of fuel, food and minerals. Price spikes will be episodic and brief, sometimes caused by the attempts of producer cartels to restrict supplies. Supplies of key commodities such as petroleum will sometimes be interrupted by war and political instability. And governments will never fully break themselves of the democratic tendency toward the inflation of money supplies to mollify debtors.

The broader trend will be restraint of prices, even brief periods of deflation in certain categories of goods, caused by fierce competition among producer nations that are more and more evenly matched. On balance, the forces of inflation and disinflation (or even deflation) will hold each other in check pretty well, resulting in a continuation of price stability in global markets.

## BROADER SHARING OF WORLD LEADERSHIP

No nation will dominate the 21st-century world economy as the United States has dominated the 20th century. The U.S. will remain the only true world superpower for decades to come, with its unique combination of military might, political influence and a compelling model of economic openness, not to mention a pervasive pop culture of great appeal to other people. But the rest of the world will need the U.S. less in the next century as a military protector and source of development capital. Other nations will flex their muscles in the world economy and be less inclined to go along with U.S. leadership.

The world's decreasing need for American help, both military and financial, will coincide with the declining financial ability of the U.S. to be the world's chief policeman and financial protector. In the five decades after World War II, the U.S. devoted an inordinate amount of its economic resources to helping rebuild Europe and Japan and to ensuring its own military preparedness. That relieved its democratic allies, especially former foes Japan and Germany, of the need to provide for their own defenses, and was an economic boon to those nations.

In the decades ahead, the U.S. will spend relatively less on military capability, directing more of its national income to infrastructure, social services, health care, basic research, public education and other nondefense needs, all of which will strengthen the economy.

In countless ways, economic leadership in the world will be more broadly shared. For example, national contributions to the International Monetary Fund, World Bank and United Nations are based roughly on a nation's share of aggregate world GDP. As the developed nations' share of total world economic activity declines, newly industrialized nations will assume more of the financial burden of assisting their less successful neighbors.

There will be broader sharing of leadership in research and technology, too. As scientists and engineers (many of them trained in U.S. universities and corporations) fan out across the globe, the awarding of patents will be spread more evenly, although the U.S., Japan and a few other developed nations will continue to dominate. The less-developed nations won't continue to be just assembly sites for products designed and engineered in developed countries. More and more of the original product development will be done on site in the newly emerging economies, integrating engineering and production as never before.

## NEW SOURCES OF CAPITAL

In the early stages of any nation's economic development, investment capital usually comes from offshore. Europe and the U.S. were virtually the only major sources for such capital in the Third World until the 1970s, when the oil-rich Arab nations began investing overseas, and the 1980s, when Japan became a significant capital provider.

All of these investors will continue to be active, but they will be joined by many new funders, giving world business a new diversity of capital sources. Much of the industrial development of Southeast Asia and China will be spurred by capital from the worldwide expatriate community of ethnic Chinese, including citizens of Hong Kong, Taiwan, Canada, Indonesia and the U.S.

As the economies of the less-developed nations grow and achieve serious capital accumulation, more and more of their growth will be financed by the retained earnings of their own businesses.

## RISING WORLD POPULATION, BUT A LOWER RATE OF GROWTH

World population will keep increasing, from six billion today to about 7.5 billion in 2020, an increase of 25%. Well over 95% of the growth will occur in the world's poorest nations.

Even as total population increases, the *rate* of growth will continue to decline, and that decline will accelerate. But high population growth in many developing nations will be a dismaying challenge. They will struggle with rapid urbanization, maintaining food supplies, and protecting air and water quality amid rapid economic development.

Most of the developed nations, including Japan and almost all of Europe, have already achieved or are fast approaching zero population growth, with low immigration and a fertility rate well below the population-replacement level of 2.1 children per woman.

The world population growth rate will decline because rising living standards—and related trends in urbanization, education and job opportunities for women—are historically accompanied by broader contraceptive use and declining birth rates.

## CONSTANT RESOURCE SUBSTITUTION

Throughout history, anxiety about dwindling resources—food, water, wood to burn or build with, metallic ores, fuels for lighting and heat—has proven to be unfounded. In every crisis of commodity scarcity, human ingenuity has led to a variety of solutions, including finding new reserves, getting more product from existing reserves through new extraction and refining technologies, and supplementing and eventually replacing the scarce resource with a new substance that works as well and proves to be plentiful and cheap.

There is no reason to believe that this process has run its course. On the contrary, it is likely that increasing knowledge in plant science, new-materials research, desalination, geology, nuclear physics and other fields will increase future generations' ability to augment and replace currently popular resources.

## ADEQUATE SUPPLIES OF FOOD, FUEL AND WATER

So despite the fact that the earth and its resources will be called on to support upwards of 75 million more people each year for decades, there will not be a world crisis of supply or price in major natural resources, including the three most basic raw materials of economic growth: water, food and fuel.

Some recent trends in world agriculture—such as flattening growth in crop yields, declining amounts of land under cultivation, and stagnant harvests of ocean fish—do raise concern. But advances in technology will accelerate in the next century and will, as they have throughout history, provide adequate food for a growing world population. What's more, world agriculture will do its job while employing a sharply dwindling number of workers.

Today, with no food crisis on the horizon, much of the world's tillable land isn't even in service. The U.S. and Canada have vast uncultivated acreage in the Middle West and Great Plains that could be pressed into service as demand and farm prices rise. In Argentina, huge tracts of rich land suitable for growing wheat are now used for grazing cattle, which are inefficient converters of protein. Lands like these in many nations will be able to boost the world's grain production to cover population growth for years to come.

As urbanization and manufacturing spread, so will world trade in food products. A nation's self-sufficiency in food may continue to be an issue of national security, but it will not be an economic necessity. A relatively small number of nations with vast land areas—including the United States, Canada, Argentina, the former Soviet republics and Australia, as well as some of the larger nations of Africa and Asia—can continue to be major exporters of food to the world.

Late in the next century, the age-old, ironclad link between land and food production will begin to be disconnected. Vegetables grown not in soil, but hydroponically, in shallow trays of nutrient-rich water, will become a significant food source. The light for this aquaculture will come from the sun or from arrays of artificial lights, and where land is scarce, the whole process will take place in towering skyscrapers, veritable veggie factories.

Energy companies continue to find vast new reserves, and technology will lower the cost of pinpointing and exploiting the most-promising areas. In addition, pressure on mounting energy demand will be eased by a relentless trend toward conservation. This doesn't mean self-denial, because virtually everything—from homes and appliances to factory systems, airplanes and automobiles—will be designed and engineered to operate on less energy.

Throughout history, commonly used fuels have been supplemented and replaced by new energy sources according to the laws of supply and demand—that is, change occurred only when a fuel became scarce and the price soared. In the next century, however, the workings of resource markets will be altered by a potent new force: environmental concern. Powerful political voices in the advanced nations will call for drastic curtailment of fossil-fuel use, thought by many scientists to contribute to global warming. This pressure for reduced energy consumption will be widely resented and resisted in the developing nations, which suspect it's an attempt to hold back their rising economic competition with the wealthier nations.

## NO WORLDWIDE WARFARE, BUT REGIONAL AND CIVIL STRIFE

There will be no massive world wars in the next century, no conflagrations of the scale that twice devastated major parts of the globe in this century. There are several reasons why the odds are against such a war. One is the broader distribution of conventional armaments worldwide. Some would argue that this increases the chance of conflict, but we believe that it's a deterrent to aggression.

And small wars will be less likely to develop into big ones because nations will be more tightly knit economically. Multinational corporations, with production, sales and customers spread all over the world, will not want to jeopardize their markets by supporting their governments through long, devastating wars. Even where there are no global economic interests at stake—such as in the Balkans—multilateral forces from the UN or NATO will be deployed to contain the conflicts for humanitarian purposes.

There will be small wars between neighbors from time to time, and maybe even the use of tactical nuclear and/or biochemical weapons by terrorist groups and rogue states. One need only look at the terrible, ongoing anguish in Kosovo to see the effects of nationalistic, ethnic and racial resentment, which in this case had been kept in check by five decades of communist rule.

Powerful neighbors may still attempt to impose their political and military will on weak neighbors, as Iraq attempted to do with Kuwait in 1990. In the coming decades, an economically and militarily powerful China will have the ability to subjugate much of Asia, as Japan did in the 1930s. And a resurgence of Russian nationalism will someday pose a new military threat to the same neighbors that the Soviet empire dominated for a half-century.

The world's major nations will continue to be reluctant to intrude in civil wars, as evidenced by international inaction in the '90s against mass murder in Rwanda, Sudan, and—until it was almost too late—in Bosnia. The NATO campaign against Yugoslavia's genocide in its province of Kosovo will stand out as an exception that proves the difficulty of international involvement in such conflicts.

## WORLDWIDE EMPOWERMENT OF WOMEN

The political and economic empowerment of women has been one of the most significant developments of the late 20th century. But because that empowerment has been limited largely to the advanced nations, it hasn't yet had the dramatic impact on the world economy that its global spread will have in the century ahead. Bringing more than half of the world's population into the global market economy as high-achieving producers, consumers and investors will make profound changes in every aspect of life in the 21st century.

Virtually all women, everywhere are already "working women," and they have been since the dawn of civilization. But until fairly recently, the vast majority have toiled outside cash economies, earning little but producing incalculable output through their management of households, rearing of children, growing and preparing of food, and making of clothing and simple crafts for the home. Whether in a cash economy or working at home, women clearly account for a disproportionate share (well over half) of all the hours worked each year. That's because women do not take as much leisure time for themselves as men have traditionally felt entitled to, by the cultural norms of most societies.

In many nations, social and legal constraints still block women's access to the same educational, occupational and economic opportunities that men enjoy, depriving the world economy of the benefits of their intelligence, creativity and entrepreneurial zeal.

Now this is all changing. In nations of Asia, Latin America, Africa and the Middle East, girls will someday have the same access to public education that boys do. Child care will become more institutionalized in developing nations, so more women will have the choice of working outside the home, if they wish. Labor-saving home appliances—stoves, washing machines, refrigerators, and so on—will become common in developing nations, freeing women to join market economies full-time or part-time.

Women will benefit from the trend toward "microcredit"—very small loans to individuals and cooperatives to create small businesses, serving first their local economies, then broader markets. A telecommunications mogul in Bangladesh, for example, has expanded the sale of his company's cellular phones by extending credit for buying phones to poor but entrepreneurial women in rural villages that have no wired phone service. The women, some of whom now own the only phone in town, charge their equally impoverished neighbors small sums to make calls, thereby paying off the loans and making a profit over time.

As they enter the market economy of manufacturing and skilled services, women will be an enormous force in the worldwide rise in living standards. The addition of so much new labor into the market economy will have wide-ranging, and not fully foreseeable, social and economic effects. For example, it could have the effect of restraining wage increases, or actually lowering wages, in the traditional, mostly male global work force. At the same time, the cash earnings of the new global corps of employed women will be a great stimulus to consumer demand for food, appliances, housing and services. On balance, the trend will be highly positive for the world economy.

# CHAPTER 3

# America's Bright Economic Future

T he U.S. will continue to set the pace for the world's most advanced nations in virtually all categories of economic success and competitiveness—total production, per-capita GDP, productivity, wealth, standard of living, trade volume, scientific research and technology. Over the next 20 years or so, the average annual rate of economic growth will rise above a two-decade average in the mid 2% range to a new, higher plateau of nearly 3%. Business cycles will be moderated by a number of new situations in the global economy, but they will not disappear. The long trend line of economic expansion will still be punctuated by occasional recessions and spurts of much higher growth.

This improvement in America's long-term economic performance will result from steady increases in the size of the labor force (growing about 1.3% a year) and—most important—a big boost from higher capital investment. This will raise U.S. productivity by an average of more than 1.7% a year—nearly double the average gains of the past two decades.

On the demand side of the growth equation, the biggest force will be robust overseas purchases of American goods and services, especially high-tech manufactured goods and sophisticated, exportable services such as telecommunications, banking and investments, health care, entertainment, education, engineering and architecture, and law.

Here are a few highlights of our U.S. economic forecast, with more detail to follow in this chapter:

**Inflation and interest rates.** Consumer inflation will average a little less than 3% a year over the next few decades. Interest rates will be pulled in opposite directions by two strong, countervailing forces—

41

restrained by low inflation and low federal deficits, but pushed higher by worldwide competition for business capital. On balance, lenders will demand the historically typical three points over the inflation rate for short-term loans to the U.S. government.

**Personal savings rates.** Savings rates, now at the lowest level in a half-century, will rise for 15 to 20 years, as baby-boomers save for retirement. Then rates will flatten or decline, as boomers draw down savings in retirement.

**Corporate profits.** American businesses with foreign competition will have difficulty raising prices, and will experience a squeeze on profit margins.

**Foreign trade.** The total value of U.S. foreign trade—both exports and imports of goods and services—will continue to grow strongly. Due largely to imports of cheap oil, the U.S. will run a continuous trade deficit in merchandise, only partially offset by its surplus in service exports.

**Capital inflows and outflows.** Foreign investment in the U.S. economy will remain a very strong and beneficial force. American firms will accelerate their overseas expansions, too.

**Manufacturing.** American production of tangible goods will continue to grow in value indefinitely. Manufacturing's share of the U.S. economy will hold level for a decade or so, then begin a slow decline. The composition of America's manufactures will continue to shift from simple, labor-intensive goods to high technology.

**Job growth and the labor force.** Rising productivity in manufacturing and services will restrain job growth to a level about matching increases in the labor force. There will be labor shortages and strongly rising pay in a variety of high-tech fields, partially relieved by immigration.

# Higher Growth Ahead

The U.S. economy is now producing more than $8 trillion worth of goods and services a year—a GDP that's virtually the same as all the nations of the European community combined, and about two and a half times the size of Japan's. The American people, with less than 5% of total world population, account each year for some 22% of the world's total production.

The U.S. is a nation of vast size—the third-largest in land area, after Russia and China, and the third-largest in population, after China and India. It also has exceptionally rich natural resources.

U.S. growth has averaged 2.4% since 1978 but 3.2% since 1991—

the best record among all the world's large economies in this decade. With the exception of a brief, mild recession from late 1990 through early 1991, the economy has expanded continually for 16 years, since the fall of 1982.

In the nearly three decades since 1970, the U.S. economy has experienced only five calendar years in which its total level of economic activity declined rather than grew—1974, 1975, 1980, 1982, and 1990. In the other years, rates of growth ranged from virtually nothing (1970 and 1990) to spurts as high as 7% in 1984 and 5.8% in 1973.

The expansion of the '90s has been remarkable both for its length and for the evenness of its moderate growth. While the paucity of exhilarating boom years (just an occasional quarter or two of 4% growth) has been disappointing to some, the smoothness of the growth has been a big key to the longevity of the expansion.

In the decades ahead, the U.S. will achieve a long-term average annual growth rate resembling the '90s—about 3% a year.

# A Surge in Productivity

The key to this long-range forecast of higher economic growth is a judgment that U.S. productivity growth—probably understated for years in government statistics—will get a big boost from heavy capital spending on automation. Overall productivity—the value of output per hour worked—took off in 1996-'98, rising by a very impressive 2% each year. This level of gain will be tough to sustain as a long-term trend, but it is much closer to what future performance will look like than the 1% productivity gains of the past two decades.

A developing nation can hike its growth rate by putting more people to work, but an advanced nation with slow growth in the labor force can boost productivity only by pairing its labor force with better and better capital equipment.

As Massachusetts Institute of Technology economist Paul Krugman puts it, "Productivity isn't everything, but in the long run, it's almost everything; the rate of growth of our living standard equals the rate of growth of our domestic productivity . . . period." If a company gets more output from each hour of labor, it can pay workers more and boost profits, too, without raising prices. Higher real wages, in turn, stimulate the economy by giving workers more money to spend on goods and services. And that is precisely what will happen in the United States (and the world) over the next decade.

American productivity growth was much more robust in the

quarter-century between the end of World War II and the inflationary spike of the early '70s than in the years since 1973.

The annual rate of productivity growth appears to have fallen by more than half, from 3.4% (1948 to 1973) to about 1.3% (1974 to 1992), according to the Labor Department. With that slower growth came a slower rise in the real wages—and therefore living standards—of many workers. There are many explanations for this, including lower capital investment (from a declining national savings rate), the new and permanently higher cost of energy, myopic leadership by both business managers and labor unions, declining public education, erosion in the work ethic, and a federal tax code that discouraged investment.

## STRONG IN MANUFACTURING, WEAK IN SERVICES

Productivity gains have been impressive in American manufacturing in the '80s and '90s, with factory automation boosting output per hour at a rate of between 3% and 4% a year. There is plenty of evidence of similar strong gains in service-sector productivity, in such fields as mass-market retailing (with a boom in catalog sales and lightly staffed "superstores"), telecommunications (fewer phone operators), health maintenance organizations (physicians and nurses seeing more patients per hour), and financial services (ATMs, online banking and online stock trading).

Nonetheless, government statistics indicate very anemic growth in service productivity—less than 1% a year until a very recent jump to about 2%. Because services are the biggest and fastest-growing sector of the economy, overall productivity growth in the U.S. economy has been averaging only about 1% a year, even during the long expansions of the '80s and '90s.

Some economists, notably Federal Reserve Board Chairman Alan Greenspan, say the full benefits of revolutionary advances in technology usually take longer to show up in productivity data than optimists had predicted. But, he adds, they eventually they do show up, and these benefits now lie just ahead for the U.S. and world economies.

Other observers, especially in business, are simply convinced that the government statistics have been wrong—failing to accurately measure the dramatic productivity gains that they see occurring in services. The accuracy of official productivity data is more than some game for academics, because it can affect policy decisions. If overall productivity continues to log something like the recent gains of 2% per year, the Federal Reserve could manage monetary policy for higher economic growth without fear of igniting inflation.

# Adequate Capital for Growth

T he main reason productivity is poised to ascend to a higher plateau of average growth is that American business has been on a capital-spending binge for 15 years—with double-digit annual increases in investments in new plants and equipment in virtually every line of work. Business investment must be fueled by private capital from many sources—retained corporate earnings, personal savings by Americans, and money invested in the U.S. from overseas businesses and savers. So let's take a look at the recent data on all of these, and then figure out whether the U.S. will have adequate capital to continue the productivity gains that are critical to a higher rate of economic growth.

## AMERICA STILL ISN'T MUCH OF A SAVER

The United States, as a nation, is not much of an achiever in the savings and investment department. About 18% of its annual GDP goes to "private investment"—money spent by individuals and businesses on things of enduring value (like construction of homes and apartments) and on things that will produce future value (like new factories, machinery, and office buildings).

This "private investment" portion of America's annual production is a relatively small share compared with that of many other nations. America's 1996 rate of capital investment was a little higher than that of Sweden (14.5%), Great Britain (15%), and Mexico (16%), and about the same as Italy (17%), Poland (17.1%), Canada (17.5%), and France (18%).

But the investment rate was substantially lower than the rates of several countries deemed to be America's major competitors: Germany (21.7%), Japan (28.5%), and South Korea (36.6%). Among the less-developed nations, India has been running a domestic savings rate of 22% and China a breathtaking 42%, as corporate earnings and personal incomes rose much faster than investment opportunities for business and the availability of sophisticated goods for Chinese consumers to buy.

National savings come from a combination of sources: business savings (retained and reinvested corporate profits, plus money set aside for replacing depreciating assets); individual savings; government savings, in the form of budget surpluses (or for most of the past 40 years, "negative savings"—borrowing—created by annual budget deficits); and capital inflows from foreigners, who either choose to invest abroad or must invest abroad to recycle the foreign currencies they amass from their trade surpluses.

America's private savings rate, both business and individual, began a steep decline in the early 1980s, and the decline has continued since then. At the same time, the government wasn't saving anything, but was borrowing heavily to cover annual deficits, diverting capital from business and contributing, to some unknown degree, to higher interest rates.

### *Anemic personal savings*

Saving by individuals hit post-World War II peaks of about 9.4% of disposable (after-tax) income in 1975 and then again in 1981. But it has plummeted in the years since, running barely 4% for most of the '90s and hitting 3.8% in 1997—the lowest level since 1946. There are many explanations for this low savings rate, including these:

• People tend to save less of their new earnings when their assets are rising strongly in value (the "wealth effect"). Soaring home equity and stock prices in the '80s contributed to low savings then, and the long bull market of the '90s has probably had a similar effect.

• For ten years the U.S. had the world's highest taxation of capital gains, a situation that improved only recently, with the 1997 tax cut.

• Borrowing is rewarded by the tax deductibility of interest on business loans and on consumers' home-equity loans, but America's corporate profits continue to be taxed twice, first as corporate income and then again, if distributed to shareholders, as personal dividend income.

• America is demographically younger than most advanced nations, and young people in their early-career and household-formation years tend to save less than older people do.

• Today's senior citizens are freer-spending, and less savings-conscious, than earlier generations were, due to strong income from social security, private pensions and investments.

• Spending on such durable products as cars and home improvements is counted in government statistics as consumption, even though these purchases have residual value. In the affluent U.S., where such expenditures are heavy, they depress the official savings rate more than in other nations.

• Individual savings rates tend to decline when people feel confident about the nation's future and their well-being, as has been the case during most of the '90s (at least as reflected in consumer-confidence polls).

### HIGHER SAVINGS AHEAD

Fortunately for America's future competitiveness, this long trend of declining national savings will not continue indefinitely. The future looks generally positive.

Business savings has been picking up in the '90s and will probably continue. A higher percentage of earnings is being retained and reinvested, rather than paid out as dividends to shareholders. Stockholders don't mind the lower yield from dividends, especially since taxation of capital gains was reduced. U.S. corporate earnings *growth* will not be as boomy in the next decade or so as it has been in the '90s, but the trend toward higher retention of earnings will continue to boost the rate of business investment.

### Government no longer a big 'dissaver'

Government at all levels—federal, state and local—will be a positive factor in a rise in the national savings rate, reversing the negative role it has played for 25 years.

While actual budget surpluses—and the resulting paying down of previous debt—will be very rare or nonexistent in Washington, federal deficits will continue to account for a relatively small share of a growing economy, on the order of 1% to 2%, rather than the 4% to 6% seen in the mid '80s. This will reduce the government's competition for capital and keep interest rates in the present moderate range.

### Aging boomers get the idea

The U.S. personal savings rates will probably tick up a little from recent all-time lows. Why? Because the 74 million baby-boomers, now in their peak earning years, finally seem to be getting serious about saving for retirement, encouraged by big gains in stocks and government incentives like Roth IRAs. While the stock market will not be as boomy in the next decade as in the '90s, most investors will take a patient, long-term view and keep putting money in on a regular basis.

## FOREIGN INVESTORS GIVE AMERICA A LIFT

For better or worse, Americans have long been relieved of some of their savings obligation by the eagerness of foreign savers to send their money here, for investment in everything from plants and equipment to financial assets. Since 1993 there has been an enormous surge of foreign capital into U.S. Treasury notes, corporate bonds and publicly traded stocks. By 1997 the annual purchases were more than three times the level of 1993.

There is no reason to believe that this flow will diminish in the years ahead, even with exciting equity investment opportunities in developing nations. Besides the need to recycle the dollars they acquire by selling us their products, foreigners have had plenty of other good reasons to invest in America. The U.S. will continue to be the world's most dynamic large economy, investment returns will be good, and—as the Asian financial crisis has shown—the safety of U.S. markets poses a stark contrast to volatility in other nations.

### AMERICA WILL DO WELL *DESPITE* LOW SAVINGS

A final word on America's low rate of domestic savings and capital investment, compared with other nations': It's been low throughout a 15-year period in which America has done better economically than most of the advanced nations with higher savings rates (Japan, for example, and several nations of Western Europe).

Part of the explanation for this seeming paradox lies in the difference between a *proportion* and an absolute *amount*. The *proportion* of America's output that goes into new investment might be low compared with other nations, but the *amount* is stunningly large, due to the immensity of the U.S. economy. And this annual increment of investment adds to a capital stock of factories, laboratories, offices and schools that is already vastly larger, more modern and more productive than any other nation's.

# Foreign Role in U.S. Growth: Customers and Investors

America has long been the world's leading exporter in value of goods and services, but foreign trade has been a relatively small part of its total economy, due to the size and affluence of its domestic market. Many American businesses didn't bother to look abroad for sales growth, as firms in smaller nations such as Japan, Germany and the Netherlands have done for years.

Now, emboldened by surging consumer and business demand in other lands, American businesses of all sizes are looking far beyond their shores, searching for newly capable customers on every continent—5.7 billion potential customers or 95% of the world's population. Stories like these are happening in every U. S. state:

• Kingsdown, a maker of luxury bedding in Mebane, N.C., exports $3,000 mattress sets to Japan, the Middle East and South America;

• Multiplex, based in Ballwin, Mo., sells beverage-dispensing equipment in Taiwan, Germany, France, Canada and England;

• Quickie, a Fresno, Cal., maker of high-performance wheelchairs, sells its equipment all over the world; and

• Pantone, a Carlstadt, N.J,. maker of color-control processes for printing, textiles and other applications, sells its products in Asia through a Hong Kong office.

And giant American companies are stepping up their foreign initiatives, too. U.S. toy maker Mattel embarked in 1998 on an ambitious strategy to double its foreign sales over the next five years, reducing its U.S. sales to 50% of total revenues, down from 65% today. "Only 3% of the world's kids are in the U.S.," Mattel CEO Jill Barad told *The Wall Street Journal*, while announcing a new line of less-expensive dolls for foreign markets, including "Global Friends" dolls that reflect the look and attire of children in major world capitals.

## EXPORTS A RISING SHARE OF ECONOMY

Commitments such as these explain why exports are a strongly rising share of the economy. From 1985 through 1997, exports rose every year, averaging double-digit growth until interrupted by a slight downturn in 1998, when the emerging markets crisis in Asia and elsewhere severely impaired the ability of foreign customers to buy U.S. goods. Sales of American services to foreign customers (either in their home country or on our shores) rose by a similar percentage. Purchases by Americans of imported goods and services rose, too, but not as much as exports.

While the total volume of foreign trade in and out of America was growing at double-digit levels, the overall economy was growing at less than 3% a year. So foreign trade's share of total economic activity nearly doubled, from about 13.8% of GDP in 1986 to 26% in 1996.

America's export boom isn't restricted to a few big manufacturing states. According to a study by the Massachusetts Institute of Social and Economic Research, 46 of the 50 states experienced varying degrees of export growth from 1992 through 1996. Several previously small exporters such as South Dakota, Hawaii, Arizona and New Mexico doubled or tripled their export volume in this period. Big industrial states such as Michigan and Missouri achieved 67% and 56% growth, respectively, in exports, and South Carolina, a hotbed of foreign investment, boosted its exports 76%.

## SERVICES EXPORTS BOOM

The U.S. is the world's largest seller of services, and its lead is likely to grow in the decades ahead, despite increasing global competition in lines ranging from commercial aviation to civil engineering.

In increasing numbers, foreign customers will travel the world on U.S.-based airlines. They will watch TV shows and movies produced in the U.S. They will come to America to have difficult surgery performed. They will study at American universities, either on U.S. campuses, at a foreign campus of a U.S. college, or through Internet or televised distance-learning programs. They will make phone calls, even in their own countries, on wireless phones tied to American-owned satellite systems. They will run their appliances on electrical current from a U.S.-owned, or U.S.-engineered, utility. Their garbage will be collected and their industrial wastes processed by American companies. Some of their biggest buildings will be designed by American architects.

Foreign businesses will hire U.S.-based management consulting firms to guide their way into global partnerships and new markets. They will buy consumer products through American retailers who operate vast, fully stocked virtual stores on the Internet, and their goods will arrive via Federal Express and United Parcel Service. And foreign tourists will keep flocking to the U.S. to spend their entertainment and leisure money in America's theme parks, wilderness areas and historical sites. Other foreign citizens will seek capital for their businesses from, and pay fees to, U.S. investment bankers, and investors all over the world will use the brokerage services of U.S. firms, whether at local offices overseas or on the Internet.

## BIG-TICKET EXPORTS AND CONSUMER GOODS, TOO

America's export strength has traditionally been derived largely from high-priced capital goods and other items bought by businesses—jet airliners, computers and scientific equipment, for example.

Sales of these products will be joined by surging trade in consumer products that, though not necessarily better than another country's similar product, carry an unusually high cachet with the new global middle class, especially young consumers. Levi Strauss, for example, is selling its jeans at some 28 retail stores in Malaysia. Teens in Asia, Latin America and Europe chat on Motorola cell phones on long-distance calls cleared by AT&T. They gobble McDonald's Big Macs and guzzle Coke and Pepsi, do homework on IBM and Macintosh home computers, and wear clothing from Nike and Champion. They carry bankcards issued by Citicorp. They use personal-care products made by Procter & Gamble and Johnson & Johnson.

And in amazing numbers, they derive their distorted view of life in America from U.S.-made movies and television programming. It is estimated that MTV's music videos are seen by more youths around the world—in nations as different as Brazil, India and China—than in the U.S. The mix of songs on MTV's overseas networks, however, is truly international and generally more wholesome than the U.S. version; American hits are interspersed with large doses of the local pop music.

## AMERICAN MULTINATIONALS SPREAD THEIR REACH

"American-brand" goods are not necessarily made in the U.S. Many of these consumer products are, and will increasingly be, made by American multinational companies in their overseas plants.

In a few decades most of the biggest American multinationals will have vastly more employees outside the U.S. than on home turf. That's true today of only two large American corporations, Ford and IBM, which have 54% and 51% of their employees in plants and offices outside the U.S. Another group of U.S. multinationals, including AT&T, General Electric, PepsiCo and General Motors, have between one-fifth and one-third of their total employment in non-U.S. facilities.

The world leaders in non-domestic employment are multinationals based in small European nations—Switzerland's Nestlé, with 97% of its employees in other nations, and the Dutch electronics firm Philips, with 82%. Over time, American companies will increasingly emulate this model of international growth.

## NO END TO TRADE DEFICITS

It is highly unlikely that American exports and imports—of goods and services combined—will be in balance at any time in the next few decades.

There are three reasons why: First, the U.S. is the world's most open economy. Second, the U.S. is the world's richest nation, and therefore able to afford all the imports it wishes to buy. Third, over half of the trade deficit is attributed to petroleum, which world producers are happy to supply at cheap prices while U.S. reserves sit in the ground to await the higher prices of another day. (Some people consider U.S. dependence on foreign oil to be a national-security issue, but it's not much of one, given the geographic variety of imported-oil sources today and in the future.)

Over the next few years the trade deficit will probably widen, due to weakness in Asia, which will impair the growth of exports to that region and flood the U.S. market with Asian goods that the continent's weak economies can't absorb.

In any event, persistent U.S. trade deficits will have no particular bearing on America's continued economic success in the world economy. In recent years, the rising U.S. trade deficit has not been due to American economic weakness. Rather, it arises from the financial capac-

ity of a booming United States to absorb the bargain-priced excess production of trading partners whose economic growth, and therefore
domestic consumer demand, have been relatively weak.

There are highly successful nations that regularly run big trade
deficits, and there are less-successful nations with big surpluses, especially poor nations whose citizens can't afford to buy goods from the rest
of the world. The enormous trade surpluses of one affluent nation—
Japan—haven't saved it from a decade of economic stagnation in the
'90s. Instead, Japan's surpluses—a symptom of its closed markets and
high consumer prices—have contributed to its economic woes.

## MAJOR TRADING PARTNERS

Among America's 20 largest trading partners in 1997, fourteen of
them sold the U.S. more goods and services than they bought, and
those 14 nations included the top four trading partners, Canada, Japan,
Mexico and China. The U.S. ran a small surplus with its number-five
partner, Great Britain. America's biggest trade surpluses were with (in
order) the Netherlands, Australia, Brazil, Hong Kong, Belgium and
Great Britain.

In total dollars, the U.S. deficit with Japan was the largest, at
about $56 billion, but the greatest percentage imbalance was with
China, whose factories and workers supplied the U.S. more than *five
times* the value of products and services that China bought from America. But much of the merchandise coming from China (as from many
of the less-developed nations) is imported to the U.S. by American
firms that contracted with Chinese companies for production or that
made the goods in factories they own in China.

The U.S. trade deficit with Japan will decline in the next few years,
as Japan gradually opens its economy to foreign capital and goods to
stimulate growth, lower consumer costs, and raise living standards in its
struggling economy. But the deficit with China will keep growing, sup-
planting the Japanese deficit as the biggest in volume—and as the
hottest issue in U.S. trade policy. The United States will press China to
open its economy to more American goods and also improve its sorry
record in the protection of U.S. patents and copyrights.

## STRONG FOREIGN INVESTMENT IN U.S.

Since the U.S. will continue to run a sizable trade deficit, it will
automatically see a high level of foreign investment, because net inflows
of foreign capital are *always* at least equal to a nation's trade deficit.
The surplus dollars earned by overseas producers will simply come

back to the U.S. as heavy—and very beneficial—foreign investment in plants, stocks, bonds and bank deposits.

In addition, if an economy is attractive to foreign investors for its sheer market size, affluence, growth prospects, investment returns and political stability—as the U.S. is—it will receive even more foreign capital than required to cover its trade deficit.

In 1996, foreign investors poured $408 billion more into U.S. financial assets than American investors placed overseas, and this was almost 200% more than the volume of just three years earlier. More than half of that foreign money went into U.S. government bonds—the ultimate safe haven for the world's capital—with the rest going to corporate bonds, certificates of deposit (CDs) and stocks (only about 3% of the $408 billion, but helpful support for U.S. stock prices).

A lot of China's $50 billion trade surplus with the U.S. in 1997—maybe as much as 40%, or $20 billion—found its way back to the U.S. in financial investments, with heavy Chinese purchases (by government and businesses) of U.S. Treasuries and mortgage-backed bonds issued by Fannie Mae and Freddie Mac. These infusions of Chinese capital helped keep U.S. interests rates low and contributed to the long boom in U.S. home sales. So far, the Chinese haven't been big direct investors in American plants, equipment or whole companies. But that will come in the decade ahead, as it develops multinational firms of its own.

### *More foreign-owned facilities*

Direct foreign investment (DFI) in the U.S.—the purchase of entire American companies, or expansion of foreign-owned manufacturing facilities—has remained very strong throughout the '90s, even as vast amounts of capital from the advanced nations (U.S., Japan and the countries of Europe) flowed into hot markets of the developing world. For example, America's total DFI greatly exceeded that of China, which has led all the developing nations in its receipt of foreign investment capital in the '90s.

The foreign companies sending this capital to the U.S. are typically multinationals starting or expanding U.S. operations or making American acquisitions in everything from chemicals, banking and textiles to computers, publishing and pharmaceuticals. Their products are either consumed in the U.S. market or exported to overseas customers, counting as American exports.

Heavy foreign investment has long been a boon to the U. S. economy, creating jobs and helping communities grow. Foreign-owned firms employ only 5% of all American workers, but in the manufacturing sector they employ more than double that percentage—almost 12%. Foreign capital is attracted to America by the dynamism of the U.S. economy, with its high consumer income, its talented, highly productive work force, its moderate wages (especially compared with Europe), and its relatively low taxes, regulation and barriers to foreign capital.

The only downside to heavy foreign investment is the possibility that the earnings of the foreign-owned businesses will flow out of the U.S. to foreign shareholders, or that foreign-owned firms will be less supportive of their local American communities than U.S. firms are. But up to now, neither situation has been a problem. Most earnings of foreign facilities have been reinvested in the U.S. market, which is a positive for America's future.

### Regional boosts from foreign money

The benefit of this foreign investment is evident everywhere, but particularly in the southeastern states—the Carolinas and Georgia especially—which have long been strongholds of heavy foreign investment from Europe and Japan and which, not coincidentally, have been among America's fastest-growing state economies. Alabama is another state much blessed by foreign investment, with a new Mercedes plant near Tuscaloosa and a British Steel iron-smelting operation near Mobile (dismantled and moved from Scotland). The latter supplies iron to a British Steel minimill in Tuscaloosa and another mill in Decatur, Georgia, that's owned jointly by British Steel, Japan's Sumitomo and America's LTV.

Despite the fact that the U.S. is a mature auto market where growth in units sold will not match that of developing nations, foreign automakers—from BMW and Mercedes to the big Japanese makers—are beefing up their U.S. production to try to gain market share. In the process, they will replace some future volume of imported cars with their American-made cars. Toyota has expanded its Kentucky plant, is planning to build another in either the U.S. or Canada, and will double the originally planned capacity of a truck plant in Indiana. Honda, with two auto plants in Ohio, is thinking about adding another one in another state, ideally a place where labor is more plentiful than in the boomy manufacturing climate of Ohio.

### Europe will stay U.S.'s biggest foreign investor

Many Americans believe Asian corporations, especially Japanese, are the largest foreign owners of business assets in the U.S. But while Asian investment took the biggest jump over the past 15 years—rising twelvefold to $143 billion by 1996—the Asian share of total foreign business assets in America is much less than that of Europe's multi-national firms—only 21% to Europe's 65%.

In the decade ahead, European multinationals are likely to maintain their number-one position as the biggest foreign owners of American plants, equipment and operating companies. While a united Europe will see a substantial improvement in its business climate and costs of production, especially with strong growth opportunities in Eastern Europe and Russia, European multinationals will continue to be attracted to the unique business opportunities in America.

Great Britain, already the number-one owner of U.S. production assets, led all nations in additions to American holdings in 1997, with $13 billion of new direct foreign investment. But 1998 has been the year of the Germans, with transnational megamergers by Daimler-Benz (with Chrysler), Bertelsmann (with Random House) and others. All told, European firms poured more money into the U.S. in the first five months of 1998 than in all of the previous year. Japanese companies, hungry for capital in their troubled home economy, invested less than $2 billion in new U.S. acquisitions and expansions in 1997, down from nearly $9 billion the year before.

## AMERICAN FIRMS KEEP MOVING ABROAD

International investment is a multilane highway, of course. While foreign businesses have been shoveling money into American operations, U.S. multinationals have also been investing increasing amounts of their capital in new or expanded capacity overseas. In the first half of the '90s, direct foreign investment by U.S. businesses overseas *exceeded* the very heavy flows from foreign firms into the U.S.

Aggressive U.S. firms are pushing further into the world economy in all lines of business in both the developed nations of Europe and Third World nations. U.S. automakers are building factories in Russia and China. Coca-Cola bottles its beverages in the former East Germany. Gillette makes razor blades in Poland. Whirlpool is making refrigerators in India, where Motorola is big in pagers. American petroleum companies are investing heavily in developing the rich reserves of former Soviet republics. Frito-Lay sells its potato chips in China and Thailand. AES, a power company based in the Virginia suburbs of Washington, D.C., acquires and builds new electric-generating plants all over the world. Otis, a part of United Technologies, has joint ventures making elevators in Vietnam and China. Anheuser-Busch makes Budweiser in China. Citicorp took advantage of financial crises, and falling prices, in Mexico and Thailand to acquire failing banks in those countries, and its credit card business is booming in Thailand.

Most significantly, the deepening financial crises in Japan and South Korea in 1998 began to open those markets, for the first time ever, to the full acquisition of their ailing local companies by foreign corporations from the U.S. and Europe.

In 1996 the total value of all U.S.-owned business assets overseas ($796 billion) was 26% greater than the value of foreign-owned business assets in America ($630 billion), measured by what those assets cost when originally purchased. But much of the U.S. business investment overseas took place long ago, when prices were much lower, while foreign assets in the U.S. are generally of more recent purchase. So the true difference in value is probably much greater than 26%.

### Destinations of U.S. investment

Canada, America's biggest trading partner by far (with nearly $1 billion of two-way trade *every day*), was once also the site of the greatest share of U.S.-owned plants and facilities. As recently as 1982, American production facilities in Canada had a value one and a half times greater than American-owned assets in all of Asia. While U.S. investment in Canada has doubled in the years since then, flows of American investment into Europe and especially Asia have been much heavier—a fourfold increase in Europe and a fivefold increase in Asia.

As a result, Canada today is the site of only 11% of American business assets abroad (down from 21% in 1982), compared with 50% in Europe, 18% in Asia and 18% in Latin America. Africa and the Middle East (including North Africa) account for only about 1% each of U.S. direct foreign investment.

## U.S. A 'DEBTOR NATION'? NO BIG DEAL

One of the silliest nonissues in American economic debate is concern about the U. S.'s being a "debtor nation"—a popular and troubling notion during the darkest days of America's "declinist" anxiety in the late '80s. While it doesn't get talked about as much in these days of greater American self-confidence, it still rears its head from time to time, with as much public misunderstanding as ever.

If your idea of a debtor is someone who owes any amount of money, then the United States is certainly a debtor. So is any individual American with a home mortgage, or any business that borrows money to expand. But if your idea of a debtor is someone whose total debts constitute a high percentage of his assets, or even exceed his assets, then the U.S. is definitely *not* a debtor nation.

In the jargon of international economics, America is called a "debtor" nation because the total value of a *single class* of assets—those owned by foreigners, such as factories, office buildings, corporate stocks and bonds, U.S. Treasury bonds and bank deposits—is greater than the value of overseas assets owned by Americans. This is true, and it has been true since 1987, but it's next to meaningless as a measure of America's strength.

"Net foreign debt," economists Herbert Stein and Murray Foss observe, "is only a comparison of arbitrarily chosen totals of assets and liabilities"—and rather minor totals, at that. If it were ever necessary for Americans to square their debts with the world—a truly remote possibility—the assets available for this reconciliation wouldn't be just America's assets *overseas*, but its total assets *everywhere*, including in the U.S.

Foreign claims on Americans—the assets foreign investors and businesses own in the U.S.—had an estimated market value of $3 trillion in 1993. That same year, U.S. assets abroad were estimated at a lower amount, about $2.5 trillion—hence the "debtor" status. But the value of U.S.-owned assets *in America* was estimated at a breathtaking $21 trillion, for a total American national wealth of $23.5 trillion. So foreign-owned assets in the U.S. represented only 13% of America's total wealth. Now, you wouldn't lose sleep at night if your family or your business had such a ratio of assets to liabilities—7.5 to 1. As Stein and Foss sum it up, the concept of America as a "net debtor nation" is "not a threat to the United States or a sign of economic weakness."

## THE MIGHTY DOLLAR

The U.S. dollar will remain strong, trading at or slightly less than its present range for years. In mid 1998, it was unusually high against the yen, due to Japan's lingering economic malaise, but it drifted down as Japan got back on its feet the following year.

The value of any nation's currency rises and falls with other people's desire to own it—to buy products and services of that nation, to invest in its assets, to visit it as a tourist, student or medical patient, or for a variety of other purposes. The strength of the dollar in recent years has been based on a robust world desire to own dollars for purchasing American goods and services, to invest in U.S. Treasuries, and to participate in the successful U.S. economy as equity investors.

But currency values are in constant flux. In 1998, the very high dollar dampened demand for American exports in recession-wracked Asia, and this eventually brought the dollar back into line. Similarly, the occasional rush of world investment capital to a hot, fast-growing region with soaring stock prices—like Asia before the crash there—will dampen demand for American assets, softening the value of the dollar.

### *Dollar a global means of exchange*

But the U.S. dollar isn't just the currency of America. It is the dominant means of exchange of the global economy.

Since the U.S. is the largest player in world trade, every transaction going in and out of the country—fully 20% of world trade volume—is priced in dollars. And because of the dollar's stability, it is trusted by so many other nations that it is used for many transactions not involving American parties at all. Some 48% of all the world's trade transactions are priced in dollars. Some 62% of the currency reserves of national governments are held in dollars. Due to the immensity of American stock, bond and currency markets, and strong foreign investor demand for U.S. assets, dollars are used in an estimated 80% of all the world's investment transactions each day. And in the informal (black) markets of developing nations, American currency is always more highly valued than local money.

This global demand supports a high valuation for dollars. While an excessively high level (as in the mid '80s and late '90s) can overprice U.S. products and trim exports, a moderately high level contributes to low American inflation and interest rates.

### *New competition to the dollar*

Over the next few years, the dollar will get its first competition for the hearts, minds and pocketbooks of the world: the euro, the new currency of 11 European Union nations (not including, at first, Britain, Sweden, Denmark and Greece). It will eventually be used not only in its issuing nations, but also in other global transactions now using the German mark, the world's second most popular currency, and the French franc. There is also the possibility that many nations of Eastern Europe that now use dollars extensively will migrate toward the euro. And there could be a parallel trend in Asia, with the emergence of the yen as the dominant currency for trade and investment.

But it's not a foregone conclusion that the euro will succeed to the extent that the 11 "euroland" nations' will abandon their own national currencies once a dual-use transition ends in 2002. There is a strong possibility that the fiscal discipline required by the member nations—especially reducing government deficits to less than 3% amid double-digit unemployment in Europe—will cause a populist backlash against monetary integration and delay or scuttle full adoption of the new currency.

The strength of the euro, like any currency, will ultimately rest on the economic vitality and dynamism of the issuing nations. And correspondingly, the strength of the dollar will depend on the future performance of the U.S. economy. As Deputy Treasury Secretary Lawrence Summers told a congressional hearing in 1997, "If the United States maintains strong and credible policies, the dollar will remain a sound currency; the fate of the dollar will be largely in our hands."

# U.S. Manufacturing: Alive and Well

Contrary to public misperception, the value of manufactured goods produced in America rises virtually every year, with occasional dips during recessions, and this long trend will continue. Manufacturing's share of the U.S. economy has not declined in recent years, but has held fairly steady in a narrow range between 20% and 23% of GDP.

The U.S. still has a significant productivity edge over its major competitors, and it enjoys an enormous superiority over the Third World nations. But as advanced manufacturing technology spreads to the developing world, this superiority will gradually diminish. The U.S. will import even more consumer goods and capital equipment than it does today.

Annual increases in U.S. manufacturing value have been especially strong over the past decade, averaging about 5% a year, with gains as high as 8.6% in 1994 and 7.4% in 1995. Strength was especially evident in high-value durable goods such as cars, appliances, electronics, machinery and aircraft, with a record gain of 12.4% in 1994. The more high-tech the manufacturing, the greater America's, but even such basic industries as steel and textiles are enjoying a resurgence, due to enormous productivity gains.

The steel industry is a good example of America's new manufacturing strength. After a terrible decline in the '70s and early '80s, American-made steel has made an amazing comeback over the past ten years, thanks to heavy capital investment in productivity, the development of highly efficient minimills using scrap as their raw material, and heavy foreign investment by Japanese and British steelmakers. Today the U.S. is probably *the* low-cost steel producer in the world. Total production in 1996 was 105 million tons, about 30% higher than a decade before, even with tough world competition and relatively low U.S. trade barriers to foreign-made steel. And U.S. steel output in 1997 was the second-highest in American history.

## THE *REINDUSTRIALIZING* OF AMERICA

America's resurgent manufacturing strength should have silenced the myth of "deindustrialization," but it lives on in public discourse. What accounts for the durability of this myth? It comes from two facts: the changing *composition* of U.S. manufactured goods and the declining number of people producing tangible goods, a function of soaring productivity in manufacturing, mining and construction.

All over America, manufacturers large and small are creating totally new high-tech products every week—in biotech, telecommunications, scientific instruments, microelectronics and countless other fields. And the rising value of these new kinds of goods more than offsets the declining value of old-style simple goods, such as apparel, shoes, dinnerware and toys. A case can be made that the U.S. is *reindustrializing*, rather than deindustrializing.

But most Americans don't notice this trend because of the prominence in their lives of foreign-made consumer goods. The American home is full of foreign consumer products—apparel made in Hong Kong, Mexico, India, Poland, Bangladesh or Mauritius; shoes made in Malaysia, Brazil or Italy; an automobile made in Japan or Germany; TVs, stereos and PCs made in Singapore or Thailand; toys, dishes and clothing (and lots of other things) made in China.

Americans who remember a time when all of this stuff had a "Made in the U.S.A." label, and imports were negligible, tend to buy into the deindustrializing myth. The products that America makes best today (and exports) are big, expensive and often used by business rather than consumers. You won't find in the home such great American products as airliners made by Boeing, high-speed commercial laser printers made by Xerox, telecommunications switching systems made by Lucent, tractors and road graders made by Caterpillar or satellites made by Hughes.

## SLOW JOB GROWTH IN MANUFACTURING

While it seems obvious that the vitality of an industry should be judged by the increasing value of its output, many Americans (especially politicians) want to make employment, rather than output, the measurement of health. Machinery doesn't vote; people do. Herein lies the root of America's misperception of its manufacturing strength.

Even the manufacturing employment issue isn't as simple as it looks at first glance; there is continuing confusion between the *actual number* of manufacturing jobs versus the *share* of total U.S. employment that those jobs represent. The number of goods-producing jobs (including construction and mining, but not farming) has been virtually flat for the past 25 years. The number of people working in the tangible-goods industries in 1996—a little over 24 million—is a little higher than the number working in such fields in 1970 and just slightly less than the numbers in 1980 and 1990. The number of people working in manufacturing has actually ticked up a little during the economic expansion of the '90s, due to the boom in high-tech manufacturing.

What's astounding is that manufacturing production has soared in the U.S. over the past 25 years with only a negligible increase in the number of workers producing it. This, quite simply, is what productivity is all about.

Because employment in the service sector is growing much more rapidly, manufacturing jobs are a shrinking share of the work force. This has been going on for years. The goods-producing sector (not including farming) accounted for 41% of jobs in 1950, 33% in 1970 and only 20% in 1996; the Labor Department estimates that its share will drop to 18% by 2005 and probably continue to head south thereafter. All other jobs are counted in the service sector, whose share of total employment has risen from 59% in 1950 to about 80%.

It is likely that the number of manufacturing jobs in the U.S. won't fall in the years ahead, but it won't rise much either. American firms—and foreign-owned subsidiaries in the U.S.—will continue to increase the number of plants, productive capacity and variety of products made in the U.S. But advances in automation will be so great that the growth in employment will be far lower than the rise in output.

# A Slow-Growing U.S. Work Force

In the next 10 to 15 years, job growth will slow a bit from the torrid pace of the '80s and '90s, according to forecasts by the U.S. Bureau of Labor Statistics (BLS). This won't result in a surge in unemployment, however, because the labor force will also grow more slowly— about 1.3% a year. Labor shortages will continue in certain highly skilled occupations—such as computers and health care—and in high-growth geographic areas. Such shortages will be relieved in part by immigration.

Changes in the work force will mirror changes in the overall population. Women, racial minorities and immigrants will account for a higher proportion of new entrants to the job market, while white males, retiring in large numbers, will be a declining portion of the work force.

Women will make up about 48% of the work force in 2010 and 50% or more by 2020. The percentage of Hispanic workers will increase from 9% now to 12% in 2010 and 14% or 15% by 2020. African-American workers will compose a bit more than 11%, a fairly steady share. The percentage of Asian and other minority workers will increase sharply, but will still make up only about 5% of the work force in 2010. Whites, now about 77% of the work force, will fall to less than 70% by 2020.

The work force will also be aging. There will be an increase in older workers, while those aged 25 to 44 will decline in actual numbers, not just in their share of the work force. The upper age levels of the work force are even more predominantly white than the labor force as a whole. So as these workers retire after 2010, the composition of the work force will shift even more toward women and racial minorities.

## ALMOST ALL JOB GROWTH IN SERVICES

The U. S. economy has shown an amazing capacity to create new jobs over the past decade, while most of its major competitors were mired in sluggish job growth and high unemployment. Employment in manufacturing has been basically flat, so almost all the growth has been in the service sector. Service employment grew by more than 20 million jobs—an average of two million a year.

A key aspect of the economic angst felt by many Americans has been a feeling that lost manufacturing jobs were replaced by low-wage jobs in services. Examples often cited include declining employment in steel or automaking and soaring employment in minimum-wage retailing, household help and fast-food occupations.

There is some validity to this concern, but it looms larger in public debate than it should. First of all, high-wage union jobs in steel and automaking were never typical of all manufacturing pay, just as the minimum wage is not typical of service-sector work today. Manufacturing does pay more on average than service work, but the differential is something like 10%, not 200% or 300%.

A lot of those new service jobs *do* pay less—sometimes much less—than the average U.S. wage. In 1993, according to the Commerce Department, about 58% of service-sector jobs were in 14 fields—including retail clerking, child care, gardening, office and house cleaning, car washing, fast food—that pay less than the average American wage. (The biggest component of this lower-wage group is retailing, which pays on average only about 60% of the typical American wage in the private sector.)

## HIGH-WAGE SERVICES, TOO

Conversely, the other 42% of service-sector workers toil in the larger number of fields (19 different lines of work) that pay a higher-than-average wage or salary. These include such fields as medicine, education, stock brokerage, real estate, banking, law, engineering, insurance, accounting, architecture, long-haul trucking, airline piloting and maintenance, telecommunications and computer-systems design and maintenance. Job growth in most of these fields has been especially strong in recent years, which should—but has yet to—dispel the myth that America's service sector boom has been driven largely by "junk jobs."

One characteristic of America's good new jobs, whether in manufacturing or services, is that they invariably require a solid education, usually beyond the high school level. If America has a job-creation problem, it's that today's economy is not creating the kinds of low-skill, moderate-wage jobs that can be filled by young people of limited education (high school or less), like the old factory jobs of the '50s and '60s.

That day simply isn't coming back, so America's critical challenge in the decades ahead is to improve education and vocational training to match the jobs that are emerging in abundance. This is in the early stages of coming to pass, as we'll show later in our discussion of education and job training.

# Low Inflation Ahead

One of the great economic debates of the late '90s concerns the long-term prospects for inflation: Could double-digit (or high-single-digit) inflation return? Or are we headed for a lengthy period of very low inflation or even deflation—that is, declining prices? The last bout of hyperinflation, in the late '70s and early '80s, was caused by a global phenomenon external to the U.S. economy—an artificial jacking-up of oil prices by a powerful cartel. That's not likely to happen again, because of diversity in oil supply. Other major inflationary factors have included loose monetary policy and federal deficits that were a very high percentage of GDP. These situations are also not likely to be repeated in the next decade or so.

## INFLATIONARY FORCES

Nonetheless, there is a deep-seated tendency toward inflationary government policies in all social democracies. Debtors like inflation a lot more than they admit, because they can pay off their obligations with money that's worth less than what they borrowed. And debtors out-number creditors by a wide margin.

World commodity prices—of everything from wood pulp and oil to metal ores and grains—will be a mixed picture. Soaring worldwide economic growth in the Third World will mean increased competition with the developed nations for these commodities. With normal lags between rising demand and increased production, there will be occasional price spikes in commodities, causing inflationary pressures in the U.S. and elsewhere. But these should level off with adjustments in production.

There will be upward pressure on wages and fringe benefits in labor-short regions of the country and in high-skill occupations needed by fast-growing technology lines. Businesses will try to pass higher labor costs on to their customers in higher prices, but in many situations it won't be possible.

While foreign competition will restrain wages and prices in many areas (especially manufacturing), there are plenty of business sectors, mostly in services, with relatively little global competition. Such sectors include housing and construction, health care, media and advertising, higher education, domestic travel, financial services, restaurant dining, household help, entertainment and phone service. These are important and generally rising shares of household budgets, and they are highly susceptible to inflationary pressure. Recent trends toward consolidation in many of these national businesses will reduce competition and make it easier for big players to raise prices.

## DISINFLATIONARY FACTORS

On the anti-inflation side of the scale, start with stable U.S. monetary policy, providing enough liquidity and credit to fuel moderate growth without encouraging over-expansion and speculation. Add in more responsible fiscal policy, with generally lower government deficits at the federal, state and local levels. In the private sectors, prices and wages will be increasingly restrained by global competition in manufactured goods, agriculture and energy.

## THE BOTTOM LINE: MODERATE INFLATION

Weighing all these price pressures and pressure relievers, the preponderance of evidence points to a generally low level of consumer inflation, not much different from what the U.S. has experienced in the past 15 years. For planning purposes, expect consumer prices to rise a little less than 3% a year on average.

But there won't be actual *deflation*. Prices will fall in particular business sectors, especially in response to automation, new technology, economies of scale and global competition, as has been seen in consumer electronics for years and is now being seen in services including telecommunications and securities trading. And prices fall due to occasional imbalances of supply and demand, as in housing and auto prices. But a long period of deflation would have to be accompanied by a collapse in personal income, credit and consumer demand—both at home and in the world economy—and that's just not on the horizon.

## REVISING THE CPI

Over the past few years a consensus emerged among economists that the government's consumer price index—the periodic calculation of the cost of a market basket of goods and services consumed by most Americans—was overstating price increases by as much as one percentage point a year. In particular, economists believed, the CPI didn't recognize that when the price of a product rises, consumers frequently make substitutions—buying a different kind of product, particular brand or container size, or shopping at a different retail outlet. So in 1998 the Bureau of Labor Statistics made changes in the CPI formula that are expected to trim about eight-tenths of 1% off the annual increase in future years.

This change will have a major effect on the U.S. economy, because the government's CPI is the standard for cost-of-living adjustments (COLAs) in countless private and public uses, including labor contracts, commercial and residential leases. Most significantly, the CPI is used in raising government pension benefits (social security, military and civil service) and adjusting the tax brackets and standard deduction on federal income-tax forms.

In its effect on the federal budget, shaving the CPI will tend to reduce future deficits. That's because it will restrain spending hikes by allowing smaller increases in government pensions, while boosting tax revenues by not raising the standard deduction or broadening the tax brackets as much as the old CPI formula did.

## INTEREST RATES WILL STAY IN PRESENT RANGE

In a fully global capital market, the price of borrowed money will be determined by supply and demand for credit not just within one nation, but among all nations.

The future cost of borrowed money in the U.S. will be restrained domestically by low government deficits, low inflation, a strong dollar, strong capital creation by business and big inflows of foreign capital. But interest rates will occasionally be pushed higher by strong world-wide competition for business capital. These two forces, which will tend to balance each other, will keep the cost of money in the present general range for years to come.

Over the past ten years, the prime lending rate has run between three and six points higher than the level of consumer price inflation in a given year. Lenders don't believe that low inflation will be a perma-nent feature in the economic landscape, so the prime rate tends to remain on the high side, especially when corporate demand for credit is strong. That's why the prime sat at 8.5% through much of 1997 and 1998, even as inflation cooled down to less than 3% and other key inter-est rates, such as Treasuries of various durations, fell to their lowest lev-els in several decades.

# Coming Squeeze on Corporate Profits

American businesses, especially the large publicly traded compa-nies that make up the major American stock indexes, have enjoyed more than a decade of strongly rising total corporate profits, running at double-digit rates of growth during the '90s. This degree of earnings growth, while still possible for smaller, fast-growing firms with surging sales, will not be consistently achieved in the years ahead by as broad an array of U.S. firms.

### CORPORATE PROFITS AS A SHARE OF INCOME

As a share of total national income, corporate profits slid down-ward in a long, irregular path from the mid 1960s to around 1980, taking a big hit from soaring energy prices in the '70s.

Profits began trending up after the recession of 1981-1982, fat-tened by slower growth in employment, surging capital spending on productivity enhancements, and strong earnings from overseas opera-tions. This has continued through the '90s, but the pretax corporate-profit share of national income, now at about 10%, is still well below its 14% peak around 1965. (On the other hand, cash wages and salaries have shown a modest increase in their share of national income over the past few decades, while fringe benefits—such as health care and retire-ment contributions—have seen a big jump in share since the '60s.)

In the past few years, corporate profits have been boosted by an unusual combination of circumstances, including a slowing in the rise of health care costs, unusually low interest rates, a stunning increase in exports to developing nations (in part due to a lower dollar), and moderate wage demands from a labor force content just to be employed after the downsizing wave of the early '90s.

## TOUGHER GAINS AHEAD

While none of these situations will go into a 180-degree reversal in the years ahead, the stars will not continue to be so perfectly aligned for American business profits. Wages and salaries in a labor-tight U.S. market, especially in high-skill technology jobs, will rise at a faster rate. Health care costs will begin to climb again, as the baby-boom generation ages and has more medical needs, and as additional efficiencies from the big shift to managed care are harder to come by.

A strong dollar will dampen the spectacular growth rate (but not the absolute volume) of U.S. exports. Earnings from U.S. operations will be under increasing pressure from foreign competitors. And even businesses that don't have much foreign competition will find their margins squeezed from ever-larger domestic rivals, who are using technology to reduce prices costs or who are achieving economies of scale by consolidating with other firms in their field.

It's important to remember the distinction between total profits—a volume figure—and profit margins—or earnings as a percentage of each dollar of sales. Margins can fall even as total earnings are growing, and that's the situation that many dynamic businesses find themselves in today and will continue to experience in the years ahead.

# Smoother Business Cycles

In the euphoria that swept over America in 1997, before the collapse of Asian financial markets, there was a lot of talk about "the new economy." There was a growing feeling, especially on Wall Street, that America had created a perpetual-growth machine, demolishing business cycles and rendering national recessions obsolete. We disagreed at the time, and want to reiterate that the U.S. and world economies are still governed by the laws of supply and demand. There will be occasional excesses that must be worked off by contractions of growth.

Having said that, we acknowledge that there are, indeed, some fundamentally different things about how business is conducted worldwide today—changes in technology, trade policy, business organization and management, global outsourcing, international finance and many other trends. Taken together, these forces will tend to smooth out the traditional cycles of boom and bust.

## MODERATING INFLUENCES

Future U.S. business cycles will be moderated by a variety of factors, including these:

• **a rising share of the economy coming from services,** for which the demand is generally more stable than for tangible goods;

• **less dependence on U.S. consumers alone** to sustain sales growth, due to rising revenues from a variety of foreign customers;

• **less inventory buildup,** due to broader use of computers, satellite tracking and just-in-time manufacturing and deliveries, allowing businesses to keep less product on hand;

• **broader outsourcing** to a variety of vendors, reducing the need to lay off a firm's own workers when sales soften; and

• **broader securitizing of American assets,** especially commercial real estate, spreading the risks of ownership across more investors and smoothing out regional boom-and-bust cycles.

## SHORTER, MILDER RECESSIONS

As a result of all this, future national recessions are likely to be fairly brief and not too deep. The severe slumps in the mid and late '70s were caused by external shocks—a tenfold increase in the price of oil and the worldwide hyperinflation that followed—events not likely to be repeated. The deep economic slump in the early '80s was a fundamental and painful restructuring of U.S. industry that also need not be repeated. Now the service sector is going through a similar restructuring, with downsizing and consolidation in retailing, financial services, telecommunications, health care and other service lines. But so far, this has been accomplished without a national recession and rising unemployment.

There will still be slumps affecting particular industries and particular regions of the U.S., as have occurred throughout the long, jagged line of expansion since 1982.

But the amazing diversity of the U.S. economy will enable robust growth in certain areas to offset weakness in others, keeping the national economy on a more even keel than in the past. The rising share of foreign trade in the U.S. economy will make it more vulnerable to severe slumps elsewhere in the world. But greater diversity in America's export markets—growing sales to an ever-widening list of nations on all continents—will temper the risks of globalization.

# CHAPTER 4

# Expanding World Markets

F aced with moderate growth in domestic consumer demand in the next century, the world's richest nations—in North America, Europe and Asia—will be heavily dependent on surging growth in the less-developed nations for their future prosperity. And the developing nations will oblige, by opening their markets to two-way trade and foreign investment on an unprecedented scale.

The most promising overseas markets for U.S. firms will be those with the biggest populations, the highest personal incomes, and the best governmental climates for foreign trade and investment. But only a few nations, most of them in Europe, offer all three of these traits. There are nations that are enormous in population but still relatively anemic in consumer purchasing power, such as China, India, Indonesia, Brazil and Russia. And there are nations with prosperous but small populations, such as Canada, the Netherlands, Taiwan, Switzerland and Australia, which by virtue of their purchasing power and open markets rank among America's top 20 export customers.

Finally, there are nations that, possessing large populations and rich resources, would have become powerful producers and consumers long ago were it not for decades of mismanagement or repression by their political leaders. Sadly, this is a long list that has included, for most of this century, such nations as Russia, China, India, Argentina, Brazil and most of the nations of Africa and the Middle East.

But fortunately for humankind's future, the general level of governmental competence and economic freedom is rising worldwide. This trend toward economic freedom will be the single most important force accelerating world growth in the 21st century.

## A World Tour of Development Prospects

This chapter offers a quick world tour of trends in economic development. While it cannot be comprehensive, it spotlights regions and nations that have significant trade and investment relations with the United States.

A useful resource for anyone thinking of investing or conducting business in a foreign nation is the annual *Index of Economic Freedom*, published jointly by *The Wall Street Journal* and the Heritage Foundation, a Washington think tank. (Visit www.heritage.org or www.wsj.com for ordering information.) This reference work describes the governmental and economic framework of every nation (taxes, tariffs, foreign investment rules, property rights, inflation, black market, regulation, and so on) and ranks them according to the degree of economic freedom enjoyed by businesses and individuals there.

Its 1998 rankings ran from top acheivers Hong Kong, Singapore, Bahrain, New Zealand, Switzerland and the U.S. to such cellar dwellers as Somalia, Vietnam, Bosnia, Iraq, Cuba, Laos and North Korea. (Hong Kong's future ranking is likely to be reduced by the Chinese government's massive intervention in the Hong Kong stock market during the stormy days of 1998.) Our references in this chapter to "highly rated for economic freedom" or "liberalization" and similar judgments are derived from data in the 1999 edition of this guide, augmented by our own staff reporting on recent political situations in these nations.

# Canada

No two nations are better next-door neighbors than the United States and Canada, especially considering the vast disparity in the size of their populations. Canada's population of about 30 million is barely one-ninth that of the U.S.'s. But the high-productivity Canadian economy creates goods and services each year with a value of more than $600 billion—almost as much as Mexico does with a population that is more than triple Canada's. Canada's per-capita GDP is in the world's top ten, on a par (adjusted for purchasing power) with that of Japan, Austria and Denmark. And it's only 20% lower than the U.S.'s (which is second to that of tiny Luxembourg).

Two-way trade between the U.S. and Canada has nearly doubled in the past decade, boosted by the North American Free Trade Agreement (NAFTA). At about $320 billion a year, the value of these transactions is the largest between any two nations on earth—about $130 billion greater per year than America's two-way trade with Japan, for example, and twice the value of the annual trade between the U.S. and Mexico.

This trade will continue to grow robustly, with Canada selling the U.S. rising amounts of natural gas and oil, lumber, grain and other farm products, uranium, hydroelectric power, steel, aluminum, paper, and other goods. U.S. producers will sell Canadians processed foods, electronics, automobiles, furniture, textiles and many other consumer products. Cross-border investment will be heavy by corporations based in both nations.

Canada will experience modestly stronger economic growth than it has over the past 15 years, as its decade-long economic liberalization programs begin to pay off. Canada will be increasingly attractive to higher investment by both Canadian and foreign multinationals.

The wild card for Canada's future continues to be the issue of independence for French-speaking Canada. It is likely that Quebec's perception of its financial self-interest will prevail over its nationalistic fervor, and it will not fully secede. But the turmoil will continue to make Quebec a less attractive locale for foreign investment than other provinces of Canada.

### *Canada comes on strong*

Free trade between two nations virtually preordains that there will be some degree of convergence in their costs of doing business, including taxes, wages and regulatory burdens. After NAFTA, Canada was faced with the choice of liberalizing its economic environment or losing a growing number of businesses and talented citizens to its giant neighbor to the south. Canada wisely chose the path of liberalization, embarking in the '80s on the path of privatizing state-run industries, cutting taxes, restraining the growth of social spending and reducing government deficits, both at the federal and provincial levels.

This progress, which has continued under both Conservative and Liberal administrations in Ottawa, has created a vibrant business climate, attractive to both existing corporations and new entrepreneurs. Canada's federal taxation of capital gains is 22%, similar to the U.S.'s long-term-gain rate, and its top corporate tax rate is a similar 46%. While the income-tax burden on middle-income taxpayers is similar to that in the U.S., the top marginal rate on high-income Canadians is higher, with a combined federal-provincial tax bite of about 53% in Ontario.

While Canada is now one of the most economically liberalized nations, it still has more barriers to foreign investment than the U.S. Foreign investments in, or takeovers of, Canadian firms must be deemed by the government to be of "net benefit to Canada," a determination that, although not often denied, has a chilling effect on purchase of Canadian firms by foreign multinationals in sensitive industries such as energy, telecommunications and media. Canada is also highly restrictive of non-Canadian banks' setting up branches there.

### Civility and order

On balance, Canada will prosper by combining its improving business climate with its traditionally high-quality social services (such as national health care), a low crime rate and a high degree of public civility. These will make Canada very attractive to immigrants. But despite having an enormous land area to settle, Canada will continue, for the foreseeable future, to restrict immigration largely to well-educated, well-heeled expatriates—ranging from Californians moving north to ethnic Chinese bringing their big bank accounts to Vancouver, British Columbia. As an aging society like the U.S., Canada will have the same need for more and more young workers, especially low-skill labor, to fill service positions and help support the retirement of a graying population. This may lead, a decade or so from now, to higher immigration quotas.

# Europe, West and East

The economies of the European Union, like most of the advanced world, will grow much more slowly than the economies of the developing countries of Asia, Latin America and Africa. They will also grow less strongly than the United States's average rate of about 3% a year—say, at about 2.5%.

But several trends—notably a slowing of wage increases and social spending, amid the increasing integration of economies—will give Europe's growth a little boost over its sluggish rates of the past quarter-century. "Eurosclerosis" is not dead, but flexibility and global competitiveness will be ascendant in Europe. And even with slow growth, the affluence of Europe—coupled with its increasing openness—will make it a very important market for foreign producers of every kind of product and service.

The integrated European Union is already as big an economy as the United States, and with Eastern Europe added in, it's much bigger. Europe accounts for a slightly higher percentage of total world trade than the U.S. (about 19% versus 17%). As trade barriers decline, Europe will become an even better market for U.S. goods.

European multinational companies will look to Eastern Europe as a source of inexpensive labor. This will boost their competitiveness in world trade but also exacerbate tensions with labor unions in Germany, France and other Western European nations. And the same European multinationals will accelerate their investment in North America and the rest of the world, in a quest for lower labor costs and a more hospitable regulatory environment than even a revitalized Europe will offer. European multinationals were already the largest foreign investors in the United States, well before the late-'90s buying binge that saw major acquisitions by German automakers, Swiss and Swedish heavy-equipment makers, German and British publishers, and a Dutch grocery conglomerate.

### The new euro

The EU's common currency, the euro, will greatly facilitate trade among the 11 members that will use it (who constitute the European Monetary Union), and its gradual acceptance will also lubricate trade between EU nations and the rest of the world. The euro won't pose much of a challenge to the dollar as the world's dominant reserve and trade currency, but it will help U.S. businesses by easing worries about currency fluctuations in so many different countries.

The fiscal discipline that the euro requires will be put to a severe test in the next European recession, whenever it comes. In times of economic contraction and rising unemployment, there will be voter pressure for higher social spending, amid declining tax revenues. Euro governments won't be able to stimulate their economies by devaluing their currency, and if they boost social spending, they will risk raising their budget deficits above the EU's 3%-of-GDP target.

Germany will lead the forces for fiscal conservatism and a strong euro, while socialists and labor unions in France and elsewhere will pose a threat to monetary integration with their calls for ever-higher wages, job protection and expensive benefits.

But the euro will survive, and eventually—years from now—the monetary union will encompass all of Europe, including the four current holdouts.

### Eurosclerosis in remission

Europe is still a continent of high pay and long vacations, high taxes, high trade barriers with the outside, overregulation by government, intractable trade unions that resist downsizing and love to call crippling national strikes, sluggish job growth, and double-digit unemployment. Joblessness averages 10% throughout the region, and in early 1998 ranged from about 5% in the Netherlands, Britain and Denmark to 20% in Spain and East Germany.

But a new spirit of competitiveness is slowly emerging. There is widespread privatization of formerly state-owned industries, ranging from power generation to telephone systems and airlines. Government deficits have been reduced so much—mostly by strong economic growth but also by controlled social spending—that virtually all the nations choosing to participate in the European Monetary Union (with the exception of Greece) will be close to the 3%-of-GDP goal.

It is getting a little easier for companies to downsize by laying off workers, and the European market for temporary labor is surging by 10% a year, bringing a new flexibility to corporate staffing. In Denmark a 50% cut in unemployment benefits has brought a big drop in unemployment among young adults.

In terms of growth rates, the shining stars of the new Europe will continue to be the nations that are moving most surely toward globalization, deregulation and reduction of their public sectors, such as Britain, Ireland, Belgium, Austria, the Netherlands and Luxembourg. European nations that have the added benefit of low labor costs—Spain, Ireland, Portugal and Greece—will enjoy especially strong growth if they can begin to move (or in the case of Ireland and Spain, continue moving) in the direction of economic liberalization. France's and Italy's growth will be impeded by their clinging to outmoded government policies. Germany, dynamic though it is, will have its hands full trying to achieve full economic integration with its eastern sector.

### Major U.S. trading partners

Because many U.S. companies are so dependent on the European market, a 1% increase in the economic growth of Europe can mean more to the companies' bottom line than 7% or 8% growth in Asia.

The United Kingdom will remain one of the best U.S. trade partners, continuing to buy computers, telecommunications equipment, software, aircraft, machinery, financial services, movies, videos and television programming. Because they speak the same language, Britons are an excellent test market for small and medium-size companies U.S. to test the European market.

U.S. companies will build more factories and distribution centers in Scotland, Wales and Northern Ireland (assuming the peace agreement holds). Intel, IBM and Hewlett-Packard already operate in Scotland, in the area dubbed Silicon Glen.

Germany has struggled with the costs of reunification, and it is hobbled by an aging population. Its economic growth will recover some of its old steam in the next decade. Germany will remain an important market for U.S. exports, including computers, telecommunications, transportation equipment, machinery, entertainment and financial services.

Along the lines of NAFTA, the next several years will see an increase in free trade between the U.S. and the European Union, probably starting with computer hardware and software, semiconductors, and telecommunications equipment and service. Europe's traditionally protected industries—agriculture, textiles and steel—will be the last to open fully. But even as governments fight over agricultural trade, often posturing to curry favor with their politically potent farmers, food trade between the U.S. and Europe has grown strongly in the late '90s, in everything from dairy products and vegetables to processed foods and bull semen. With the World Trade Organization taking a stand in favor of trade openness—and against non-tariff barriers such as scientifically dubious health concerns about U.S. food additives—the volume will continue to rise.

### Europe's big challenges

Europe still has a lot of challenges ahead, besides integrating its monetary systems and continuing to resolve its high costs of production and government spending.

Workers in the EU will face increasingly tough competition from low-cost labor in Eastern Europe and the former Soviet Union, and unions will resist the steady shift of manufacturing by western European multinational companies into those lower-cost centers.

With birth rates so low, Europe will face worsening labor shortages, which it will meet in part with immigration from Turkey and North Africa. But that immigration will aggravate social welfare costs and cultural assimilation tensions. And even with immigration, a decade or two from now Europe will be facing the dilemma of how to support a growing retired population with a relatively small work force.

The big issue, in the end, will be the future of European economic integration. Like welfare reform in the U.S., the euro is being launched in the best possible economic climate. An economic downturn will bring back old national rivalries, as farmers and manufacturers try to boost production and grab market share from neighboring nations.

Eventually, the nations of Europe will have to do more than just meet targets on lower government deficits. They will have to achieve more convergence in their tax rules and total tax burdens, internal business regulations, labor costs, and social safety nets. To achieve real competitiveness in the world economy, vis-à-vis North America, Asia and Latin America, this convergence should be toward liberalization and lower costs. But that means great pressure on the high-cost societies—especially Germany and France—and that means great political risk to their leaders.

In short, there is a lot more turmoil ahead for an integrated Europe. While the survival of European monetary integration is not a foregone conclusion, we believe that the necessary, sometimes painful, adjustments will be made.

### Rebirth for Eastern Europe

The former Soviet satellites of Eastern Europe are all making progress toward economic and political liberalization, with especially notable success achieved by the Czech Republic, Hungary, Poland, Estonia and Latvia.

Multinational firms from all over the world view Eastern Europe as both a reservoir of skilled, low-wage labor and a consumer market of vast potential—that is, once personal incomes begin to rise strongly. But multinationals are also finding that the socialist traditions of Eastern Europe are still an impediment to doing deals there. For example, General Motors decided to walk away from a planned deal to privatize a Polish auto plant when the government insisted that GM retain several thousand more workers than were needed. Significantly, South Korea's Daewoo car company took over the plant on the Polish government's terms, but Daewoo ended up using the deal as a ruse for importing nearly complete Korean vehicles, probably at a loss, to gain market share in Eastern Europe.

# Asia

Over the next two decades, the earth's economic center will shift thousands of miles—from the Atlantic Ocean, bordered by Europe and North America, to the Pacific Ocean, on whose shores sit the two great national powers of the next century, the U.S. and China.

Asia will recover in a couple of years from the financial crises that enveloped the region in 1997-1998 and dampened economic growth worldwide. Years from now, the crisis will be remembered as an event that changed forever the fundamental economic structure and way of doing business in much of Asia. Plunging stock prices, rapidly eroding currencies, defaulted bank loans—these all combined to accomplish in a few years what decades of political pressure and diplomatic cajoling had failed to accomplish: significant first steps toward the dismantling of Asian "crony capitalism" and the opening of closed economies to heavy foreign investment.

The foreign lenders and investors who fueled rapid growth in East Asia in the '80s and '90s—inflating the balloon that burst in 1997—will be extra cautious about their choice of projects for several years. But the conditions that fed Asia's economic miracle are still in place, including geography, large and youthful populations, cheap labor, and great determination to become manufacturing giants. The continent's long-term prospects remain excellent.

### *Gigantic world markets*

By 2020, it is likely that five of the world's six largest economies will be Asian—China, Japan, India, Indonesia and a reunited Korea (the U.S. will occupy the number-two position). China will pass Japan as the continent's dominant force, then pass the United States as the world's largest economy—in sheer volume of annual production, but not on a per-capita basis. Even if growth in China, India and Indonesia averages just 6% a year—a fairly conservative projection—Asia will soon produce the economic output of the U.S. and Europe combined.

Just as the U.S. was the big, affluent market of choice for the world's exporters in the late 20th century, so Asia will be the focus of multinational manufacturers and service companies seeking new customers. Prosperity will produce a huge new middle class over the next 20 years, nearly a billion strong. Many will be young, well educated and eager to spend some of their earnings on a better standard of living. They will buy automobiles, television sets, VCRs and a range of home appliances. They will subscribe to cable or satellite TV services and watch American movies and other entertainment fare.

At the same time, trade barriers will be coming down all over the Pacific Rim. The 18 nations of the Asia Pacific Economic Cooperation group (APEC) will remove barriers and tariffs among themselves for environmental products, energy goods and services, chemicals, telecommunications equipment, medical devices, lumber, toys and gems by 2010.

### *The Asian miracle comes back to reality*

The rise of Asia in the second half of the 20th century has been the most amazing economic-development story in history. No other people in any era raised their average standard of living so much in so brief a period of time.

Just fifty years ago, most Asians were living at a bare-subsistence level, lower than the average citizens of Latin America or Africa. While that still defines the material lives of hundreds of millions of Asians, especially in India, China and much of Southeast Asia, many others have achieved a middle-class standard of living. And a small but rapidly growing number have achieved considerable wealth, in many lines of work.

The big questions, as this decade and century come to an end: Will the Asian miracle continue? Yes, but at a lower rate of growth. Will the long-awaited restructuring and opening up of these notoriously clubby economies continue after the current crisis passes? Yes. As Asian production costs rise, will foreign capital, the driving force of world growth today, look for ever-greener pastures, with even lower wages, on other continents, such as Latin America and Africa? Yes, and that will give Asia tough competition in simple manufacturing and drive down the cost of consumer products worldwide.

## CHINA RISING

For a number of years to come, China will remain a communist society with a high degree of government direction of the economy, political repression and social control. But political and economic liberalization will slowly emerge, resulting in something resembling democracy within two decades. China will gradually develop commercial and political ties to Taiwan, which will become a semi-autonomous affiliate of a greater Chinese empire.

By 2010, Shanghai will surpass Hong Kong to become the financial hub not only of China but also of the entrepreneurial network of 100 million overseas Chinese, who are important business leaders and holders of wealth throughout Southeast Asia and even in such far-flung spots as Los Angeles and Vancouver.

China's determination to become a global power may be best symbolized by its frenzy of skyscraper construction. Four of the world's five tallest buildings are being built in China. The Shanghai World Financial Center will soar 95 stories into the sky and become the world's tallest building (counting its antennas) when it is finished in 2001. All five of the world's tallest structures, including the Petronas Towers in Malaysia, were designed by American architecture firms—evidence of mounting U.S. strength in the export of high-value services.

*Doing business in China*

In the shorter run China, with its 1.2 billion consumers and producers, will be a tantalizing, baffling and frustrating market in which to do business.

While the Japanese model of central planning, tough import controls and restricted access is discredited in most of Asia, it is alive and well in China. Most big foreign-financed projects (those over $30 million) must have national and local government approval (too often lubricated with bribes). And China often insists that in a joint venture, the Western partner transfer its technology to the Chinese partner, through elaborate education and training programs. It is widely assumed that the purpose of this is to enable China to develop locally owned, competing industries in everything from autos to aerospace. But it's no longer necessary for every foreign investor to have a Chinese partner for every venture, and new wholly foreign-owned firms have recently outnumbered new joint ventures.

*Heavy investment in China*

Multinational companies will keep rushing into China, more tempted by the size of the market than turned off by the government's foreign-investment ground rules. Intel, Kodak, Microsoft, Coca-Cola, Hewlett-Packard, GE, IBM, McDonald's, AT&T, Nike, Boeing and United Technologies are just a few of the major American corporations already active there.

Some multinationals are beginning to have second thoughts about how much new production the Chinese consumer market can absorb in the near future. For example, many of the world's automakers—Ford, GM, VW-Audi, Suzuki and others—rushed in to create joint ventures, but some of them, such Daimler-Benz and Chrysler (separately, before their merger), have either pulled out or trimmed their plans considerably, concerned that production will race ahead of the Chinese consumer's ability to afford cars. But GM remains committed to building midsize Buicks in China, as well as electric cars. And its research centers—practically full-blown universities—are teaching Chinese engineers how to use the latest U.S. technology in fuel-injection and braking systems. (A GM executive wryly notes that many of the young Chinese automotive engineers don't know how to drive a car; they still ride bicycles to work.)

Importing technological expertise, especially from the U.S. and Japan, is part of China's master plan to build the basic industries vital to its future. The government vigorously defends key sectors from foreign competition, including autos, chemicals, aerospace, electronics, machinery and building materials. But China also wants to join the World Trade Organization, and to impress the world with its readiness to do so, it plans to reduce its tariffs from an average of about 23% to 15% within the next two years. This will boost China's imports of products from the advanced nations.

Another kind of technology transfer between the U.S. and China is taking place every day in the classrooms of America's finest universities, where an estimated 42,000 Chinese students come to study each year. They contribute to the U.S. trade surplus in services, but unlike students from other Asian nations, who are free to remain in the U.S. as high-tech workers (which many do, happily for our economy), the Chinese students are ordered by their governments to return home with their new and valuable American education.

### *Trade strife with China*

While the multinationals in China are producing in part for the domestic Chinese market, a lot of their products come back to the U.S. as Chinese exports, albeit of American brands. China rationalizes its enormous and growing trade surplus with the U.S. as a natural "stage of development" situation for an emerging economy: America has a voracious appetite for the cheap consumer goods that China makes so well, but the Chinese can't yet afford to buy as much of the high-value products that are America's specialty. America's exports to China, especially expensive capital goods, will indeed rise strongly with that country's growing affluence, but not nearly fast enough to erase China's enormous trade surplus with the U.S. for years to come.

So America's toughest trade battles will be with China, not Japan. Tension were already high over the lackluster effort by Chinese government officials to crack down on its country's thriving software-piracy industry and the U.S.'s continuing criticizism of China over its human-rights record (treatment of dissidents), forced abortions, use of child and prison labor, and supplying of missile technology to such volatile nations as Pakistan, Libya and Iran. Relations were further strained in 1998 by revelations of attempted Chinese influence on Clinton administration trade policy through illegal campaign contributions. Then in 1999 came the scandal of probable theft of nuclear weapons secrets from the Los Alamos laboratory. Finally, there was the Chinese outrage over the accidental NATO bombing of the Chinese embassy in Belgrade, Yugoslavia.

In the end, however, the economic objective of increased two-way trade and investment with China—and continued diplomatic rapport with an emerging giant—will override all other foreign-policy considerations.

### China's rate of growth will decline

China's double-digit annual growth of the '90s is likely to diminish significantly, for a variety of reasons.

As the financial crisis of 1997-98 was unfolding elsewhere in Asia, it was widely assumed that China would be unaffected by the debacle. But it was not immune from the spillover effects. Foreign investment still poured into China, but at a lower rate than its mid-'90s peak. China's desired membeship in the World Trade Organization was derailed in '99 by growing tensions with the U.S. But China will eventually be admitted in the WTO, after showing evidence of its commitment to honor the organization's open-trade rules. Having China in the WTO will be a great long-term benefit to the United States and other advanced nations in their attempts to gain access to the enormous Chinese market.

Then there's the issue of geography in China's development. Much of its recent growth has been in coastal areas of the south, near existing transportation and ports. As development spreads inland, the cost of modernizing China's infrastructure will be monumental. China plans to spend up to $1 *trillion* over the next several years on highways, bridges, dams, sewers, power plants, railroads, airports, telecommunications and other needs of a fast-growing society. This less-glamorous but vital investment will divert money from China's export-manufacturing sector. It will also create enormous selling opportunities for multinationals, many of them American-based, in engineering, construction management, heavy equipment, phone equipment and many other fields.

### Challenges big challenges

A recent study by the Organization for Economic Cooperation and Development identified several other big challenges for China, including feeding its population (as farmland is converted to other uses) and avoiding environmental disaster from pollution. The Chinese banking system needs a major overhaul, too, with clear accounting rules and less cronyism in lending. State-run monopolies are in need of major employment pruning or outright privatization.

The Chinese government still owns and operates an astounding number of businesses—an estimated 118,000—most of which are unprofitable. But state-run enterprises employ some 114 million Chinese, approximately two-thirds of all urban workers, so drastic downsizing could lead to social unrest. Further, even a mild slowdown in economic growth could leave many of China's newly minted college graduates without work. There is also the issue of growing political tension between the booming coastal areas and the mostly rural and poor interior.

As China enters the economic big leagues of world competition, it cannot ignore any of these challenges. Managing and financing them all simultaneously will tax the ingenuity and social control of the Chinese government. Since it will be impossible for central planning to accomplish these tasks, the very complexity of China's economic development will hasten its transition to decentralized markets and a growing degree of political freedom.

## JAPAN: FINALLY OPENING UP

The Japanese economy of ten years hence will be a very different organism from today's tightly knit circle of business and government planning. The long stagnation of the '90s, aggravated by the Asian financial crisis of 1997-99, will finally open Japan to foreign investment far faster than most people thought possible.

And while Japan is not likely to resume the torrid pace of growth and capital formation it achieved in the '80s, it will emerge from its long economic malaise a stronger nation and bolder global competitor.

### Lingering recession, not world domination

In the late '80s it was widely assumed, in Japan and in the U.S., that the following decade would be the one in which Japan clearly sprinted ahead of the United States as the world's most dynamic economy. Then the bubble of inflated Japanese asset values—stocks, real estate, the yen—burst, and the economy still hasn't recovered its old vitality. For a year or so, in 1995 and 1996, it seemed to be back on track, with an occasional period of growth stronger than America's.

But then the collapse of the Southeast Asian economies—big customers, borrowers and investment partners of Japanese manufacturers and banks—helped push Japan back into recession. Of the more than $100 billion owed by South Korean corporations and banks to foreign lenders at the end of 1996, an estimated $24 billion was owed to Japanese banks, whose books were already loaded with uncollectable (but not yet written-off) loans in their own nation.

How the mighty have fallen. A 1998 ranking of national economies in the *World Competitive Yearbook* dropped Japan nine places to 18th in global competitiveness. In the early '90s, it ranked second behind the U.S., which has held the number-one spot for a decade. Japanese newspapers in 1998 bemoaned a rapid succession of Japanese asset sales to U.S. firms, calling it the "third American invasion," after Commodore Perry in 1853 and General Douglas MacArthur in 1945. By the summer of 1998, the yen had fallen so low against the dollar that the U.S. Treasury felt compelled to buy yen. A year later, with the Asian crisis waning, Japan appeared to be back on the path of growth.

### Slow to take its medicine

Japan's big problem has been its reluctance to acknowledge, and proceed to undertake, the painful restructuring that every advanced nation must go through to remain competitive in the new world economy. The United States was the first to take the bitter medicine in the early '80s, followed by Great Britain and other nations in Europe, where the process is ongoing.

Japan knows what it must do—cut taxes and government regulation, write off massive amounts of bad debt on real estate, abolish lifetime corporate employment and automatic seniority raises, open up its markets to foreign investment and cheap foreign goods, and continue to move manufacturing offshore. It is now doing some of these things, and it will keep doing more, but all of it so tentatively and slowly that its seven-year stagnation will drag on for a while longer.

### Down, but far from out

With all the excitement about China and the concern about Japan's weakness, it is easy to count Japan out. That would be a mistake.

Japan has an enormous economy of great diversity, either the second largest in the world (using current exchange rates) or the third, behind China (adjusting for purchasing-power parity). It is a major investor of capital overseas, from which it derives a mounting flow of dividends and interest. The educated work force, technological know-how, savings ethic and hard work that built Japan's economy from the devastation of World War II into a global power will continue to give Japan a crucial role in the world economy. In technology, Japanese multinationals continue to target key industries of the future—including robotics, new materials, biotech and microelectronics. They have no intention of slipping from the world stage.

It's clear that Japan won't again match its awe-inspiring growth of the '70s and '80s. Its economy and its society are more mature. Due to a virtual absence of population growth, which will lead to a declining population in the next century, Japan faces the prospect of relatively few workers supporting a large retired class, to a much greater extent than the U.S. does.

As slowly as it is restructuring, the changes *are* proceeding, producing impressive productivity (and profit) gains in steelmaking, shipbuilding and other heavy industries, and keeping Japan competitive with rivals in South Korea, the U.S., and Europe. The long-protected telecommunications and financial-services industries are feeling the heat of competition from a number of foreign-owned firms. Japanese consumers, long forced to pay high prices at protected specialty retailers, are now enjoying lower prices at highly efficient convenience stores (such as Japanese-owned 7-Eleven stores) that sell a wide range of groceries, drugs and even travel services. And more companies are following Honda's lead, begun in 1992, in replacing seniority-based promotions and raises with merit pay and advancement.

### *Foreign purchases of Japan's companies*

For years it has been relatively easy for an American company to establish a subsidiary in Japan or form a joint venture with a Japanese firm. But one kind of foreign investment has been exceedingly difficult to make—the outright acquisition of a Japanese company. Japanese firms have not sought foreign acquirers, nor have they had to, with so much Japanese capital available. Occasional foreign acquisition attempts were rebuffed, tangled up in red tape or thwarted by a friendly offer (not necessarily for a higher price) from a Japanese company.

But the economic woes of the late '90s changed this. When stock prices were down, struggling Japanese companies couldn't find the easy domestic capital they needed, and foreign offers suddenly looked very tempting. When Yamaichi Securities collapsed in late 1997, Merrill Lynch stepped in with $300 million to acquire 30 branches staffed with 2,000 employees. GE Capital acquired the more lucrative parts of Toho Mutual Life Insurance Co., and Bass PLC, a British company, bought the prestigious Inter-Continental Hotel group from Saison, a once high-flying Japanese retail and services conglomerate. Daimler-Benz, fresh from its deal with Chrysler in the spring of 1998, began negotiations with Nissan to acquire its diesel-truck division. Ford's consumer credit division bought the financing operations of a major Japanese retailer, Daei. Foreign acquisitions such as these will accelerate, and the biggest change they will make will be exposing Japan's business leadership and consumers to the more free-wheeling, fast-moving management style that characterizes today's transnational corporations.

To find workers at a moderate cost for its auto, electronics and other manufacturing industries, Japan will continue to shift production to lower-cost Asian countries, Eastern Europe, Latin America and, yes, the United States. Decades from now, Japan will prosper largely from collecting dividend and interest income from the vast overseas investments of its multinational corporations and its personal savers, as the tiny European nation of the Netherlands has done for generations. Significantly, the U.S. will take a similar path, as its multinationals spread manufacturing all over the globe and American workers recognize that the best way to benefit from global competition is as stockholders.

## INDIA AT A CROSSROADS

India—with 950 million people, a fast-growing middle class, and some three million scientists, engineers and technicians eager for work—is destined to be a major world power in the 21st century.

But in 1998, a year of enormous change in India, it was not clear what kind of a world power would emerge under the muscle-flexing Hindu nationalism of the Bharatiya Janata Party (BJP). Will India continue on its new path of developing nuclear weapons that threaten neighboring Pakistan and China, both of which India has fought in territorial disputes during the past three decades? Will India continue the trend of economic liberalization and openness to foreign investment that has progressed in fits and starts since 1991? Which wing of the BJP will prevail—the internationalist group which favors foreign investment, or the protectionist wing, which seems to view multinational corporations as neocolonial successors to the British imperial rulers who controlled India until 1947?

Perhaps not even the BJP leaders know the answers to these questions. But we believe that, over time, pragmatism will win out over ideology, and cooperation will prevail over belligerence. India will come to see that its self-interest lies in openness, international cooperation and repudiation of the use of nuclear weapons. The alternative would result in isolation and a terribly expensive arms race with its neighbors. India would risk a long-term loss of foreign investment, international aid and loan guarantees that are crucial to raising its woefully low standard of living.

### India compared with China

At the end of the 1940s, India and China had much in common— the two largest populations in the world, largely agrarian economies and a majority of their people living in appalling poverty. Thereafter their paths diverged, politically more than economically. While China was ruled by a communist dictatorship and India became the world's largest democracy, both economies were planned and tightly controlled by their governments, with state-owned industries, barriers to foreign investment, high tariffs, wage and price controls, bureaucratic regulation of everything. And as a result, both India and China suffered very slow improvement in living standards.

Strangely, it was communist China that moved away from economic closedness and control sooner and more boldly. China had been liberalizing its economy (but not its political freedoms) for nearly a decade before India's long-ruling Congress Party, spurred by a financial crisis in 1991, began taking tentative steps toward openness.

### Getting India on track

Over the following several years, as barriers to foreign goods and capital declined and modest privatization of industry gathered momentum, foreign investment (heavily American) poured into India. The economy grew at a rate averaging nearly 5% a year, peaking at almost 8% in 1996. This pales in comparison with China's double-digit growth spurt, but it was a major improvement for India.

American exports to India soared, especially in capital goods such as telecommunications equipment, planes and aircraft parts, electric-power plants, computers and software, plastics and chemicals, and equipment for mining and steel making. American multinational energy firms AES and Enron (with Bechtel and GE Capital as co-investors with Enron) each began developing massive electric generating plants that they would own and operate, selling the power to state-run distribution systems. Many U.S. firms are entering the Indian market by joint venture. Harris Corp., a Florida-based electronics manufacturer, has forged alliances worth close to $1 billion with four partners in India to provide basic telephone services.

### Sultans of software

India has become a world-class giant in software production, with activity centered in New Delhi and especially in Bangalore, the Silicon Valley of Asia. Programmers working for multinational software firms and home-grown Indian companies write millions of lines of code used by the likes of American Express, Citibank, IBM and Hewlett-Packard. Satellite links enable Indian programmers to create, revise, repair and transmit software to clients all over the world instantly. "If a neighborhood ATM swallows your bankcard because of a problem with the machine's new software, the problem may be fixed overnight by experts in Bangalore," says John Stremlau of the Carnegie Commission. And a lot of the reprogramming to fix the computer world's "millenium bug" is also being done in India.

India's fast-growing software industry, with annual sales exceeding $1.5 billion a year, exemplifies the tough challenge that the advanced nations will face in high technology in the next century. India has the English-speaking world's second-largest work force of scientists, engineers and technicians, and is turning out an estimated 20,000 computer-science graduates each year. Many of them are willing to start work for about $10,000 a year. That's about one-fourth the pay of their counterparts in the U.S., but it enables the young Indian professionals to live like kings in Bangalore, where the average annual income is about $400.

While the U.S. will continue to be the creativity leader in software of all sorts, including artificial-intelligence agents and virtual-reality programs, a lot of the heavy lifting—the tedious writing of code—will be done in developing nations. As *The Economist* has noted, while other nations of Asia provide world business with "cheap hands" that can assemble electronics, apparel, shoes and toys, India aims to be the world's "cheap brains" in the information technology business. The challenge for Europe and North America will be to continually upgrade public education to keep their labor forces a step ahead of the ambitious youths of the developing nations.

### India's nuclear-testing shock

When the BJP came to power in 1998 and shocked the world with its underground tests of nuclear weapons, the U.S. and some of its allies—notably Japan, which is India's most generous provider of unilateral foreign aid—immediately announced a variety of financial sanctions, such as an end to foreign aid and loan guarantees. In the short run, these restrictions will cut into investment in India by the U.S., which has been India's largest foreign investor in recent years. If other nations, especially American allies in Europe, don't follow suit but use the sanctions as a selling opportunity for them, the U.S. sanctions will end up hurting American exports more than they will hurt the Indian economy. (Private-sector trade and investment not dependent on U.S. government assistance won't be affected by the sanctions.)

The crisis over India's nuclear testing and the subsequent sanctions came at a time when foreign investment—and India's growth rate—were already beginning to cool from the torrid mid-'90s pace. The BJP's future economic policies are hard to read. On the one hand, the party attracts the young professional elite with pro-business rhetoric that calls for an attack on bureaucratic red tape and corruption. But it also champions a kind of economic nationalism that favors limiting foreign investment (welcome only for big infrastructure projects) while continuing to protect Indian firms from import competition or acquisition by foreign multinationals.

It is possible that the crises of 1998 foreshadow a broad retreat from economic openness and the beginning of a dangerous period of military tension on the Asian subcontinent. The pro-Hindu BJP could turn up its anti-Muslim rhetoric and actions, alienating India's large Muslim minority and further inflaming relations with Muslim-majority Pakistan. Pakistan and China could start new rounds of nuclear testing to match India's. There could even be warfare between India and Pakistan, India and China, or both.

But there is another very different—and more likely—scenario that could unfold over the next few years: Having proven its point that it is a power to be reckoned with, India will rejoin the world community and forswear deployment of nuclear weapons. Eventually, it will sign the Comprehensive Nuclear Test Ban Treaty of 1996, which still awaits ratification by several nuclear powers, including the U.S. India is likely to follow this path because it cannot easily do without international aid and loan guarantees.

### India's long-range future

The challenges facing India are still enormous. While some 240 million Indians—ranging from the newly rich to the desperately poor—jam into sprawling, unsanitary cities, three-quarters of all Indians live in rural areas, trying to eke out a subsistence living farming small plots. Agriculture, by far India's largest industry, has not shared in the new prosperity resulting from economic reforms. Many smaller farmers have had to deal with declining government subsidies for seed, energy and fertilizer at the same time that they are whipsawed by drought and wide fluctuations in world crop prices.

In its internal economics, the BJP will have little choice but to resume the stalled liberalization and privatization of the early '90s if it wants to match the high rates of growth—on the order of 8% a year—that are necessary to raise living standards in a nation where most people are desperately poor. Still to be privatized is all of India's banking industry. India's tariffs average about 48% (more than a third *higher* than in 1991), but the government plans to eliminate tariffs on telecommunications equipment and electronics by 2000.

As India grows in economic power in the decades to come, it will retain and lure back more of its best and brightest engineers and entrepreneurs, who today are attracted to America, Europe and other advanced economies. It is significant that one of the world's fastest-growing multinational steel companies, Ispat International, was founded in Calcutta but is no longer headquartered in India. Frustrated by governmental regulation, steel magnate Lakshmi Mittal moved his home to England and Ispat's headquarters to the most international of all European nations, the Netherlands. Over the past 25 years, Mittal has built Ispat into one of the top five steel producers in the world, with mills in Indonesia, Mexico, Kazakstan, Canada, Germany, Ireland, Trinidad and Tobago, the U.S. (Inland Steel, acquired in early 1998) and, yes, India. In a generation or two, this kind of Indian enterprise will start, grow big, and branch out into the world—without ever moving its headquarters from the home country.

## AILING, BUT NOT TOOTHLESS, TIGERS

The smaller economies of Asia tend to be lumped together in the public mind, but they are vastly different in their histories, scope of industrial power and governmental structures. Not surprisingly, the effects of the Asian financial crisis have varied enormously from nation to nation, and their postcrisis prospects will vary a great deal as well.

### Crisis in Indonesia

The near-term outlook is bleakest for Indonesia, where currency collapse and demise of Suharto's corrupt and repressive rule was followed by social, political and economic chaos. The very survival of Indonesia as currently constituted is in doubt. Rebels in East Tibor and Irian Java are emboldened in their campaigns for secession. Consumer purchasing power has plummeted. The military has lost its ability to prevent widespread looting. And ethnic Chinese, the backbone of the retail economy, have been violently driven out of this predominantly Muslim nation of 210 million people.

### Taiwan emerges stronger

Not every Asian nation suffered badly in the regional meltdown. Singapore and Hong Kong had big drops in their stock markets, but they emerged relatively unscathed. (Hong Kong saw a modest contraction in its economy in early 1998, accompanied by a 25% drop in tourism.)

89

Taiwan has been another opportunistic survivor. It stayed out of trouble by keeping its external debt low, accumulating massive reserves of foreign exchange—an estimated $90 billion—and avoiding the over-building and fantastic run-up in real estate prices that afflicted Malaysia, Thailand and Indonesia.

Taiwan found itself in the enviable position of being able to buy into the troubled economies of its neighbors at bargain prices. The small island nation went shopping for luxury hotels in South Korea and Thailand, a bank in Thailand, and manufacturing facilities all over Southeast Asia. By these and other investments, Taiwan will seek to bolster its claim to be regarded as a powerful independent nation in the region, not a rebellious province of the People's Republic of China.

China deeply resents Taiwan's "Go South" strategy of investment in other Southeast Asian nations, and it will continue to threaten its small neighbors with trade reprisals if they expand their commercial relations with Taiwan. In the very long run, commercial ties between China and Taiwan will grow, eventually bringing Taiwan into China's political sphere without military conquest by the mainland.

### South Korea tries openness

The nation that will be most changed by the Asian crisis will be South Korea, whose precrisis economy was most closely patterned after Japan's, a neighbor both resented for its past domination and admired for its remarkable economic success. On the insistence of the IMF, as a condition for massive bailout funds, the Korean government embarked on an ambitious plan to privatize many state-owned businesses, and it eased restrictions on foreign investment in several key business sectors, including commercial airlines, oil refining and investment banking.

Debt-ridden Korean *chaebols* (powerful interlocking conglomer-ates with close ties to the government) began selling operating divisions to such multinationals as Coca-Cola, Procter & Gamble and Germany's BASF chemical and fiber firm. AES invested nearly $900 million in elec-tric-generating operations, and Germany's Commerzbank bought a 30% interest in the state-run Korea Exchange Bank. Daewoo, the Korean automaker whose loss-leader expansion strategy has given U.S. automakers fits, was reduced to courting General Motors to acquire a big chunk of the company for assumption of some of Daewoo's massive corporate debt. Other big buyers in Korea in the wake of the Asian con-tagion included U.S. paper companies, GE, DuPont and Kodak. The stronger Korean *chaebols* have also been buyers, cherry-picking the assets of their bankrupt brethren.

### *Sustainable growth ahead*

And so it will go throughout East Asia for several years to come—the forced internationalization of economies, with the Asian nations emerging stronger for it.

South Korea will recover and strengthen its position as a world player in many key industries, including electronics, steel, shipbuilding and car manufacturing. The International Iron & Steel Institute forecasts that the Asia-Pacific region will account for 44% of world crude-steel production by 2005, up from 33% in 1995.

Singapore already enjoys a standard of living that rivals or surpasses most European countries. It has attracted investment from many multinational electronics giants, including IBM, Texas Instruments, Motorola and Plessey. Ethnic Chinese dominate the business community in this city-state, which has a diverse population that includes Malays, Hindus and Muslims. Singapore often rates near the top among the best places to do business, despite (or because of) an authoritarian government that is quick to punish those who dissent from official state views. The military, police, legal system, press and trade unions are firmly under the control of the ruling People's Action Party.

The signs of Malaysia's rapid growth in the '90s are everywhere in Kuala Lumpur, even after the bubble burst. The skyline is going straight up, the streets are packed with Mercedes and Jaguars, a new $4 billion international airport is nearing completion, and an entirely new capital city is being built on the southern outskirts of Kuala Lumpur.

Malaysia's ascent was made possible by an infusion of $20 billion in foreign investment in the mid-'90s. When the yen was strong, many of Japan's largest electronics companies opened facilities in Malaysia to make televisions, camcorders and VCRs. But Malaysia's long-term outlook may not match that of its neighbors. Its work force probably can't remain competitive very long against China and Indonesia. And its labor costs are already rising because skilled workers are in short supply. These trends will dampen foreign investment over the long term, with investors preferring to bet on Thailand, Singapore and other Asian countries.

Keep an eye on two future tigers, Vietnam and the Philippines. The World Bank estimates that Vietnam will grow at or above 8% a year over the next decade, with industrial sectors growing at a 10% clip or better. Sony, Toyota and U.S. multinationals are building factories and entering joint-venture deals there. Eventually its tightly controlling communist government will go the way of all repressive regimes, but not soon.

## Anglo-Asia: Australia and New Zealand

These two Anglo-Asian nations will become more Asian and less Anglo in the years to come. Rich in natural resources, with plenty of space to grow and well-educated populations, they are also geographically well positioned to be important links between the mature economies of the Old World and the surging Asian economies that will be ascendant in the next century. In the judgment of Hamish McRae, associate editor of the *Independent* in London and a keen analyst of the world economy, both nations will hitch their wagons to the rising stars of Asia, and they "have a golden future ahead of them."

### *Australia goes multiracial*

Under a succession of governments since the early '80s, Australia has firmly embraced the goals of open markets, denationalizing industries, lowering tariffs, reducing government deficits and encouraging foreign investment.

Most significantly, Australia began to embrace a new vision of itself as a multiracial, multicultural society—with better treatment of not only its aboriginal people, but of people from any background. It opened its vast expanses to more and more immigrants, especially from Asia and Eastern Europe. More than half of all immigrants in the '90s have come from Asia, with large numbers from Hong Kong, Vietnam and the Philippines. Many of these immigrants, from both Asia and Europe, are well educated and highly entrepreneurial, contributing strongly to high-tech business in Australia and building economic links with their former homelands.

Australia has been welcoming foreign investment, too. In the 1980s Japanese capital poured into Australian real estate, with extensive purchases of hotels and resorts, office buildings and raw land. Then came heavy investment in manufacturing, especially electronics, from multinational firms based in the U.S., Europe and Asia. Workers of all sorts—from assembly-line workers to skilled engineers—can be hired much less expensively in Australia than in Europe and North America, with some engineers receiving only half the salary of their U.S. counterparts.

But Australia is determined not to become just a source of cheap skilled laborers, who assemble sophisticated components made elsewhere. As a condition for government approval of new foreign-owned electronics facilities, for example, it set rigorous standards that skirted the edge of illegality under international trade rules. The government required that companies doing more than a certain volume of manufacturing in Australia also set up research and development laboratories. And at a time when "domestic content" laws are being found to be virtually unworkable in a global economy, Australia has tried to hold to a 70% local-content rule for electronics exported from foreign-owned plants in Australia. Foreign firms grumble about the requirements, but nearly three dozen of them wanted to be in the Australian market badly enough to agree to the terms.

Australia is among the 20 top trading partners of the U.S., buying vastly more from U.S. firms—in aircraft, computers, chemicals, machinery and lots of high-tech stuff—than it sells to America in meat, wool, wine, aluminum and other products. Over time, however, Australia's dominant trade will be with the other nations of Asia. It will be a major provider of natural resources and food to the continent, especially a few decades from now as food prices rise and much of Asia's farmland has been converted to human habitation. Japan is already a big customer for Australian resources, buying about half of its coal imports and 40% of its iron ore from Down Under in some recent years. Australia will also be an increasingly favorite playground for the world, capitalizing on its beautiful mountains, beaches and unusual marine and inland ecosystems.

In a world in which most advanced nations have stagnant populations and face the problem of how to support the increasing number of elderly people, Australia has the luxury, like Canada and the U.S., of growing as much as it chooses to without getting crowded. The odds are good that Australia will opt for moderate growth by immigration, and it will be one of only two major nations in the world (along with the U.S.) that will do so. As in the U.S., this policy will be highly favorable to Australia's economic future.

### New Zealand blazes a new trail

New Zealand has lots of land, lots of sheep and fewer than four million people. It also has a highly progressive economy—rated among the half-dozen least restrictive in the world. Having come a long way from its social-democratic roots after independence in the 1930s, New Zealand has been a world leader in scaling back the high cost and personal dependency associated with welfare states.

Successive governments have cut taxes to a point where the top rate on personal income is 33%, with plans to drop it to 30% in 1998. Rare among advanced nations, New Zealand levies no taxes on capital gains or estates. It has exceptionally low tariffs, with plans to abolish all tariffs by 2004, but other marketing barriers still exist in the important agricultural sector. Direct foreign investment, especially in fishing facilities and farmland, requires government approval, but it is not often withheld, and foreign banks can set up shop with considerable ease.

Like Australia, New Zealand will be a significant provider of food, wool and other natural products to the soaring middle-class populations of Asia in the decades ahead.

# Latin America

Three big developments will occur in Latin America over the next decade or so. First, free enterprise and free trade will extend throughout the western hemisphere, with more and more nations emulating the pro-business governmental policies of Chile, Argentina and others. NAFTA will be expanded (and no doubt renamed) to cover all of Central and South America. This will bring political dividends, too. Countries that trade together will find it easier to cooperate in a range of other areas, including antidrug efforts. A major beneficiary in this country will be south Florida, a hub of trade, finance and transportation throughout the hemisphere. More than 350 multinational companies, including many European giants, have set up shop in Miami.

Second, Mexico and Brazil will become strong, dynamic players in the world economy, providing rich markets for exports and proving to be tough competitors in manufacturing.

Third, Cuba, one of the world's last die-hard communist systems, will make tentative steps toward capitalism well before Fidel Castro's death, and then move quickly toward democracy and free enterprise after his demise. Over the next few years, the U.S. will resume trade and investment relations with Cuba, ending decades of economic isolation.

## INTERRUPTED PROGRESS IN LATIN AMERICA

It will take Latin America a few more years to fully recover from the severe recession that engulfed most of the region's nations in '98-'99—a slump caused by depressed global commodity prices and a fall-off in once-booming foreign investment. All of this resulted in wildly fluctuating currencies, rising unemployment and declining personal incomes.

The economic pain was all the worse because it came at the end of a decade-long surge in economic growth and living standards, stimulated by free-market reforms in Chile, Argentina and other nations. The recession led voters in numerous countries to question the wisdom of the reforms and elect new leaders with old-style leftist agendas. This backswing of the pendulum won't be permanent, however. Latin America will eventually resume its economic liberalization of the '90s.

Relatively few Latin American countries rank in the very top echelon of nations with governmental climates hospitable to business and investment, but two of them do—Chile and the Bahamas (though the latter may be a little *too* hospitable to a variety of shady enterprises seeking a haven from international scrutiny). Other Latin American nations with good rankings for economic freedom today include Argentina, Uruguay, Bolivia, Peru, Ecuador, Panama, El Salvador, Costa Rica, Barbados and Trinidad and Tobago.

One of the most dramatic turnarounds occurred in Argentina. Before World War II, this well-educated society, blessed with fertile land and rich resources, had been among the world's half-dozen wealthiest nations, with a standard of living on a par with the U.S. and the more-affluent nations of Europe. But a half-century of governmental mismanagement and social disorder took a terrible toll on Argentina. Finally, free-market reforms, begun by President Carlos Menem in 1990, laid the foundation for long-term economic stability.

## MEXICO RECOVERS FROM CRISIS

Mexico will continue its accelerating recovery from the banking crisis that began in December 1994 and was followed by a drastic peso devaluation. The devaluation crippled the ability of the emerging Mexican middle class to afford foreign goods, and U.S. sales to Mexico suffered, deepening the U.S. trade deficit with Mexico.

But Mexico is now back on track. Lowering tariffs, cutting state subsidies and selling government-owned companies will gradually energize more of the Mexican economy, which by 1997 was growing at an annual rate of more than 7%. The *maquiladoras*, or twin plants, straddling the U.S.–Mexico border will prosper due to proximity to U.S. markets. Many American retailers will find success in Mexico.

Mexico passed Japan in 1998 as America's second-largest trading partner after Canada, with two-way trade easily exceeding the 1997 figure of $157 billion ($71 billion of exports to Mexico, $86 billion in imports). U.S. automakers will expand operations south of the border. Mexico will export more agricultural goods, cement, steel, textiles and apparel to the U.S., causing a loss of low-skill jobs in the U.S. But these losses will be offset by the creation of jobs in capital and consumer goods and services, which the U.S. will increasingly export to Mexico.

Mexico still has serious problems that will take years to solve. Its political elites must find ways to bring more Mexicans into the governmental process. The nation has a low savings rate, a heavy debt load, a poorly managed banking system, and undercapitalized small and medium firms. The booming drug trade—Mexico is both a major source and a transit country for illegal drugs sold in the U.S.—will plague U.S.–Mexico relations, including trade. Bribery and corruption, violent crime, and environmental degradation along the border also present serious problems for Mexico's government.

But Mexico eventually will break away from one-party political rule and will fully privatize its economy. Mexican immigrant labor will remain important to the U.S., but America's problem with illegal immigration will ease, as Mexico becomes more prosperous and creates more jobs at home.

### ANOTHER NEW DAWN FOR BRAZIL

Brazil—an industrial giant with 164 million people and an economy nearly twice the size of Mexico's—has been widely touted as a rising global star several times in recent decades, only to crash and burn amid government mismanagement and runaway inflation.

It's difficult to know whether Brazil is in the midst of another such false hope, or whether the fundamental restructuring going on now will lay the groundwork for a new era of high growth with stability. The odds favor the latter.

President Fernando Cardoso seems serious about stunting hyper-inflation, privatizing state-owned industries (selling off some $70 billion of public assets), cutting bloated government payrolls, diminishing the power of labor unions, and reducing the cost of the world's most generous pension systems (with benefits beginning after 25 years of work for women and 30 for men, regardless of the retiree's age).

These and other reforms are curbing high inflation, but at a cost in the short term of slower economic growth, rising unemployment and political unrest. If Cardoso and his successors can stay the course, the restructuring will finally allow Brazil to achieve its long-predicted success. Once protected from outside competition by high tariffs and import quotas, industries such as cars and computers are opening to the world. Foreign investment is now welcomed. Brazil is the single largest destination for new U.S. investment in South America. Over the next decade or two, Brazil will import huge amounts of machinery, electrical material, crude oil, chemicals, grains and coal.

### VENEZUELA BANKS ON OIL

Venezuela is a top-20 trading partner of the U.S. on the basis of one product: petroleum. It sells the U.S. more oil than any other nation, and Citgo, a subsidiary of Venezuela's state-owned oil industry, recently ranked as the largest retailer of gasoline in the U.S. Venezuela has gone on an oil investment binge in recent years, expanding state-owned exploration and production and inviting in foreign producers—Chevron, British Petroleum, Conoco, Atlantic Richfield and Mobil, among others—for the first time since nationalizing its energy industry in 1976.

Venezuela's stepped-up production has angered fellow oil exporters Mexico and Saudi Arabia, but it seems determined to become an even bigger force in world oil supply, pinning the nation's future on energy. That is a risky strategy that assumes very strong future oil prices. Economic liberalization has not progressed in Venezuela to the same degree as in many other Latin American nations, and inflation has been unusually high. Populist president Hugo Chavez threatens to roll back some of his predecessor's reforms—lower trade barriers, privatization and job cuts in the bloated public sector. But the imperative of attracting foreign investment will eventually trump the left-wing rhetoric.

## COSTA RICA: A CENTRAL AMERICAN SUCCESS STORY

After decades of almost nonstop civil war and forced migrations of refugees from nation to nation (including northward to the U.S.), Central America is in a relative state of peace. For a glimpse of what many years of peace and democracy (when fully achieved) could do for all the nations of Central America, one has only to look at tiny Costa Rica.

Costa Rica is rapidly becoming a high-tech manufacturing center. It has a population of only 3.5 million, smaller than that of Kentucky or Arizona, but it boasts a 95% literacy rate. While its neighbors have squandered their money on large militaries and years of civil war, Costa Rica has used its funds for education and infrastructure to facilitate a transition from agriculture to manufacturing.

A decade ago, almost all of Costa Rica's exports were farm products such as coffee, bananas and sugar. Today high-tech exports totaling some $1 billion a year surpass agricultural exports. Most of these high-tech products come from about 150 U.S. companies manufacturing and distributing there, including Monsanto, Motorola, Hewlett-Packard and soon Intel, which is building a $500 million computer-chip plant that will eventually employ 2,000 people.

Not surprisingly, labor shortages have arisen for skilled work in Costa Rica, and wages are rising strongly. Traditional manufacturing industries that depend on low-wage labor, such as apparel factories, are leaving Costa Rica for less expensive economies, such as Guatemala, Nicaragua and El Salvador, which will benefit from this migration.

In this way Central America is displaying the same progression of economic development—fueled by foreign investment—that has occurred throughout the world, from Europe and North America in the 19th and 20th centuries to Asia, Latin America and Africa today. This progression is the engine that has always driven the rise of global living standards.

## A WINDING ROAD FOR LATIN AMERICA

Economic progress in Latin America will continue to be uneven, hampered by undemocratic regimes, government corruption, vast disparities in wealth, and drug cartels that siphon off valuable resources, fail to pay taxes, and undermine the integrity of law enforcement and courts. Many countries can't create enough jobs for their fast-growing populations. Investors will have to be ready to absorb unexpected shocks and setbacks. In addition, many Latin countries have weak education and banking systems and low domestic savings rates, according to Pedro-Pablo Kuzcinski, former finance minister of Peru and now an investment banker in New York. In the Caribbean, drug cartels are moving in from Mexico and Colombia, filling a trade and investment vacuum that was left by declining U.S. governmental aid and waning agricultural exports to Europe.

## THE EUROPEAN TRADE CHALLENGE IN LATIN AMERICA

A key challenge for U.S. government and business will be making sure that South America doesn't tilt strongly toward Europe in trade. While Congress dilly-dallies on giving the President "fast track" authority for NAFTA expansion into South America, European companies such as Fiat, Electrolux and British Telecom are increasing their presence in South America, especially in Brazil and Argentina.

In 1996 total trade between the European Union nations and the Mercosur trade group—Brazil, Argentina, Uruguay and Paraguay—was greater in volume than Mercosur trade with the United States. This served as a wake-up call to American business (but apparently not yet to the U.S. Congress) that, after several decades of American dominance in Latin American business, Europe was reasserting its historical ties with South America.

# The Middle East and North Africa

This region's primary importance to the United States and the other advanced nations can be summed up in one word: oil. Although the region provides a declining share of America's imported oil, the U.S. still gets significant quantities from Saudi Arabia, the United Arab Emirates, Kuwait and Algeria, all of which rank (along with oil-less Israel and Egypt) among America's top 50 two-way trading partners.

In addition to oil, the world's interest in the area has focused on tension between Israel and the Palestinians, Saddam Hussein's evil reign in Iraq, and Muslim fundamentalists' attempts to create theocracies wherever possible. But there are also profound economic developments quietly taking shape all over the Arabic world of the Middle East and North Africa. Many nations are finally, slowly, getting their economic acts together, beginning to take the proven path to success through privatization, lower trade barriers and encouragement of outside investment.

## STILL RECOVERING FROM LOW OIL PRICES

After leading the world in income growth during the oil boom of the '70s and early '80s, the Arabic nations went into an economic tailspin when the price of petroleum collapsed in 1986. In the decade that followed, while economies grew at varying rates in almost every other region of the world, the region experienced contracting GDP and personal incomes. The economies not dependent on oil fared better, but even their growth was anemic compared with the rest of the world's.

In an unusually harsh judgment from an international organization, a 1995 World Bank study said that the Arabic nations "for too long have squandered their potential" due to governmental policies that were "ill-suited to a world economy that is fundamentally different from that in the past."

In the whole region, and notably in Egypt and Algeria, governments have been slow to privatize inefficient, overstaffed state industries. But the nations that embraced economic liberalization and diversification first—especially non-energy producers such as Morocco, Jordan and Tunisia—have shown that it can pay off in growth, attracting foreign investment, creating jobs and reducing poverty. The nations with the most-open markets and with economic climates conducive to growth also tend to have governments that are politically progressive, though not necessarily democratic. These include Jordan, Bahrain, Morocco and Tunisia. The nations with the worst business climates also have the most politically repressive regimes: Libya, Iraq, Iran, Syria and Yemen.

## ISRAEL'S ENTREPRENEURIAL BOOM

Israel, the largest recipient of American foreign aid (primarily military), has been hampered economically by being in a state of virtually constant wartime preparedness since its founding in 1948. It also has little land and few natural resources, making it highly dependent on imports of fuel, food and raw materials. Entrepreneurship was stymied for years by heavy government regulation and ownership of business, but the current government is moving slowly toward economic liberalization.

Coupled with a high level of education, this new spirit has spawned a rather impressive high-tech boom, with many new start-up firms in computers, software and other advanced fields. As it manages to achieve a lasting peace with its Arab neighbors and the Palestinians within its borders, it will devote more of its resources to productive investment.

## MANY HURDLES TO CLEAR

The nations of North Africa and the Middle East still have a long way to go to join the world community economically, and the bumps along the road are many and rough. These nations have among the world's highest rates of population growth—running more than 2.5% a year, with labor-force growth at over 3% a year.

Fertility rates will decline over time, but in the short run, creating enough jobs will require significant reforms to attract foreign investment. The need will be great for low-skill and moderate-skill jobs in manufacturing goods for export; Morocco has had some success in exporting textiles and clothing and the Persian Gulf states are exporting chemicals. A good start would be to bring home to the region some of the estimated $350 *billion* in capital that the oil-exporting nations invested in overseas assets during the past 25 years.

Muslim fundamentalism, with its bedrock antagonism to Western values, including economic openness and full rights for women, will be an impediment to foreign investment and economic growth for years. It will keep a grip on Iran and continue to foment open warfare in Algeria and terrorism in Egypt, Tunisia and the Gulf states. Ultimately, however, secular rule with expanding civil rights and liberties will prevail in the Muslim world, as it will elsewhere. There are already encouraging signs of a subtle shift in Iran, which will lead to improved U.S. relations with that nation.

# Sub-Saharan Africa

The people of Africa have endured the worst kinds of repression and exploitation for more than a century, first at the hands of colonial powers and then, for the past half-century, by home-grown despots. Often these rulers were propped up by distant Cold War antagonists in the global struggle between the expansion and containment of Soviet communism.

Africa's recent history is a story of lengthy civil wars, dependency on paternalistic foreign aid from the West, extravagant theft of the public's wealth by corrupt government officials, vicious ethnic conflicts and genocides, the AIDS epidemic, and widespread famine.

## THE SLOW DEMISE OF AFRICAN SOCIALISM

But now the winds of change are beginning to blow across Africa, as a new generation of pragmatic, market-oriented leaders replaces the deposed and dying strongmen who created dictatorships in the postcolonial era.

The 54 nations of Africa that lie south of the Sahara, while continuing to lag far behind the rest of the world in living standards, are slowly beginning to develop the free markets that will give them, for the first time in a quarter-century, a taste of serious economic progress.

Sub-Saharan Africa is consistently achieving annual economic growth of about 5%, and this is likely to continue and even accelerate. The countries making the most progress in economic liberalization, such as Uganda, are achieving growth rates substantially higher.

## MORE FOREIGN INVESTMENT AND TRADE

Foreign investors shunned most of Africa throughout the postcolonial era, because foreign-owned or -financed facilities were not safe from government seizure, and it was difficult or impossible for investors to bring profits home. In the 1990s Sub-Saharan Africa received less than 5% of the world's total foreign investment, compared with about 45% for Asia.

South Africa—both before and after the end of white rule—has been the exception. It had long been the largest recipient of foreign investment, and it had long enjoyed governance that, although racially unjust, was stable. As a result, today's democratic South Africa is the African nation with the continent's highest standard of living for people of all races.

The nations of Africa account for only about 2% of U.S. trade. As small as this seems, just one African nation, South Africa, trades more with the U.S. than all of the nations of Eastern Europe combined. And 12 nations at the southern end of the continent trade a higher value of goods and services with America than do the 15 republics of the former Soviet Union. U.S.-Africa trade will explode in value in the decade ahead, with the development of Africa's rich natural resources and the growth of manufacturing of all kinds.

## AFRICAN PROGRESS

Uganda has instituted economic reforms and is now experiencing strong economic growth and substantial foreign investment. Much of the new capital has returned with thousands of merchants of Indian descent, whom former dictator Idi Amin banished from Uganda in the '70s.

Ghana has officially turned away from socialism and is developing a wide range of industries, including banking and financial services, manufacturing, and mining (including the first black-managed multinational mining company, Ashanti Goldfields, which is listed on the New York Stock Exchange). But an enormous, inefficient government sector still owns most large industries, and the privatization program seems to have run out of steam.

Botswana, a nation small in population, has the big advantage for foreign investors of being close to the large, highly developed nation of South Africa. This has attracted financial-services investors as well as manufacturers such as Volvo and Hyundai, which are making cars there for sale all over Africa. Tanzania has drastically reduced its public sector, cutting spending and privatizing or closing about a third of its 400 state-run enterprises.

Eritrea, which finally won its hard-fought independence from Ethiopia in 1993, has taken the unusual step of turning aside most international aid, trying to avoid the economic dependency that helped ruin so many other African nations. It is building a new government will little debt and little corruption, with unusual peace among its many disparate religions and cultures. But its progress was jeopardized by a resumption in 1998 of border disputes and combat with Ethiopia.

Varying degrees of economic revival are also being achieved in numerous other African nations, including Benin, Namibia, Swaziland, Gabon, Kenya, Mali and Zambia. The tiny island of Mauritius, in the Indian Ocean east of Madagascar, is a booming exporter of apparel to the U.S. and Europe.

One of the interesting characteristics of the African revival now under way is the important role being played by women in business, government and education. One of the most prominent businesswomen is Ghana's Sarah Hage-Ali, who returned from England to acquire and revitalize the nation's only manufacturer of sanitary napkins.

## A DILEMMA FOR AMERICAN LIBERALS

A key to Africa's continued economic progress will be the willing-ness of the advanced nations to buy more manufactured products from the continent, not just Nigeria's petroleum, Botswana's diamonds, the Ivory Coast's cocoa and the sugar produced by several nations.

U.S. multinationals in textiles and apparel are eager to invest in Africa, where some nations have lower wages even than China. But American labor unions are resisting the lowering of trade barriers to such imports, even from a continent that accounts for only 1% of Amer-ican apparel imports. This creates the peculiar situation of U.S. foreign aid being used by Kenya to build shirt factories, but the U.S. govern-ment instituting a dumping complaint against the shirts produced in those same factories, declaring them to be illegally low-priced.

The nations of Africa, and many members of Congress, support a free-trade bill that would, for ten years, eliminate American barriers to products of African nations that pass tests relating to human rights, eco-nomic reform, labor conditions and protection of intellectual property.

Among the opponents of the bill (in addition to pro-union con-gressmen and representatives from textile and apparel states) are a number of liberal black congressmen and activists, who fear that it would lead to the "recolonization" of Africa by multinational corpora-tions. The bill narrowly passed the House in 1998, just before President Clinton's tour of Africa, but will encounter stiff resistance in the Senate, despite the addition of safeguards for American labor.

## UNFINISHED BUSINESS IN AFRICA'S REVIVAL

Africa is on its way to a new era, but it still faces staggering chal-lenges. Despite the continent's vast farm acreage and rich soil, only two of its nations, South Africa and Zimbabwe, can feed their own people without imports, and almost half the nations require interna-tional food aid.

Nearly half the nations are ruled by dictators and suffer from the wholesale theft of foreign-aid funds and tax revenues by small ruling elites—as much as an incredible 90% of the continent's aggregate GDP, according to one United Nations study. Two of the continent's most populous and resource-rich nations, Nigeria and Congo (formerly Zaire), continue to be plagued by astounding governmental corruption and repression. The new strongman in Nigeria has promised free elec-tions and other political and economic reforms. But change will be very difficult in a nation where for years the military elite has been accus-tomed to stealing most of the nation's $10 billion of annual oil revenues, leaving the economy in financial ruin and the people in abject poverty.

There are also thorny unresolved issues surrounding the wealth of small white minorities compared with enormous black populations. It is unclear how South Africa, blessed by heavy foreign investment, a well-educated population and relative harmony, will fare as crime rises and more and more whites choose to emigrate. In Zimbabwe, a potentially prosperous nation whose economy is in disarray, the government has proposed seizing, with only minimal compensation, the rich farmland owned by the nation's large commercial farms. The dominant owners are the 2% white minority who control about 70% of Zimbabwe's most productive farmland.

# Russia and the CIS

Ever since the disintegration of the Soviet Union nearly a decade ago, Russia has lurched from crisis to crisis, both political and economic, and this is likely to continue for years to come.

There are still considerable doubts about whether its experiments with free markets and democracy will take hold permanently, or whether Russia will someday revert to its historical roots of authoritarian government control over both the economy and poplitical system. Many of its average citizens seem to yearn for the stability of the old communist order, however drab and repressive it was. A return to dictatorship would likely be accompanied by some degree of confiscation of private property, both Russian- and foreign-owned.

After contracting substantially—possibly as much as 43%—between 1989 and 1996, the Russian economy got on track again briefly, only to plunge into near-chaos in 1998. The government of Boris Yeltsin raised interest rates to breathtaking levels to bolster the ruble and stem the outflow of private wealth, but only a new IMF bailout averted an economic meltdown. After virtually defaulting on its government debt, Russia found itself without access to international credit except at prohibitively high interest rates.

Russia is plagued by huge problems, including widespread discontent due to the widening income chasm between newly rich entrepreneurs and the great masses suffering declining living standards. Its once-proud military is growing outdated, inept and demoralized. It has tense relations with its neighboring republics in the Commonwealth of Independent States (CIS), which fear that a future Russian government might try to distract the public's attention from declining living standards by waging a nationalistic campaign to reassemble the former Soviet empire. The government's ability to provide basic servises is undermined by widespread tax evasion and capital flight by the capitilist elite. Russia is one of the few nations—and certainly the only large, advanced nation—in which average life expectancy is actually falling, due to deteriorating diet and health care and rising rates of alcoholism and suicide.

Uncertainty will remain the watchword for investment in Russia for years to come. But over the long haul, Russia will offer selective opportunities for the patient, risk-taking foreign investor, due to a richness of natural resources and a well-educated work force. There is great wealth locked away in huge oil and gas reserves in Siberia and several of the CIS nations. Exports of gold, diamonds, platinum, palladium, chrome, rhodium and timber will continue to bring in hard currency. Workers with good scientific education will make valuable employees for multinational companies in computers, aerospace, software programming, telecommunications, banking and financial services.

## RUSSIA: A TOUGH PLACE TO DO BUSINESS

Still, Russia will remain a very tough place for foreigners to do business for many years. Having gone from a czarist monarchy to a seven-decade communist regime, Russia has no tradition of respect for private property and contract law. The country lacks an effective legal, financial and tax systems, which makes foreign investors unsure of how or if they'll get their profits out of the country. Corruption and payoffs are common. The black market flourishes, and there is widespread copying of intellectual property. Competing companies physically threaten their rivals and try to extort money from them. Corporate funds mysteriously disappear from bank accounts, and the income of the new capitalist elite gets shipped out as soon as it is earned—before taxes are paid. The Russian mafia has its tentacles everywhere, demanding protection money from businesses both local and international. Those who resist, or fail to hire comparably strong protectors (security services staffed by former Russian military and intelligence officers), are at risk of bodily harm or even murder.

Despite all this, a lot pf international businesses will continue to put up with the hassles and the dangers of doing business in Russia, because of its enormous population, making it a potentially lucrative market for everything from capital goods to consumer products.

But private stock markets exist (with a lot of securities fraud), state-owned businesses are being privatized, and foreign capital will eventually return to modernize Russian industry and business. More important, a legal and financial system will slowly emerge to support

economic rights and liberalization. The Russian people are well educated and industrious, and technology created to support military and
space research is being adapted to a variety of commercial purposes.

## THE CIS REPUBLICS

The Commonwealth of Independent States comprises Russia and
11 republics that chose to remain in a loose—very loose—alliance for
their mutual benefit. All the CIS nations suffered broad declines in
economic activity after the collapse of the Soviet Union, and only about
half of themhave resumed their earlier growth.

With the decline of sales to the Russian government (especially the
former Soviet military), trade among the CIS nations has actually been
contracting as they increasingly look outside the bloc for consumer
goods, capital equipment and investment capital.

Most of the CIS nations are lagging behind Russia in the liberalization of their economic systems, and most, including Ukraine, have
suffered even deeper drops in living standards than Russia has. Arme-
nia and Moldova are exceptions, doing substantially better than most of
their CIS colleagues in creating a governmental climate hospitable to
free enterprise, but even they would rank below world norms for economic openness and freedom.

The CIS has proven so far to be a weak, disorganized alliance, and
it is not likely to get much stronger. Many in Ukraine, for example,
desire a closer relationship with Europe, including possible NATO
membership. Most of the CIS nations still resent their long domination
by Russia and their present reliance on Russian energy, and many of
them fear a resurgence of Russian nationalism and a possible attempt
to forcibly reassemble the Soviet Union.

In the years to come, the CIS will exist largely to reduce trade barriers among the 12 republics, and in this it will succeed. A growing
Russian economy will once again look to its neighbors for a variety of
raw materials and cheap manufactured goods.

# CHAPTER 5

# Government's Role in the U.S. Economy

I t would be easy and tempting to forecast that government—federal, state and local—will continue on its 15-year-long path of diminishing power over American life and business. But that would be shortsighted. In fact, the record of the past decade and a half isn't a clear picture of diminished governmental involvement. It's quite a mixed record, and the outlook for the next few years is similarly mixed—a crazy-quilt combination of waxing and waning involvement, with the federal and state governments pulling back in some places and plunging boldly into new areas.

All over the world, national governments that have long exerted high levels of control over their economies—higher than ever practiced in the United States—are privatizing, deregulating and gradually reducing the size and scope of their public sectors. But in the U.S., which led the way in the late '70s and early '80s, there are signs of a slow pendulum swing back toward more governmental regulation and more control over unfettered capitalism.

For example, in response to a surge in business consolidations and allegedly anticompetitive behavior, federal and state governments have stepped up antitrust efforts. The assault on the tobacco industry is unprecedented since Prohibition. And Washington is putting forth more, not fewer, new regulations covering the environment, the workplace and health care. On the other hand, trade barriers will continue to decline. And the federal government will never return to the old days of tight market regulation in agriculture, transportation, banking and telecommunications. The pendulum might swing back, but in a very narrow arc.

The public sector in America—governments at all levels—won't shrink in the years ahead. It will maintain its present share of the U.S. economy for the next 15 years and then begin to enlarge, as the retiring baby-boom generation puts more social-service and health care demands on the economy. Mandatory federal spending—entitlements and interest on the debt—will allow virtually no real growth in discretionary spending on everything else—from defense and education to infrastructure and the environment.

Government budgets will hover around a rough balance, dipping into deficit in times of recession and falling revenues. Many states will be in balance or run surpluses. The federal budget won't regularly achieve an authentic balance—that is, one that doesn't depend on using surplusses in the social security trust fund to make ends appear to meet.

The total federal tax burden will remain in the present range, and the present graduated income tax will not be replaced by a flat tax, valued-added tax or consumption tax.

Looming deficits in medicare and social security accounts will be corrected over the next few years by a variety of fixes, including raising the age of eligibility, applying a means test and raising the wage base on which taxes are levied. Social security will be partially privatized, with the government investing some of the current surplus and future payroll taxes in the U.S. stock and bond markets.

# A Public Sector of Stable Size

Total government spending in the U.S.—federal, state and local—has risen strongly over the past few decades, more or less in lock step with a growing economy, personal incomes and tax receipts. This is likely to continue for years.

The federal government typically consumes a share of annual American output (GDP) in the high-teens-to-20% range (though recently it's been down to about 16%), and state and local government together consume about 10% to 15%, putting total government spending at about 30% to 35% of GDP, on average. There will not be any major change in this share, as there will be countervailing forces at play. On the one hand, restraints in government spending amid strong economic growth will tug this consumption rate downward a little. On the other hand, the health care needs of a graying population, plus the constant costs of interest on the federal debt, will push it up a little.

Despite the recent wave of tax cutting by state governments, the long-term trend in state and local government will be toward modestly higher taxation, as "devolution" comes home to roost with nonfederal government units forced to shoulder more of the burdens that were once met by Uncle Sam.

## SMALLER IN THE U.S. THAN IN EUROPE

Spending by the public sector accounts for a smaller share of total economic activity in the U. S. than in virtually any other large industrial nation. It's substantially lower than in the European nations, where heavy social-welfare spending puts the governmental share of GDP into the 45% to 50% range.

There seems to be some correlation between economic growth and relatively small public sectors, at least in the major industrial nations, and this augurs well for the United States in its competition with Europe. But the European Union nations are beginning to come to grips with their bloated public sectors, which will be a boost to their economic growth.

## DOWNSIZING AND PRIVATIZING

Since the growth of government spending consists primarily of surging payments to individuals—which are handled primarily by computer systems—government employment in the U. S. will continue its long downward trend as a share of the total work force. Federal employees made up more than 6% of the labor force in the mid '60s, but that's down to near 3.5%.

At all levels of government, the trend is toward privatizing public services in virtually every field, including garbage collection, management of schools, prison and welfare systems, office cleaning, street repair, and public transit.

Privatization will move in fits and starts, slowed by occasional public opposition (to privatizing police and firefighting, for example) and the resistance of public-employee unions. In many jurisdictions, government agencies will be invited to bid on the services they are now performing, and the more entrepreneurial agencies will sometimes win contracts over private competitors. The U.S. Department of Agriculture, for example, won a contract to run the payroll computer system of the Federal Aviation Administration, beating out several private-sector bidders.

Privatization will restrain or even reduce direct government employment, but in a sense it merely shifts employment to the books of private firms, which will often pay lower salaries and benefits than the government workers once earned. The record of taxpayer savings from privatization will be mixed but generally favorable to continued outsourcing.

# The Government Spending Outlook

When President Clinton announced in early 1996 that "the era of big government is over," what he probably meant was that the era of big government budget deficits is over. And that's probably true. A remarkable consensus has emerged in Washington, in both major parties, that the U.S. economy runs better with balanced governmental budgets, or at worst, occasional federal deficits of barely 1% of gross domestic product (GDP), the value of all goods and services produced in America each year. More to the point, this new consensus holds that budgetary balances should be achieved primarily through spending restraint rather than higher taxes.

But remember this: A government with its spending roughly in balance isn't the same as a smaller government or a less-intrusive government. It's still "big government" by any definition.

## THE DISAPPEARING FEDERAL DEFICIT

Over the last four decades, the U.S. government achieved a true balance between current revenues and current expenses only twice, in fiscal 1960 and 1969. Deficits of varying magnitude became the norm. Government spending rose virtually every year, but tax revenue would occasionally dip during recessions and periods of sluggish economic growth, deepening the annual budget deficit. The deficit exploded in the '80s, when Congress and the White House agreed on deep marginal tax cuts but let defense and social spending soar. Deficits amounted to 3% to 6% of GDP—an unhealthfully high level—in every year but one from 1982 to 1994.

In absolute dollars, the federal budget deficit peaked in '92 and seemingly declined to almost nothing by the end of the '90s. Credit for this feat should go primarily to the American private sector...surging corporate profits, capital gains from a dazzling stock market, and a strong rise in personal income. Congress and the White House did their parts by showing a higher degree of budgetary discipline than at any time since the early 1960s. But even more credit should go to a hidden ally—the social security surplus, which created the illusion of balanced budgets in '98 and '99.

In fact, the budget won't be in true balance until all the costs of general government operations are being covered from general tax revenues, without having to borrow funds from the social security system, which has been running an annual excess of payroll taxes over benefits paid out. This true balance hasn't been achieved yet, but it could happen as early as fiscal 2000, with a total budgetary surplus of $5 billion—modest in magnitude, but the first genuine surplus in 30 years.

## SURPLUSES FOREVER?

So are federal budget deficits gone forever, destined to become a footnote in the history of late 20th century America? No. While surpluses won't be the rarity they've been since 1960, don't expect an eternal string of them. There are bound to be occasional economic slumps accompanied by classic Keynesian deficit spending—periods when tax receipts fall but social spending holds level or, more likely, rises to pay for relief and to stimulate the economy. Even in good times, it will be difficult for Congress and the White House to resist the pressure to raise spending or slash taxes to use up a surplus—both voter-pleasing moves. Washington will succumb in varying degrees to both temptations.

The alternative—running consistent but small surpluses year after year, except in the rare severe recession—lacks political sex appeal. But a significant portion of political leaders and voters will argue for leaving the surpluses alone, to accomplish two important objectives: 1) paying back the federal borrowings of previous decades (about $5.6 trillion), which would reduce the government's annual interest cost (about 14% of the total annual budget) and free up revenue for other federal programs; and 2) keeping social security flush, to pay for the baby boomers' retirements, beginning around 2010, when benefit costs will begin to exceed payroll taxes.

## PAYING DOWN THE FEDERAL DEBT

The federal debt represents about 60% of GDP. After World War II, the debt was equal to 122%, but steadily declined to a low of 24% in '74. From there it grew two and a half times to today's level. Now there's a strong sentiment in favor of paying down these old debts, rather than saddling our grandchildren with that burden.

It's not that the federal debt represents unabashed profligacy in Washington, however. The U.S. government, unlike some state governments and other nations, doesn't have separate accounts for current operations (money that is paid out to individuals and businesses and therefore consumed each year) and for capital spending. Much of the government's debt represents borrowing that financed things of lasting value to America—highways, dams, national parks, armaments to maintain world order, education and training for our work force. So in a sense, some of the national debt represents investment in future growth, world peace and other objectives of society.

## A TILT IN HOW MONEY IS SPENT

The structure of federal spending has changed dramatically in the past few decades. National defense was once the biggest share of the budget, but today, at a six-decade low (about 15% of the budget), it's only about the cost of annual interest on the debt. And it's a fraction of the cost of federal payments to or in direct support of individuals. There is no big jump foreseeable in military spending, which will continue a modest downward path as a share of the budget.

Payments to individuals, both direct and indirect, account for 50% to 60% of federal spending. They include social security benefits, medicare and medicaid payments, pensions for civil service and military retirees, student grants, and welfare assistance. The lion's share of these transfer payments—about 60%—goes for social security and medicare, and welfare spending accounts for a very small share.

## CRUMBS FOR EVERYTHING ELSE

What's left—only 10% to 15% of the annual budget—must fund *all other* functions of the government—interstate highways, housing aid, farm subsidies and research, education and job training, foreign aid, medical research, space exploration, environmental and food safety, law-enforcement assistance, aviation control, drug interdiction, weather tracking, and on and on.

When you hear members of Congress fighting over the hottest new legislative proposal or funding continuation—for child nutrition, aid to developing nations, a volunteer teacher corps, a new space mission, whatever—keep in mind that they're fighting over the table scraps. Look at these percentages of federal spending: support for the arts (a fraction of 1% of the budget), foreign aid (1%), farm subsidies (less than 1%), education (2%) and health research (2%).

The main course—the real meat of the federal budget—is the entitlements that Congress can reduce only by hard-fought changes in program rules. Throughout the budget battles of the '90s, Congress chose to put off the tough choices relating to social security and medicare, which if not modified in the years ahead, will plunge the government much deeper into red ink. Congress won't be able to put it off much longer, so it will take steps to fix these programs over the next few years.

In light of the rising cost of programs for the elderly, it is highly unlikely that Congress will be able to find significant additional funds—beyond simple inflationary increases, if that—for any of the other functions of government.

# Supporting Tomorrow's Elderly

In all the demographically graying economies of North America and Europe (and even in China, with its low birth rate), maintaining the health and welfare of tomorrow's elderly will be the greatest financial challenge facing government for decades. Those over 65 compose about 12.5% of the U.S. population, and public support systems at all levels of government are already beginning to groan under the burden of meeting their needs. By the year 2020, the elderly will account for 16.5% of the population, and that will rise to 20% by the year 2030. The enormous, aging baby boom population will put considerable political pressure on Washington to meet its needs, especially in health care. The cost of these needs will be magnified by advancing medical technology. It will be difficult (but financially essential) to limit, through rationing or denial, access to the latest life-extending and life-improving procedures.

## BENEFIT 'CUTS' OR JUST SLOWER GROWTH?

Changes in social security and medicare will typically be decried as "benefit cuts" by opponents in senior-citizen lobby groups. But Congress won't ever cut the current benefit being received by anyone on social security. Washington will merely restrain the *growth in future benefits* for current retirees and cut the *anticipated benefits* of future retirees.

However, medicare recipients will face increases in premium expenses, especially through means testing for upper-income retirees. And greater taxation of social security benefits—one of the options under discussion—will have the same net effect as reducing cash benefits.

And despite all the new restraints on the rate of spending growth, total spending for all senior-citizen programs will continue to mount for decades, both in absolute amounts and as a percentage of the federal budget, continually putting the squeeze on everything defined as discretionary spending.

## MEDICARE AND SOCIAL SECURITY *WILL* BE STABILIZED

Ultimately, the government will have to pay back to the social security trust fund the money it has been borrowing to cover previous government spending. The pay-back money—principal and interest on the Treasury bonds owned by social security—will come from one source: taxes on future generations of workers.

The problem is, there will be a declining ratio of workers to retirees, falling from an estimated 3.3 workers per beneficiary today to 2.4 in 2020 and 2.0 in 2050. Unless changes are made in the present social security system, the tax burden on future workers will be staggering.

According to public-opinion polls, many Americans apparently believe the task of shoring up social security is insurmountable. Young adults say they don't believe that social security will "be there for them"—meaning, presumably, that it will have collapsed by the time they retire, or that the return to them in benefits will be a negligible portion of the payroll taxes they will pay in over a lifetime of work.

Their pessimism is unwarranted, but it has fueled a groundswell of support for full privatization of social security—that is, dismantling the entire system and replacing it with a requirement that workers invest the equivalent of their combined employer-employee payroll tax in market investments, through a kind of mandatory super individual retirement account.

Full privatization has a lot of political appeal, after several years of soaring stock prices, and it's especially appealing to high-income younger workers, who would benefit most from privatization. But it would require the creation of separate programs for fulfilling the special income needs of low-earners, widows and orphans, the disabled and the elderly divorced, who all get special treatment from the present system. In the end, these concerns, coupled with congressional anxiety over having to bail out retirees who made bad investment choices, will induce Congress to take the more cautious approach of partial privatization.

### Small fixes will do the trick

In fact, the future solvency of the program, and its ability to provide a decent return to future generations, can be assured by some relatively small changes in the current program. "Fixing the financial problems of social security is not rocket science," argue Henry Aaron and Robert Reischauer of the Brookings Institution. "There are many ways to do it that don't require intergalactic thrust"—that is, full privatization.

However, even the relatively modest changes advocated by social security preservationists like Aaron and Reischauer won't be enacted without political courage and cooperation among parties who heretofore have dug in their heels and resisted making tough choices. Over the next several years the social security and medicare reform debate will be marked by acrimonious debate. The political struggle will often pit an alliance of today's retirees and older baby-boomers against the relatively smaller age cohort of young adults in their twenties and early thirties.

## OUTLOOK FOR SOCIAL SECURITY REFORM

When the dust settles, Congress will probably adopt some combination of the following changes. It will be a mix-and-match process, since a greater reliance on one kind of fix would reduce or eliminate the need to adopt a different one. In any event, here's the menu of likely changes:

**An increase in qualifying ages.** The age at which an early retiree may first receive a reduced benefit is now 62, and the age of full benefit is 65. These will both be raised, in stages over many years, to 65 for reduced benefits and nearly 70 for full benefits. These increases will reflect the great strides in American health and life expectancy since the program was created in 1935. Many workers will want to work well past 65 anyway, for their own self-fulfillment or financial need.

**A substantial hike in the social security wage base.** In 1999, workers paid social security taxes on all income up to $72,600, and that wage base is set to increase automatically each year by about 4%. But some members of Congress have called for a big jump in the wage base, up into the $90,000s, or even the taxation of all earnings, with no upper limit. (The 2.9% medicare portion of the 15.3% FICA tax already applies to all earnings.) In addition, there may be an increase in the number of years of earnings used to calculate the retiree's benefits (instead of using the last—and highest—years of the person's career).

**Broader taxation of social security benefits,** at least for upper-income recipients (so-called "means testing"). Some proposals call for taxing everyone's social security benefits the same as private-pension income—that is, normal taxation of the portion of benefits that exceeds what the retiree contributed in payroll taxes while working. Taxation of everyone's benefits isn't likely to fly.

**Partial privatization of social security.** Eventually Congress may direct that some of the social security trust fund assets be invested in publicly traded stocks and bonds, not just in U.S. Treasury securities. Given the stock market's historical advantage over Treasuries, this should result in better returns for social security with minimal risk. Or Congress will mix in some individual responsibility, going along with calls to let workers invest a small portion of the combined employee-employer payroll tax—say, one-fifth of the 15.3% FICA payroll tax (meaning about 3% could be invested by employees).

### Ideas that probably won't fly

Take note of what we think Congress will *not* do about social security:

**Raise the 12.4% social security payroll tax** (included in the combined 15.3% FICA tax) that is now divided equally between employers and their workers. It is a highly regressive tax, meaning that it falls much more heavily on low- and middle-income taxpayers than on the affluent. Most Americans of moderate income already pay more in social security taxes than they do in federal income tax, and there will be enormous pressure to leave the tax where it is or even reduce it, perhaps in combination with a big hike in the taxable wage base.

**Trim the annual, automatic increase in benefits.** This is now equal to the annual rate of consumer inflation, as measured by the consumer price index (CPI). A reduced cost of living adjustment (COLA), maybe just a half-point less than the CPI, would save social security vast amounts of money each year. But this probably won't happen because senior-citizen lobbies will resist it mightily. More to the point, the Bureau of Labor Statistics may have accomplished the same result with its recent changes in the calculation of the CPI, which cumulatively will probably lop nearly a full percentage point off the official rate of inflation.

**Include public employees in social security.** It's estimated that one-quarter of all state and local employees are outside social security, in pension plans of their own. While putting new public-employee hires into the system would help stabilize it financially, unions and pension plans will probably block this change.

### A stable but less lucrative new system

Some mix of the changes listed above will guarantee that social security will "be there" for future generations with a substantial monthly benefit. However, it will not be the sweet deal it has been for retirees over the past few decades, when payroll taxes were low and Congress kept boosting benefits. Past retirees recovered all the taxes they paid in, plus a modest rate of interest, in a relatively few years of benefits. A retiree who was born in 1895, and who worked until 1960 at a minimum level of earnings for social security credit, got all his taxes and interest back in less than one year of benefits. But the situation changed dramatically when social security payroll taxes were jacked up in the '80s.

Under the present rules and taxes, a worker born in 1965, now 33 and working at an average level of earnings, wouldn't get all her money back in social security benefits until 19 years after she retires at 65 in 2030. And if her earnings were at the upper end of the amount taxed by social security, the length of payback would expand dramatically, to 33 years, or age 98—if she starts getting benefits at 65, which is not likely, given the probable increase to age 70 or so. If most of the projected changes are implemented, the payback will take even longer. For practical purposes, many workers will not live long enough to get back in benefits what they paid in, plus a modest interest return.

These numbers are the most potent argument for partially privatizing social security. Private investing of some amount of the social security surplus would likely improve the return to beneficiaries, not to mention creating an enormous pool of capital for the growth of American business.

### Fixing the health care programs too

Medicare and medicaid will present a more immediate problem for Washington. Both programs have been growing rapidly for years. Left unchanged, they would soak up *all* federal tax receipts by about 2015. Congress and the White House will fight for the next several years over reforming the health plans. Likely changes include raising medicare's eligibility age, pushing most seniors into managed care such as HMOs, and instituting some kinds of benefit reductions for high-income retirees. Possible but less likely options include privatizing medicare by giving seniors vouchers for health care and cutting medicaid payments to middle-class nursing-home patients. You can probably rule out an increase in payroll taxes for medicare.

# The Structure of American Taxation

In the coming years, Congress will debate whether to replace the current multirate graduated personal income tax with something entirely new: a flat-rate income tax, a national sales tax at point of sale, a European-style value-added tax (VAT, a tiny sales tax added on to every product as it moves through stages of production), a consumption tax, or something else. None of these approaches will be adopted as a substitute for the present income tax in the next decade or so. It is possible, however, that a very low VAT could be added to the income tax for a revenue boost that would be largely invisible to voters, hidden as it would be within the final price of goods.

## THE DEVIL WE DON'T KNOW

When push comes to shove, there will be public anxiety about replacing the devil we know with the devil we don't. Broad-gauged tax reform would entail an enormous risk for an economy that is functioning pretty well with the highly flawed, bizarrely complex tax system America has now.

Radical change would create new classes of winners and losers. For instance, homeowners (and the real estate industry) are big winners under the current tax code, because interest on a mortgage and local property taxes are deductible, and profit on the sale of most homes escapes taxation. Charities are also big winners, because donors get a deduction for giving. To retain these and other popular breaks in a flat-tax system, the rate on all taxpayers would rise well beyond 20%, quickly losing its appeal to many voters. At the very least, charities, real estate and every other industry would insist on complicated "transition rules"—phasing out the breaks they now enjoy—that would make today's tax code look simple. Sales of real estate, government bonds, life insurance and other tax-favored investments would be severely curtailed while Congress debated overhaul, perhaps causing a recession.

So lawmakers will continue to cast its lot with the devil it knows—today's tax code and its amazing collection of incentives and disincentives for all kinds of human behavior. Politicians will make changes here and there. Many of the changes will be designed to boost savings, something Congress has tried before, as when it created individual retirement accounts in the '80s, expanded them in the '90s and restored in 1997 the capital-gains tax preference that it unwisely abolished a decade earlier.

### A STABLE TOTAL TAX BURDEN

Any changes in the tax code, no matter how modest they seem at first, will have to be judged by how much money they raise or forfeit for the government. As a share of the nation's output, taxes have been remarkably stable since the end of World War II, right around 20% of GDP. Assuming that support for defense, health care, environmental protection, highways and bridges, parks, and thousands of other items won't decline, taxes as a percentage of GDP will remain fairly constant.

It will take substantial cost restraints in the fast-growing medicare and medicaid programs to prevent taxes from rising, so it is reasonable not to expect any significant tax cuts in the years ahead.

# More Regulation of Daily Business Life

D
on't confuse the general trend of market deregulation with the government's increasing inclination to tell businesses how they must conduct their affairs internally. In the decades ahead, Washington and state governments will have more, not less, say in environmental controls, land use, product liability, health care, food and drug safety, occupational health, hiring discrimination, and the treatment of workers (and customers) with disabilities.

## PUBLIC CLAMORING FOR MORE REGULATION

The American public and business have always had a love-hate relationship with government regulation. They decry regulations that infringe on *their* rights and well-being. But they keep petitioning government for new rules, subsidies and trade protection to shield them from free markets and give them an edge over someone else.

They pay lip service to the benefits of laissez-faire, but they seek the shelter of government assistance when Darwinian capitalism gets too harsh. This ambivalence will continue indefinitely, but more people and businesses will be forced by the realities of modern competition to fend for themselves.

As recently as 20 years ago, the federal government set or approved industry pricing in such fields as banking, aviation, trucking, rail transport and agriculture. But a wave of deregulation established market pricing and opened up competition in these and other industries, including partial deregulation of telecommunications and the beginning of interstate branch banking.

Market deregulation isn't over, with the electric-power and financial-services industries still to finish the process. The states are taking the lead on power deregulation, and market consolidation is forcing Congress's hand on financial-services restructuring.

## THE EPIC TOBACCO STRUGGLE

One of the most significant regulatory developments in recent years was the decision of the Food and Drug Administration to define cigarettes as a delivery system for the addictive drug nicotine, thereby giving itself authority to regulate the tobacco industry. That action, followed by related state and congressional initiatives, marked the first time since Prohibition that government had undertaken an attack on an industry that legally makes and sells a substance that the government later deemed to constitute a hazard to society.

But rather than ban tobacco outright—an approach that didn't work well with alcohol 80 years ago—governments seek to discourage use through heavy taxation, sales and advertising restrictions, elaborate education campaigns, and surveys of which brands young people are smoking most. The eventual settlements probably won't make much of a dent in teen smoking—which is based more on adolescent rebellion than on ignorance of the risks—but they will raise a lot of money to help defray the public costs of smokers' medical care.

Emboldened by the lucrative outcome of the tobacco initiative, governments and consortiums of class-action attorneys will continue to look for ways to restrict the sale of other products, now legally available, that are believed to pose health risks with large costs to taxpayers. This led in 1999 to the first lawsuits filed by city governments against handgun manufacturers. It is likely that the alcoholic beverage industry will someday face lawsuits aimed at further restricting the advertising and sale of products that, while salubrious when used in moderation, can be abused.

## THE INCESSANT URGE TO INTRUDE IN MARKETS

Congress won't be able to resist the urge to micromanage business when there is a public clamoring that "something should be done" about a hot new issue with broad voter appeal.

When parents began complaining about pornography on the Internet, Congress swung into action with the Communications Decency Act in 1995, only to see it struck down by the Supreme Court as unconstitutional two years later.

When women complained to Congress about being rushed out of hospitals after giving birth, Congress legislated minimum stays.

When it was revealed that confidential personal financial information was being peddled on the Internet, Congress began considering new federal protections, despite the fact that enforcement of existing laws would probably suffice.

When voters began to complain about coverage restrictions in their managed-care health plans, Congress embarked on a broad regulatory program for health maintenance organizations. And all across America, most states are creating growing lists of medical conditions that an employer must cover if it offers health insurance to its employees. Thirteen states, for example, require coverage of infertility.

And so it goes on Capitol Hill and in the statehouses. When the public—or some vocal portion of the public—wants action, government will oblige. States and local governments will be especially active. Other states will emulate California's requirement that all automakers manufacture and sell electric cars as a condition of selling any kind of vehicles there. When such new regulations are imposed in a massive market such as California, they can have the effect of creating nation-wide changes in the ways big companies do business.

## A TORRENT OF NEW RULES FROM WASHINGTON

And even when Congress is not enacting new regulatory laws, the federal agencies of the executive branch will be expanding their authority with a widening stream of new rules and regulations.

With much fanfare in 1996, Congress gave itself a unique power to review and overturn new federal regulations that it deemed to over-step the authority of original legislative intent. Since that time, some 6,000 rules have been issued by regulatory agencies, of which about 120 could be rated as major new regulations. The number disapproved so far (as of mid 1998): zero.

The torrent of new rules affecting business can be seen in the growing bulk of the Federal Register, whose 1997 total of 67,000 pages was 33% greater than a decade earlier—after ten years of government "deregulation."

## THE HIDDEN COSTS OF REGULATION

Government regulation adds enormously to the cost of doing business in America. Because the cost is passed on to consumers in the price of their goods and services, it constitutes a kind of hidden taxa-tion. Some estimates put the cost as high as $700 billion a year—almost as much as Americans pay in income taxes.

For that price, American consumers and workers get a measure of protection from a variety of hazards and risks of varying magnitude. But there will be endless debate about the cost-benefit ratios of various kinds of regulations, many of which seem to impose a far greater cost than they are worth. Risk analysis and cost-benefit equations will become more common in debate over new regulations, but public concern and pressure over new risks, real and imagined, will always trump economics.

# The Antitrust Revival

The U.S. is now seeing the rebirth of antitrust activity after a decade of quietude. In fact, the most significant economic battle of the next few years will be the emergence of a new U.S. antitrust policy to fit an era of rapid technological change, globalization and increasing consolidation in world business. The crafting of this new policy will involve all branches of the federal government, from the White House and Justice Department to Congress and especially the federal courts, where the toughest cases will be decided. States will get in on the act, too. Antitrust policy will become internationalized, with antitrust officials all over the world increasingly coordinating their actions on transnational mergers and price fixing by international cartels.

## DISAGREEMENT WITHIN WASHINGTON

The debate will become a struggle between advocates of unbridled capitalism and proponents of government as referee of markets. Each side will claim to be the genuine champion of open competition.

And there will be considerable disagreement among powerful voices within the government itself. At a congressional hearing in mid 1998, for example, Federal Reserve Chairman Alan Greenspan and White House Council of Economic Advisers Chairman Janet Yellen expressed concern about the new antitrust zeal at Justice and the Federal Trade Commission. Greenspan noted that mergers often give the combined firms a short-run advantage over competitors, but "evidence of sustained dominance where markets are open are few."

### *Do markets eventually erode monopolies?*

Foes of antitrust note that governments have a poor record of predicting sudden shifts in technology that can catch "monopolists" by surprise, quickly eroding their market shares and reviving competition. One of the great follies in antitrust history was the government's attack in the 1970s on IBM's dominance in mainframe computers. The attack came on the eve of the personal-computer revolution that would put IBM into a long slide for a decade. Growing competition in microprocessors (for both PCs and other appliances) could do the same to Intel, without federal intervention. Similarly, the rise of the Internet, networked PCs, smart phones and cable-TV modems might erode Microsoft's operating-system hegemony, regardless of the outcome of antitrust efforts.

Economist Yellen cautioned at the hearing that "large size is not the same as monopoly power." No one disputes that contention, so future antitrust policy won't hinge on the populist concept that "big is bad" per se. On the contrary, there is a broad consensus that American multinationals must get even bigger to compete effectively with foreign rivals in nations that don't have a tradition of concern about monopolies, whether government-run or private.

## BEHAVIOR, NOT SIZE, IS THE ISSUE

Significantly, landmark government suits against Microsoft and Intel focus not on their sheer size or even their market shares of more than 90% in PC operating systems and microprocessors. The issue is not their size but their behavior: Intel's withholding of product-development information from companies with which it is feuding, and a variety of Microsoft practices that limit the freedom of computer makers to do business with its competitors, etc. But Microsoft's sheer size—in cash wealth—is also an issue, because competitors believe that its war chest of $12 billion in cash enables it to ignore short-term profits and add more and more free software features to its Windows operating system. This, they charge, is a kind of predatory pricing that will put makers of similar, stand-alone software out of business.

## TRADITIONAL ANTICOMPETITIVE PRACTICES

Most cases won't blaze new trails in antitrust theory, but will focus simply on whether traditional mergers will reduce competition and enable the consolidated firm to raise prices to the detriment of customers.

That's what was behind the government's blocking of a merger of Office Depot and Staples in the national office-supply market, and a variety of initiatives in the defense and aerospace industries (Lockheed Martin's attempted takeover of Northrop), airlines (joint marketing agreements among carriers), telecommunications, pharmaceutical wholesaling, local radio stations, and satellite and cable TV.

After a 1996 law relaxing restrictions on the ownership of multiple radio stations in the same market, the Justice Department was able to force the abandonment or restructuring of a dozen proposed mergers among radio station-owners, alleging that the concentrations of owner-ship would allow one company to dictate advertising rates in local mar-kets. But despite these efforts, there has been, and will continue to be, concentration of most radio stations in the hands of a few giant owners.

The least controversial area of antitrust policy will be stepped-up attacks on alleged price fixing by international cartels in such industries as agriculture, chemicals, food additives, metals, paper, ocean shipping and commercial aviation. The Justice Department was presenting evi-dence on price fixing to more than two dozen grand juries in mid 1998, and a slew of charges will result over the next year or two.

## ISSUES TO BE EXAMINED

The new antitrust policy will probe many issues that have arisen only in the past few years. Someday, for example, it will venture into the area of biotechnology and the patenting of DNA sequences. Here are some of the issues now facing regulators:

• Does the consolidated ownership of both media outlets (such as broadcast networks and local stations) and content that airs on those outlets (say, sports team and movies) deprive other content providers of getting air time in major markets?

• Is a large retailer with vast purchasing power getting markedly lower prices from suppliers than smaller companies can negotiate? Is the giant retailer trying to punish its suppliers for doing business with the big buyer's competitors?

• Is it anti-competitive (as the feds charged in a '99 suit) for a big carrier such as American Airlines to slash fares and add flights at a hub it controls, to meet the competition of low-fare start-up airlines?

• Did Congress intend, when it deregulated telecommunications, to allow the Baby Bells to combine into enormous regional phone systems, or AT&T to control cable TV access to a majority of households?

• Is it legal for real estate brokerage firms to raise and lower their commissions in lock step?

• Does a computer or software company essentially force consumers to buy new versions of its market-dominant products by failing to support earlier versions?

## UNDERMANNED ANTITRUST STAFFS

Government antitrust staffs and budgets—at the Justice Department and Federal Trade Commission in Washington and attorney general's offices in the states—will be sorely overburdened in a climate of accelerating corporate mergers.

Even with more staff requested from Congress, Justice and the FTC will not have the resources to investigate and pursue even half the potentially anticompetitive consolidations that come along. In 1976 the Justice Department challenged 31 mergers; in the middle of 1998 it had 93 court cases in the works and 415 investigations going in many different industries. And it was doing all that with only 343 attorneys in the antitrust division, 100 fewer than in 1980.

### Settlements rather than litigation

So trustbusters will often have to rely on saber-rattling inquiries and threats of litigation to discourage consummation of announced mergers or to require that the merged companies divest themselves of overlapping divisions. The idea is to avoid lengthy and expensive court battles. Threats will be an effective deterrent in many cases, but some giant companies (like Microsoft) will rather fight than give in.

In most cases, merger partners will agree to sell off the problem operations, as MCI and WorldCom did with MCI's Internet business while keeping WorldCom's valuable UUNet franchise. And the Justice Department's main condition (among others) for allowing the $58 billion combination of phone giants SBC and Ameritech will probably be greater access of rival phone companies to their local service areas.

# Standardization of Laws

D espite all the talk about "devolution" in America's federal system—Washington's return of governmental power to the states (for example, in welfare reform)—a more important but less visible trend will bring about the opposite: the preemption and overriding of state and local authority by new federal policies in countless fields. This preemption will typically be requested of Congress by businesses that are having trouble dealing with countless conflicting, and often more-stringent, standards in different state and local jurisdictions around the U.S.

## FEDERAL/STATE/LOCAL RELATIONS

Washington will struggle with its "partners" in the federal system over issues such as whether Internet access providers can be locally taxed like a utility (probably not); whether local zoning can block the siting of new towers for wireless phones and high-definition TV (probably not); whether a new federal law on electric deregulation—when Congress finally gets around to passing it—will preempt state utility authority (to a degree, yes); whether federal housing antidiscrimination laws can override local zoning on the siting of low-income housing and group housing for handicapped people and troubled youths (probably yes); whether eventual financial-services deregulation will override state insurance regulations (to a degree, yes); whether property-compensation cases involving land use, such as wetlands, can bypass state and local courts and go right into the federal judicial systems (probably not); whether new national industry standards in construction materials and techniques can override local building codes (sometimes).

There will be a lot at stake for business in all of these issues, and they will ultimately be decided in the federal courts. The states and cities will win some, but Washington will win more. The broad trend will be toward the convergence of governmental regulations along federally mandated lines, which will make it generally easier to do business in 50 states and thousands of municipalities.

The governmental assault on the tobacco industry is a possible harbinger of future jurisdictional conflicts between Washington and the states. While the FDA did the theoretical spadework, state attorneys general—in Mississippi, Florida, Texas and other states—showed the way in their health-cost lawsuits. While Congress bloated its tobacco settlement bill to the point of legislative collapse in 1998, several states moved ahead with their own antismoking programs, such as Florida's $11.3 billion agreement with the tobacco industry and New Jersey's doubling of cigarette taxes.

# A Trend Toward Freer Trade

Advocates and opponents of free trade will do constant battles in Congress, with each side winning its share of skirmishes. The political clout of free trade will often seem muted and diffused compared with the focused opposition from trade protectionists, led by organized labor and its Democratic allies.

Protectionism will fade in boom times but enjoy sudden revivals when world economic conditions soften and when excess capacity in manufactured goods and raw materials floods into markets that are relatively more strong.

Unions will be joined by other special interests, such as environmental groups and human rights activists concerned about low wages, working conditions, child labor and industrial pollution in such rapidly developing nations as China and Mexico. Trade sanctions will eventually fade as an instrument of U.S. foreign policy, due to competitive commercial pressures from other nations.

The antagonists of freer trade will slow, but not halt, the inexorable rise in American two-way trade, which will increase both in absolute value and as a share of a growing economy. In a few years, after the long-delayed granting of "fast-track" presidential authority to increase the scope of the North American Free Trade Agreement, all the major nations of South America, starting with Chile and later including Brazil and Argentina, will be folded into an enormous Pan-American free trade zone.

# CHAPTER 6

# Upheaval in Education and Training

The U.S. has, on average, the world's best work force, but it will have to be much better educated and trained than it is today to maintain America's economic leadership in the century ahead. This will require substantial change in an education system that simultaneously harbors the best and worst schools in the advanced world.

American industries that depend on less-skilled labor will continue to migrate to the low-wage markets of Asia, Latin America, Africa and Eastern Europe. The U.S. will protect and raise its world-leading standard of living only by excelling at high-productivity tasks in both manufacturing and services. And all these jobs require highly educated workers. American education and job training will meet this daunting challenge in the decades ahead, but not without enormous effort, will, controversy, turmoil and political struggle.

Of all the major enterprises in America, public education is the only one that has changed little in the past 50 years. Its structure (monopolistic), management style (top down) and basic delivery of service (teachers imparting informaton in a classroom) has been largely unaffected by the technological, deregulatory and entrepreneurial revolution that has swept over virtually every other business and profession. But this is all about to change.

Public education is now in the early stages of a broad, dramatic restructuring not unlike what has already been achieved in manufacturing and is still underway in such service sectors as health care and financial services. Already well in evidence, the following educational trends will become better established and accelerate, in fits and starts, over the years just ahead:

**Lifelong learning,** with a boom in adult education and mid-career retraining.

**Toughening of curriculum and educational standards,** from elementary school to college, with national tests as benchmarks for student achievement.

**Improved vocational education and de-emphasis of four-year colleges** as the only path to high earnings.

**More choice in public education,** including easier transfers, publicly funded charter schools and vouchers to attend private schools.

**Home schooling,** with the ability of at-home students to selectively use public school programs.

**Boom in private schools** at the elementary and secondary level, with and without the support of publicly funded vouchers.

**More-rigorous teacher evaluation,** accompanied by higher pay for the best teachers and administrators.

**Return of character and values education** in public schools.

**Distance learning,** with students taking courses over the Internet from the finest lecturers in any field.

**Cooperation between business and education** in improving education and tailoring curriculum to the kinds of jobs being created.

**Less racial integration** in public schools, as court-ordered busing for racial balance falls from favor with parents of all races.

**Total-immersion English instruction** replacing bilingual education for Latin-American immigrants.

**Restructuring of higher education** to restrain cost hikes and improve productivity.

## LIFELONG LEARNING

Whether they're industrial workers, clerical personnel or managers, employees will need constant retraining—sometimes to change jobs or industries in mid career, other times to hone skills and adapt to ever-changing technology. And education won't take place only in schools and colleges. Many adults will be educated on the job or at company-owned schools run under contract by community colleges.

Colleges all over the nation are creating special divisions for adult students, with classes at night and on weekends. Universities are establishing branches far from their main campuses, renting space in major employment centers handy to prospective students. Competition for adult students will be fierce, with success going to the colleges that have the most-practical programs, at the most convenient locations and times, at the lowest prices.

Traditional nonprofit colleges, both public and private, will face growing competition from for-profit education programs, such as the fast-growing University of Phoenix, a 22-year old "virtual college" whose parent company trades on the New York Stock Exchange. Phoenix has 48,000 night students using rented facilities in more than a dozen states, a part-time faculty of working professionals in many fields and a library consisting of materials posted on the Internet. Its tuition rates are higher than those of many public colleges but lower than the privates. Phoenix's applications for accreditation are typically opposed by nonprofit colleges, which always claim that they are adequately meeting their state's adult-education needs.

## DISTANCE LEARNING

At the college level, many lecture halls will give way to "distance learning," a kind of high-tech correspondence school in which students rarely, if ever, set foot on campus.

On their home or office computer, students will call up a lecture complete with charts, video and other visual and audio aids. They'll be able to ask questions and engage in discussions with other students or e-mail questions to the professor after hours. Tests will be conducted by computer. Many colleges have already begun to offer some courses over the Internet. The implications are far-reaching.

Online college courses will be a boon for working adults who don't want to interrupt their careers to go back to school. They'll be able to update their skills, expand their horizons, even earn advanced degrees while staying on the job. Already 45% of college students are 24 years or older, and that figure will rise as demand for adult learning skyrockets.

Colleges will use Internet courses to cut costs—fewer expensive new buildings will be needed, for example—and increase enrollment. Even prestigious universities, which have always attracted more good applicants than they could handle on campus, will be able to enroll more students without increasing costs. Internet instruction will be marketed to working professionals who can afford to pay tuition, and many employers will contribute financially to the surge in Internet study. At the University of Phoenix, for example, 75% of the 40,000 students get tuition help from employers.

The traditional college campus will not disappear. Most Internet courses will be offered by colleges that still have classrooms. Further, the college experience combines education with social and personal growth. Many young people straight out of high school yearn to spread their wings, leave their parents' home and socialize when they're not hitting the books. Besides, it's more fun to root for State U's football team than Internet U's chess squad.

### INTENSE BUSINESS INVOLVEMENT IN EDUCATION

Business woke up to the need to get involved in improving education when it started getting applicants holding high school diplomas (and sometimes college degrees) who could barely comprehend passages of text and do simple business math.

Today local businesses support their public schools in a variety of ways—encouraging employees to volunteer as tutors and part-time teachers, paying for school supplies and equipment in needy schools, and helping review curriculum, for instance.

Business recognizes that community colleges are prime feeders into their work forces. With labor tight in many markets, businesses are raising their profiles at local colleges to get a head start in recruiting the graduates. They are working closely with college administrators to create the right courses and the technical training that they need in their work force. They are setting up apprenticeships and work-study programs, and holding job fairs to encourage applications at their business.

Finally, businesses are becoming significant educators in their own right, conducting remedial education and performance-enhancement classes on their own premises, with instructors either in their employ or under contract from private firms or local colleges.

### NEW RESPECT FOR VOCATIONAL EDUCATION

It's dawning on Americans that not every kid wants, needs or is cut out for a traditional four-year college education focusing on the liberal arts and social sciences. And it's also dawning on them that many good-paying jobs of the future, especially in manufacturing, won't require a college education. But these jobs will require the ability to read instructions and computer screens, run CAD-CAM programs (computer assisted design and manufacturing), operate numerically controlled machine tools, and picture how various aspects of the manufacturing process fit together.

This is what the new vocational education (voc-ed) is all about, and it's getting new respect in educational circles. It will begin to attract better students who like working with their hands as well as their brains, who don't want to work in offices, and who are interested in good-paying jobs in such fields as machinery repair and high-tech manufacturing. Many graduates of high school voc-ed programs will go right into apprenticeships with manufacturers, and their earnings will eventually match those of college graduates who choose to study liberal-arts subjects—say, English literature, sociology or French—for which the employment demand is not as great.

### *Business support of voc-ed*

To train students for real employment and ease labor shortages at the same time, more and more businesses are getting together to create innovative voc-ed and apprenticeship programs for both high school and community-college students. Here are some examples:

• **Home builders** in Florida, Michigan, North Carolina, Ohio and South Carolina are working with community colleges and high schools to train students in framing. Hundreds of students have gone right into carpentry jobs after finishing the course.

• **A dozen plastics-processing firms** in Rhode Island got together and, with some state money, built their own cooperative training lab.

• **The National Tooling & Machining Association** works with high school and college students in Rochester, N.Y., and other cities on training and apprenticeship programs to augment the critically low supply of labor for metal-finishing and fabrication jobs.

• **A community college tech center** in Pueblo, Col., does training at simulated work sites that replicate a firm's actual working conditions.

• **Local contractors and a labor union** in southern Illinois are teaching high schoolers how to operate excavating and grading equipment.

A glimpse of the future of combined education and job training is on display at Arthur Hill High School, in Saginaw, Mich. From 7:45 A.M. to 10 A.M., students take typical academic courses. They spend the next two hours learning how to operate lathes, drills and mills at a nearby career center. In the afternoon, they work at manufacturing plants. When they graduate, students will get a certificate, listing their proven skills, which they can take to employers. If a student decides to attend college, participating employers will pay part of the tuition. For employers, the payoff comes in developing a source of skilled labor, which will often be in short supply. The Arthur Hill model will be replicated all over the country to train students in graphic arts, computer-aided drafting, auto repair, electronics, child care, home health care and other fields.

## A BROADENING GAP BETWEEN THE WELL-TRAINED AND THE ILL-EDUCATED

There is a growing correlation between education and income, due largely to rapid technological advances and, to a lesser degree, to growing competition from low-cost foreign manufacturing. Robert Solow, of the Urban Institute, downplays the role of foreign competition, noting that wage inequality—the gap between haves and have-nots in the United States—began to grow even before low-wage countries developed large-scale manufacturing industries.

Men with only a high school education now earn about 60% of what college graduates do, down from 80% in the late 1970s. This trend won't change anytime soon. Growth in the next ten years will be concentrated in what economist Lester C. Thurow of the Massachusetts Institute of Technology calls "brainpower industries," such as biotechnology, telecommunications, microelectronics, robotics and new materials. Employers have an important role to play in upgrading both public education and the skills of their current employees. According to Thurow, the rate of return for industries that invest in the skills of their workers is twice that of industries that focus on plant and equipment spending.

# Improving Our Public Schools

Raising the standards and performance of public schools, a high national priority for decades, has proven to be a formidable challenge and elusive goal. Countless reports over the past 30 years have documented shortfalls in our schools, including declining test scores and anecdotes about high school graduates who can't read or do simple math.

Particularly alarming were international test results released in 1998 that showed American high school seniors performing at or near the bottom in mathematics and science, trailing virtually all advanced European nations and Canada. By contrast, American fourth graders performed well above the average, and eighth graders were in the middle of the pack, suggesting that American scholastic performance gets worse relative to other nation's with every passing year of school.

## BEHIND THE TEST SCORES

Explanations abound for these results, including the fact that, compared with the high school students of Canada and Europe, U.S. students take fewer and less-demanding science and math courses, and a high percentage of American high school math and science teachers did not major or minor in those fields. There are cultural factors, too, including the fact that, compared with other nations, American homework loads (lighter than other nations') are often squeezed out by after-school extracurricular activities and paid employment. About 55% of the American high school seniors who took the tests reported working three or more hours each day at a paying job, compared with only 18% of the European test-takers.

Some analysts believe that these results paint too bleak a picture of how public school kids are doing. They argue that, while the tests certainly show weakness in course content and calculation skills, tests can't measure the free-wheeling creativity and problem-solving skills that seem to emerge from American education and culture in larger doses than in more-rigorous educational systems. Gerald W. Bracey, a research psychologist and education analyst, notes the puzzlement in America when the education minister of Singapore came to study the U.S. public education system. In an interview with *The New York Times*, Bracey recalled people asking the visitor, "'What are you looking here for? Your kids consistently score on top of all the international tests.' And he said something like, 'All that our kids can do is take tests.' He understood that we are nurturing more creativity here than the Asians."

These explanations cannot be dismissed as easily as the apologias of the public-education establishment, whose consistent response to all low test results is a call for more money, more and higher-paid teachers, and smaller classes. Some of America's most brilliant scientists are also suggesting that there may be something to the idea that U.S. education, both public and private, does a better job than statistics indicate. Dudley Herschbach, a Nobel Prize winner who teaches chemistry at Harvard, put it this way (in remarks to *The New York Times*): "I have noticed that graduate students who get straight As are often lost when it comes to research. Like America, science is a fundamentally optimistic endeavor, where little attention is paid to getting it right immediately, and there is little stress on canons. Maybe we let kids wander all over hell in high school, but that preserves some energy for later, when it is better spent."

This may explain in part how America, with supposedly mediocre public education, can be doing so well in an increasingly competitive global economy, especially in high-tech research and engineering. Another explanation focuses on the sheer number of gifted students America produces, even if they are a small percentage of all students. It's generally agreed that students in the very top echelon—say, the top 5% to 10%—are as sharp as any in the world, and since the U.S. is a very big nation, that's a lot of really smart and creative kids—more than enough to invent breakthrough technologies in biology, microelectronics and other high-tech fields. Then there's the undisputed quality of American universities, which do a good job of motivating the late bloomers with untapped intellectual potential.

But before we begin feeling smug, we should acknowledge that America's deficiency in educating American-born youths in science and math is greatly offset by the immigration of brilliant foreign students. More than half of all U.S. graduate students in science and engineering are foreign-born, and between 25% and 33% of all doctorates in these fields over the last decade have been awarded to foreign-born students. Fortunately for America, a lot of them have stayed in the U.S. to staff our high-tech industries, and this might mask the shortcomings of our native-born and U.S.-educated youths.

## NEW APPROACHES FOR PUBLIC EDUCATION

In any event, it's broadly agreed that America's biggest education problem isn't the performance of its better schools and their graduates, but the chasm between them and the woefully undereducated youths in the weakest high schools, especially in poverty-ridden inner cities.

Even in decent school systems, there is mounting concern about issues that aren't strictly academic but that certainly affect the climate for learning, such as incivility, disobedience and even violence, plus the lack of any discussion of character and values.

So the U.S. public-school system is about to go through its biggest changes in years, driven by dissatisfaction from all angles. Taxpayers, many of whom don't have school-age children, think they're paying too much for bad schools. Federal and state governments can't or won't dramatically increase funds for education, since there are many competing demands for that money. Employers who hire the products of our school system say they're seeing more young people who lack basic skills to succeed on the job. Parents worry that the schools won't prepare their children for the highly competitive world.

### Back to basics—and good behavior

In the next decade, schools will be under pressure to emphasize basic skills and core content (even by memorization), beef up homework assignments, and improve discipline. Champions of the two main methods of teaching reading and writing—phonics and "whole language"—will bury the hatchet and recognize that different kids learn best with different styles. Eventually both methods will be used in the same classrooms.

Schools will find ways to inject fundamental human values and morality into the curriculum, despite the risks of offending people of different religions, cultures and belief systems. Security will become more visible and widespread in response to highly publicized violent incidents. High schools and junior highs will tighten dress codes, and many elementary schools will institute school uniforms. Schools will also expel troublemakers more quickly, which improves the learning atmosphere in schools but doesn't address the problem of what to do with the miscreants.

### Ethnicity, race and separation of sexes

Bilingual education will fade everywhere. Its demise has already begun in California with the 1998 passage of a referendumthat abolished it. It will give way to the total-immersion approach, starting with English as a Second Language (ESL) courses, after which students will be mainstreamed into full English-only classes.

Busing to achieve racial balance has proven unpopular with both black and white parents, and courts will move away from insisting on it. Schools will become more racially segregated, not by law but according to neighborhood racial patterns. Fewer people will care much, if the educational quality is satisfactory—a big *if*. School systems will use high-quality magnet schools to try to achieve the racial balance that courts couldn't create by edict.

More and more public schools will experiment with separating boys and girls at the junior high and high school levels, especially for teaching science and math, on evidence that teens of both sexes learn better without the distraction of adolescent role-playing and social pressures. Baltimore has done this since 1994 in some schools, and a handful of other cities are trying it too, despite legal challenges from the American Civil Liberties Union and the National Organization for Women.

### Ways to control costs

More decisions, including those on curriculum, will be made at the school level, fewer at the district level or higher. But local leaders will be responding increasingly to statewide and national demands for higher performance, with tough accountability for principals and superintendents.

To make ends meet, schools will cut central-office bureaucracy and focus resources on teaching. As both an economy and an aid to teaching, schools will use more technology—computer programs, movies, Internet courses—to supplement human teachers.

More schools will run year-round to take full advantage of their expensive facilities. In some school districts, long summer vacations will give way to more-frequent short vacations, improving the retention of information (and giving relief to many beleaguered parents of summer-bored kids).

There will be a trend back to smaller schools. Large high schools, a popular idea in the 1960s and 1970s, will be divided into smaller, specialized "campuses" and magnet schools for arts, science and other fields. Magnet schools will be increasingly criticized as elitist enclaves of super-bright kids, but they will continue to be the public schools' major weapon for stemming the defection of smart kids to private schools. Since many of the differences in school quality relate to vastly different resources among school districts, based on local property-tax revenues, courts will try to force the equalization of expenditures among neighboring school districts. These controversial measures will entail some sort of pooling of local taxes or state assumption of more of the cost of local schools.

### More testing of kids—and teachers

There will not be a mandatory national curriculum, but Congress will eventually approve national tests of content and skills against which states and counties can measure their students' performance. States and school districts will set their own standards in reading, writing, math and science, and students must meet them to move up in grade, easing out the age-old practice of "social promotions." Individual schools will have some flexibility in designing curricula to meet those standards. There will be more reliance on testing—and publicity about the results—to hold schools more responsible for educating their pupils. Standards, assessment and accountability will become the building blocks for reform movements. The periodic testing and evaluation of teachers and principals will spread, despite the opposition of teachers' unions, and such evaluations will be key to holding jobs and getting raises.

### Computers in schools

Computers will change the dynamics in the classroom and the role of the teacher. Instead of being primarily lecturers, teachers will become managers of information, guiding youngsters to acquire their own knowledge. "Teachers will have to learn how to incorporate technology into their teaching, not just turn on a video in the afternoon and call that technology," says Michael Resnick, an official of the National School Boards Association.

Schools will be linked to libraries, hospitals, fire stations and other institutions in town, allowing students to reach information on a wealth of subjects from the weighty to the whimsical, from downloading encyclopedia passages to checking local movie listings. This is already under way in a few communities and will spread rapidly, thanks to financial and technical assistance from government, business and volunteers.

# Alternatives to Public Education

Public schools are clearly feeling the heat of public disapproval: Enrollments of private and parochial schools are rising. And home schooling is surging, fueled by parents who are concerned about not only the lack of discipline, safety and moral education in many schools but a lack of academic rigor as well. Eventually, home schoolers in many areas will win the right for their kids to participate selectively in local school activities and academic courses, despite the opposition of school officials. Home schooling will get an added boost from technology, enabling kids to take Internet courses in the subjects that their parents may be weak in.

All the public-school reforms listed above will make a positive difference in the quality of education over time, but for many parents, government officials and education reformers, it's too little too late. Their impatience—and in some cases, an ideological desire to break up the public school monopoly—has triggered an avalanche of alternatives to traditional public education.

## FREE-MARKET CHALLENGES

The challenge to public education takes many forms—expanding private-school enrollment, voucher plans, home schooling, charter schools—and the assault will accelerate in the years ahead. At least 16 states have created "school choice" plans that allow students dissatisfied with their local schools to transfer out of district, space permitting. In other cities, school boards have turned the operation of wretched local schools over to for-profit businesses or local universities.

And in every community, the demand for private education is growing, with rising enrollment in all kinds of schools, including religious schools. One such school, the Islamic Academy of New England, in Sharon, Mass., enrolls children from Middle Eastern, Indo-Pakistani and African-American Muslim families, all of them attracted by, among other traits, the school's insistence on good manners and respect for elders. For many immigrant families, these religious schools are a haven from the heavy influence of American pop culture in the public schools.

### Vouchers for attending other schools

A few cities, notably Milwaukee and Cleveland, have launched voucher programs, in which public-school students are given a cash stipend they can use as partial tuition at any private school, including religious schools—inevitably inviting court challenges on the separation of church and state. And the concept of a federally funded voucher continues to inflame Congress, where it is supported by many Republicans but opposed by most Democrats and their allies in the teachers' unions.

While politicians fight over the future of publicly funded vouchers, a handful of corporations, foundations and philanthropists across the nation, operating independently of each other, are launching their own private voucher plans—essentially, non-selective scholarships (first-come, first-served, using lottery selection) for any inner-city kid to spend on tuition at any private or parochial school. In early 1998, these programs were spending more than $45 million on vouchers in 32 cities, giving an estimated 14,000 students the chance to flee their local elementary and secondary schools.

Voucher programs, both public and private, will spread in the coming years, despite the challenge on religious-entanglement grounds. And eventually there will be federal funds going into the effort. But the implementation of voucher programs will create vexing problems. There won't be enough room in private schools—existing or new—to accommodate all the kids who want to transfer, and in most programs, the private schools won't be obligated to accept anyone who applies. Cities will find, as Cleveland is discovering, that the cross-city transportation costs will be enormous. In the end, the greatest legacy of voucher programs will be the stimulus they provide to public-school systems to clean up their acts. The schools that students seek to flee in large numbers will come under the glare of public disapproval, eventually forcing changes in leadership, curricula and standards.

### The charter-school movement

By far the most ambitious and fervent attack on public schools is coming from charter schools—privately operated schools that get public funds to teach through any of countless educational philosophies and styles. In the words of journalist Thomas Toch, writing in *U.S. News & World Report* magazine, charter schools are creating a "hybrid free-market system, in which students and parents exercise choice but the public pays the costs."

The first charter schools were launched in Minnesota in 1992, and today there are an estimated 800 such schools in 23 states and Washington, D.C., with an enrollment of about 165,000. Some 350 of these schools operate in just two states, Arizona and Michigan, which grant charter-school organizers unusually broad freedom over the style, curriculum, staffing and budgets of their schools.

Charter schools run the gamut from conservatively traditional to wildly progressive. They celebrate every ethnic, religious and cultural heritage, from African to Armenian. In Michigan, most of the charter schools are run by state universities. In several states, a large proportion of charter schools are formerly independent private schools that converted to charter schools and, in the process, received a big infusion of public funds.

The charter movement is passionate about its mission, and even voucher opponents such as President Clinton are calling for a dramatic expansion of charter schools nationwide. This will certainly happen, and in the process, charter schools will be constantly embroiled in controversy. There will be debate over whether charter schools should take all applicants or be allowed to select their students, and policies will vary from state to state. States will have to come up with ways to evaluate the education that takes place in charter schools. It remains to be seen whether charters will be revoked if educational performance lags the public schools'—or if officials will simply leave it to parents to decide for themselves, allowing a school to fail the market test. Will charter schools be required to serve students with special needs and handicaps? Will charter schools be allowed to teach religion and still get public funds? These and more questions remain to be answered. But along with vouchers, the growth of charter schools will give the public-school establishment its first real taste of competitive pressure, and the results should be positive for all concerned.

## THE BALKANIZATION OF EDUCATION

The net effect of these tumultuous changes will be the transformation—indeed, probably the demise—of the traditional role of public elementary and secondary education.

Public schools have been the homogenizing force in American life, giving a shared experience to millions of Americans of different cultural and national backgrounds, income levels and aptitudes. For decades, accelerated courses and "tracking" of bright students satisfied the most demanding parents, while the less capable students at least got a decent grounding in math and reading. The public schools served America very well, and, on balance, they still do.

But a variety of situations—the "dumbing down" of curriculum, the phasing out of high-achievement tracks, the erosion of discipline, and most of all, the conspicuous and tragic failure of schools in the inner cities—planted the seeds of dissent and rebellion.

The breaking up of public education into special spheres of interest with different educational styles and philosophies for different groups is not unlike what has happened in many other areas of American life, such as the fragmentation of television viewership by cable TV, the decline of mass-circulation magazines once read by "everyone," the rise of ethnic marketing, and the explosive growth of new evangelical churches to challenge mainstream Protestant sects.

These are all forces of increasing choice—and disunity—in an increasingly diverse nation. They are not, in themselves, signs of decay. They may even be evidence of America's constant adaptation and reinvention of itself.

# Big Changes Ahead for Higher Education

College enrollment will grow from about 12 million to 14 million by 2005, as children of the "echo baby boom" of the '80s reach college age. Also, more adults will return to college to earn advanced degrees, polish their skills or prepare for midlife career changes.

The number of foreign students at U.S. colleges, now about half a million, will continue to grow. Higher education is a significant service "export" for the U.S. because the young foreigners spend plenty of money here, on tuition and living expenses. They are often sponsored by wealthy families or governments back home. Other nations are taking notice. Japan, for one, is actively recruiting foreign students (especially from Asian nations), and this will cut into the growth of this component of U.S. enrollment.

## THE MANY MISSIONS OF COLLEGE IN AMERICA

America democratized higher education, and is stronger for it. In most countries, college is reserved for a small percentage of elite students to become versed in core academic subjects, such as science and the humanities. But in the U.S., even students of average aptitude and academic achievement can find a place in a college, often a two-year community college, to study nontraditional courses such as law enforcement, fashion design, drafting, physical therapy, sports medicine and restaurant management.

Today a record-high percentage of American high school graduates go on to some kind of college—67% overall, including 70% of young women and 64% of men. (In 1960, the comparable figures were 38% of females and 54% of men.) Not surprisingly, a college degree in the U.S. is less emblematic of high intellectual achievement than it is in other nations, or than it used to be in America. In a sense, America has debased the college degree as a valuable credential, but in the process it has kept many more of its young people involved in post-high school education than other nations have. And many of these youths catch fire in college and go on to great success in many fields.

There are many reasons why a higher percentage of youth in America go on to college than in any other nation, among them a belief in equality and self-determination, our national wealth, and the recognized financial advantages of a college education.

As a society, we benefit from this emphasis placed on higher education. It has made our universities the envy of the world, fueling the discoveries and advances that help secure the U.S.'s position of leadership in many fields. And it has created a skilled labor force for American businesses, enhancing the nation's output and productivity.

In the next two decades, America's colleges will continue to lead the way, conducting important research and churning out millions of skilled graduates. That isn't to say, however, that there aren't serious challenges facing U.S. higher education.

## TOUGHER STANDARDS FOR COLLEGE ACCEPTANCE

The toughening of academic standards that will occur throughout American education will make fundamental changes in college admissions and enrollment patterns. Public colleges will move away from open admissions for any student with a certain grade average, out of a distrust for the meaning of those grades. More and more public colleges will use admissions and placement tests to establish basic proficiency in reading and math, and they will stop providing remedial education to freshmen who didn't master these skills in high school. Applicants who can't demonstrate basic proficiencies will be directed to two-year community and vocational colleges, which will expand enrollments to meet demand.

This trend is seen in the 1998 decision of the City University of New York (CUNY) to abandon its three-decade experiment with open admissions, requiring all freshman to pass placement tests and phasing out remedial education by 2002.

The tightening of college admissions standards, accompanied by a movement away from formal affirmative-action programs, will have the short-term effect of reducing enrollment of African-American and Latino students at more-rigorous state universities. But students of all races will find plenty of opportunity at community colleges and less-prestigious state colleges, from which the most successful students will transfer and continue their academic careers.

## FINANCIAL TURMOIL AHEAD

The cost of a college education will remain a burden to middle-class families. The good news is that cost increases will roughly track inflation for the next several years, after bigger jumps in recent years. Government will take steps to lighten the load by encouraging more tax-assisted savings for college.

Competition will limit how much colleges can charge, and private colleges, with their high tuitions, will face increasing pressure from public colleges. Top students from middle-class and even well-to-do families, weighing acceptances from both expensive private colleges and excellent state universities with lower tuition, will increasingly choose the public institution. To fight back, private colleges will boost their financial aid to families of higher income, especially those that have more than one child in college.

Private technical colleges will spring up to compete with some state-run schools. And private colleges in the Northeast, facing flat enrollment in that part of the country, will open campuses in the Sun Belt to compete with existing private and state colleges.

## THE DOWNSIZING OF HIGHER EDUCATION

Price competition among colleges will lead to a major restructuring of higher education. Over the next decade colleges must, and will, find ways to control costs, boost productivity and enhance revenues, much as American manufacturing and other service sectors have already done. Higher education is simply the last of the major service industries to embark on this painful, but ultimately therapeutic, process.

Restructuring will take many forms. As in other businesses, there will be more outsourcing of support functions, including marketing, admissions processing, financial-aid management, food service, and maintenance of all sorts. Revenue will be boosted by adult education and distance learning, gathering in new students from all over the world. Academic departments that don't attract enough students will be closed or consolidated. Many colleges will cease trying to be all things to all applicants, instead selecting a few areas in which to excel. Small liberal arts colleges will buck the trend, however, continuing to give their students a sampling of important core subjects and encouraging them to defer specialization until graduate school.

Tenure for professors—the only workers with guaranteed life-time employment in any American enterprise—will come under increasing attack as an expensive and ossified system that stymies the freshening effects of performance accountability and occasional turnover. But it will last for years before finally succumbing to a system of multiyear faculty contracts, renewable based on performance. In addition to taking on tenure, colleges will seek to boost the productivity of their faculty by demanding that professors not heavily engaged in research spend more time teaching.

State university systems will not be able to afford to offer duplicative programs, majors and professional schools (law, medicine, dentistry, nursing) on numerous campuses, if enrollment can't support them all—or if they're mediocre. So they will trim and consolidate, directing applicants to a smaller number of stronger programs on particular campuses.

Hungry for revenue, colleges will forge even closer relationships with large corporations, to educate their employees, share sponsored research, and create incubator businesses that share personnel—and the profits of the products developed there. This will lead to frequent disputes among all the participants—the universities, professors and corporations—over ownership of patents and the commercial fruits of their research.

Many of these restructurings will be fought tooth and nail by various interests, including labor unions, alumni groups and affected faculty members. But the imperatives of rising costs and heightened competition will eventually steamroll the opposition.

## 21ST CENTURY MBAS

Business education is booming in America, and the boom will continue for years. In the process, business education will change dramatically. It will become less academic and theoretical and much more hands-on and practical.

The student population will change, too, getting older, more female and more diverse by race and nationality. The average age is now in the upper 20s, even higher among part-time students. Many business schools now require applicants to have worked for several years and an estimated two-thirds of all MBA candidates are mid-career students who take classes at night or on weekends while working full time.

Business schools will do more to emphasize entrepreneurial training and practical learning in fields such as computer science, information technology, international marketing and investment portfolio management. This is a reflection of the corporate downsizing of the past ten years. Today's business students are more likely than their predecessors to work for a small company, perhaps a start-up. Students need to learn how to get a business going, create or market new products and services, arrange for financing, and so on. The most-sought-after MBA graduates will be those who combine business education with a science or engineering degree, creating gilt-edged credentials for a rapid rise in the world of high technology.

Many B-school students will shift away from traditional management and finance courses to learn more about start-ups and strategic planning. Some of them have watched their parents work for years at one company, then struggle to adjust after being laid off in a corporate restructuring.

To differentiate themselves in a crowded market, schools will specialize in certain areas of business. For example, Washington, D.C- area MBA programs, with many foreign students, are strong in international trade. Virginia Tech and the University of Maryland, located near the hotbed of information technology and telecommunications firms in the suburbs of Washington, specialize in those fields. Vanderbilt, located in Nashville, one of the cradles of the managed-care industry, plays up its expertise in health care administration. Stanford's MBA students benefit from its Silicon Valley location at ground zero of the computer and software industries. And the University of South Carolina's MBA program emphasizes international business, reflecting the high concentration of European and Japanese multinationals in the Piedmont region of the Southeast, from the Carolinas through Georgia.

# CHAPTER 7

# America's Standard of Living

Question: Which generation will be the first in American history to live materially less well, over a whole lifetime, than its parents did? a) The baby-boomers; b) Generation X, born from the late '60s through the mid '70s; c) Children of the boomers, born in the '80s and '90s; d) none of the above.

The resoundingly correct answer is d, based on both the economic record of the past 50 years and the likelihood of increasing productivity, rising personal income and stable prices for years to come. In short, the U.S. standard of living—the highest among all large nations—will continue to rise for all Americans, rich and poor, male and female, no matter what race they are or how long they've been in the country.

## VARIATIONS IN PROGRESS

But within various groups, the rate of improvement will vary greatly, depending on each individual's education, choice of career and family structure. The poverty rate—a matter of tricky definition—will remain in the present range for years to come. And income inequality will continue to widen—depressing no one's absolute standard of living but heightening feelings of relative poverty (falling further behind) and social unfairness.

The greatest gains in living-standard improvement will be achieved, in general, by women, racial and ethnic minorities, and the elderly. Those with limited educations and job skills—especially unwed mothers and their children—will continue to fare badly.

The overall rate of improvement in U.S. living standards will continue at the moderate (some would say sluggish) pace of the past two decades. That's because average wage gains will be restrained by downsizing and foreign competition, even as they are pushed up by accelerating productivity and labor shortages in some fields. Improvements in purchasing power will come as much from stable or declining consumer prices (and increasing product quality) as from real income growth.

The baby-boomers, now ages 34 to 52, have achieved a much higher standard of living than their parents, and their well-being will be swelled further by the largest average inheritances in world history (an estimated $50,000 per person from their parents' home equity, financial assets and insurance). Meanwhile, the Gen-Xers have a higher standard of living at their age than any previous generation in history, and they will continue to do fine. (They don't live as well as their parents do now—who does in their twenties and early thirties?—but they live a lot better than their parents did at the same age.) This is also likely to be true of today's adolescents, the children of the baby boom echo.

## SIGNS OF MATERIAL SUCCESS

Homeownership will rise above the present record-high 66%, with continued robust gains by first-time buyers, singles and racial minorities. Multiple car ownership, once an emblem of great affluence, will become common. Average Americans will travel, dine out and consume entertainment in record numbers. And ownership of financial assets by Americans—already at a record-high 44% of all households (not including indirect ownership through pension and profit-sharing plans)—will climb even further.

Most tellingly, Americans will increasingly define as necessities a widening range of goods and services that their parents considered luxuries. Some analysts have calculated that today's bottom 20% of households in income have a lifestyle that is the material equal of the average American family in 1955. In short, there is no evidence that the American dream of "living better than your parents" is in any jeopardy.

## NON-ECONOMIC ISSUES, TOO

But America will continue to face tough social challenges that will dampen improvement in living standards: births to mothers without male support; a high level of divorce; drug addiction and crime; and poor urban education. Many of these problems, fortunately for America, seem to be in the early stages of improvement, and this improvement will probably continue for a number of years.

# Global Comparisons

First, let's define terms: A nation's "standard of living" is the level of material comfort—housing, food, clothing, appliances, entertainment, travel, and so on—that can be bought with an average level of earnings.

A good starting point for proving America's current number-one position would be per-capita GDP (national output divided by population), even though GDP in itself doesn't address personal income—that is, the share of GDP that goes to citizens for their own use—or the distribution of that income among citizens.

If every nation's annual economic activity is converted into dollars at current exchange rates, America's per-capita GDP is nowhere near the highest in the world. In 1995, for example, it ranked 10th, behind Switzerland, Luxembourg, Japan, Norway, Denmark, Germany, Austria, Belgium and France.

But these nations all have costs of living considerably higher than America's. The general price level in 1996 was 29% higher in France, 37% higher in Germany, 59% higher in Japan and 65% higher in Switzerland. A market basket of consumer goods and services that cost $100 in the U.S. would have cost $159 in Japan, for example.

To account for differences in living costs, international economists make adjustments for "purchasing power parity." By this calculation, the U.S. jumps to the near-top of the list of advanced nations in per-capita GDP, ahead of all the big industrial nations and second only to tiny Luxembourg.

Further evidence of America's world-leading living standard is found in international comparisons of material well-being, such as homeownership, square footage of home or apartment, ownership of cars and appliances, and ability to afford vacation travel.

By all these measurements, the middle-class American family has a lifestyle that would be deemed affluent in most other nations, including the advanced economies. In the late '80s, George Gilder showed that the bottom one-fifth of American households (by income) had a higher material lifestyle than the average Japanese family, and there is no reason to believe this has changed during the '90s, which has been a particularly difficult decade for the Japanese economy.

## THE HIGH-CONSUMING U.S. SOCIETY

If per-capita GDP is the right starting point for judging a nation's standard of living, the next step is determining what part of the nation's annual production goes for personal consumption, rather than government operations, investment in future production and exports to consumers elsewhere. In the U.S., personal consumption runs a rather high percentage of GDP compared with other major nations, about 65%. (It should be noted, however, that some spending officially defined as "consumption"—such as college tuition, mid-career training and even some kinds of medical treatment—is really more like investment.)

### What Americans buy

In recent decades, as personal income has continuously risen, Americans have been spending relatively smaller shares of their budget on food and housing, slightly larger shares on clothing and private education, and much greater shares on health care, cars, leisure travel and recreation (including home electronics).

The most dramatic jump has been in health care spending, which has soared from only about 1% of personal-consumption spending in 1963 to 15% in 1993, reflecting the broader availability of quality medical treatment, rising prices for sophisticated procedures, technology and drugs, and—not least—the fact that most consumers of health care aren't paying their own bills but are passing the burden to employers and government.

In general, America's spending tilt away from the basics and toward higher discretionary spending on "the good life" is historically typical of rising affluence, and it will continue in the years ahead. And the same phenomenon will be seen in nations all over the world.

The developing world's increasing consumption of higher-priced consumer goods and services such as automobiles, processed foods, pharmaceuticals, entertainment and foreign travel will present rich opportunities for America's multinational corporations and their sought-after American-brand products.

# Higher U.S. Living Standards Ahead

So the average U.S. standard of living is clearly the highest in the world. But is it still rising, or is it stagnating—or worse, falling? Remember that the standard of living is a measurement of purchasing power. So if earnings are rising faster than consumer prices, so is the American living standard. The living standard can also rise even if wages are stagnant, so long as average prices of consumer needs—housing, food, clothing, appliances, fuel—are falling.

Living standards can also rise if wages and prices ascend at the same rate but consumer products get better in size, performance or durability. For example, the average new home costs considerably more today, even adjusted for inflation, than it did 20 years ago, but the square footage of the average home increased about 39% between 1970 and 1990 and is still rising, and new homes are better equipped today than back then.

Today's cars, while giving everyone sticker shock at purchase, are better built, more fuel-efficient and longer-lasting with less maintenance than cars of two decades ago. Ditto for home computers and other home appliances, whose prices have mostly fallen on an inflation-adjusted basis. Similarly, today's Americans have a substantially lower real cost of groceries than 20 years ago, and a much lower cost of fuel, too. The real price of gasoline today may be at its lowest level in history.

## PERSONAL INCOME KEEPS RISING

Real, inflation-adjusted earnings will continue to grow at the moderate rate of the past quarter-century.

All groups of Americans, of all ages and races, have substantially higher incomes than their counterparts of 50 years ago, even after adjusting for inflation. In 1997 dollars, median family incomes more than *doubled*, from $19,700 in 1947 to about $42,000. But the dramatic improvement in real incomes came during the first half of that period, from 1947 through about 1972.

In the quarter-century since then, improvement of real earnings has been much slower, due to slackening productivity growth, periods of high inflation, foreign competition and a surge in the size of the labor force. The labor force has been swelled by enormous numbers of new workers—baby-boomers, adult women working for the first time, and immigrants from Latin America and Asia—but job growth has more than kept pace, reducing unemployment to record-low levels.

## CONFLICTING WAGE STATISTICS

Some people believe that the average American's earnings, adjusted for inflation, are actually a little lower than in the early '70s. They point to statistics showing that average hourly cash wages (generally, the pay of lower-level workers) have indeed declined in real terms—after inflation—in recent years. But this apparent decline masks a shift in compensation from wages to benefits, especially for health insurance. When wages and benefits are considered together, total hourly compensation has risen anywhere from 2.9% to 4.8% a year since 1989, higher than the consumer price index in every year but one.

Another figure suggesting an erosion of pay in America is the Bureau of Labor Statistics (BLS) calculation of average weekly real earnings. But this figure, like the hourly-wage number, excludes the earnings of as much as one-third of the American work force. Missing from the data are all self-employed people, government employees (including publicly employed professionals like nurses, teachers, lawyers, scientists and engineers), agricultural workers, and all managerial personnel— broadly defined as anyone who supervises another worker. While the BLS weekly earnings figure gives an accurate picture of income stagnation among the lowest two-thirds of American workers—especially production, clerical and service workers—it isn't equivalent to the entire American work force.

Federal data on family and household income is also misleading— with some data showing stagnation and others showing solid growth. Most relevant are figures that include the value of noncash employer benefits, which have risen more strongly than wages in recent years.

Data on average household income is skewed downward by the changing definition of a household. Years ago it tended to be synonymous with a "typical" family—father and mother, at least one of whom held a steady job, and their children. In households that still meet that description, earnings growth has been excellent, especially where both parents work full- or part-time. But a growing share of households consist of one person with low income, or a single mother and her children, also with meager income. This has depressed the income data for all households.

## BIG GAINS FOR WOMEN, RACIAL MINORITIES AND SENIORS

Women as a group have fared very well in earnings growth in the past two decades, as have most racial minorities. (But due to heavy immigration of low-skill Hispanics in the '80s, Hispanic households as a group have a lower real income today than 20 years ago.)

African-Americans, the largest racial minority group, have seen remarkable progress made among those who have gotten a good education and created stable families. In 1950, just 17% of African-Americans were in the middle class; now, 66% are in a middle class that itself is considerably more comfortable. And the high school dropout rate for blacks has fallen 50% since 1968, to about 14% today, just two percentage points higher than for whites.

The elderly have fared particularly well. Thanks to inflation-indexed social security benefits, company pensions, individual savings and strong appreciation in home prices and the stock market, today's elderly enjoy substantially higher incomes than any earlier generation of retirees. Men ages 45 to 64, at the peak of their careers, have done well in recent decades, too.

The coming years will see continued improvement in the living standards of all these groups—women and racial minorities due to higher levels of education and improved career opportunities, and the elderly due to the same forces that have boosted their fortunes in recent decades. The elderly will live and work longer, have better medical care, and benefit from continued appreciation in financial assets and home prices.

### BIG LOSERS: MEN AGES 25 TO 44 WITH LIMITED EDUCATION

This group's after-inflation wages really have stagnated, possibly even declined, since the early 1970s. Since they had been a large portion of the labor force during that period, their moderate decline has been a big statistical depressant on the picture of general wage improvement by other groups.

Their plight is mostly a reflection of the decline in a certain kind of manufacturing job—one that used to pay a high wage but didn't require much education. These jobs, filled by high school graduates and even drop-outs, were once plentiful, but they are rare today. They've been replaced by high-skill manufacturing jobs that require the ability to operate sophisticated machinery on automated assembly lines and interpret computer-generated production data.

### OTHER LOSERS: SINGLE MOTHERS WITH NO SKILLS

As the elderly have moved up in comfort, the disproportionate place they once held in lower income levels has been taken over by young, unmarried mothers and their young children, typically unsupported by the children's fathers and not educated or trained enough to earn a decent living. Divorce has been particularly hard on women and children, too, who typically experience a major drop in living standards, unlike the divorced husband.

### MORE WAGE GROWTH AHEAD

The conditions that led to diminishing rates of real wage growth over the past 25 years aren't about to change much in the years ahead. On the plus side, there will be strong improvement in productivity growth. And growing labor shortages in high-tech manufacturing jobs and high-skill service positions will bring strong wage gains in many fields.

Young men and women with the most-sought-after skills will achieve higher incomes earlier in life than any previous cohort of young adults in history, as is already happening in such fields as Internet services, software design and the biological sciences.

### Restraints on wage growth

But other trends will continue to restrain wage and salary gains. Wage growth in manufacturing will be moderated by intense foreign competition, whether from U.S.- or foreign-owned plants. As labor supplies tighten and wages rise in high-tech fields, U.S. businesses will lure to this country more and more well-educated immigrants, at the same time they outsource increasing amounts of skilled work—such as computer programming—to foreign subsidiaries. This will moderate U.S. wage gains in high-tech and high-skill manufacturing.

Wages at the bottom of the skill ladder will be restrained by immigrants who will be willing to do the most menial jobs for little pay. Finally, automation and downsizing will be the relentless norm of American business.

The huge corporations that often lead the way in pay and benefits are still shedding jobs. Since 1979, employment at Fortune 500 companies has shrunk by a third, from 16.5 million to 11.5 million. But at the same time, the U.S. has created about 30 million new jobs, many of them at fast-growing large- and medium-size firms. The majority of new jobs pay strong wages and benefits, but many are at small businesses that are hard pressed to raise pay and benefits. In the years ahead, more companies will restrain regular raises and load more compensation onto year-end performance bonuses and stock ownership, linking pay more closely to the company's success.

Continued slow growth in earnings will induce more and more Americans to try self-employment, in which their earnings potential is limited only by their own creativity and hard work. Working for yourself is no bed of roses, as many once-salaried people find out fast, but at least you're not dependent on someone else's assessment of your performance and your value to the company.

## THE BOTTOM LINE: RISING STANDARDS OF LIVING

Rising real wages, a stable tax burden, flat or falling consumer prices for food, clothing, gasoline and consumer appliances, plus improving product quality and durability—it all adds up to a continually rising standard of living.

While the typical family must work more hours in a year to pay for certain expenses, such as housing and college, on balance their purchasing power has greatly increased over time. The late Fabian Linden, while director of consumer research at the Conference Board, said that, historically, Americans have doubled their real (inflation-adjusted) incomes every 35 to 40 years, and he saw no end to this long-term trend.

## HOMEOWNERSHIP

Homeownership has long been a foundation of a middle-class American lifestyle, and it will continue to be. Affordability of homes is at a two-decade high, thanks to low mortgage rates and moderate increases in home prices in the '90s, after the rapid run-up in the '70s and '80s. While married couples still account for almost two-thirds of all homes purchased, single people are buying homes in record numbers, too, accounting for an all-time high of 35% in 1997 (up from 30% the year before). Members of racial minorities, many of them immigrants, are getting the homeowner habit, too, buying almost 23% of homes in 1997, up strongly from 19% the year before.

# The Distribution of Riches

Wealth and income have always been rather unevenly distributed in America; it's a trait of a diverse, fluid, capitalistic society in which there is substantial economic mobility both up and down.

The distribution of personal wealth has changed less than you might think over the past several decades, and it's changed a lot less than the distribution of current income. In 1963, the richest 1% of households owned about 32% of the nation's wealth. In 1992, the richest 1% owned a slightly *lower* share—about 30%. The strong stock market of the past several years has probably pushed that figure back up, possibly even above the level of 30 years ago, but not by much.

The role of small-business ownership in creating personal wealth comes across very clearly in the data. Among the richest 1%, ownership of their own businesses accounts for about 40% of their wealth, real estate 20%, and publicly traded equities only 12%.

## A BIGGER SHARE FOR THOSE AT THE TOP

The distribution of income among American households moved in a fairly narrow range between the '40s and the late '80s. The bottom one-fifth of households by income typically earned 5% to 6% of total

American income, and the top one-fifth received 40% to 44% of income. The middle three-fifths got the remaining chunk, ranging over the years between 55% and 60%.

But during the 1990s, the upper-income fifth has broken out of its traditional range of income share, picking up a big chunk of the income previously received by the lower four groups. In 1995, the top fifth of households claimed 48.7% of total personal income, an increase of more than three percentage points since a decade before and a gain of five points since 1975. The other quintiles showed a steady loss of income *share* (though not *actual* income received) between 1975 and 1995. The smallest drop in income share was experienced by the bottom fifth of households (from 4.4% to 3.7%), with the biggest loss coming from the middle three quintiles, (from 52.4% to only 47.6%).

Before assuming that this growing inequality of income is primarily a result of fat paychecks for sports stars, bond traders, surgeons, corporate lawyers and CEOs, let's take a look at just what level of income puts a household in the top 20%. In 1995, an income a shade over $65,000 did the trick; today it's probably about $70,000.

The shift of income share to the upper tiers has been especially pronounced at the very highest income level—the top 5% of all households. In 1975 this group claimed 16% of all household income, and by 1985 its share had advanced only one percentage point. But in the following decade, this group gained an amazing four percentage points of share, accounting for 21% of all income in 1995. What level of income places a household in the top 5%? It took $113,000 in 1995, maybe $125,000 today. That's about three times the median American household income in the low $40,000s. (Because the top 5% includes many superhigh-income individuals, the average annual income is about $250,000; in 1995, about 87,000 tax returns showed incomes of $1 million or more, a 30% increase over 1993.)

In many parts of America, especially in high-cost metro areas on the east and west coasts, families with household incomes in the $120,000 range don't consider themselves rich. Nonetheless, they are better off than 95% of their fellow citizens.

## REASONS BEHIND GROWING INCOME INEQUALITY

What's going on here? There are many reasons for this increasingly uneven distribution of income. One of the most significant is the growing linkage between education and income. People with college degrees and postgraduate education, especially in technical fields, have always earned much more than high school grads and dropouts, but the pay premium for higher education and special training is broadening at a quickening rate.

The entrepreneurial boom has contributed to this trend. So has strong earnings growth in the skilled services—health care, financial services, law, engineering and others. And the atypically strong gains in stock prices over the past decade and a half have increased not just the wealth but also the current income of affluent Americans. That's because realized capital gains are included in annual personal income, along with salaries, dividends and interest.

Another factor has been strong executive pay in the '90s, especially in publicly traded companies that have shifted compensation from base salary to lavish stock options. While in no sense typical of all executive pay, the total compensation packages of CEOs at the nation's 365 largest corporations (including stock options) averaged $7.8 million in 1997, up 35% from the previous year. Whether in business, sports, entertainment or professions such as law and medicine, America has evolved toward a star system in which large organizations bid aggressively for the talents of the most exceptional performers.

### *The big, invisible factor in inequality*

While all these forces have contributed to growing income inequality in recent years, they all pale in comparison with the biggest—and least acknowledged—factor. It's a combination of sociological, rather than economic, forces: the increasing education of women, their surge into the workplace, especially into high-income professions and executive jobs, and finally, the growing tendency of men and women with similar education, occupations and incomes to marry each other.

A generation ago, women made up a tiny portion of America's physicians, lawyers and business managers and owners. Today there are almost equal numbers of men and women enrolled in college and graduate schools. Women's pay gains have been impressive, and there is virtually no difference between the average earnings of young men and women with similar educations and job experience. More than half of all women continue their careers after marriage and during motherhood (with occasional breaks when the kids are young), so the two-income family is the rule, not the exception, in America. This is what has pushed so many families from the middle class into the upper-income stratum.

This phenomenon has been accentuated by the fact that more men and women are marrying an educational, occupational and earning equal. In decades past, a man in business or a profession typically married his high school sweetheart (who maybe never entered the work force), or a secretary or clerk he met at work, or another woman with lower or no earnings. And typically the wife didn't work after marrying. This all had the effect of spreading household earnings more evenly.

Today, however, men tend to marry women they meet in college, graduate school or the workplace, where they often hold jobs of similar status and income. And the wife continues earning after marriage and childbirth. So two single-person households with strong earnings combine into a new dual-earner household, often with very high income. An example: A thirtyish man and woman, each a college graduate earning about $42,000, would constitute two middle-quintile households if living separately. But if they marry, their combined income would vault them into the top quintile of households, and if they get raises or bonuses (or capital gains) that add another $20,000 or so to each of their incomes, their combined income would put their household into the highest 5%.

### *Affluent dual-earning couples*

This is precisely what is happening in millions of highly educated, dual-earner households. There is no downside to this, except for the concern—hard to substantiate—that children of dual-career parents may get lower-quality child care than they would if one of the parents stayed home with them during the early years.

"Much of the purported inequity (of income inequality) would disappear if married women simply stayed home," or if more dual-career couples got divorced, observes Diana Furchtgott-Roth. "Those who favor women's progression up the career ladder should not bemoan the resulting income gap." Furchtgott-Roth, who has analyzed this trend for the American Enterprise Institute and the Independent Women's Forum, writes, "It is a natural outgrowth of improved opportunities. So-called income disparities are often a sign of progress, not decline."

In any event, these trends show no signs of abating, and they are, taken together, the biggest single force in the increasing unevenness of income distribution.

### SOCIAL MOBILITY

The composition of each income quintile—the particular individuals and families in each income group—does not remain the same over time. There is enormous socioeconomic mobility, both up and down, especially during the stages of life. Young adults start off in a lower-income quintile, and with hard work and luck (and by uniting in marriage with another earning adult) climb into a higher quintile.

This is especially true of the immigrant experience, where upward mobility is alive and well. On the other hand, the changing composition of an ethnic group can affect the appearance of their progress. For example, Hispanics' median real household income (expressed in 1995 dollars) fell from $26,000 in 1973 to $22,900 in 1995, but that's not saying that the same Hispanics who lived in America in 1973 have a lower median income today. Those who have been here for 25 years probably have substantially higher incomes than the median, but the median is depressed by the lower incomes of newly arrived immigrant families.

### The upwardly mobile middle class

In the late '80s it was fashionable to bemoan the "shrinking middle class"—a presumed demotion of once middle-class families into the lower tiers of income. While the size of the traditional middle class really *has* declined, if not in actual numbers of households, then certainly as a share of all households, this has little to do with people getting poorer. It's really about the *upward* mobility of middle-income families into the ranks of the upper-middle classes.

Take a look at those families who were in the bottom one-fifth of income during the mid 1970s. Of that group, an estimated 80% have experienced upward mobility, with 29% moving into the top fifth of income, 30% into the second fifth and 21% into the third fifth. For some of those who remain in the bottom fifth, there is no easy solution. Breakdown of traditional families is a frequently cited culprit, and in fact, two-thirds of the families in the lowest income group are headed by single mothers.

## MORE INCOME INEQUALITY AHEAD

The dominant trend in the distribution of income will continue to be this: The greater the gap in education and training, the greater the gap in earnings. Generally, education deficits explain the larger income shares of college graduates versus high school grads, older workers versus younger ones, whites versus racial minorities, men versus women. Adjusted first for education, then again for length of job experience, most of these income gaps shrink to negligible margins. This underscores the need to improve education and job training—and broaden access to them—as America's key to wage growth, rising living standards and more-even distribution of income in the 21st century.

Income maldistribution will be a hotly debated topic in the next few years. Some Republicans dismiss it as being irrelevant to rising living standards, and others even tout it as a positive force that motivates people to work hard and emulate more-successful fellow citizens. Many Democrats decry maldistribution of income as an evil that must be rectified by higher marginal taxation of the rich or by elaborate social programs to improve the earning capacity of the poor.

### A feeling of falling behind

So are the "rich getting richer and the poor getting poorer?" No, it looks as if the poor are getting less poor as the rich are getting richer—and as the rich are also increasing their share of total income.

But for many people, their concept of getting ahead is relative—not whether they're actually doing better than they used to, but whether they're doing as much better as someone else is. This is the foundation of the "politics of envy" which colors all debate on Capitol Hill. In the coming struggle over whether to replace our present tax code with something else, Democrats will use evidence of the growing gap between rich and poor to block Republican proposals for a flat tax to replace the progressive income tax.

# The Outlook for Poverty

The United States has: a) one of the lowest rates of poverty among advanced nations; b) the highest rate of poverty; c) both. Answer: c) both, depending on which of the two common international definitions of poverty you use.

Poverty can be defined either by an absolute standard—say, the inability to afford a certain amount and quality of food, shelter and clothing, which will vary from nation to nation; or by a relative standard, typically a household income that is only half of the nation's median income.

Compared with most other advanced nations, the U.S. has a low rate of poverty by the absolute standard, because it is a very wealthy society and even its poorest people have a lifestyle that would be considered comfortable in most other nations. In a study of European and North American nations by economist McKinley Blackburn, using 1980s data, only Canada and Luxembourg came out lower than the U.S. in absolute poverty rates, based on each nations's standards. The U.S. rate was much lower than those of the Netherlands, Italy, Britain, Australia, Germany and France.

But the U.S., as a wealthy nation with high inequality of income, has one of the world's highest rates of *relative* poverty. If, for example, poverty is defined as having only half of a nation's median household income, 25% of U.S. households (those with incomes under about $20,000) would be considered poor. As Blackburn points out, a focus on relative poverty can lead to the "curious policy suggestion that a successful method for 'fighting' poverty may be to increase taxes on the middle class—thereby lowering their standard of living and (also) the relative threshold necessary for low-income families to escape poverty."

## POVERTY TRENDS

The U.S. measurement of poverty uses an absolute standard that attempts to measure the percentage of households whose income is less than three times the cost of a subsistence food budget.

Adjusted each year for changes in the price of this subsistence diet, the poverty-income level today is about $16,000 for an urban family of four. The poverty rate fell for decades, from about 25% in 1960 to an official low of 11% in 1973. It rose to about 15% in 1983, after the severe recession, and it has hovered in the 13% range since. The poverty rate doesn't take into account noncash income from housing subsidies, food stamps, school lunches, and health care from medicare and medicaid. With the value of these government programs added in, the poverty rate is probably between 9% and 11% of all households.

## FEMALE-HEADED HOUSEHOLDS AND POVERTY

The poor in America once included mostly older people, who had a poverty rate of some 35% in 1960. That rate has steadily fallen, thanks to corporate pensions and social security, and today a record-low 10% live in poverty.

The opposite situation has occurred with children, whose poverty rate has steadily risen for 25 years, from about 15% in 1970 to about 21%. This trend has clearly coincided with the enormous rise in births to unwed mothers, many of whom receive little or no financial support from the children's fathers. In households headed by single mothers, more than 60% of the children live in poverty. Most other advanced nations have a much lower incidence of single-female-headed households, but a higher portion of their female-headed households are in poverty—for example, about 75% to 80% in Britain and Germany in the late '80s, and 90% in the Netherlands. Any way you look at it, intact two-parent families are key to the material well-being of people everywhere.

## ASSETS DON'T COUNT IN CALCULATING POVERTY

The American definition of poverty is based only on current income, without regard to net worth—what possessions a household owns. When you look at census data that matches a household's income with its possessions, it becomes clear why America's concept of being poor doesn't square with how the rest of the world defines poverty, or even with how America defined poverty a generation or two ago.

Certainly many of the Americans who are classified as poor are truly destitute—having little or no income, owning virtually nothing, unable to earn enough to provide a nutritious diet for their children or afford even the smallest, shabbiest rental apartment. This includes America's relatively small number of homeless street people, as well as many teenage mothers with no means of support.

But it also appears, from census data, that many poor Americans own possessions—presumably acquired during an earlier period of sufficient income—that give them what would be considered a middle-class lifestyle in other countries or in earlier eras of American life.

Analyzing census data on homeownership, Robert Rector of the Heritage Foundation drew these startling conclusions: In 1995 41% of poor households owned their own home, and the average home owned by poor households had three bedrooms, a garage, and a patio or porch. About 750,000 officially poor households owned homes valued at more than $150,000, and 200,000 of the poor owned homes valued over $300,000.

As for auto ownership, 70% of households with incomes below the official poverty line owned a car, and 27% owned two or more vehicles. This data probably reflect the higher-than-typical asset ownership of elderly people now considered poor who once, during their working years, had higher incomes and still own homes and cars free of debt.

# A Nation's Health Is More Than Wealth

We don't want to give the impression that a nation's well-being is entirely, or even largely, a matter of material comfort. Indeed, there is no ironclad link between economic and social health. Throughout history there have been financially poor, "primitive" societies in which there was (and still is) a high degree of social cohesion, harmony and happiness. And there have been affluent societies with high levels of crime, degradation and conflict, coupled with low levels of personal and civic integrity.

In America's history, there have been periods of low crime and considerable social order amid dire economic circumstances—for example, during the Great Depression, when there was no noticeable increase in crime. But for the past several decades, many of the indices of U.S. social health have declined amid rising prosperity.

## FEARS ABOUT AMERICA'S FUTURE

When many Americans talk about the standard of living, their talk often strays to the nation's social, spiritual and emotional health. They talk about "quality of life" issues and human values.

And they are worried—deeply concerned about trends of the past quarter-century in crime, drug use, suicide, divorce, adolescent sexual activity, unwed motherhood, abortion, tension between the races, the growing vulgarity and violence in pop music, movies and TV, and a general erosion of civility in all human affairs.

Their greatest concern is for America's youth, because statistics relating to their well-being seem to be running counter to encouraging trends in adult society. On the TV news and in the newspapers, there is plenty of anecdotal evidence of increases in teen crime, depression, pregnancy, drug use at earlier ages, binge drinking, and eating disorders such as anorexia and bulimia.

### *Elusive reasons—and solutions*

There are as many explanations of these trends as there are shades of opinion on all things ideological, social, political and cultural. Some point a finger at the divorce rate, or inadequate supervision of children in dual-career families, or overly permissive parenting by mothers and fathers insecure in their traditional authority roles, or the decline of the influence of churches, schools, neighbors, youth groups and even grandparents in shaping the values and character of youths.

Some point to low parental expectations, and others cite excessively high expectations. Some point to material indulgence amid emotional deprivation. Some blame the unwholesome influence of pop culture, and others the easy availability of guns and drugs. Some fault the shallow materialism of an affluent consumer society, and others point to poor education and lack of job opportunities in inner-city neighborhoods. Some point to overspending by adults on their own entertainment—such as professional sports and leisure travel—and underinvesting (of both money and time) in the education and guidance of American youth. Still others bemoan a culture of blaming others for one's own failures.

The odds are pretty good that all of these factors, and others not cited, have contributed—to some degree, in some unknown mix of proportions—to social problems in America today.

### *A pendulum swing ahead?*

But as market imbalances tend to be self-correcting, similar forces are at work in social trends. When a situation reaches crisis levels, a public outcry mounts, corrective actions begin and—a few years later— changes begin to appear. There is often a lag between the perception of change and the reality. Well after improvement is under way, public-opinion polls still show a perception of worsening conditions.

The pendulum may already be swinging back in a positive direction on several troubling situations in America. Here's a look at the mixed pictures on several of them:

**Violent crime.** There was a shocking increase in violent youth crime in the '80s—for example, a tripling of juvenile homicides from 1984 to 1994, far outpacing the increase in the youth population. But overall national rates of violent crime, including murder, rape and armed robbery, have been falling during the 1990s, and there are recent indications of a drop in youth crime, too.

But a high percentage of all crimes are still committed by young adults ages 18 to 24, and this age cohort will grow in numbers by 20% between now and 2010—not a good omen for crime, barring a significant change in attitude or crime deterrence.

**Drug use and alcohol abuse.** Studies indicate declining drug use and alcohol abuse by adults, but increasing use among youths at younger ages. Girls, in particular, are drinking and smoking at a higher rate and earlier age than ever before. But alcohol-related auto accidents are now at an all-time low.

**Suicide.** The suicide rate for adults hasn't changed much, but for adolescents it's vastly higher than it was in 1980, especially for African-American males, whose traditionally low suicide rate has doubled since then. But over the last few years teen rates seem to have peaked and possibly declined slightly.

**Divorce.** The national rate of divorce, while still high, has declined since the early '80s. Divorce is now coming to be recognized as devastating to children both emotionally and financially. No-fault divorce will lose favor, and more states will create programs for so-called "covenant marriage," requiring extensive premarital counseling and allowing divorce only for a narrow range of causes.

**Teen sexual activity.** Two recent surveys showed a decline in teen sex between 1988 and 1995—the first such decline in years. It was most pronounced among suburban youths, but there was also a leveling out among urban and rural teens.

**Births to teenaged girls.** The number peaked in 1970 and has fallen in a jagged line ever since. Births declined between 1991 and 1996 in all states, for girls of all races. It seems to be due mostly to increasing abstinence and contraception use by teens, but not to abortion, which is falling in both rate and total numbers.

Black teenaged girls have twice the birth rate of whites, but their rate has fallen 21% since 1991 and is now at the lowest level ever recorded. Hispanics have the highest teen birth rate, with one of every ten teenage girls giving birth in 1996. About 70% of all births to all teenaged girls are out of wedlock, and the fathers are typically at least 20 years old.

The recent decline suggests that teenagers are slowly getting the message that abstinence from sexual activity until adulthood or marriage is critical to developing their self-esteem, completing their education and achieving middle-class material well-being.

**Births to unwed mothers.** The percentage of babies born to unwed mothers—whatever their age or race—dropped one percentage point, from 33% in 1994 to 32% in 1997, the first such drop in decades. (The rate was only 18% in 1980.) There is now reason to believe that illegitimacy will be further reduced by abstinence, contraception and welfare reform, with its emphasis on job training and capping of benefits for additional out-of-wedlock children.

Rates vary greatly by race: 16% of Asian births are out of wedlock, 26% of white births, 41% of Hispanic births, and 70% of African-American births. The greatest increase in recent years has been to middle-class young white women. Most births outside marriage are to women in their twenties, not teens; births to teens account for only about 30% of the total, births to cohabiting couples make up 25%.

**Abortion.** Both the rate and total number of abortions have declined in the '90s, probably due mostly to a drop in the incidence of unintended pregnancy, which in turn is due to either less sexual activity (in and outside marriage) or more contraceptive use. Abortion-rights activists also believe that clinic picketing and the absence of medicaid funding also play a role in the decline (although some states still fund abortions for the poor).

## WHAT LIES AHEAD

It is impossible to know whether recent improvements in several of these trends are just aberrant blips in a long decline or harbingers of a major turnaround. Without lapsing into wishful forecasting, there is reason to be hopeful that something significant is happening. You can see it in the education reform movement, renewed interest in religion and character among youths, a growing willingness to accept individual responsibility, and more discussion of ethical conduct in business and government (if not yet visible improvement).

Advancing economic prosperity cannot in itself create a moral and cooperative society, as America has painfully learned in recent decades. But it lays a good foundation for the difficult work on other fronts. Progress against social ills is much easier to accomplish in an environment of broadly rising living standards—which, fortunately for the United States, is what still lies ahead for the vast majority of its citizens.

# CHAPTER 8

# World Population Growth

The early 21st century will be marked by sweeping demographic changes on a global scale, with huge impacts on business, politics and the environment. The world will add another 1.5 billion citizens by 2020, boosting population 25%, to more than 7.5 billion. Almost all of this growth—about 95%—will occur in the less-developed nations, especially in Africa, Asia and the Middle East.

This projection means that, over the next 20 years, the earth's population will increase by 70 million to 80 million people every year. To picture the magnitude of this annual increase, consider that it's more than the population of the Philippines today, and more than the combined populations of South Korea and Peru.

While it is highly conjectural to look much beyond 2020, the odds are good that world population will peak at about 8 billion at mid century. Then, due to steadily falling fertility rates, it will begin a gradual decline to around 7.2 billion by 2100.

As dramatic as the absolute increase will be over the next 20 years, the rate of world growth will keep slowing—from a peak of 2% a year in 1970, to 1.3% today, to less than 1% by 2020. This slowdown will result from stunning drops in fertility rates—the average number of children born to a woman in her lifetime—in the developing world.

Population growth, while presenting many challenges to the world economy and environment, will not halt the steady rise in world living standards, nor even slow it down. Nor will it lead, in and of itself, to any of the crises predicted by population pessimists—widespread famine, severe environmental degradation, world war, resource depletion and predatory industrial competition.

There is no reason to believe that population growth limits economic growth; in fact, there's plenty of evidence of a positive relationship between them. Where a negative connection seems to exist, a closer examination usually reveals other factors at play, such as market-stifling economic policies, political tyranny, an absence of resources or capital, and poor, narrowly available public education.

These new people on earth will be part of an expanding global market of producers and consumers. And most of them will live in or around ever-sprawling urban areas, especially in Asia, where many cities will reach sizes once thought to be wildly unmanageable. Making these megacities safe, sanitary and decent places to live will require vast amounts of expensive new infrastructure.

# Young Nations, Old Nations

With relatively high birth rates and low life expectancies, developing nations will continue to have high percentages of young people and low proportions of elderly. The opposite is true in the developed nations. Each situation poses different sets of challenges. Historian Paul Kennedy describes the dilemma very well: "As prosperous nations grapple with the problem of allocating more and more resources to the elderly, the rest of the globe begs for help dealing with demands flowing from the boom in young children and infants," such as medicine, day care, public education and, later on, jobs for the young adults they will become.

These nations will add the most people, in this order: India, China, Nigeria, Pakistan, Indonesia, the United States and Bangladesh. But many other nations, those with birth rates below replacement level, will probably lose population in the decades ahead. These include Japan, Germany, Great Britain, Russia, Italy, Spain, Ukraine and several other European nations. They will have to deal with tough issues such as maintaining adequate labor supplies and supporting a large retired population with a smaller group of workers.

The United States will be the big exception to the pattern of stagnant populations in the advanced nations. Growing at a rate of a little less than 1% a year, it will add more than 50 million people by 2020. While the U.S. population will gradually age, this will be nothing compared with the graying of other high-income industrial nations, due to their very low birth rates and resistance to immigration. So the U.S. will be in better shape than Japan or Europe when it comes to the ratio of workers to retirees, with less strain on pension and health care systems. The median age in the U.S.—35 in 1997—is already two years younger than Britain's, four years younger than Germany's and Sweden's, and five years younger than Japan's. China, by contrast, has a median age of only 28. But with its fertility rate plunging, it will join the ranks of the graying nations before long.

To maintain the 1990 ratio of workers to retirees in the year 2025, workers in most industrial nations would have to stay employed much longer than previous generations have—working to about 75 years of age in Japan, the low seventies in Canada and Finland, about 70 in Spain and Germany, and the high 60s in Great Britain and France. In the U.S., which is graying less rapidly, the typical retirement age would have to rise to about 68. This will probably happen anyway, because some healthier seniors will choose to work longer, and will be sought-after by a labor-hungry economy, and because others won't have saved enough for retirement. And continued employment will be encouraged by a gradual increase in the age of eligibility for social security benefits.

Today's Japan gives a glimpse of what lies ahead for the economies of Europe and North America. It has the world's highest percentage of workers over 55, with many of them retiring from their long time employer and then signing on as part-time workers because there aren't enough younger Japanese to fill the jobs they're leaving.

# No Doomsday Ahead

Population growth has been the focus of doomsday predictions since Thomas Malthus warned in 1798 that population would outpace food production, leading to wide-scale starvation. Malthus's famously gloomy vision (which he later repudiated) has been repeatedly averted due to stunning increases in farm productivity, industrialization and migration of poor people to areas of better opportunity. There are still some forecasters, among them ecologist Paul Ehrlich and the Worldwatch Institute's Lester R. Brown, who believe that Malthus was simply ahead of his time and is now on the brink of vindication. They fear that the doomsday scenario is poised to come true in the next few decades due to dramatic improvements in world health, declines in mortality rates and—despite declining fertility rates—enormous population increases each year.

But the cataclysm is not likely to happen. Even at numbers unimaginable to Malthus, the world's population will have enough to eat in the coming decades. Advances in farming that have boosted production in developed countries, including the coming benefits of the biotech revolution, will keep spreading to the developing world, helping nations feed their own people and even export food.

## PLUMMETING FERTILITY RATES

The breathtaking pace of population growth since 1960, when the world's population stood at three billion, has occurred because advances in public health, medical science and agricultural production raced way ahead of changes in Third World social customs—that is, attitudes toward birth control, the role of women in society and traditional concepts of ideal family size. In earlier eras, high mortality among children was a given, so families had many children to assure the survival of enough of them to provide labor in a largely agricultural economy and to support the parents in their old age.

In the next century, public health and longevity will continue to improve, but family size will be restrained. Why? Because historically, fertility rates have declined as personal incomes, urbanization and the status of women have risen. Women who have substantial education, civil rights, job opportunities and access to entrepreneurial capital tend to have fewer children than women who don't. Add in the greater availability, safety and ease of use of birth control, and it all equates to a substantial decrease in the rate of population growth.

These forces are already combining to achieve significant drops in fertility rates in many developing nations. For example, Bangladesh nearly halved its rate between 1985 and 1997, going from an average 6.2 children per woman to 3.3. In Kenya, the rate plunged from 7.5 to 4.5 in the same period. Nonetheless, there are still 33 nations—25 of them in Africa—with fertility rates of six or more children per woman of child-bearing age. India continues to grow at a rate that may make it the most populous nation in a few decades, passing China.

Where the natural process of economic development fails to curb population growth, governments will occasionally intercede, as many do now, with incentives and edicts. China has lowered its birth rate in part through coercion, leading to a high level of abortion and infanticide, especially of newborn girls. Iran limits government aid for housing and health care to three children per family. Other nations simply mount education campaigns and provide free birth control.

It would be wonderful if the continued slowing of world population growth were to result entirely from positive forces. Unfortunately, it's also possible that rising death rates, especially from infectious diseases, will also be a factor. New strains of rapidly mutating diseases will be a constant challenge to medical science and public health. But biotech research will develop an amazing array of vaccines for all the major infectious diseases that ravage the developing nations, including AIDS, malaria and cholera. Some of these vaccines will be designed into the genes of common foods such as bananas and potatoes.

# Relentless Urbanization

The developing countries will have to cope with the demands of rapid urbanization, which will test their resources and resolve. As megacities reach virtually unmanageable size, governments will take aggressive steps, in cooperation with private business interests, to disperse population by locating new manufacturing facilities in less-congested regions. Typically, that means drawing population to smaller cities in interior areas and away from densely settled coasts.

This dispersal of population will entail an enormous investment in new infrastructure—transportation, sanitation, telecommunications, and so on—to keep the new urban areas knitted together. This world-wide trend will be not unlike the dispersal of population going on now in the United States, with older metro areas on the coasts experiencing out-migration of businesses and residents to smaller, fast-growing metro areas in the heartland.

But until this movement begins in developing nations, they will continue to experience a profound shift in the residency and occupations of their citizens away from rural areas and farming and toward big cities and jobs in manufacturing and services. Forty years ago, fewer than one person in three lived in a city. Now it's nearly one in two. The world's urban population will more than double over the next 30 years, to more than five billion. In just 15 years, there will be about 500 cities with populations of more than one million. There are already 24 cities with more than eight million people, and before 2015 there will be 33, most of them in the less developed nations.

The urbanized world, over time, has also shifted its center of gravity, from the Europe to North America and now to the emerging nations of Asia and Latin America. Earlier in this century, most large cities were in Europe. Now two-thirds of all city dwellers are found in developing countries.

Cities offer plenty of promise and peril. Since the dawn of the industrial age, they have been the engines of economic wealth and social enrichment. But they also breed poverty, lack of jobs and housing, poor infrastructure, traffic congestion, pollution and other problems. "One need only mention Manila, Jakarta, Cairo, Sao Paulo or Mexico City to conjure up images of severe pollution, traffic jams that slow commuting to a crawl for hours, shantytowns mushrooming on every spare square foot of available land," writes Mira Kamdar, a senior fellow of the World Policy Institute.

But such cities are also vibrant commercial and cultural centers of growing nations, places of opportunity for the ambitious. Of her native city of Bombay (with a population between 12 million and 15 million), Kamdar says, "the city is a place where a landless peasant, an untouchable or an indentured laborer starving to death in rural or small-town India can find work, eat, maybe even buy a television set one day." Despite their enormous problems, she observes, the sprawling metropolises of the developing nations "are centers of wealth, industry and entertainment, and as such, they continue to attract far more millions of refugees than they can possibly accommodate decently." Their teeming slums are just vastly larger versions of the miserable conditions that existed in parts of London and Paris in the 18th century and in the tenements of New York at the turn of this century.

### THE INFRASTRUCTURE CHALLENGE

Some countries have tried to ease or reverse these trends through migration controls, land-use planning, location of manufacturing facilities in rural areas, and other measures, but with mixed results. Multinational corporations may end up being more effective than governments at decentralizing urban areas by siting their new plants in "greenfield" locales far from the megacities, and providing sanitation, housing and other urban amenities built at the same time as the plants. The concentration of people in urban areas will, ironically, aid in solving some of the problems of economic development in a cost-efficient way. Advances in sanitation, water supply, health care, energy and education will cost less per person in urban areas than if the population were broadly dispersed.

Rich countries have developed technology to deal with these needs, and over the next 20 years the developing world will rely on the industrial nations to help them acquire this technology. The building of urban infrastructure in less-developed nations will be a powerful economic activity. It will provide enormous employment for engineers and construction managers in both the advanced and developing nations, with giant multinational design, engineering and construction firms leading the way, joined by firms in power generation and telecommunications.

In the early stages of economic development, nations tend to neglect infrastructure; factories to make goods for domestic consumption and export sprout in muddy fields before the coming of good roads and public sanitation. But when environmental degradation and congestion get bad enough, every nation does what it must to make life more comfortable for its citizens. This is what happened over the past 100 years in places as diverse as London, Pittsburgh and Tokyo, and it will happen in the Third World. The economic demands of developing infrastructure will, over time, take some of the competitive pressure off manufacturers in the advanced nations. The less-developed nations will have to divert resources from their recent rapid surge of industrialization, moderating their economic-growth rates and giving their competitors a little breathing room in fierce world trade competition.

## THE MICRO-ENTERPRISE ALTERNATIVE

Improvements in urban living need not involve massive government assistance, and sometimes the process works better without it. In 1970 two civic activists in Karachi, Pakistan, fed up with bureaucratic corruption and inaction on new sewer lines for their poor neighborhood, mobilized local residents to do the work themselves. The Orangi Pilot Project flourished, despite harassment by government officials, police and big contractors. Its example was eventually emulated in some three dozen other communities in Karachi and elsewhere in Pakistan. An estimated two million poor Pakistanis have benefited from the do-it-yourself sewer lines, with a 75% reduction in infant mortality in some neighborhoods. Families with annual incomes of only $1,200 willingly contribute about 15% of their monthly earnings to build and maintain the sewer lines. This and many similar stories in the Third World show the power of locally initiated micro-enterprise to improve lives.

## MORE INTERNATIONAL MIGRATION

In a politically freer world with expanding global trade, there will be more migration of poor people to places with job opportunities—generally, a flow of younger people to advanced economies with aging populations and shortages of labor. This means more guest workers (lifelong aliens) from Turkey, North Africa and the former Soviet republics coming to western Europe; more Filipinos, Thais and Pakistanis working in Japan; and more Mexicans and Central Americans arriving in the United States. Much of this migration will be illegal, as the demand for labor outstrips immigration quotas.

Most of the advanced nations will continue to feel ambivalent toward heightened immigration, both needing the labor and fearing

171

the cultural and economic changes that come with it. Relatively few, spacious advanced nations, such as the United States and Australia, will accept large numbers of immigrants and offer them the opportunity for full citizenship. In most other nations, they will remain barely tolerated guest workers. Eventually, advanced nations will figure out that the most effective way—indeed, the only way—to reduce the pressures of unwanted immigration is to help improve the economies of low-income neighboring nations.

# A Declining World Population after Mid Century?

All long-range population projections are based on highly speculative assumptions about fertility rates and death rates, which are affected by economic conditions, technology, political developments and other aspects of human behavior.

Forecasts of ever-rising world population, without any flattening or decline at mid century, make one critical assumption: Fertility rates in the poor, less-developed nations will never fall to the low levels typical of today's advanced nations. But this assumption is flawed, because of the socioeconomic forces of modernization discussed above. Ben Wattenberg, a perceptive student of demographics at the American Enterprise Institute, goes even further, calling it "preposterous" to think that most developing nations won't soon (in the next decade or two) achieve the 2.1 children-per-woman fertility rate that simply replaces the mother and father and maintains a fairly static population. Wattenberg notes that "19 less-developed countries have already gone below replacement, including China, Cuba, Thailand, Malaysia and, any minute now, Brazil." And this trend is appearing all over the world: "Never have birth and fertility rates fallen so far, so low, so fast, for so long, in so many places."

Of the various population-growth models used in official circles today, the one that looks most plausible is the United Nations' "low-medium" forecast, which reflects a rapid decline in developing-nation fertility. This model shows world population peaking at 8 billion in 2050 and then, with humankind not even replacing itself, beginning a slow decline to 7.2 billion at the end of the next century.

This would be the first time since the Middle Ages that world population contracted for any lengthy period. This decline won't result, like that one, from plagues, famine and warfare, but from the free choice of a more prosperous humankind to have smaller families, ease crowded living and lighten demands on the world's resources.

# CHAPTER 9

# Constantly Changing American Population

D emography is destiny. A nation's future depends to a great extent on the people who inhabit it—their numbers, their ages, their education, their health, their ambition to achieve. All forecasting must start with demography, because the changing composition of a people—especially by age segments—drives almost everything else.

The *aging* of America gets so much attention that it's easy to overlook the sheer impact of a *growing* population. Imagine an America in 2020 with 53 million more citizens. They'll have to live and work somewhere, buy food, shelter, clothes and cars. More than a third of these additional Americans will be immigrants, whose diversity will enrich the culture and whose ambition will help drive the economy, but whose assimilation into mainstream American life will be a constant challenge economically, socially and politically.

Meanwhile, baby-boomers are destined to be the new century's trendsetting elders, just as they've been the 20th century's trendsetting youngsters and middle-agers. Most boomers will be gone by 2050, but not long gone. Average life expectancy, now about 79 years for women and 73 for men, will climb to 84 and 80.

The number of elderly people over age 85 will quadruple, from roughly four million to more than 18 million. Their demand for assisted-care lodging, medical services and recreation will be immense, and they'll have the financial ability to pay for it. As America ages, the proportion of married couples in households with no children at home will soar, stoking the fires of political conflict over taxes for schools, playgrounds and other services for kids, and making today's intergenerational squabbles look like patty-cake.

## GROWING, BUT MORE SLOWLY

The rate of America's population growth will decline a little over the next few decades, from about 0.9% a year now to about 0.75%. That may not seem like a lot of growth, but it means the U.S. will add more than two million people *every year*, going from a population of about 270 million today to 286 million by 2005, 298 million by 2010, 323 million by 2020 and 394 million by 2050.

There will be plenty of room for all these new Americans. The U.S. that many consider to be overcrowded is actually a rather sparsely settled country by the standards of other nations. With only 28 people per square kilometer, U.S. population density is just 60% that of Mexico's. It's only 22% of China's density, 12% of Germany's and Great Britain's, 10% of India's, 8% of Japan's and 6% of South Korea's. (If you really want to spread out, Australia has only two residents per square kilometer.)

In the process of slowly growing, the U.S. will also become, on average, older and more racially diverse. These trends will be accompanied by an accelerating rate of intermarriage, gradually rendering today's racial classifications pointless (and, in the process, hastening America's progress toward a truly color-blind society).

The fertility rate will remain low, due to widespread contraception, legal abortion, and the tendency of women of rising education and income status to have fewer children. Native-born white Americans of non-Hispanic descent are not even replacing themselves; these women will have, on average, about 1.8 children, well under the 2.1 children that maintains population at a constant level. Immigrant Hispanic women and African-American women have higher-than-replacement fertility rates, but theirs, too, will probably fall in the years to come.

Despite low fertility rates, more than 60% of the population growth will come from natural increase, the surplus of births over deaths. The other nearly 40% will come from immigration—about one million newcomers a year, mostly from Latin America. About one-quarter will enter illegally, and most will stay indefinitely. All told, immigrants and their children will account for more than half of the nation's future growth.

# Life Stages of Generations

Whatever field you are in—baby supplies or life insurance, selling cars or educating kids, stock brokerage or home building, health care or real estate sales, retailing or travel—there are enormous implications for your business or profession from the swelling and contracting size of various age cohorts. The planning and marketing of new products must always start with demographic analysis—the sheer number of prospective customers—then proceed to their financial wherewithal, needs and consumer tastes.

Not all age segments will grow much in actual numbers between now and 2010. For example, due to the small, "birth-dearth" years of the '70s, there will be relatively small increases in kids under 13 and only about 1.4 million more 14- to 17-year-olds.

The dominant age cohort of the first decades of the new century—until around 2025—will be the baby-boomers, the same generation that strained schools and colleges in the '50s and '60s; gave business an ample supply of new workers in the '70s and '80s; is now reaching its peak earnings years and driving the stock-market boom; and will begin retiring (and straining health care and retirement systems) around 2015. Americans born during the birth dearth years will be less significant demographically, but worth watching for their attitudinal impact.

In the late '80s and extending through the early '90s, many late-marrying baby-boomers hit their childbearing stride. At the same time, Generation Xers (those born between 1965 and 1983) began having children. This combination is creating a "baby-boom echo" generation that will have a great impact on the future demand for goods and services.

## RECORD BIRTHS A DOZEN YEARS FROM NOW

Total births hit a robust 4.2 million in 1990, just a little below the previous record high of 4.3 million in 1957.

But the younger boomer moms are nearing the end of their child-bearing years, so births will trail off below four million until around 2005, when the young adults of the large baby-boom echo and the immigrants who came to the U.S. as children in the '80s begin to have children of their own.

By 2012, total births will top the all-time high of 1957, rising to a level of 4.6 million by 2020.

## THE GRAYING OF AMERICA

Still, this high level of births will represent a smaller *portion* of the U.S. population than in the '50s and '60s. That's because the adults of the baby-boom and their young-adult children—the biggest age cohorts now—will live a lot longer than previous Americans did. Lengthening life expectancy adds a lot to a population. If mortality rates today were what they were in 1900, the U.S. would have a population of only 139 million in the year 2000, instead of a projected 275 million.

Due to advances in medicine and healthier personal habits, life expectancy will gradually tick upward from today's levels of 73 years for newborn boys and 79 for girls. Of course, the longer you've lived already, the higher the age at which you're likely to die. For American men and women who have already reached the age of 65, life expectancies are 81 and 84, respectively.

The median age of the population will *gradually* rise. The concept of a graying America may suggest a nation in which everyone is scooting around in wheelchairs, but this image overstates the reality. The median age is now about 35. As recently as 1990, it was 33, and in 1980 it was just 29. By 2020 the median age will rise to about 38—which, incidentally, is the median age today of America's most-elderly state, Florida.

## THE AGING BOOMERS

By the end of the next decade, the aging of the baby-boomers will result in 23 million more Americans in advanced middle age—ten million more aged 45 to 54 and 13 million more aged 55 to 64.

There won't be as many retirees in the next ten years because of the low birth rate and total births in the "trough" period of the Depression and early years of World War II. But around 2010, and accelerating thereafter, boomers will begin to retire, and the sheer number of people in their sixties and seventies—and their percentage of all Americans—really takes off. They will be the most affluent group of retirees in history; because so many of them were two-earner couples, they'll be cashing two pension checks each month, two social security checks, and drawing money out of two IRAs and 401(k)s. And a lot of these seniors won't fully retire in their sixties, or possibly ever, preferring—for financial or self-fulfillment reasons—to move continuously from one kind of career to another or from full-time to part-time employment.

They will make up a consumer market of awesome size and wealth, with needs in health care, financial services, law, travel, housing and a variety of specialized products to make life more comfortable. Aging boomers are also more likely to have expenses that their parents didn't. Some boomers who married particularly late will be paying off their kids' college loans and their parents' nursing-home bills at the same time.

Ultimately, the boomers will be assisted in handling this burden by receiving inheritances at their parents' deaths. Today's seniors became homeowners in the 1950s, and they have enormous equity in those homes, plus significant financial assets—in all, more than a third of America's total personal net worth. To maintain a comfortable lifestyle, some seniors are liquidating assets by selling their homes and moving to apartments or life-care communities, or by drawing down the equity in their homes with reverse mortgages. Nursing-home and hospital care will consume a big chunk of the seniors' financial resources in the last years of life. But even with these drains on the net worth of seniors, their children will be the recipients of the biggest intergenerational transfer of wealth in history. And 20 to 30 years from now, the boomers' children will begin receiving the same windfall from them.

## The Baby-Boom Echo

This large age cohort, mostly now in adolescence, has swelled public school enrollments and created an especially fertile market for upscale kids' clothing, games, entertainment, sports equipment, summer camps and private education. Why? Because, on average, these children were born to dual-income couples relatively late in life, have few or no siblings, and often get financial support from living grandparents.

Keep an eye on these kids as they move through their life stages. They will swell the ranks of the 18- to 24-year-olds over the coming decade; by 2010, there will be five million more Americans in this age bracket. They will be the most-educated young Americans in history—in length of schooling, if not necessarily in quality of education—and they will be coming of age in tight job markets that are hungry for labor. As a result, their young-adult earnings will be very strong (if their education and training warrant), making them avid consumers of the sorts of things people their age buy—cars, home electronics, clothing, travel and, later on, a starter home. But later in life, like the Gen-Xers, many of them will find that their path into leadership jobs will sometimes be blocked by aging boomers who won't retire, legally free to work forever and with a strong financial incentive to do so.

## Super Seniors

There is significant growth ahead in the oldest demographic group in America—the over-75 bunch—continuing a trend that has been growing stronger every decade. It's estimated that by 2000 there will be 1.6 million Americans age 90 or older, and 72,000 of them will be centenarians. Most of them will be women, but according to Cynthia Tauber, an expert on aging at the Census Bureau, in another decade or two enough couples will live long enough together that 60th and 75th wedding anniversaries will be as common as today's golden anniversaries.

By 2010 there will be nearly three million more 75-plus citizens, and over the following 20 years, their numbers will almost double, hitting about 32 million in 2030. The oldest of the old—those 85 and up—will double in number by 2025 and increase fivefold by 2050. Even though generational spans will lengthen, due to later marriage and child-rearing, many children will know their great-grandparents very well.

### Retirees will spread out

It's difficult for forecasters to figure out if a higher percentage of future retirees will move away from where they lived as working adults. Due to longer life expectancy and concern about having adequate retirement savings, many people will work longer, reversing the recent trend toward earlier and earlier retirement, so more will stay longer in the communities where they raised their families. But retiree relocation strongly correlates with affluence and education, according to Reynolds Farley of the University of Michigan's Population Studies Center. "While there are always forces that keep people in an area—family, friends, ties—when boomers retire, there probably will be an increase in movement."

Future retirees probably won't make the beeline for Florida or Arizona that past retirees have. They will spread out, particularly as today's popular destinations for retirees become overcrowded and more pricey. Many will look for places where they can practice an energetic lifestyle of hiking, biking or skiing, which accounts for rising retiree interest in non-Sun Belt areas such as Oregon and Colorado.

Among locations that have recently seen gains of more than 2% a year in retirement relocations are North Carolina (from the Atlantic coast across the Piedmont to the mountains), northern Georgia, the Ozarks (Missouri, Oklahoma, Arkansas), Michigan's Upper Peninsula, southwest Utah, Oregon (both coast and "high desert" in the east), and the Puget Sound area of Washington. College communities, ranging from Chapel Hill, N.C., to Ithaca, N.Y., are also seeing a boom in retired alumni coming back to live near their alma maters, where they take courses, go on college-sponsored foreign trips and attend sporting events.

The states that will have the biggest percentage gains in 65-and-over population between now and 2020 are:

| | | | |
|---|---|---|---|
| Nevada | 123% | Utah | 104% |
| Arizona | 113 | Alaska | 104 |
| Colorado | 109 | California | 102 |
| Washington | 105 | Texas | 100 |
| Georgia | 105 | New Mexico | 99 |

Source: National Conference of State Legislatures.

## GENERATION X

As for age segments that will see declining numbers (and therefore customers for age-specific products), the one that stands out most vividly is the 35 to 44 age group. By 2010, there will be nearly six million fewer adults of that age than there are today. This small "birth dearth" subgroup of Generation X will be moving beyond the child-raising, household-building years.

Among today's young adults now in their twenties and early thirties, an unusually high number are "boomerang kids" living with their parents: nearly 60% of 20-to 24-year-olds, and 25% of those in their early thirties. Assuming that their parents aren't charging their grown children rent, it's easy to see why many of these young people have high disposable income, even if they hold jobs that pay modest wages. This makes them an attractive target for marketers of all kinds, including big-ticket items such as cars, computers, entertainment and travel. And they also influence their parents' decisions on less-costly items, such as groceries.

This generation will continue the trend toward later marriage. The average groom is now nearly 27, the average bride, 24½, both all-time highs. By saving money while living at home and marrying later, when they're likely to be earning more, today's and tomorrow's brides and grooms will spend more on weddings, from fancy rings to lavish receptions, and on honeymoons. Later on, they will buy homes, appliances and furniture, too, but remember that the total size of the baby-bust cohort is relatively small compared with the generation that preceded or follows it.

## INTERGENERATIONAL CONFLICT AHEAD

If the politics of Florida and other high-retiree states are any indication, future retirees will not show much magnanimity toward younger generations. Seniors will be resistant to taxes to fund improved public education and other programs for someone else's children. Some intergenerational rifts will be exacerbated by differences in race. Old people, in general, will be white, and younger people, in general, will be members of racial and ethnic minorities. By 2030, three-fourths of all Americans 65 and older will be whites of European descent, and only 10% will be minorities. The predominantly white oldsters may balk at funding programs to improve the education, job training and general well-being of younger Americans who will be very different in cultural background from themselves.

And seniors will back their preferences with political action. Generally, the older, better-educated and richer people are, the more like-ly they are to vote. In the 1996 presidential election, for example, 67% of seniors voted, but only 31% of 18- to 20-year-olds did. Homeowners voted in larger percentages than renters, and 73% of college grads voted, compared with only 49% of high school grads (many of whom were older people with high school educations).

So seniors will be an ever-more-powerful political lobby. And, human nature being what it is, they will use that power to press for pro-grams that benefit themselves. These will include such things as broad-ening health care coverage to include extended nursing-home stays and sophisticated surgical procedures—including organ and joint replacements—that greatly extend and improve life more than they combat disease and disability.

Tomorrow's seniors will not be particularly sympathetic to the financial burden they will impose on younger Americans, despite the fact that 30 years of federal budget deficits created a national debt that eats up in interest alone nearly 15% of each year's tax receipts.

Tension will be augmented by the fact that many seniors won't ever retire and turn over to the next generation top-paying jobs that used to be automatically vacated at a legal retirement age of 65. While the phenomenon of seniors' continuing to work well into their sixties and even seventies will ease the otherwise short supply of labor, it will inhibit the earnings growth of generations coming along behind them.

# Surging Racial Diversity

About 50 years from now, non-Hispanic whites will still be the largest single racial group in America. But they will have just become a racial minority, outnumbered by all nonwhite races combined. Whites not of Hispanic descent make up nearly three-fourths of the population today, but that share will decline to less than two-thirds by 2020 and fall below 50% around 2050. African-Americans won't increase their share much, going from about 12% to about 13% in 2020.

The great growth in both numbers and share will occur in the Latin-American community, which every day adds more new people than any other group—even more than the majority white popula-tion. Hispanics of all races will probably overtake African-Americans as the largest minority group within the next five to seven years, with 12% to 13% of the population, and that share will increase to 19% by 2030. The percentage of Asian-Americans will nearly double, although it will remain a relatively small group.

These dramatic shifts are due entirely to the higher level of immigration (half of it Hispanic) that took off in the 1980s and has continued strong. In addition, foreign-born Hispanic women have, on average, one more child in their lifetimes than women born in the U.S.

## MAJORITY-MINORITY STATES

While it will be five decades before America as a whole has a majority of racial and ethnic minorities, the same is not true of individual states and cities. Hawaii and New Mexico already have majority nonwhite populations, due to large native populations rather than immigration. Immigration and high nonwhite birth rates will give both California and Texas nonwhite majorities in a few years, and they may be joined shortly thereafter by New Jersey, Maryland and Nevada.

California will add about nine million Hispanics and six million Asians by 2020. Texas will add more than five million Hispanics and nearly a million Asians. Florida will add more than two million Hispanics, and Illinois, one million. At the other end of the scale, Vermont, South Dakota and North Dakota will add fewer than 20,000 Asians and Hispanics.

## WAVE UPON WAVE OF IMMIGRANTS

This change in the racial mix is the result, quite simply, of the enormous Hispanic and Asian immigration of the last 25 years. It is already the second-largest wave of immigration, exceeded in total numbers only by the Eastern European exodus that spanned the decades around the turn of this century.

By 1910, the foreign-born percentage of the U.S. population hit a peak of about 15%—more than one out of every seven Americans—and nativist sentiment surged. Immigration policies were tightened to give preference to Canadians, western Europeans and, in general, white people with good education and job skills.

That's the way things stayed for the next four decades or so, and immigrants made up a steadily declining share of the population, bottoming out around 1970 at less than 5%. In 1960, a list of the top ten nations of origin for America's largest foreign-born groups included eight European nations, two nations of the Americas (Canada, in second place, and Mexico, fifth), and no nations of Asia or in Central or South America.

In 1965 Congress made a change in immigration policy that, unforeseen by most policymakers at the time, would forever change the face of America. They made it easier for the immediate family of earlier immigrants to join them. This stimulated immigration from the poorest nations closest to our borders, as well as from other poor nations. Immigration was boosted by a strong U.S. economy pulling in Mexican workers, the communist takeover of Southeast Asia, civil war in El Salvador and other Central American countries, liberalized emigration from the Soviet Union and Cuba, and violence and grinding poverty in Haiti.

So for the past quarter-century, immigrants (both legal and illegal) have surged into America in numbers not seen since the turn of the century, regularly topping one million a year since the early 1980s. America's percentage of foreign-borns has risen to 10%, more than double its 1970 low.

And the new wave of immigration is every bit as controversial as the earlier waves of Irish, Chinese, Italians, Slavs and Russians. But this time, the resentment might be even more intense, because the vast majority of the new arrivals not only speak a different language but are of different races, too.

Today's list of nations that have sent the most immigrants now living in the U.S. is quite different from that of 1960. Germany is the only European nation still on the list, due to the many immigrants (now rather elderly) who came before or after World War II. Canada is still on, but it has fallen to eighth place. The other nations are all Latin American or Asian, most of them in the less-developed world. In first place, sending nearly seven million immigrants, is Mexico. The numbers trail off sharply after Mexico, with a million immigrants from the Philippines, and less than a million each from China, Cuba, India, Vietnam, El Salvador, Canada, Korea and Germany.

### The challenge of assimilation

The problems associated with heavy immigration are well known. Many immigrants are poor and ill-educated, and most don't speak English. Although the vast majority find work very quickly, a higher percentage are unemployed at any one time than native-born Americans, and a higher percentage need public assistance, straining social-service budgets at every level of government. The new arrivals are often willing to work long hours for low pay, so they can drive down local wages in low-skill occupations and take jobs from other less-educated Americans.

Immigrants aren't evenly spread around America; they tend to gather in urban areas where others of their nationality have settled. As they spread into neighborhoods that were once working-class white or black, tense rivalries arise for control of local government and public schools. In their neighborhoods, the immigrants' native languages and traditions take over, giving the impression that they are uninterested in learning English or joining the mainstream culture.

All of this suggests an American nation splitting into islands of racial and ethnic self-interest, without common ground and common aspirations. Concern about the prevalence of Spanish has led more than 20 states to pass laws requiring that English be their official language, the only one to be used in all local government and educational affairs. Congress, however, hasn't reached agreement on a similar national law, and we don't expect it to.

But in all of these respects, the immigrant experience today is not significantly different from that of earlier decades. Native-born Americans concerned about slow assimilation of Hispanic or Asian immigrants should remember that there are still ethnic enclaves in Detroit, Chicago and Boston where very elderly immigrants and their middle-aged children speak their native tongues among themselves, in stores and churches and social halls, and read foreign-language newspapers. But their grandchildren have become fully assimilated into American life, as today's Hispanic and Southeast Asian children will, too, and probably faster than earlier generations of immigrants.

The assimilation of Hispanic immigrant children, which has been hampered by bilingual education in many communities, will get a boost from the rapid demise of this ill-conceived social experiment in the years ahead. It was significant that the California movement that resulted in the banning of bilingual ed in 1998 gathered momentum after Mexican immigrant parents, frustrated by the slow progress of their children in school, pulled 90 kids out of a Los Angeles elementary school. "Home is for speaking Spanish, sure, but school is for learning English, and so we did the boycott," one of the parents, garment worker Juana Jacoba, told *The Washington Post*. That school now teaches English as a second language (ESL) with a total-immersion approach.

### *Why immigration is good for America*

The benefits of immigration are enormous, but they're usually short-changed in the public debate. America needs the immigrants' labor, and even more, it needs their (and their children's) *future* earnings. An America without high immigration would be aging as fast as Japan and the European nations, and it would be difficult for a relatively smaller future labor force to support the growing mass of elderly Americans in retirement 25 years from now.

Immigrants are essential to achieving even the modest sub-1% annual population growth that is crucial to America's future success.

Without a high level of immigration, the economies of California, Texas, New York City and many other locales would have stagnated years ago. And if the immigrants all left tomorrow, those economies would grind to a halt.

Immigrants provide valuable labor at both the low and high end of the skill spectrum. They fill the low-paid drudgery jobs—picking vegetables, washing cars, clearing tables and washing dishes in restaurants, mowing lawns, cleaning office buildings and hospitals late at night, digging ditches—that native-born Americans are often unwilling to do.

On the high end of the skill scale, immigrants play a vital role in health care and high-tech fields such as computer science, telecommunications and genetic engineering. Without highly educated immigrants, hospitals and clinics would not have enough doctors, nurses and medical technicians. Without Asian-born scientists and engineers (and soon, their American-born children), many software and hardware companies would have to close their doors—or, more ominously, move their research operations to Asia. Why? Because the youths of comfortable, middle-class American-born families—whether white, African-American or Hispanic—are not studying science and math in sufficient numbers and with sufficient seriousness to staff America's high-growth technical industries.

Fortunately for America, a large percentage of the foreign students studying science and engineering at U.S. colleges stay in our country and become citizens. But there is a trend developing that could be troubling for the U.S.: Increasing numbers of these U.S.-trained scientists and engineers are going back to their home countries because of improving job opportunities in high technology.

### *Making their way in America*

While immigrants rank lower than native-born Americans in many indices of social and economic success, the differences are not as great as one might expect, considering the recentness of their arrival and the enormous barriers to rapid acclimation.

Nearly two-thirds of all foreign-born Americans have high school diplomas (from their home country or U.S. high schools). That's substantially lower than the 84% rate for U.S.-born citizens, but not a bad start for getting a toehold in their new country. On the high end of the education level, some 12% of foreign-born Americans have postgraduate college degrees, a rate 50% higher than for U.S.-born Americans.

Public-opinion surveys often show that native-born Americans believe that most immigrants, especially Hispanics, are on welfare. In fact, while their public-assistance rate is twice that of U.S.-born Americans, it is a surprisingly low 6%. Since the most recently arrived immigrants have a poverty rate estimated at more than 30%, it appears that immigrants as a whole take less advantage of public assistance programs than other poor Americans—either because of embarrassment, the support they get from extended families or fear of detection as illegal aliens.

The typical household earnings of immigrant groups vary greatly with their socioeconomic and educational level in their country of origin, their previous knowledge of English, the emphasis they place on education, and the number of earners in the household, which is often an extended family with numerous adults. For those who arrived here between 1987 and 1990, Japanese families earn on average about $51,400; Indians, $26,100; Koreans, $17,300; Salvadorans, $16,000; Chinese, $15,600; Mexicans, $15,000; and Cambodians, $11,800. But after immigrants have lived here awhile, their incomes rise strongly, as evidenced by the fact that immigrants who arrived before 1980 have earnings roughly equal to U.S.-born residents of similar education.

Immigrants as a group have always been highly entrepreneurial, perhaps because self-employment avoids the barriers to advancement often found in working for American-born bosses. Immigrants run far more than the mom-and-pop grocery store, painting crew, lawn service, dry cleaner and taxi company. They are starting businesses in financial services, real estate, publishing, and high-tech businesses of all sorts. And with stronger savings rates than other Americans, immigrants are buying and renovating homes in record numbers. Their small businesses and homeownership are revitalizing once-blighted inner-city neighborhoods from Brooklyn to L.A.

For all the economic benefit that immigration provides, the greatest value may be intangible: a rejuvenation of the American spirit. In our 1989 book *America in the Global '90s*, we said that "the new immigrants will provide vigor and an appreciation of our freedoms. They will help us rekindle the American spirit of self-reliance, commitment to family, hard work and high educational standards for our children." Nearly a decade and some ten million new immigrants later, we still believe this to be true.

### *Barriers to immigrants*

Nonetheless, immigration will continue to be a very contentious issue, and there will be periodic attempts, occasionally successful, to reduce total numbers, give preference to immigrants with higher education and job skills, and cut the social-service benefits to which new arrivals are entitled before they attain full citizenship (as Congress did in the welfare reform bill of 1997). Employers will be subject to tougher sanctions against hiring illegal aliens, including increasing the number of official IDs that aliens must show to get hired. There will also be occasional bursts of activity to better secure the U.S. boundary with Mexico, despite the fact that it is a sieve-like border, virtually uncontrollable.

Immigrant groups and high-tech businesses that hire skilled foreigners will lobby for higher quotas on legal immigration. They'll be opposed by labor unions, some African-American interests and many regular citizens concerned about the racial fragmentation of America. But the huge backlog of people who have already been accepted for admission and are awaiting visas—now 3.5 million—will ensure immigration exceeding a million new arrivals each year (legal and illegal) for several years to come.

### GROWING EMIGRATION, TOO

America experiences a high level of emigration, too. Each year, some 250,000 to 300,000 people leave, sometimes for a few years, often for good. Most emigres are immigrants returning to their native countries for a variety of reasons—homesickness, an inability to make their way financially in the U.S., or fulfillment of an original plan to return after saving enough money to live well in a less-expensive land.

A trend that bears careful watching is the growing departure of highly educated young immigrants—and children of immigrant parents—who can earn a good living in the booming high-tech sectors of their home countries. The pay is much less than in the U.S., but so is the cost of living. In addition, they get the benefit of culturally familiar surroundings and excellent opportunities for advancement.

An increasing number of emigres are U.S. natives deciding for a variety of reasons to pull up stakes and live overseas. Many are retirees who can live extremely well in low-cost foreign societies on a combination of pensions, social security and private savings. Each month some 370,000 U.S. social security checks are mailed to retirees living overseas.

# The Major Racial and Ethnic Groups

There will continue to be significant differences among America's racial and ethnic groups in their average education and income levels, but all will achieve great progress in the years ahead.

Since there is no evidence of any differences among racial groups in basic aptitudes of any kind—whether intellectual, athletic or artistic—

differences in achievement will relate to cultural and historical experiences. These factors include how long a given group has been in America, the strength of the family structure, the economic and educational level the immigrants had when they arrived, the degree of discrimination they faced in America, the quality of the schools where they settled, and the emphasis put on education and entrepreneurship in their native cultures and families.

## HIGH-ACHIEVING ASIAN-AMERICANS

The highest-achieving racial and ethnic group will continue to be Asian-Americans, including both immigrant families and those who have been in the U.S. for several generations.

They will keep setting a sizzling pace for others to match. In the Virginia suburbs of Washington, D.C., for example, Vietnamese immigrant youths, most of whom spoke no English on arriving in the U.S., are greatly overrepresented as valedictorians, salutatorians and other honorees at high school commencements.

Some 42% of Asian-Americans (all of them, not just immigrants) have college degrees, compared with 25% of whites, 13% of blacks and 10% of Hispanics. Even though their enrollment numbers are artificially restrained by racial preferences designed to benefit other races, Asians account for disproportionately high percentages of the student bodies at America's finest colleges—for example, 29% of freshman at MIT in 1997, 26% at the University of Chicago, 25% at Stanford, 20% at Harvard and 19% at Cornell. (There are much higher percentages in the state system of California, such as 60% of the freshman at the University of California at Irvine.)

And Asian-American kids are pushed by their families to study the hardest subjects—science, engineering and medicine—which prepare them well for the highest-paying professions. That's one reason (another being multiple breadwinners in the household) that Asian-Americans have the highest median household income at $43,300, well above whites of European descent at $38,800, Latin Americans at $24,900 and blacks at $23,500.

For all of their economic success, Asian-Americans have been a quiet minority. They tend to assimilate into the majority culture, without being very active in political affairs or pressing for any special governmental favors. There is some indication of greater political activism among Asian-Americans in California as their numbers rise, but we don't foresee their playing a significant role in public affairs in the future, except through their growing power in the corporate world of high technology. They will continue to focus on achieving success through individual performance rather than group action.

## HISPANIC-AMERICANS BECOME MORE VISIBLE

In the decades ahead Latin Americans will grow in power and cultural influence—commercially, politically and as a social force.

Hispanics account for nearly 11% of the U.S. population, just a percentage point and a half less than the share of African-Americans and *three times* the percentage of Asians. But Hispanics are greatly underrepresented—almost to the point of invisibility—in virtually every high-impact, high-status area of American life. It's largely a matter of their relatively recent arrival in large numbers and their lower socioeconomic status upon arrival.

Their participation in the political process as voters has also been hampered by the fact that many immigrants have not achieved citizenship and therefore the right to vote. In California, for example, Hispanics make up about 28% of the population but only 10% of the electorate, due to the large percentage of immigrant children and the alien status of many parents.

Because they are united by a common language, and perhaps because they feel shut out of job opportunities in mainstream media, Hispanics have developed successful national media to showcase their own popular culture. There are two highly successful cable television networks, Telemundo and Univision, the latter being the fifth-most-watched network in the U.S. The audience for Spanish-language TV is growing at a rate estimated at four times that of English-language television. It airs soccer matches, salsa entertainment, news of Latin America and the immensely popular "telenovelas," soap operas produced largely in Mexico and viewed by millions all over the world (even, with translation, in Russia). In Miami, a talk-show host who goes simply by the name Christina has a magnetism and immense following that has earned her the nickname "the Latina Oprah."

Hispanic Americans will not be content to remain a silent, invisible minority, as they draw even with and then move past African-Americans as the biggest racial minority in the next five years or so. Their political power will rise first in those regions, such as South Florida and parts of California and Texas, where they are already the most-populous minority. More Hispanics will be elected to local and state offices and to Congress, as a continuing southwestern population shift takes House seats away from the northern states and assigns them to the Sun Belt. In California, 14 out of 80 seats in the state assembly are now held by Hispanics, up from a mere four seats a few years ago, and a Mexican-American, Antonio Villaraigosa, was elected speaker of the House.

Hispanics will continue to vote as moderate-to-liberal Democrats. As they grow in power, they will be a force supporting high government spending for social-service programs, especially for children in low-income families and for recently arrived immigrants who are not yet citizens. But as a larger middle class and entrepreneurial core develops, we will see the same divergence of political views that developed in other immigrant groups, with the high-achieving members veering toward the small-government, lower-tax position of the Republican party.

## AFRICAN-AMERICANS COMING ON STRONG

African-Americans compose only 12% of the U.S. population and are facing just a small increase in their share—about one percentage point—over the next 30 years.

They are a predominantly urban people, and now their upwardly mobile families, like all middle-class groups before them, are fanning out into the suburbs around large cities in search of nicer homes for a reasonable price, safe neighborhoods and better schools. For example, blacks (mostly middle- and upper-middle-class families) are a majority in the Washington, D.C., suburbs of Prince George's County, Md., the home of the University of Maryland and several federal research and security agencies.

African-Americans are achieving impressive gains in education, job advancement, earnings and entrepreneurship. Their entrepreneurs are building successful businesses in virtually every field, including computer systems, fast-food franchises, investment management, auto dealerships, publishing, broadcasting and many others.

When the average earnings of African-Americans and whites of similar age, education and job experience are compared, income gaps attributable to race alone virtually disappear. In short, the progress of black Americans has been remarkable, given that, until 35 years ago, they were effectively excluded from normal participation in American life and even today experience significant discrimination.

### Social ills to be addressed

Despite the impressive progress made by most African-Americans, this race will continue to be plagued by socioeconomic problems that are impeding the broader enjoyment of these gains.

There is a single, troubling reason why the median household income of black Americans, as a group, lags behind that of all other major racial and ethnic groups, even Latin-Americans, a group heavy with recent immigrants who hardly speak English.

That reason is childbearing outside of marriage, especially by teens who are still children themselves. The rate of out-of-wedlock black births—about 70% of all African-American babies—is both a cause and effect of family disintegration, welfare dependency, crime, drug use and other woes of the black urban "underclass."

Since many of these young mothers and their children are counted as independent households in census data, their lack of earnings greatly depresses the median household income data for all black Americans. By contrast, the average household income of intact black families, with mothers and fathers both earning money and raising their children together, is surprisingly close to the national average for all families.

### Signs of improvement

There are some hopeful signs on the horizon—for example, the recent slight decline in childbirth outside of marriage, a figure that had risen relentlessly (among whites and Hispanics as well as blacks) for several decades. The message is slowly getting through to teenage girls that having babies they cannot support will likely consign them and their offspring to unhappy, uncomfortable lives. Another factor in a possible future decline in unwed motherhood will be welfare reform, including the demise of a once-common provision that support payments would automatically increase with each additional child born to a mother already on welfare.

Finally, a new generation of African-American leadership is talking more about individual initiative and self-reliance, and less about governmental support, than ever before.

# Where Americans Will Live

For business managers, owners and investors, figuring out where people will be living in the future—and in what numbers—is almost as important as figuring out changing characteristics of age, race and income.

## HIGH GROWTH IN THE SUN BELT

Americans will continue to migrate to areas experiencing strong economic growth and job expansion, and most of these high-growth areas will be in the South and West. For decades, the northern states fared badly in the economic-development derby, losing the factories, expansion facilities and even headquarters of their major employers to aggressive recruiters in the Sun Belt. This is still going on and will continue for years, as long as significant differentials in business operating costs remain between the North and South.

## THE NORTH MAKES A COMEBACK

But the Frost Belt is now fighting back with a vengeance. The cost gap is narrowing, due to both the rising costs (of land, wages and taxes) associated with booming economies in the Sun Belt and to the northern states' great success in improving their own business climates by lowering corporate taxation and worker's-compensation costs, streamlining permit and approval processes, improving public schools, and other programs.

The North's strength has always been manufacturing, and so the industrial states of the north central region have contributed to, and benefited from, the resurgence of manufacturing might in America over the past 15 years. The North is now winning its share of the economic-development battles, finding ways to keep big employers from leaving, and inducing them—and newcomers—to create new facilities and jobs in their states. And the South is discovering that low operating costs and fat incentive packages won't always be enough to lure the best employers; these firms also want to see a community's commitment to strong social services, including high-quality public schools.

## RELENTLESS SUBURBANIZATION

Americans have long tended to congregate in metropolitan areas, and this trend is going to continue in the decades ahead. The smaller metropolitan areas will experience the most rapid rate of growth, while the biggest metro areas will show the greatest gains in absolute numbers of people.

So when you think of expansion and marketing possibilities for your businesses, don't focus just on the biggest urban areas—say, the top 50 or even 100 metro areas. Defining a metro area as a city of at least 50,000 people plus surrounding suburbs, the federal government counts more than 300 such places. They account for only 17% of America's land area, but they are home to 80% of the population and generate an estimated 83% of America's annual economic output. Not surprisingly, their economies also create the most new jobs—80% of total U.S. job growth between 1992 and 1997—and therefore the greatest population growth as well.

## SMALLER CITIES COME ON STRONG

One of the most remarkable, but still little-appreciated, trends of the past decade is the economic revival of America's smaller cities—in all regions of the country. This trend—which will accelerate for years to come—is being driven by many forces, including telecommunications technology, supply and demand for labor, and lifestyle considerations such as crowding in cities and worries about crime and declining school quality.

In the final analysis, it is technology that's behind this small-city comeback, just as it was technology that led to the original decline of small-town economies. Early in this century, soaring agricultural productivity reduced the number of workers needed for the production of food, and the surplus labor flowed into the cities, where jobs were plentiful in heavy industry.

Now this population loss is flattening out, and many small towns are growing again, albeit at modest rates. In states like Alabama and Mississippi, African-American young adults with good educations are returning to the towns of their childhoods, after going away to college and working for a few years in a city in the North. They've come back to a "New South" with improved race relations, small-town friendliness, solid economic growth and better opportunities for black community leadership than many big cities offer.

The small-city turnaround is most evident in the agricultural Great Plains states, which suffered an almost-continuous population stagnation or drain for decades. The growth isn't dramatic, but the stemming of the loss is certainly notable. In Kansas, for example, the state's 79 rural counties grew a minuscule 0.3% during the 1990s—a heartening turnaround only in contrast to the population decline of 7% that these same counties suffered in the 1980s. In Nebraska, all 52 rural counties lost population in the '80s, and two-thirds of them continued to decline in the '90s. But the other one-third have gained population in this decade, by an average rate of 3%, according to the Center for the New West, a Denver research group.

### Manufacturing comes to small towns

The biggest factor in this population growth is the increase in non-farm job opportunities, especially in light manufacturing, including food processing, and assembly work, ranging from simple consumer goods to high-tech products like computers. Manufacturers like the low operating costs—wages, land and utilities—and the diligent, trainable work force they find in rural America.

So small-town America is a full participant in the rebirth of American manufacturing in the '80s and '90s. According to the U.S. Bureau of Labor Statistics, South Dakota has led all states in its percentage increase in factory jobs over the last decade, at 74%. North Dakota is third at 47% and Nebraska seventh with 31%. Nowhere is this trend more evident than on the outskirts of booming North Sioux City, S.D., where the quonset hut-style assembly and shipping plants of the Gateway personal-computer company sprawl across a rural landscape of dairy and corn farms.

### Some businesses can locate anywhere

One of the dominant world trends of the coming century—the broad dispersal of business to distant corners of the globe—will be at work in the U.S., too.

Today, with instant communications, colleagues at sites in several states can work together, designing projects, sharing their concepts and executing production with ease. Dispersing facilities allows an employer to take advantage of labor surpluses in other regions, lower costs, and the greater security that multiple sites offer (from bad weather, power outages, production bottlenecks, etc.) More and more, you find a spatial separation of corporate headquarters and back-office operations, with financial-service firms centered in New York City or Chicago but doing their data processing and statement preparation in Florida, South Dakota or Nebraska.

This dispersal of business has been a boon to small-town America, and the success stories are legion. Cypress Semiconductor, for example, designs computer chips in Starkville, Miss., at a small research center next to Mississippi State University. Cypress found that it can hire recent graduates in electrical engineering (many of them immigrants from Asia) for less money than at its headquarters in San Jose, Cal., where engineers are constantly being hired away in the high-turnover labor force of the Silicon Valley. In Fargo, N.D., Great Plains Software works closely with local colleges in developing computer courses and training many students whom it later hires. EnvisoNet, another software company, finds good help in Augusta, Me. Fitch Investor Services, a New York City-based company, opened a facility in Powell, Wyo., where it hired 40 young people savvy in both finance and computers; they like living and working near the Rocky Mountains and Yellowstone Park.

More than any one kind of business, teleservices—customer service and sales over toll-free numbers—has brought great vitality to small cities (and some large ones, too) throughout the West. The operators—

efficient, friendly folks with the unaccented English that their clients desire—make reservations for hotels and rental cars, take orders for catalog merchandise, validate new credit cards, handle changes of address on magazine subscriptions, straighten out billing errors, and do anything else that a human being can do over the phone. There are enormous colonies of teleservice firms in large cities like Denver, Omaha, Oklahoma City and Des Moines, and smaller ones all over the West.

### Labor shortages in small towns

Economic development involves an intricate interplay between the supply and demand for labor, and the small-city revival could be threatened, in the near future, by growing labor shortages.

The surplus rural labor that attracted manufacturing and services firms to smaller communities in the first place is now ancient history, and many of the recent college grads from less-urban states still gravitate toward the big cities—as much for the exciting lifestyle as the job opportunities. Meanwhile, the unemployed of large cities are largely African-Americans and Hispanics who are leery of moving to small communities in the West where they fear they would feel culturally out of place. So the region with the lowest unemployment rate—the Midwest, led by Nebraska, the Dakotas and Iowa—will find strong economic growth harder to come by unless it can increase its labor supply by attracting stronger migration from other states.

## MOBILE AMERICANS

One factor that will help these smaller metro areas continue to maintain adequate labor supplies is the willingness of Americans to move to greener pastures. Most relocations are driven by job opportunities, so the dispersal of business away from large cities to smaller communities, mostly in America's heartland, will encourage more big-city dwellers to move there as well.

There is also mounting evidence that middle-class, native-born Americans, both white and African-American, are leaving large cities such as New York, Chicago, Los Angeles and Miami in roughly the same numbers that new immigrants, mostly Hispanics, are moving in. Most of those leaving are moving to suburbs of the same cities, as upwardly mobile people have always done.

But an increasing number are moving out of the state and even the region. Many of "the Ozzie and Harriets of the 1990s are skipping the suburbs of the big cities and moving to more homogeneous, mostly white smaller towns and smaller cities and rural areas," William Frey, a University of Michigan demographer, said in an interview with *The Washington Post*. This trend is fueling both the small-town revival and the rapid growth of large metro areas such as Las Vegas, Orlando, Salt Lake City, Seattle and Portland, Ore.

*Migration among states*

When the Census Bureau tracks migration, it calculates a "net migration" figure for each state, the difference between the number of people moving in and the number moving out. The top gainers are typically Sun Belt states, and the biggest losers are northern states. In 1997, the top gainers from domestic migration were Florida (141,000), Georgia (82,000), Arizona (68,000), North Carolina (67,000) and Nevada (56,000). The states that lost the most residents were New York (223,000), California (143,000), Illinois (69,000), Pennsylvania (51,000) and New Jersey (40,000).

For decades, California was a magnet for migrating Americans, and it probably will be again. But this longtime trend was reversed for several years in the early to mid '90s, the result of a severe recession in aerospace and defense work, soaring prices (and then a bust) in residential real estate, growing concern over urban dilemmas (rapid immigration, crime and declining school quality), and, finally, very strong job growth in neighboring states. The California economy bounced back strongly in 1997, and out-migration slowed to about half the 1996 level. Meanwhile, due to both high immigration and natural increase, California's population continues to grow robustly—by 410,000 in 1997, the same year that it was second-highest in the net loss of residents.

But other factors will restrain the traditional wanderlust of Americans. One of the most important will be the continued growth of two-career families. With both a husband and wife pursuing careers, it is more difficult for either to accept a job-advancement opportunity in a distant locale without making sure the working spouse can find comparably satisfying and remunerative work in the same place.

## STATE-BY-STATE OUTLOOK

Over the next 20-plus years, the more than 50 million people who will be added to the U.S. population will not be evenly distributed around America. As a matter of fact, about 70% of the growth will occur in only eight states with expected population gains of two million or more people: California, Texas, Florida, Georgia, Arizona, Washington, North Carolina and Colorado. Add in just another eight states that will grow by one to two million each—Virginia, Tennessee, Utah, South

Carolina, Oregon, Nevada, Minnesota and Maryland—and you've accounted for 90% of America's likely population growth between now and 2020. The biggest gainers will be those states that are both large in land area and already the most populous. California is estimated to gain more than ten million new residents, Texas and Florida more than seven million each.

But there will be no population losers. The smallest gainers— such as Delaware, Connecticut, Rhode Island, North and South Dakota, Vermont, Wyoming, Montana, Iowa and Nebraska—will generally add between 100,000 and 200,000 new residents each over the next two decades.

### Rate of growth versus actual growth

In looking at where population growth will occur, business planners must distinguish between *rates* of growth and growth in the *absolute numbers* of people. If you focus on rate of growth only, you might rush into a fast-growing area only to find that the total number of prospective customers (and workers to staff your business) is still rather small. And competition for these customers (and workers) will be fierce among many businesses that rushed in, as you did, in hopes of growing with the community. An extreme example of the difference between growth rate and actual growth is Alaska, which, while probably ranking second among the 50 states in growth rate (58%), will add only about 357,000 residents over the next 20 years.

So don't turn your back on large, slower-growing states and metro areas, where the absolute growth level—numbers of new residents—will exceed that of many small, high-growth areas. For example, the slower-growing industrial states of Michigan (one million growth, 11% growth rate by 2020) and Ohio (834,000, 7%) will probably add substantially more residents than such "faster-growing" Sun Belt or western states as Alabama, Kentucky, Louisiana and Oklahoma. Some of the best states for business expansion will be those that combine a strong growth rate with high absolute population gains, such as these million-plus gainers: Minnesota, Maryland, Michigan, Wisconsin and Oregon.

## HOT METRO AREAS

The same consideration about disparities between rates and sheer numbers in state population growth applies to metro areas. The list of metro areas that will add the most people over the next 20 years is dominated by urban areas that are already among the top 20.

Here, from the projections of NPA Data Services in Washington,

D.C., is a list of the 12 metro areas that will likely experience the strongest population growth between now and 2020:

| Atlanta | 1,748,040 | Dallas | 1,198,070 |
|---|---|---|---|
| Phoenix | 1,638,680 | Washington, D.C. | 1,147,620 |
| Houston | 1,617,840 | Tampa/St. Petersburg/ | |
| Riverside/ | | Clearwater | 1,139,980 |
| San Bernadino | 1,495,670 | Denver | 890,380 |
| San Diego | 1,327,780 | Orlando | 883,630 |
| Los Angeles/ | | Seattle/Bellevue/ | |
| Long Beach | 1,283,400 | Everett | 883,330 |

Not surprisingly, a list of the major metro areas expected to add the most new jobs is very similar. The top 15 such cities include, besides the 12 above, Minneapolis-St.Paul, Chicago and Boston.

But the list of metro areas that will experience the highest rate of growth tends to be a collection of smaller metro areas:

| Provo, Utah | 59% | McAllen/Edinburg/Mission, TX | 53% |
|---|---|---|---|
| Orlando | 58 | West Palm Beach/Boca Raton, FL | 52 |
| Las Vegas | 58 | Ft. Myers/Cape Coral, FL | 51 |
| Daytona Beach, FL | 56 | Sacramento | 50 |
| Austin/San Marcos, TX | 56 | Tucson | 49 |
| Phoenix/Mesa | 56 | Sarasota/Bradenton, FL | 49 |

## POLITICAL IMPACT OF REGIONAL GROWTH

Since the House of Representatives is frozen at 435 seats, congressional districts keep getting bigger and bigger in population, and by law, they should all have roughly the same number of residents, today about 620,000 per district. Even if a state is holding its population level, it will lose House seats—and therefore political clout in Congress—to other states that are growing faster.

The next national census will determine which states will lose or gain House seats, and then the losers will engage in the every-decade legislative brawl to redraw the lines of their districts to determine which incumbents will have to run against each other. It's likely that New York and Pennsylvania will each lose two seats, and there may be one-seat losses in Ohio, Michigan, Connecticut, Illinois, Mississippi, Oklahoma, Wisconsin and Indiana. These dozen or so seats will likely be picked up by Texas, Georgia and Arizona (two seats each), with one-seat gains by Florida, Nevada, Colorado, California, and maybe Utah and Montana.

## THE GROWTH WILD CARD: ANTI-GROWTH SENTIMENT

When the Census Bureau and research groups like the National Planning Association project population gains, they start with such data as current population, death rates, the number and age of women of childbearing age in the area, and the area's recent experience with in-migration both from overseas and from other states. Then they try to crank into the formula some assumptions about economic growth, job gains and the state's business climate.

What forecasters can't predict is how current and future residents of a given high-growth area will react, psychologically and then politically, to the enormous population gains that lie ahead. Thus, the wild card in all population forecasting is public opinion, especially the rising tide of anti-growth sentiment in many high-growth areas. This spirit is often strong among the most-recent arrivals, who fail to see the irony in their attitude that other people—would-be newcomers like themselves—shouldn't be allowed the same opportunity to find a new job, home and life in their community. This sentiment is called, appropriately, "Last one in, lock the gate," and it is found in regions ranging from New England to Washington, D.C., from Colorado to the Pacific Northwest.

Even the modest level of population growth forecasted for America as a whole—less than 1% a year on average—will be controversial, because it will be concentrated in the suburbs of existing metropolitan areas. Already, many residents believe their quality of life is being degraded by overcrowded schools, jammed roads during rush hour and lengthening commutes.

While the growing popularity of small, "livable" cities and towns is taking a little pressure off urban growth, the outward growth of the big metro areas will continue largely unabated. Ironically, in many metro areas, the same "no-growth" proponents who oppose the gobbling up of rural land by low-density development also oppose the natural antidote to suburban sprawl—high-density "in-fill" projects in cities and older, close-in suburbs where people can use existing infrastructure, such as mass transit, to live, work and shop in compact neighborhoods.

In the years to come, the anti-growth forces will gain strength in many metro areas, from Florida and Washington, D.C., to San Francisco and Portland. Environmentalists and Zero Population Growthers will join with less-focused but equally committed growth opponents who simply want to continue using low-density, large-lot zoning to block compact, high-density, multi-family housing—zoning that very effectively excludes less-affluent newcomers from their communities.

## THERE'S STILL PLENTY OF ROOM

But the truth is, America has plenty of room to accommodate future population growth. The next time you travel by plane, look at the vast expanses of habitable but lightly inhabited America, whether it's the wooded Appalachians, the farmland of the Midwest and Great Plains, or the still lightly populated Pacific states. Even America's most densely populated state—New Jersey, with more than 1,000 people per square mile—still has large amounts of room to grow: farmland along the southern end of the New Jersey Turnpike, the horse country west of Newark's suburbs, foothills of the Kittatinny Mountains on the Delaware River, and the edges of the scenic Pine Barrens of South Jersey.

If America's most densely settled state has so much room to grow, the U.S. will have no trouble accommodating another 50 or 60 million people over the next 25 years—provided that they don't all want to live within a few miles of the Atlantic or Pacific Ocean.

The distribution of population isn't simply a matter of putting people where there is cheap land and room to spread out. People choose where they live mostly on the basis of where they can support themselves and their families, so the distribution of economic growth and job opportunities is more important than space. Since large regional and metro economies spawn ancillary enterprises of all kinds, that's where the additional population growth tends to be concentrated. This heightens existing concerns about crowding and fuels the fires of the anti-growth movement.

Many of the lowest-density states are sparsely settled for good reasons, and not just because of lack of job opportunities. Some have large expanses of arid and mountainous land that aren't especially hospitable. Some western states have shortages of surface and ground water that already limit residential development and will continue to do so.

But when all is said and done, America has a spaciousness that can be a big plus for its future economic prosperity, if—and this is a big "if"—Americans are willing to use their land in ways that accommodate both growth and good living.

# Households, Marriage and Divorce

Household formations—a figure closely watched by apartment owners, builders and makers of appliances and furniture—will grow more slowly over the next ten years, because of the small age cohort from the '70s birth dearth. But even at this slower pace, there will be 15 million more households by 2010, on top of the

100 million today. After 2010, household formations will soar, as late-marrying Gen Xers are joined by the first wave of marriages among the big baby-boom-echo generation.

American households, on average, will continue to get smaller—falling from 2.6 persons to 2.5 in the next decade. And they will bear less resemblance to the traditional nuclear family of mother, father and children. At present, about 70% of all households consist of some kind of family grouping—that is, people related to each other; the other 30% are singles and groups who aren't related. In ten years, family groupings will have fallen to 68% of all households, and singles and unrelated individuals will be 32%. An increasing number of single-person households will be widows and widowers.

## MARRIAGE AND REMARRIAGE

Despite an increase in the never-married portion of the population, marriage will remain the norm, with the U.S. continuing to have the highest rate of marriage of any industrialized nation. This rate includes serial marriages, not just the first one; America's rate of *re*marriage, after one or more failed matches, is an emblem of Americans' incurable optimism. Most divorced people remarry within a few years, and in a typical year, about half of all marriages are a second try (or more) for one or the other partner.

The average age of first marriage will continue to rise over the years, as both men and women wait to complete their educations, get settled in their careers and sow some wild oats as footloose singles.

## A FALLING DIVORCE RATE

Later marriage correlates with a lower rate of divorce, due (apparently) to the greater maturity, education and financial stability of the couple. So the advancing age of brides and grooms at first marriage should augur well for a continued decline in the divorce rate, from about 50% a few years ago to an estimated 40% for couples married in the '90s. Another factor in a gradually declining divorce rate will be the mounting backlash against easy, non-fault divorce. This will be fueled by mounting evidence that divorce—however amicable and whatever the child-custody arrangement—takes a severe toll on the psychological well-being of children and the financial stability of women.

## MORE NEVER-MARRIEDS

An estimated 90% of today's young women will marry at some point. That may sound high, but it means that the rate of never-married women will be double today's rate of 5% for women in their fifties. The simplest explanation for this is that more and more women, with the benefit of higher education and unprecedented career opportunities, won't have to marry to live a financially secure life, as most women had to do and still do in less-developed nations. And in a society in which premarital sexual relations are common, people don't have to marry to enjoy steady companionship and conjugal relationships.

In addition, as evidenced by the rising rate of births to unmarried women of all ages and socioeconomic levels, a small but increasing number of women are coming to believe that their children don't need a father any more than they themselves need a husband. Taking their independence from men to an extreme, a rising number of single women are having children by artificial insemination, without ever knowing the biological father, either literally or in the biblical sense. It remains to be seen whether this trend will continue in the face of mounting research that suggests that boys and girls without a father in their lives—whatever their mother's education and income level— experience far more trouble in adolescence (academic problems, law-breaking, substance abuse, and so on) than kids raised by a mother and father together.

## MORE INTERRACIAL MARRIAGES

Given the increasing contact between people of different races in college and in the workplace, it's not surprising that interracial mar-riage is growing. While it's only about 3% of all marriages, that's more than ten times the 1960 level and twice the 1990 level. Hard data is sketchy, and these marriages are probably greatly underreported, but all evidence points to a long, strong surge, as young Americans of all races show an unprecedented willingness to judge others more by the content of their character—and affinity of mutual interests—than by the color of their skin or country of origin.

### Less single-race classification

Increasingly, young Americans of mixed racial parentage are resisting being pigeon-holed as one race or another on college and job applications, standardized tests, driver's licenses and census surveys. For the first time, the census of 2000 will allow people to check more than one box under race. An estimated 2% will do so, but vastly more could, given America's long history of racial mixing.

This category will undoubtedly grow by the censuses of 2010 and 2020, especially with the gradual phasing out of racial quotas and affirmative-action programs that require specific racial identity. This will put increasing political strain on the remaining racial preference programs, as more and more racially mixed Americans qualify and only white, non-Hispanic Americans are left out.

# Business Implications

The business implications of all these demographic trends are too numerous to list in any comprehensive way. Every change in American demographics is full of opportunities and pitfalls for business.

If your products or services are aimed at a particular age segment, be mindful of that group's rising or falling population and its share of U.S. population. Ask yourself and your colleagues if your products appeal to people of different races, or if they are easy for older Americans to use. Focus on the gradually shrinking size of the average American household and the rising share of two-career families, with implications for housing size and type, products that are conveniently sized and services that substitute for the householder's own labor at home.

Finally, recognize that the North American and European consumer markets, as big and affluent as they are, account for a very small—and rapidly shrinking—share of the total world population. While most of the world's people are poor and unable to afford consumer goods we take for granted, this situation is rapidly changing. Whatever your line of business, from consumer goods to services such as education, medicine and investments, your best opportunities for strong growth lie far beyond America's borders.

# CHAPTER 10

# Threats to the World Boom Ahead

T he world boom ahead could be slowed or even temporarily derailed by any of several calamitous setbacks of a noneconomic nature—widespread war, devastating epidemics, nuclear or biological terrorism, a paralyzing global computer or telecom breakdown caused by either equipment failures or sabotage. While none of these risks is likely, any is possible. And were such a crisis to occur, economic progress would take a hit, as capital and human talent, time and energy were diverted to conflict, destruction, and repair of damage to lives, property and social institutions.

## Military and Political Concerns

I t would be a mistake to assume that the 21st century, although free of Soviet communism and the expensive military rivalry it sparked with the United States, will be a much safer world not requiring the same vigilance as previous eras. Indeed, it might be a more dangerous place without the stabilizing effect of the American-Soviet stalemate. Threats will be constant and varied, and the United States, as the world's only military superpower, will be involved in deterring, combating, or mopping up after all of them.

The promotion of American commercial interests overseas has been the dominant objective of American foreign policy throughout the '90s, as noncommercial considerations—military security, human rights, environmental concerns—have taken a back seat.

But troubling events in 1998-'99—including the war in Kosovo and evidence of two decades of nuclear weapons espionage by China—

will lead to a reassessment of U.S. foreign-policy priorities. The result will be a gradual, modest ascendance of noncommercial concerns.

## AMERICAN MILITARY ALLIANCES AND PREPAREDNESS

U.S. foreign and military policy will continue to emphasize the protection of Europe. Although NATO was formed to oppose the Soviet Union and the Warsaw Pact, its role of mutual security is still important. Extending membership to former Warsaw Pact members will help those Eastern European nations become secure and stable.

Sharply downsized after the fall of the Soviet empire, the U.S. armed forces will hold steady for several years at just over one million active-duty uniformed personnel and about 900,000 troops in the reserves and National Guard. Defense spending will remain around 3% of economic output, the lowest levels since before World War II. That means more than $300 billion a year early in the next decade.

American military-preparedness strategy will focus on the ability to put forces of modest size—superbly equipped—into small crises and conflicts on very short notice, using aircraft carriers to show force and put high-tech, missile-firing jet fighters into the air. In a restructuring announced by the Army in 1998, each "heavy tank" combat division will have about 13% fewer soldiers overall, equipped with fewer tanks and armored vehicles. But within a division, more troops with be assigned to intelligence and surveillance, and there will be more high-tech artillery and small rockets guided to their targets by satellites and unmanned drone aircraft.

Even more than military preparedness, the United States will emphasize innovative intelligence to identify and combat entirely new kinds of security threats, including biological sabotage and attacks on critical government and commercial computer systems.

## THE 'NEW WORLD ORDER'

The next 20 years will bring many changes in the balance of military power. New regional powers, such as China, will arise, but military might will be more evenly spread and decentralized. Resurgent nationalism will roil the landscape in many places, especially in the former Soviet empire. So will religious and cultural rivalries, many of them involving the Islamic world. For every breakthrough of peace, such as the 1998 accord in Northern Ireland (still a very fragile peace), there will be dismaying setbacks, such as the growing conflict between Israel and its Palestinian minority after several years of improving relations.

On the positive side, the international community will be tied together as never before. Increasing world trade, instantaneous global communications and the trend toward democracy almost everywhere will keep most nations pulling in the same direction. Economic growth will result in fewer have-not nations vulnerable to takeover by extremists. But radicals with political agendas—both right-wing militarists and frustrated leftists—will seize every economic crisis as an opportunity to grab power. The United States will have strong partners on every continent to help deal with the conflicts that inevitably will occur.

## THE DILEMMA OF CIVIL WARS

Some threats will be largely internal to one nation, stemming from economic instability and political chaos, as in Algeria, torn by bloody massacres amid religious conflict. Some conflicts, as in the Balkans, will bear the marks of both civil war and war between neighboring sovereign states. In Africa, the worst conflicts will continue to be tribal wars. As in the century now coming to a close, civil unrest will be an enormous impediment to improvement in living standards in the years to come.

These crises are the kind the world will have the greatest trouble dealing with. While there will be reluctance to get involved in civil wars, both because of issues of sovereignty and because of the financial cost and military risks of doing so, television will bring these wars and genocides into living rooms each night, generating enormous public pressure for other governments to "do something." Most often—unlike the response in Kosovo—the world will do what it has usually done with civil wars—persuade, cajole, threaten, take sides verbally, prevent neighbors from taking unfair advantage of the chaos and, finally, do very little to stop the carnage. Afterward, there will be the traditional handwringing, accusations and guilt that more wasn't done earlier.

## MOUNTAINS OF DEADLY WEAPONS

The world's stockpile of deadly weapons—conventional armaments of great sophistication, nuclear warheads, missiles and tactical weapons, and materials for chemical and biological warfare—is enormous, and it includes arsenals held by opponents of the U.S.

There will be periodic calls in the U.S. for limits on the sale of American weaponry to other nations, even our allies. But such sales contribute strongly to the U.S. balance of payments, and besides, if American defense contractors don't supply the stuff, it will be purchased instead from some other nation, diminishing American influence in the world. That's the cold reality of the world munitions trade—not a pretty picture.

While the world's democracies will feel restrained from using force to settle disputes, totalitarian regimes, such as Milosevic's Yugoslavia, will be under no such constraints, but will be deterred only by the threat of punishment. To make that threat credible, future administrations will keep the U.S. armed forces the world's best by a large margin, able to intervene in hot spots wherever American self-interest or humanitarian principles are in jeopardy.

## MORE INTERNATIONAL PEACEKEEPING

Virtually every foreign operation will be coordinated with other nations, often through the United Nations but under strong American leadership. The Persian Gulf War of 1991 and the conflicts in Bosnia and Kosovo will be looked on as prototypes—not because they were conducted perfectly, but because many nations agreed on the use of force and shared the financial burdens and military risks.

## THE NUCLEAR THREAT

There is a very real danger of the use of nuclear weapons some-where in the world in the next 10 to 20 years—maybe sooner rather than later, if Pakistan and India go to war over the disputed territory of Kashmir. The best hope for forbearance in that region is the knowledge that nuclear fallout, wafting across their common borders, would poison millions of innocent citizens in both nations.

Some experts think an atomic military event is at least a 50-50 chance, because nuclear technology and arms are likely to spread to more nations and even to terrorist groups, despite the efforts of the U.S. and others to stop proliferation.

The known nuclear powers now include, as of 1998, the U.S., Russia, France, Britain, China, India and Pakistan. Israel is undeclared but is known to have warheads and the means of delivering them. Nations thought by world intelligence to have nuclear aspirations and programs in some stage of development include North Korea (which may already have bombs), Iraq, Iran and Libya.

Under the 1992 START II treaty between the United States and Russia—ratified by the former but not the latter—these two nations are committed to major reductions in the total number of warheads and a ban on all multiple-warhead, land-based intercontinental ballistic missiles (ICBMs). All major members of the world's nuclear club—not yet including recent testers India and Pakistan—are also committed to a ban on further testing, either in the atmosphere or underground.

There are hundreds of tons of plutonium and highly enriched uranium around the world. Depending on the bomb maker's skill, as little as three pounds can yield a very destructive device. Bomb-making know-how is readily available to anyone determined to seek it out, with a fair amount of detail available in libraries and on Web sites.

The demise of the Soviet Union has greatly increased the danger of nuclear proliferation, because much of the world's plutonium and bomb-grade uranium is held in former Soviet republics (now independent nations), where accountability is poor, and smuggling, abetted by political corruption, is a possibility. This makes it much more likely that a dangerous regime such as Iran's could get the material or weapons through porous borders with the ex-Soviet republics.

In 1993, to accelerate the removal of weapons-grade fuel from the former Soviet Union, the U.S. agreed to buy it from the Russian military for reprocessing into atomic-reactor fuel for U.S. power plants, even though the price is higher than alternative sources of fuel. This processing is done by the government-owned U.S. Enrichment Corporation, one of four such reprocessing plants in the world. The Clinton administration has plans to sell this facility to private investors, but the odds are good that Congress won't permit this $1.6 billion divestiture in a time of growing concern over nuclear proliferation.

The U.S. and the Soviet Union were afraid to use their nuclear weapons on each other for fear of counterattack—the doctrine of mutual assured destruction. Such deterrence won't be so strong against regimes or terrorist groups motivated by radical (indeed, irrational) ideology, making it much harder for any nation to defend itself. It will take good surveillance and intelligence and quick response to prevent attacks. The failure in 1998 of U.S. intelligence to spot India's preparations for underground nuclear tests and alert military officials in Washington was not reassuring.

Over time, all the major nuclear powers—including India and Pakistan—will agree to stop further development and testing of nuclear weapons, and they will work together to limit nuclear proliferation and reduce current stocks of warheads. The United States, however, will continue to develop a variety of space-based defenses for intercepting and exploding incoming missiles.

## TERRORISM AND 'WEAPONS OF MASS DESTRUCTION'

Chemical and biological weapons capable of killing thousands of people with even a limited attack will also present danger to the world.

Iran, Iraq, Libya, Syria and North Korea are among the outlaw nations that already possess these weapons, which some describe as the "poor man's nuclear bomb." Several of these countries also have contacts with extremist and terrorist groups, increasing the chance that non-governmental groups will gain access to these kinds of weapons.

Terrorism, much of it sponsored by radical Islamic groups, will remain a grave threat at home and abroad. While basic civil liberties in the United States will be preserved, Congress and the courts will give law enforcement more leeway to infiltrate and stop groups suspected of terrorism, or to catch perpetrators after an attack.

The active-duty military and national guard units around the nation will be given new training and responsibilities for dealing with possible chemical and biological terrorism in the U.S., involving threats to water supplies, transportation systems and large gatherings of people (such as in stadiums).

## THE SPECTER OF CYBER-SABOTAGE

With so many of the world's mechanical systems and military operations run by complex computers, and with so many of those computers interconnected, terrorists using the services of computer hackers could badly cripple gigantic chunks of world commerce, energy supply and military readiness.

This is not a remote theoretical risk. There have been several instances of mischievous hackers, probably meaning no harm but thrilled by a challenge, breaking into supposedly secure national-defense computers. One notorious group, the Masters of Download (with members probably in the U.S., Russia and Great Britain), are thought by U.S. intelligence experts to have penetrated various computer systems that track U.S. submarines and control the satellites of the Global Positioning System, broadly used to monitor world aviation, ocean shipping and trucking.

Computer experts at the U.S. National Security Agency (NSA) conducted an elaborate exercise in 1998, in which they demonstrated that, using software obtained from public hacker sites on the Internet, they could gain access to computers that control the entire American electric-power grid and U.S. military communications in the Pacific.

There is no reason to believe that cyber-sabotage played any role in the 1998 malfunctioning of the Galaxy IV communications satellite, which crippled some 80% of America's pagers, interrupted cable TV's Weather Channel and interfered with the operations of National Public Radio, credit card clearances, ATMs and hospital communications all over the U.S. But with communications satellites numbering more than 650 and proliferating at a quickening pace, the vulnerability of world communications and financial operations to hackers is a real concern.

The United States will begin to take more seriously the possibility that ingenious terrorists could plunge whole continents into the dark, disable missile defense systems, shut down world financial trading, or even worse, plant viruses in major computer systems that would prevent their normal operation for long stretches. This threat is called information warfare, or "infowar," and the only possible defense—not necessarily foolproof—is constant changing of access codes, passwords and other locking devices. But it is possible that high-speed decoding programs of the future will always find a way, by trying enough combinations at blinding speed, to crack any lock.

## THE EXPLOSIVE MIDDLE EAST

It would be hard to find more hostility anywhere in the world than exists between Islamic extremists and Israel. The Mideast and the Persian Gulf region will pose the greatest danger of nuclear conflict in the new century.

This deep-seated antagonism, combined with the region's huge oil reserves, will make the Mideast the most vital area of the globe to U.S. interests. While Middle East oil production is no longer as important to American oil supply as it was a quarter-century ago, disruption of that production would be viewed as a calamity with potential to weaken the entire world economy. For that reason, the U.S. and its allies will go to great lengths to support friendly Arab states, such as Saudi Arabia and Kuwait, against threats both internal and external, despite the fact that none of them would be mistaken for democratic regimes.

Despite the obvious dangers, there is reason for optimism that new wars between Israel and its neighbors can be avoided. Few would have predicted that Israel and the Palestinian Liberation Front would agree to Palestinian authority in the West Bank and Gaza. Peace won't come easily or quickly, and relations will sometimes deteriorate just when things are looking up, as in the heightened tensions of 1998. Terrorist groups with ties to Iran and Syria will disrupt and delay progress. But eventually Israel and most Arab states will agree to coexist, and someday, many years from now, Palestinians will have a true, self-governing homeland encompassing parts of Israel and Jordan.

Iran, Iraq and Libya will remain threats to regional stability, backing terrorist groups and resisting U.S. influence. All three have chemical weapons, and Iran and Iraq will keep trying to acquire nuclear weapons. Having passed up the chance to overthrow Saddam Hussein at the end of the Gulf War, the West will wait for him to do something to justify another military action against his regime. But if he doesn't provoke the West further, the odds are good that he will maintain his repressive hold on Iraq for years, unless a determined (and suicidal) patriot manages to assassinate him.

There are signs that radical Islamic fundamentalism may have peaked in some nations, due to a broad public desire (if not shared by clerics) to improve civil rights and the status of women, as well as relations with other nations. Even in Iran, a more moderate president was elected by landslide in 1997, and many Iranians profess to welcome American visitors.

## CHINA'S GROWING MILITARY MIGHT

The top world-affairs headline of the next 20 years will be China's emergence as both an economic and military power. China's neighbors fear it will become a military threat, projecting its strength throughout the region and beyond. Indeed, China will probably change the balance of political and military power for the whole world.

China's leaders are determined to improve the nation's nuclear and conventional military power. The key for the U.S. will not be in stopping this buildup—it can't—but in persuading China to use its power responsibly. In fact, U.S. policy toward China could backfire if it becomes too confrontational and runs headlong into Chinese nationalism.

China is already exerting more influence on the Indian subcontinent and the Persian Gulf, through economic ties and the sale of arms and nuclear know-how to Pakistan and Iran. Chinese arms exports to these and other nations will continue to grow, leading to periodic tension between Washington and Beijing.

Even a moderately aggressive China would create enormous problems for its neighbors and the rest of the world. With Hong Kong back under Chinese control and Macao soon to follow, China will turn more attention to annexing Taiwan. This won't necessarily lead to a military showdown, but resolving the Taiwan issue will involve careful diplomacy by China and the U.S., which already recognizes a "one China" policy.

As China gradually liberalizes its political and economic systems, and as investment ties between Taiwan and China take root and flourish, the two nations will reconcile their differences and come together. Years from now, it is likely that Taiwan will be a semi-autonomous province of China, without having been annexed by military force.

## CONFLICT ON THE ASIAN SUBCONTINENT

A great risk to world peace lies on the India-Pakistan border, especially in Kashmir. Both countries have many nuclear weapons and the missiles to fire them. India's growing productivity and developing middle class give it every motive to avoid war, but its new ruling party is dominated by Hindu nationalists who seem determined to act belligerent toward Muslim Pakistan, which is inclined to act similarly. Pakistan will remain a desperately poor country, susceptible to civil war or takeover by Islamic militants. Even if a military confrontation between these two rivals is averted, the continuing tension will limit investment and economic growth in the region.

## TENSION IN EAST ASIA

Japan will continue to play an important economic role throughout Asia. It will also be more active in regional foreign and military policy. If China becomes aggressive and threatening, Japan will dramatically increase its military power, including the acquisition of missiles and nuclear weapons, with the assistance and encouragement of the U.S.

Ties between Japan and the U.S. will grow, and the two will work together on regional problem spots such as North Korea. Japan's military growth, in fact, will be accomplished by buying U.S. weapons and taking on a larger share of the regional defense burden, now borne overwhelmingly by the U.S.

The divided Korean peninsula will remain the most dangerous spot in the region, and the U.S. will continue to have a large military presence there. North Korea's communist regime will eventually collapse, although the timing is hard to predict. The biggest U.S. concern will be making sure that North Korea doesn't go out in a blaze of violence aimed at South Korea. Even if war can be averted, South Korea will still face the enormous economic challenge of integrating into its economy and society one of the world's poorest and most repressed peoples. The cost of this reunification will someday be a big drag on the economic growth of South Korea, even more than German reunification has been on West Germany.

## RUSSIA WILL RISE AGAIN

It may be hard to see the makings yet, or just how it will happen, but Russia will regain its footing as a great military power and someday, many years from now, an economic power, too. It remains the U.S.'s closest rival in nuclear strength, with intercontinental missiles and armed submarines capable of causing overwhelming destruction over great distances. There is growing evidence, however, that a politically weakened and underfunded Russian military is having trouble maintaining the functionality of its armaments, especially its nuclear-armed submarine fleet.

As Russia gets on its feet economically, it will seek to play a greater role in world diplomacy, to recapture its central place on the stage. It has better relations than the U.S. with some regions, such as the Arab world, which will at times make Russia a valued partner for peace. On the other hand, Russia will seek closer political and security ties with China—a concern in Washington.

And the U.S. and its allies will have to make sure Russia's reinvigorated nationalism won't turn expansionist and once again seek to threaten and dominate neighboring states, either its former Soviet republics or the nations of Eastern and Western Europe.

That danger helps explain the Western rationale for including the old Soviet satellite states in NATO, which is, of course, opposed by Russia. It is not inconceivable that, years from now, a much stronger Russia—whether democratic or totalitarian at the time—will be ruled by nationalists nostalgic for the old empire and desirous of reassembling the Soviet Union.

In the short run, U.S. policy toward Russia will also involve watching over the military debris of the old Soviet Union. Russia's military decline has increased the chance that nuclear weapons or know-how could be sold on the black market to rogue nations or terrorist groups. The same goes for other ex-Soviet republics. There will be more U.S. actions like the purchase of Kazakh plutonium and MiG-29 fighter jets from Moldova, to keep weapons out of dangerous hands.

# Overpopulation, Famine and Disease

It is possible that world population growth will outstrip improvements in productivity and agricultural output, as well as the ability of the natural environment to support rapid urbanization and industrialization. The result would be widespread famine and environmental disaster. We do not believe this to be likely, for reasons discussed in chapters on population growth and agriculture (see Chapters 8 and 16).

But there will be occasional outbreaks of new strains of infectious diseases that will raise death rates in some areas. These epidemics will divert more of a nation's financial resources to health care, depressing productivity and economic growth in particular regions for indefinite periods of time, until the diseases run their course or are controlled.

Infectious diseases account for more than one-third of all deaths in the world each year, led by pneumonia, diarrheal diseases such as dysentery, tuberculosis, malaria, measles, hepatitis B, AIDS and exotic contaminations such as Ebola, Hanta virus, E.coli food infections and Lassa fever.

Some of the worst diseases, after years of declining death rates, are making comebacks in mutating, drug-resistant versions, in part because of broad overuse of antibiotics for nonspecific effects. Infections are jumping from species to species, including animal to humans, such as cryptosporidium from cattle to people. HIV is thought to have originated in monkeys in Africa, from which the viral infection spread all over the world. Antibiotic-resistant strains of pneumonia and TB are giving health care professionals a hard time from New Guinea to Hungary to the United States.

The microbes that cause infections can mutate faster than modern medical science can come up with new antidotes. And the global economy, with booming world trade and travel for both business and recreation, will contribute to the faster circulation of infections.

The development of new vaccines and better sanitation in developing nations will accomplish much more than will fighting infectious diseases after the fact. Biotechnology will improve the outlook with a variety of new vaccines, including preventives for influenza, cholera, malaria, hepatitis B and herpes.

# Government Corruption and Organized Crime

The developing nations will continue to be plagued for decades by widespread governmental corruption—the systematic looting of national income by entrenched elites well supported by taxing authority and police and military power. This will be a problem not just in authoritarian regimes but also in emerging democracies.

Much of the 20th century's multinational foreign aid has been siphoned from infrastructure projects into the lavish living and overseas bank accounts of ruling families and their cronies. This theft and capital flight have been major factors in the dismal economic performance of many developing nations, especially in Africa and Latin America.

But systematic governmental corruption and capital diversion will gradually decline with the establishment of democracy and modern civic administration in many nations. The scale, if not the prevalence, of governmental embezzlement will ebb as massive foreign-assistance programs are replaced by private corporate investment. However, foreign companies will have to continue offering bribes and kickbacks as a standard cost of doing business in the developing world for years to come.

The growth of global organized crime will require increasingly sophisticated techniques and international cooperation. Global crime includes a wide range of activities, all of which threaten economic vitality. Drug cartels provide debilitating substances to an estimated 190 million customers worldwide—sapping them of their personal health and income, eroding their productivity, and imposing enormous costs on governments to fight crime, support dependent children and pay for medical care.

Organized crime is also heavily involved in the piracy of intellectual property, through the illegal production of brand-name and patented products. Counterfeiting of currency, especially American dollars, is equally dangerous to the world economy. Better and better counterfeiting, using the latest color laser printers and good-quality paper, will keep the U.S. moving toward uncopiable paper money, using a variety of special markings that are revealed to the naked eye or special counter-top scanners.

Finally, run-of-the-mill theft will divert vast amounts of merchandise from global commerce—directly from factories and loading docks, as well as from piers, ports and airports.

There is growing evidence that organized criminals are moving from traditional rackets of theft, smuggling and drugs into new kinds of ventures, especially financial fraud. Using the talents of crooked computer geniuses, criminal syndicates will be able to rob banks and brokerages electronically, without pulling a gun or cracking a safe. Or they can simply manipulate stock trading the same way as dishonest traders have done. The losses in assets, insurance settlements and tax revenue will be enormous. And stemming the boom in hot merchandise, computer embezzlement and stock fraud will tax the ingenuity of law enforcement everywhere.

# CHAPTER 11

# World-Changing Technology

S cience and technology have always been the driving forces in the steady rise of humanity's material well-being. This improvement will both accelerate in speed and broaden in geographic scope in the next century, which will be marked less by new scientific breakthroughs than by improvements in, and dissemination of, existing technology. The democratization and dispersal of technology—leading to mass production in many nations, declining prices, and rising affordability by a growing middle class in less-affluent nations—is a world-changing trend.

Over the next decades, today's two most important technologies—telecommunications and biotechnology—will have a greater effect on more lives, in more countries, in a shorter period of time, than any previous technological impact (even more than steam-driven machines had on the Industrial Revolution, which played out over a longer period and was confined to a relatively small portion of the world's population).

Telecommunications, broadly defined as the two-way transmission of digitized information, will be a force for political and economic liberalization, the dispersal of education and scientific knowledge, and the spread of manufacturing to every nation. Biotechnology will accelerate established trends in rising food production and reduced disease and death rates, dramatically improving life in less-developed nations.

Later in the century, a similar effect will be achieved by energy technologies that will revolutionize the generation and transmission of electricity, with breakthroughs in atomic fusion and superconductivity. And underlying all of these technologies will be the creation of totally new materials from the convergence of chemistry, biology and physics—new combinations of molecules arranged to provide particular benefits in specific industrial uses.

## THE BOUNTY OF TECHNOLOGY

Technology harnesses research, design and production to create products of greater utility at ever-lower prices. Technology boosts productivity, and productivity gains are what raise human wealth and living standards. Technology improves and extends life by enriching diets, preventing and curing disease, and giving new freedom to people with disabilities. It enables us to generate electricity with less pollution and to transmit that electricity over long distances with less loss of power. Technology helps people communicate faster, more clearly and less expensively. It gives the power of complex computation and problem-solving to people with limited training. Technology allows businesses to locate branch operations in far-flung locations, breathing new life into small towns and rural areas. Technology makes it possible for humankind to counter scarcity by either finding more of the scarce natural substances (such as fossil fuels) or creating new substances to replace them.

## TROUBLING TECHNOLOGY CHALLENGES

At the same time, fast-changing technology poses dismaying dilemmas. By rendering conventional products obsolete, it undermines the livelihood of those who make them, even as it creates new jobs making the replacement goods. And by increasing productivity, technology reduces the demand for certain kinds of labor, even as it creates new jobs and raises the wages of workers who make and use the new techniques. While it expands personal freedom and power, it reduces our basic self-sufficiency, making us dependent on complex devices that as individuals we don't know how to make or fix. Almost all of these devices run on electricity, for which, until the advent of photovoltaic home generators and fuel cells, we are totally dependent on outside commercial sources.

In the short run—possibly in the next decade—rapid technological advances in the developed nations, coupled with the inability of poorer nations to afford them, will broaden the existing chasm between rich and poor, educated and uneducated, both within each nation and among nations. But over a longer period, the declining prices of core technologies and their spread to every corner of the globe will be a force for the convergence of living standards at higher levels.

In the medical realm, advances in technology will clash with affordability. It will be difficult for even the most well-to-do patients, let alone third-party payers like employers and governments, to pay for the wonders that medical science will make possible. This will lead inevitably to intergenerational conflict over the allocation of health care funding and, ultimately, to the rationing of expensive techniques for the rejuvenation of aging bodies or the creation of genetically improved babies. Ethical debate will rage over the emerging techniques of "germline gene therapy," in which genes for a particular human characteristic can be added to not just one individual but to future generations of that person's offspring.

New technology, especially in information dissemination, will exert stress on traditional ways of living, earning a living and relating to one another in society, diminishing the influence of social structures—family, schools, churches—that have been important forces in civilization.

Changes in food production that will be wrought by biotechnology will accelerate the age-old trend of declining employment in agriculture, especially in developing nations. To some futurists, this raises the specter of massive worldwide unemployment in agriculture. But this trend will unfold slowly, and it will coincide with rising job opportunities in manufacturing in those same nations, averting widespread joblessness.

Owners of intellectual property—copyrighted text, movies, music and photos—will struggle to find technologies to help protect their assets from illegal copying, or at least to collect small fees for such copying. And information technologies of growing importance in mass marketing—such as databases of personal information—raise troublesome implications for individual privacy.

In the world of information technology, an avalanche of instant information will be a mixed blessing. It will be easy to find information on virtually any subject, but, as the volume explodes, it will be harder and harder to find *useful* information and evaluate its quality.

The democratization of information will reduce the influence of society's traditional gatekeepers of knowledge—scholars, teachers, scientific researchers, physicians, journalists, book editors, "experts" of all kinds. People have long relied on such modern mandarins to sift through information and use their education and judgment to direct our attention to ideas that they deem useful, original and uplifting. In the process, a society built a base of commonly shared information and values. This whole process has been undermined in recent decades by several forces in addition to technology, such as the increasing diversity of the U.S. population and changes in education and popular culture. But information technology has accentuated cultural fragmentation by creating smaller and smaller bodies of knowledge and spheres of interest for ever-smaller audiences.

In the new Internet world, reliable information will vie, often unsuccessfully, with information that is unreliable—untested science, uninformed judgments and advice tainted by the commercial interests of the disseminator. In a kind of Gresham's Law of information, content that is heavily promoted and superficially appealing may crowd out information of higher quality that, due to a lack of well-funded sponsors, will be harder to find on the Internet.

But it is futile to bemoan the onslaught of new technology, because we are powerless to hold it back. Throughout history, it has been axiomatic that everything that can be done will be done. Every invention, however destructive to a traditional practice or livelihood, will be put into use by someone, somewhere. By legislation or fiat, governments can merely slow the adoption of a new technology they deem dangerous, but they cannot stop it forever, if it proves useful to any large group of people. The challenge facing every people, in every epoch, is adapting to technological changes that they are powerless to impede.

## A TECHNOLOGY SAMPLER

The core technologies fall loosely into two broad groups: those based on the physical sciences (electronics, robotics and manufacturing technology, aerospace, telecommunications, new materials, electrical generation and storage) and those based on the life sciences (the overlapping of biology with chemistry in agriculture, medicine and new materials).

But most new products result from the combination of several core technologies. The creation of ever-faster and higher-storage computer chips blends electronics and materials science in the quest for ever-thinner printed circuits and new compounds, other than silicon, that can conduct electricity with ever-diminishing resistance and heat. Telecommunications involves microelectronics, broadcasting, space and satellite technology, and fiber optics, which is a combination of the technologies of laser-light generation and materials science (plastics and glass). The manufacturing technologies, such as robotics and automated assembly lines, combine microelectronics with old-fashioned mechanical engineering. Most new medical inventions are likewise combinations of electronics, materials science and mechanical ingenuity. The energy technologies—for example, nuclear fission (and someday fusion) and electricity from solar energy, batteries and fuel cells—combine the sciences of physics and chemistry.

And all these technologies require computer controls, based on microprocessors, which in turn require instructions from software. In a sense, computer technology and software languages are the core technologies upon which all the others depend.

The next few years will see amazing advances in software, in the fields of artificial intelligence, parallel processing, intelligent-agent systems, optical character recognition and translation, voice recognition and translation, and virtual-reality systems.

The next few chapters present our sense of what lies ahead in the core technologies. Entire books are written about each of these fields. Our aim is to give you a quick, broad overview of major developments that will have a special impact on business and consumers.

# CHAPTER 12

# Ubiquitous Computers

The computer and microprocessor industries are on the verge of changes as earthshaking—both to them as businesses and to their users—as the rise of the personal computer in the 1980s.

The changes will be wrought not by accelerating chip speed and power—which will actually flatten in their rate of growth—but by a variety of forces, including the growing power of the Internet, advances in artificial-intelligence software, commercial and governmental challenges to PC-dominators Microsoft and Intel, and the arrival of simpler, cheaper information appliances that will supplant the PC for most home uses. The highest-growth segment of the chip market will be non-PC microprocessors—very fast, limited-function brains that will cost a lot less than today's full-featured Pentium chips. American companies will continue to dominate innovation in software, but they will keep spreading their programming operations all over the world.

## How Far Computers Have Come

Consider the increase in computing capabilities since the first powerful, commercial digital computer, UNIVAC, was unveiled in 1951. UNIVAC was the size of a small room and cost $930,000—the equivalent of more than $6 million today. But as for computing power, it had only the speed of today's simplest hand-held calculator costing a few dollars.

After transistors replaced vacuum tubes, and after scientists figured out how to etch microscopic circuits onto ever-smaller wafers of silicon, computing power took off in a steep slope of seemingly limitless duration. Gordon Moore, co-founder of Intel, looked back a few years ago at the rate of growth in computer speed and figured out that it was increasing at a nearly constant rate of about 60% a year—that is, doubling about every 18 months. This historical fact, and the tacit assumption that it would continue indefinitely, came to be known as Moore's Law.

# Flatter Growth in Computing Speed Ahead

But now the longevity of Moore's Law is being called into question by no less an authority than Dr. Moore himself, as well as by top scientists at such microelectronics leaders as Lucent Technologies, Hitachi, Intel and Fujitsu. They're well aware that earlier predictions of a flattening growth curve in chip speed turned out to be premature, but they cite a number of reasons why it is now likely. One involves the increasing difficulty of controlling streams of electrons as they bounce through ever-thinner circuits. Another is the staggering cost of the machinery and factories needed to make silicon wafers, an investment that now runs several billion dollars for one state-of-the-art plant. Even if vastly faster microprocessors can be made, will they be cost-competitive with the alternative—harnessing several slower microprocessors together to work as a unit? Perhaps not.

## TOTALLY NEW KINDS OF CHIPS

A search has been under way for years to invent totally new kinds of microprocessors, using wafer materials other than silicon and energy sources other than electrons. There is promising research on semiconducting polymers (plastics) that might be easier and cheaper to make than silicon chips. This has led to the invention of clear-plastic sheets of semiconducting materials with nearly invisible circuits etched on them—a flat, flexible computer you could roll up and stuff in a pocket. To deal with the problem of uncontrollable electron streams, researchers are working on switches that would be turned on and off by a single electron. An even bolder approach would replace electrons (electricity) with beams of light as the power source, using pulsating lasers to control optical switches etched three-dimensionally in tiny blocks of clear glass or plastic. Yet another avenue of experimentation focuses on perfecting "neural net" processors, which seek to mimic the flexible, adaptive reasoning of the human brain. Rudimentary versions of neural net processors are actually in use, controlling the touchpad pointer that replaces the mouse or trackball in some laptop computers.

But while the most fertile minds in microelectronics hunt for ways to extend Moore's Law with totally new technology, the old war horse— the electrically controlled silicon microprocessor—keeps getting faster. Even the most cautious authorities in the field believe there are still several more years of 60% annual increases in computing power ahead.

But even if Moore's Law hits a wall far sooner than expected, the effect on computer applications will not be unduly negative. In a few more generations of improvement, the speed and capacity of a single microprocessor will be sufficient to run artificial-intelligence and virtual-reality programs of a sophistication unimaginable a decade ago. Ways will be found to boost the parallel-processing speed of several microprocessors working together. And software creators, long spoiled by the soaring speed and falling prices of processors and memory chips, will begin to design operating systems that are less voracious in their appetite for memory and electrical power.

Whether or not microelectronics research comes up with startlingly new chip designs and materials, and whether or not computing speed increases according to Moore's Law, appliance designers will have all the horsepower they need for years to come—and at falling prices.

# Fast Growth in Non-PC Chip Markets

It's not at all clear that computer and appliance manufacturers need substantially more-sophisticated microprocessors than exist now, capable of executing more and more complex instructions simultaneously. What they really seem to want are chips that do a few tasks very fast, are cheap to make and can run several different operating systems.

Indeed, the fastest-growing segment of the computer-chip industry will be microprocessors for non-PC uses, such as smart phones, high-definition TV, set-top cable-TV modems, video games, hand-held computers and organizers, digital cameras, home appliances, cheap network computers (NCs), automotive computers, avionics, and factory robots. These chips won't need to execute the many varied and complex instructions of a Windows PC, as Intel's powerful and expensive microprocessors do so well.

While Intel dominates the PC market with its expensive Pentium chips (with an astounding market share of nearly 90% in 1997), it will face tough competition in consumer appliances from rivals that are focusing on this lucrative new market with fast, cheap microprocessors—rivals such as Advanced Micro Devices, Hitachi, IBM, LSI Logic, Motorola, National Semiconductor and NEC. The new generation of low-cost microprocessor is no slouch in performance, either. A new $15 Motorola chip for Microsoft's WebTV system, according to a report in *The Wall Street Journal*, runs at 200 million instructions a second, processes movie-quality video and serves as a high-speed data modem. Intel, not surprisingly, will work on simplifying and reducing the price of its chips for the consumer-electronics market, just as Microsoft has created new versions of its Windows operating systems for hand-held devices and other small non-PC appliances.

# 'Wintel' PCs Versus Network Computers

With the possible exception of employees and large shareholders of Microsoft and Intel, hardly anyone is comfortable with the firm grip these two companies have on home and office computing today. While the prices of these "Wintel" computers continue to fall, their growing power and complexity make them dauntingly difficult for many consumers to use and increasingly expensive for businesses to upgrade, repair and administer on their local area networks (LANs). Many consumers and business managers are looking for new kinds of computers that are less expensive, more reliable, and simpler to learn and maintain.

That might turn out to be the network computer (NC), a stripped-down, less-versatile terminal that loads its software from a corporate mainframe or Internet site and runs Java, the universal Internet programming language developed by Sun Microsystems. Some formidable companies have put their money behind the NC concept, including IBM, Netscape, Oracle and Sun. The NC concept of less-intelligent terminals linked to powerful mainframes is slowly catching on with corporations. IBM, for example, had sold more than 100,000 of its NCs by early 1998, but products from Oracle and Sun have been slow out of the starting gate. Microsoft is proving to be a heavyweight contender for this new market, too, with a new version of the Windows NT operating system that runs on less-full-featured "thin terminal" PCs. But Sun got a big boost in 1998 when cable giant TCI selected its Personal Java as the software TCI will install in most of the 18 million set-top Internet TV controllers it will provide its cable customers.

COMPETITION FROM NEW INFORMATION APPLIANCES

The PC-versus-NC battle is far from over, and it's likely that the popularity of terminals that are cheaper and easier to learn, use and service will continue to grow. More important, this fight is just one skirmish in the larger war over what kind of device or "information appliance"— PC, smart phone, cable-TV box, HDTV set, or something altogether new—will become the dominant one for receiving, sending and processing information. (The next chapter explores the distinctive role of each of these appliances in various segments of the market.)

# Antitrust and the Computer Industry

The government's antitrust suits against Microsoft and Intel were still dragging on in 1999, and no one knows how they will turn out. But the result will probably be a reduction in their current market power. Microsoft will probably be limited in its freedom to add new features, for free, to its operating system, a practice that has effectively kept other software makers from selling certain competing applications (especially Netscape's Web browser) that run on Windows. On the "first-screen" issue—that is, the question of what users will see when they first turn on their computers—manufacturers will probably be allowed to modify and customize the Windows start-up screen to highlight non-Microsoft products, if they wish. And Intel will be required to keep computer makers fully apprised (with technical specifications) of upcoming changes in its Pentium chip designs and features, so the makers can plan their future generations of computers. Intel will also be ordered not to punish companies for doing business with its chip competitors by withholding such information .

In the end, however, the commercial challenge from competing products—new operating systems for the Internet, new microprocessors at lower prices—will be more effective than government action in renewing competition in computer and software industries.

# Superintelligent Software

Microprocessors do the heavy lifting in computing, but software is the brain telling the microprocessor what to do. It is software that learns enough about chess to tie up a human chess champion. It is software that learns to translate foreign languages, predict hurricanes or understand the spoken voice.

The most basic software is the computer's operating system. The trend in operating systems will be toward products that can run the most applications without incompatibility problems, especially on the Internet. In future decades, most software won't be purchased at a store on disc, but will be stored on Internet sites and downloaded, for a fee, to the user's computer.

The new frontier in software will be "intelligent agents" that can screen information and perform tasks for the user, much like a robot. Examples of intelligent agents already exist, in the form of online financial-information services that you program to alert you to news about a particular industry or a sharp drop in a stock you own. Agents operate by letting your computer talk to someone else's computer, on your orders. Over the next few decades, these agents will come to be known as "knowbots," programmable personal assistants that will execute a broad variety of tasks on your behalf, using their stored knowledge of your interests, tastes and preferences to think and act as you would. Knowbots will use programs involving highly sophisticated artificial intelligence, which simulates human thought processes. Your knowbot will buy your airline ticket after you've told it where you want to go and how much you're willing to pay, or arrange luncheon appointments by checking other people's calendars. Agents will also be used to find items of interest in a newspaper, shop for cars within a certain price range and filter out unwanted phone calls (a kind of super caller-ID).

One field attracting much interest in computer science is genetic algorithms, first developed in the 1960s, in which computers are programmed to come up with the best possible solutions to a problem while rejecting weaker solutions. The most promising solutions are then combined to yield even better answers, much the way scientists believe species evolved through a process of natural genetic selection. John Deere & Co. is using genetic algorithms to revise factory schedules when a machine breaks down. Others hope to use this process to predict stock market and currency fluctuations.

### DICTATION AND TRANSLATION FROM PRINT AND VOICE

The major barrier to easy communication in the global economy is the many different languages spoken all over the world. While simple business English has emerged as the common language of world commerce, coming breakthroughs in language-translation software will make social and business conversation much easier.

In a few years, there will be highly reliable programs that can quickly scan any printed material in any language, in any type font, and translate it almost simultaneously into any other language, with vocabulary and syntax that comes close to colloquial usage.

Programs approaching this skill exist today, including some on the Internet where people can chat at once in various languages; at present, the translations can be hilariously awkward, especially when attempting to make sense of slang, but improvements will come quickly. Someday these translation programs will make foreign news, books, business reports and research materials readily available all over the world, while also aiding companies in translating their in-house materials for use by employees in different countries.

The perfection of today's voice-recognition technology will decrease the importance of typing skills. Dictation software already on the market for just a few hundred dollars can quickly learn your own accent and pronunciation of common words and remember them. Voice-activated systems can now dial preset phone numbers, take messages and talk to callers on instruction from the owner, and in the future you'll be able to call people without dialing, simply by saying the name of the person you want to speak with. Other programs will mimic your writing style, inserting favorite phrases when appropriate.

Within ten years voice-recognition technology will be joined by eye-recognition software. A computer will be able to track the movement of the user's eyes, permitting it to perform the command the user is looking at.

## VIRTUAL REALITY

Computerized three-dimensional simulations will make you feel as if you're present in another place, sensing the sights, sounds, feel (and perhaps, with artificial-aroma generators, even the smell) of exotic venues, historical times, and activities you wouldn't think of experiencing in person. Wearing special goggles and gloves that pick up your eye and body movements, you will be able to experience the thrill (or terror) of skydiving, scuba diving, spelunking, downhill skiing, walking on the moon, playing a tennis match with a future Pete Sampras or being on the battlefield during Pickett's Charge at Gettysburg. You'll be able to preview vacation spots or walk through your architect's design of an addition to your home to see how you'd like living in it.

Virtual-reality control devices will give new freedom and occupational power to paraplegics and quadriplegics, enabling them to use tiny movements of fingers, hands, mouth and eyes to control motorized wheelchairs, cars and appliances and to experience physical activities and sensations enjoyed by able-bodied people.

# The Ultimate Goal: Ease and Transparency

Personal computers are used in only about 40% of American households, and a much smaller percentage worldwide. One reason is cost, but falling prices will take care of that issue. The other big reason is difficulty of use and questionable reliability. Computers will really become a part of our lives only when they are as easy to use as the TV or CD player: No more seized-up screens, crashes, "illegal operation" messages and lost data. And software that is fully self-guiding and doesn't require lengthy manuals or tutorials before it can be used.

Computer makers know this, and so do competitors in consumer electronics. So the dominant trend will be the design of simple, user-friendly devices that do most of what people want, such as access home entertainment and news on the Web, call their friends on the phone, manage their personal finances and play games.

# Full Globalization of the Computer Industry

The manufacture of computer components is already the world's most globalized business, with multinational firms making chips, hard drives, monitors and other parts in dozens of nations. And the writing of software code has spread worldwide too, with U.S. software giants setting up programming operations in India, Ireland, Israel, Mexico, the Philippines, Russia and many other nations.

This trend will continue, as American companies experience shortages of computer engineers and programmers at home but are able to hire all they need, at much lower salaries, in other nations. And the American labor force in computer engineering and software design will include a rising proportion of immigrant workers. Foreign-born people account for an estimated one-third of all computer and software workers in California's two major centers, the Silicon Valley and Orange County, and this share will keep rising, because not enough U.S.-born youths are choosing to prepare for these mentally rigorous careers.

# CHAPTER 13

# Telecommunications and Information Technology

I magine being in constant contact with anyone, anywhere, even someone not on Earth but in a spacecraft far above, or even in a colony on the moon. Imagine that this easy contact doesn't depend on your being near any kind of antenna or electrical-power source. Consider yourself being able to talk with a friend, co-worker or stranger in a different nation, each of you speaking your own language and hearing a simultaneous translation of the other's words. Envision being able to see that person's face in fluid, live-action video as you converse, or view any kind of graphic image just as easily.

Imagine being able to receive any information—audio, text or graphic—on a device that combines traits of today's personal computer, telephone, radio, CD player and color TV. This device could be small enough to wear on your wrist or large enough to cover the wall of your living room. And suppose all of this technology was available at constantly falling prices, affordable to virtually any middle-class person in any country.

This vision is surprisingly close. Some of it is here now, some of it will be realized in just a few years, and all of it will be a part of everyday life within 20 years. The revolution in telecommunications and information technology that erupted over the past ten years will proceed at a quickening pace, bringing fundamental changes in the politics and economics of the world.

## A FORCE FOR FREEDOM AND OPEN MARKETS

The biggest impact of the telecom revolution will be in relatively closed societies. Repressive governments will find it almost impossible to block out progressive ideas and culture, and to keep their citizens from learning of the freedom and prosperity beyond their borders.

And if the essential feature of efficient markets is a similar degree of information among buyers and sellers, instant global communication will help level the playing fields of commerce, narrowing the broker's and speculator's historical advantage—the gap between ignorance and knowledge. Farmers in remote areas of Bangladesh, for example, are already benefiting from the coming of cell phones to their poor villages. They don't have to accept a low-ball offer from a local grain buyer if they can determine, with a quick phone call, that harvests are poor in a neighboring region and higher prices are being offered there.

## COLLABORATING WITH FELLOW WORKERS ANYWHERE

It will be easier for people anywhere to be co-workers, toiling simultaneously on the same creative tasks of invention, design and production. This will be a force in the dispersal of research, design and manufacturing to far corners of the globe, taking advantage of lower labor costs for programmers, technicians and factory workers in less-developed nations.

Meetings, whether involving heads of state, business colleagues or the PTA, will increasingly be conducted by videoconference. David Farber, a telecommunications professor at the University of Pennsylvania, predicts that within a few years you'll be able to "attend" a meeting, college lecture or art exhibit virtually anywhere on earth, via your computer or TV screen. Video cameras and microphones positioned throughout the lecture hall will allow you to wander around, Farber says, looking at exhibits and talking to other attendees.

# The All-Powerful Internet

The Internet will become the common pathway for every kind of electronic communication—phone calls, radio, TV, movies, and home and office computing.

Some see the Internet as the dawning of a wonderful day, giving new power to each of us. "The Internet is going to be the thing that frees us from monopolies—telephone, broadcast TV, the local newspaper; it's an equalizer," says Gene Mondrus, a New York computer consultant. "We'll all own the presses."

Others are less sanguine about the Internet's playing a fully positive role in everyday life. They point to the potential for invading the privacy of others, spreading false information about people or companies, pirating copyrighted books, music and movies, and enabling compulsive gamblers to lose their shirts at virtual casinos. Then there is concern about possible domination of the Internet by a handful of powerful companies controlling Web browsers and search engines. All of these worries, some of which are already becoming reality, will spawn a slew of new privacy and copyright regulations on Capitol Hill, as well as antitrust initiatives. But Congress will always be playing catch-up with technology.

## FASTER AND FASTER VELOCITY OF INFORMATION

Internet data, coursing through ultrafast modems, will arrive in your home or office through any of several competing transmission technologies—high-capacity phone lines, cable-TV connections, direct-satellite signals, broadcast TV, even electric power lines. Internet speed will be so great that today's long waits for downloading complex Web pages will become a distant memory.

And you won't have to dial into the Internet and wait for a connection. Most service will be "constant on" or "instant on." The appliance will sense when you're not using it and cut back on the power or speed available.

The Internet will send live-action video without the slightest jerkiness. As worldwide use expands and language-translation software improves, e-mail, Web-site content and even spoken phone conversations will be instantly translated. Voice-recognition software on your computer will allow you to navigate the Web with voice commands rather than keyboard instructions.

Today's e-mail—mostly text, with some graphic files available as attachments—will be supplemented by v-mail—visual mail—a video recording of you delivering the message. With a tiny camera mounted just above the screen of your PC monitor, phone or TV, you and your electronic penpals and business colleagues will be able to chat on the Internet, face to face in real time.

### *Home entertainment*

All your favorite entertainment—movies, music, games, sports events, art exhibits, TV shows, dance recitals, symphonic concerts—will be available whenever you want it, with single-use payments charged automatically to your master account with the phone company, cable-TV vendor, satellite broadcaster or other purveyor of information. For a higher fee, you'll be able to capture the video and high-fidelity sound on mini CDs that you'll record at home. Copyrighted material will be coded to prevent unauthorized copying and reselling.

You will be able to select from vast databases of virtually every movie ever made, every piece of music ever recorded, every football game ever televised, every painting in every major art museum in the world—searchable by a variety of characteristics, including movie director, actor, conductor, painter or author. You will also be able to buy whole books online, creating your own printed volume on your home printer, in whatever type style, font size and page dimension you prefer (a plus for elderly readers who like large-type books).

All this content—editorial, graphic and audio—will continue to be owned by the original copyright holders, who will license it to online companies and receive fees ranging from a few cents to a few dollars for consumer and business use. Most Web sites will be free to visitors, with advertisers picking up the cost of maintaining the site. But other sites will be supported by a combination of advertising and subscription fees, just as most newspapers and magazines are today.

Home entertainment will be fully interactive. You will be able to edit recorded music with your own synthesizer, changing instruments and tempos. Interactive TV shows will allow you to play Jeopardy! at home, competing with the contestants on the show or your friends in their homes; change the outcome of mysteries; cast yourself into a role in a sitcom; or select the camera angles during a football game the same way the director does in the control booth.

In addition to pay-per-view offerings, which will become a significant force in home entertainment, conventional TV—free to the viewer but still larded with commercials—will live on for years. But the audience of today's major broadcast networks will continue to erode in both size and demographic desirability, surpassed by growing viewership of specialty channels. Advertisers will continue to gravitate toward easily targeted audiences for special-interest channels, with programming on investing, hobbies, history, wildlife, cultural events, and so on.

### Personal finance online

Most financial services will be marketed and managed on the Net. Online trading of stocks and mutual funds will continue to grow, with smaller and smaller commissions. People needing insurance will fill out questionnaires to help them determine what kind they need and how much to buy, then get price quotes from several insurers and finally, apply for coverage online.

Most consumer banking transactions—paying bills, making deposits or withdrawals, checking balances, moving money from account to account—will be done at the Web sites of banks. Money will be easily transferred from your checking account to online holding accounts, from which "micropayments" of a few cents or so will be made to providers of information content on the Web.

### *Shopping on the Net*

The sale of merchandise over the Web will continue to soar, led by business-to-business merchandise and strong retail sales of computers and software, stocks, airline tickets, gambling wagers, books, flowers, music CDs and pornography. Retail shopping on the Internet will someday be as pervasive as catalog shopping is today.

Most people will get comfortable with charging Internet purchases on their bankcards, as thousands of customers worldwide are now doing with "virtual retailers" such as the Amazon.com bookstore, CDNow.com and 1-800-FLOWERS florist Web site. They figure that giving their credit card number to a Web merchant that uses number-scrambling software is no more risky (and probably less so) than handing their card to a waiter or store clerk, or reciting the digits to a telephone operator.

Online ordering of automobiles is also coming on strong, with car buyers kicking the tires at a local dealer but then shopping hard for the best price at Web sites operated by national buying services or dealers. (The actual sale is almost always executed through a dealer, who gets a referral from the Web broker.) Internet gambling is also a boom field. It remains to be seen whether it will continue to be legal, but banning it would be difficult, given the fact that the Internet is a truly international market, and many of the gambling sites are located outside the U.S. Businesses will increasingly use the Web to put out bid invitations, receive proposals from vendors and close the sale.

Shoppers will also have the option of paying for their purchases using a prepaid cash account online, or they will insert a prepaid "smart card" into a box attached to the computer, much like using an automated teller machine. Want to buy your son a jersey of his favorite British soccer team, purchased online from a London shop? No problem; the smart card will also take care of the currency exchange.

The Internet is ideal for transforming a retail specialty store or unusual service into a fully global business. A small North Carolina map seller, for example, put its catalog on a Web site and now sells maps of every nation to customers all over the globe. A Rochester, N.Y., restorer of vintage stringed instruments sells to collectors around the world via his Web site. A young Mississippi entrepreneur conducts real-time cattle auctions on the Internet, with bidders watching video clips of the cows standing in their home fields all over the nation.

## DIGITAL IDs, TOO

The spread of commerce by e-mail and on the Internet has created a need for ways to reliably identify the person you're dealing with on purchases, contracts and affidavits, to prevent fraud and misrepresentation. So the American Bar Association has developed guidelines for digital signature verification. Part of the solution will be digital markings that can be made only on the computer owner's appliance, if the proper password is given.

## REGULATORY ISSUES APLENTY

The big regulatory issues facing Internet commerce are taxation, consumer privacy and encryption software. The U.S. government generally favors a hands-off approach to state and local taxation of Internet commerce so as not to hinder its explosive growth, and despite strong disagreement from the nonfederal governmental units, Washington will probably prevail on this.

As for consumer privacy, Uncle Sam will probably try to put in place a variety of safeguards against the gathering, analysis and sale of personal information about Internet use. It is questionable, however, whether these safeguards will work in an environment in which marketing is increasingly dependent on database compilations.

The encryption issue is a thorny one that pits various government officials against each other. The ability of software to scramble and then decode computer data is essential to protecting the privacy of digital phone calls and Internet commerce, preventing thieves from eavesdropping on your calls or cleaning out your bank account. So encryption is favored by many Commerce Department officials, banking regulators and others in government. But some military and law-enforcement officials favor strict limits on encryption technology—such as export controls on software—so crooks and terrorists won't be able to use it to shield their illegal activities from government surveillance techniques such as wiretapping. We believe that the pro-encryption forces will prevail, in the interests of privacy and financial security.

## INTERNET AS AN ADVERTISING MEDIUM

As more people spend more time visiting Web sites, as opposed to watching broadcast TV or reading their local newspapers, the efficiency (and cost) of advertising on the Web will continue to rise. It is the ultimate form of impulse-driven, direct-response advertising, because the customer is able to do everything except handle the product. (Eventually Web retailers will be able to display the product in 3-D, which will be the next best thing to holding it in your hand.)

Today many of your personal characteristics and commercial habits—including your birth date, driving record, mortgage and catalog purchases—are readily available to mass marketers through burgeoning databases. So likewise will be information about your Internet habits— which sites you visit, what kind of information you seek there and what you buy. This data is being captured now by Web-site operators, and unless prohibited by Congress, it's likely that it will be repackaged for use by other marketers, especially for advertising on other Web sites.

# New Modes of Data Transmission

The information flowing to and from our homes and offices— and those of people and businesses throughout the world— will move in torrents of data compressed into ever-smaller streams. The data will follow a variety of paths, sometimes using several transmission technologies on the same trip, with instant relays from one system to another. The revenue generated by each transmission will be shared (as tiny fees) among all the companies that helped the data on its way.

Competition will be fierce among all segments of the telecom industry—the wired firms (the Baby Bells, AT&T's newly acquired empire of cable TV firms, Comcast cable, etc.), the long-distance firms (MCI/Worldcom, Sprint, etc.) and the pure wireless companies (including direct-from-satellite TV and phone companies, such as DirecTV, Iridium, Globalstar, etc.). The wired firms have enormous customer bases and dramatic new technologies for passing more and more data through existing wires, both copper and fiber-optic.

But most of the half-billion households wired for phone service are in the developed nations, leaving an estimated 70% of world households without phone service. Given the high cost of installing and maintaining phone lines in every household and shop in the developing world, it's a good bet that much of the currently unwired world will remain that way for years to come—or even forever. These areas will be brought into the global telecom community through wireless carriers—digital mobile phones, satellite systems, and interactive broadcasting. The high cost of infrastructure will be saved, but the unit cost per call will be higher than the cost of today's wired service for some time to come, until economies of scale and competition brings it down.

The wireless companies will benefit from data compression and radio-wave bandwidth narrowing, enabling vastly more channels to be carried on the public airwaves. Low-power local transmitters and receivers will enable offices, schools and even homes to have their own local-area networks (LANs) up and running instantly, without any cables linking the terminals and file servers. There are already digital wireless phone systems that enable a traveling salesman to pull off the highway, turn on the laptop computer and connect to the company's Web site, without having to plug into a wired phone jack.

The biggest companies, such as AT&T, will push the concept of bundling every telecom service—local and long-distance phoning, Internet access, cable TV, etc.—into one customer relationship. But the odds are good that, years from now, many households will still be buying services from several different vendors.

# The Wired World

A fierce battle for the future of a vast telecom market will be waged between combatants that were once part of the same empire—AT&T versus its former affiliates, the Baby Bell local phone companies. AT&T's strategy is to reconnect itself to the American home by acquiring most of the nation's large cable TV firms and using those cables for every sort of telecom service—local phoning, long distance, Internet access and television. The Baby Bells want to use their existing phone lines to accomplish the same ends, and they will seek to block, by legislation or antitrust filings, AT&T's spreading national power.

The wired telephone systems of the Baby Bells now serve some 94% of U.S. households. Copper phones lines and moderately fast modems (28.8 or 56 kilobytes per second) are now the dominant Internet access method. But today's phones and modems are frustratingly slow in processing data through increasingly complex Web sites. Businesses can use high-speed leased T1 and T3 lines, but they're too pricey for home use. The Baby Bells will stake their near-term future on so-called digital subscriber lines (DSLs), which are more than 100 times faster than standard phone lines and, best of all, allows both voice and Internet use at the same time over a single phone line.

### A new kind of phone service

But the new frontier, unveiled in 1998, will be a totally different data-transmission service for home and office—one that will replace the conventional circuit-switch phone system used for more than a century. Rather than tying up a single phone line for each call between two points, this new system will use the Internet method of bundling data in "packets" that are mingled together, routed through ultrahigh-capacity fiber-optic cables along the cheapest paths, and finally sorted out and reconstituted at the receiving end.

Sprint dubbed its version of this approach the Integrated On-demand Network (ION), enabling all kinds of data originating in one household or office—phone calls, Internet connections, full-action video—to emanate simultaneously from one copper phone line in the home. Sprint and others adopting the packet-router technology (such as Qwest, Frontier, IXC and Level 3) will need the cooperation of the local phone companies—mostly Baby Bells—because they have the customer relationship with most households, and their copper wiring already in the home will be the starting point for the new system.

The odds are good that in a few years Sprint's vision will be the norm in the telecom world, with everyone from AT&T to the Baby Bells abandoning the old circuit-switch system and moving to packet-router transmission. Eventually, there will be no more long-distance phone charges varying by the length of your call or the distance to the city you called. A meter on your telecom line at home will simply measure the flow of data into and out of your house, whether the bits of information are converted to voice messages, video or computer text. And in a ferociously competitive market, the price of the data flow will keep coming down, down, down.

## CABLE TV

Today's cable TV systems have the potential to be a significant force in the integrating of all voice, Internet and video services, using cable modems that promise to be about 20 times faster than 56K phone modems. Current cable customers may have to pay a surcharge for Internet access, but they won't have to get an additional phone line.

Because the cable modems and set-top units will be connected to the shared lines of the cable operator, there's a possibility that speed would be slowed if everyone on the cable system were online at the same time—a problem not likely for a number of years, and perhaps solved by new technology in the meantime.

In just 12 months spanning '98-'99, AT&T spent some $130 billion to buy all or parts of the biggest cable operations in America, including TCI, MediaOne and cable units of Time Warner. These acquisitions give it access to an estimated 60% of all households in America. (But in mid-'99, it was still not certain that AT&T's buy-out of MediaOne would pass muster with federal communications and antitrust officials.)

## ELECTRIC UTILITIES

In 1997, Nortel and a British power company announced a breakthrough technology that will allow electric utilities to transmit data over power lines, by screening the data from electrical interference. They believe that transmission speeds of one megabit per second—about ten times faster than today's highest-speed home service with ISDN (Integrated Services Digital Network)—will be achievable.

In the United States, many utilities that now sell power, water and natural gas are exploring entering the telecommunications business, but some are meeting with skepticism from state utility regulators. National utility companies, especially the gas-pipeline industry, have already begun using their valuable rights of way to lay or string fiber-optic cable, with more than one million miles now in place.

## INTERNATIONAL CALLS THROUGH OCEANIC CABLES

For years to come, most of the international traffic in voice and data messages will travel not through the air—via land towers or satellites—but by land and across ocean floors through fiber-optic glass strands now circling the globe.

There are an estimated 90,000 miles of such international cables now in use, and in the next two years another 177,000 miles will be laid, with an additional 200,000 more miles planned by 2003. And the carrying capacity of each strand of cable is growing enormously. A transAtlantic fiber-optic cable is currently able to carry 2.4 million phone conversations simultaneously, according to a report in *The Washington Post,* and a planned seabed cable between China and the United States is expected to be able to transmit four million phone calls at the same time.

In 1998 Lucent Technologies announced that it had achieved a nearly fivefold increase in the number of wavelengths of light that could simultaneously carry different streams of data through one hair-thin glass fiber. The practical result: ten million phone calls moving simultaneously through a single strand of fiber, at a speed of 400 billion bits of data per second. Lucent claims that, at this speed, a single strand handling 80 channels could carry all the world's present Internet traffic at one time.

# The Wireless Challenge

While wired phone service enjoys a 94% market penetration among American households, wireless phones have only a 25% penetration. But that's growing rapidly. The total number of wireless-phone accounts, including business use, has soared from only five million in 1990 to an estimated 70 million, with a projected growth of 50 million over the next five years.

Some of the same companies that run wires into your home or business are also providers of wireless portable phone service, either cellular (analog signal) or PCS, the newer digital portables. And Sprint, the number-three long-distance phone company, is betting big on both PCS wireless and its new ION wired service.

Analog cell service is on the way out, eventually to be surpassed by digital phones for clarity, security of conversations, and popular features like paging, voice mail and caller-ID. But for now, analog cellular has much broader coverage, so it will be around for quite a while. Digital service will cover virtually all of the country by 2001. And users of both systems are benefiting from the competition, with cell-phone charges declining by about half where PCS has entered the market. Some phone makers, such as AT&T, are making portable phones that will work with both analog cell systems and digital systems, but the three different digital protocols in use now (GSM, CDMA and TDMA) are not expected to be compatible.

## TV AND THE INTERNET COME TOGETHER

Only half of American homes own a personal computer, but TV ownership is virtually universal. So it's likely that the familiar, easy-to-use TV set will play a big role in bringing Internet access to virtually every American home over the next decade. The signal will come to the TV set either by cable, through the airwaves from a local broadcaster, or direct from a satellite to a small dish on the roof.

Microsoft's WebTV, the first popularly priced experiment in combined TV and Internet access, has fewer than one million subscribers today, but it shows what is possible. Users can simultaneously watch TV and visit a Web site on the same screen. This kind of technology will make possible interactive viewing, in which viewers can play along with quiz shows, participate in public-opinion polls after a political debate, look up the stats of baseball players while a game is going on, or register their own verdict on a boxing match after each round.

## BROADCAST TV

Coming soon: video of amazing clarity and brightness, the long-awaited high-definition TV. During the transition to full digital HDTV broadcasting between now and 2006, the owners of more than 1,500 TV stations will be deciding whether to go into the business of providing full telecommunications services—Internet access, telephone service and data—to America's homes and businesses.

For those owners, the government's encouragement to begin broadcasting HDTV as soon as possible is a mixed blessing. On the downside, the stations (and programming networks) must invest millions of dollars in new equipment for HDTV broadcasting, with no prospect of recovering the cost in higher advertising rates from their sponsors.

But there is a silver lining: Uncle Sam will give every station, free, an extra TV channel for HDTV broadcasting, along with the analog channel the station is currently using. Employing the new digital data-compression technologies, a broadcaster will be able to use the new channel in any of several lucrative ways. It could split the bandwidth into a half-dozen new TV channels and compete better with cable-TV operators. Or it could use the bandwidth to go into the data and voice businesses, in competition with local phone companies and Internet-access providers. Most stations will use their bandwidth for both HDTV and some additional kind of service.

The current government plan is for TV stations to broadcast in both analog and HDTV formats until 2006, at which time they would cease analog broadcasts and turn their original channel back to the Federal Communications Commission, which will sell it to someone else in a government bandwidth auction. But six years from now, there will still be millions of today's analog TV sets in homes around America, and their owners won't be left stranded, or forced to buy an HDTV set; dual TV broadcasts are likely to continue long after the 2006 deadline.

Sales of new HDTV sets will start slowly, since the price can run $6,000 or $7,000, and HDTV programming will be very limited for a few years. But, as with the new color TVs of the 1950s and '60s, the price will fall substantially with mass production. Giant-screen sets, which will showcase the improved picture quality, will become a mainstay of the consumer electronics industry, which hasn't had a hot new "must-have" product since VCRs and CD players.

HDTV broadcasts began on about 26 stations in the ten largest U.S. metro areas in late '98, but start-up will probably be delayed at many stations by a variety of problems, including squabbles over signal interference and citizen opposition to the very tall transmission towers that are required. But it's possible that half of America's households will have access to an HDTV signal by the end of 2000, with the rest following within a couple of years.

## DIRECT TV COMES ON STRONG—AND THEN RADIO, TOO

The direct-from-satellite broadcasters (such as DirecTV, Primestar and EchoStar) will soon be able to use data-compression technology to offer a lot more than 200 different sporting events and movies each weekend. They can, if they wish, be full-service providers of all kinds of data, from voice to Internet access.

DirecTV, for example, joined forces with America Online in 1999 as part of the "AOL Anywhere" strategy, under which AOL will try to wean itself from total dependence on local dial-up phone connections for linking its millions of subscribers to the Internet.

Someday, it's also possible that companies engaged in Global Positioning Systems, used now mostly for tracking transport vehicles, monitoring agriculture and controlling navigation systems (including the new systems for automobiles), will be transformed into full-service communications providers for home and business.

### *New kinds of radio broadcasts*

The different ways of building and operating a wireless telecommunications network are limited only by the bandwidth available on the public airwaves—which, in an era of narrowcasting and data compression, seems to be an almost unlimited resource.

One of the newest contenders is the Local Multipoint Distribution System (LMDS), which transmits microwave radio signals, not unlike current TV stations but with more power, from a network of antennas spaced every five miles or so. LMDS has potential for TV and phone service, and one company is now offering TV service in New York City. But a 1997 FCC auction of licenses and bandwidth didn't generate as many bids as expected, perhaps because of the difficulty LMDS will face in competing against other entrenched technologies.

Separately, there are plans afoot by several companies (including CD Radio and Worldspace) to use satellites for a new kind of pay-radio broadcast—high-fidelity music and news would be received on special small antennas mounted on your car or home. On a subscription basis, they will offer every kind of music and information in many different languages, opening up a world of programming choices in competition with free commercial and public radio stations.

### INFORMATION BY SATELLITE

The first "sat phones"—direct-to-satellite portable telephones—came into use in 1998, at high prices and with mixed reviews on performance. But in a few years, as reliability improves and prices fall, there will be lots of competition in the "personal satellite communications" market, making telephone and Internet connections possible literally anywhere on earth, without the need for land antennas to relay the data.

Iridium, the first small "sat phone" on the market, is the brainchild of visionaries at Motorola, which owns about 18% of the system and operates it for a consortium of communications firms that have invested billions in it. It will be joined soon by a competing system from Globalstar, and later on, the Teledesic project, bankrolled by cellular mogul Craig McCaw, Microsoft's Bill Gates and a Saudi Arabian prince.

Blanketing the globe with a network of 66 low-orbit satellites, Iridium enables users of its chunky phones (which can cost from $2,300 upward, depending on the country of purchase) to place calls to and from any point on earth, with per-minute charges running a couple of dollars or more, depending on location and the method of routing required. Some calls move through 14 "gateway" transmission facilities around the world, but others will go directly to and from the satellites.

In its first year of operation, Iridium's phones were plagued by technical difficulties, such as frequent dropped calls and weak signals that didn't allow for use inside buildings. Sales were lower than expected, and operating losses mounted. Iridium also faces competition on some continents from a cheaper, lower-tech but more reliable rival, the Inmarsat phone system. Its phones (laptop sized, with a detachable window-sill antenna for indoor use) communicate through only two stationary satellites over the Atlantic and Indian oceans, originally placed there for maritime navigation.

# Pricing and Regulatory Battles Ahead

The biggest governmental battle will be whether the local phone companies will be unleashed to go into long-distance calling and the long-distance companies will be allowed to offer local service. This would complete the total deregulation of telecommunications envisioned by Congress in its landmark act of 1996.

While the industry, federal courts, FCC and state regulators will fight this battle for several more years, the odds are good that, in the end, every industry will have relatively free access to each other's turf, with resulting savings for users in all areas of telecommunications. AT&T, trying to hold antitrust actions at bay during its roll-up of America's cable TV companies, talks of dramatic savings to consumers from its planned bundling of all phone, TV and Internet services into one bill. Customers might be charged simply for their total hours of telecom usage—whether phone calls, TV viewing or Web access—all at the same rate, regardless of the usage mix.

One of the biggest issues to be resolved in the coming clash of competing technologies is how all these services will be priced, and what role government regulators, both federal and state, will play in the process.

Take, for example, the simple question of who should pay for calls made to a wireless phone. In most nations, the caller pays for all calls, to any phone, based on the length of the call—even local calls made from a wired home phone. But the United States has a double standard. Local calls between wired phones (at home or the office) are essentially "free"—that is, untimed and covered by the monthly service charge. But calls made both to and from a wireless phone are timed and billed to the wireless account. So every call to a wireless phone is a "collect" call. The resulting high usage fees discourage many potential customers from getting wireless service and deter current customers from using their wireless phone as a true substitute for their regular home phone.

So the wireless industry will push for adoption of the European-style "caller pays" system. They believe this could lead to people using wireless phones for all their voice calling, reserving their wired home service for Internet connections or home entertainment.

There is no U.S. law against "caller pays," but it's likely to face some formidable barriers. First of all, the wired phone companies may not want to give wireless such a big competitive boost by agreeing to the plan. And state utility regulators will probably want a say in this pricing revolution, if it spreads beyond a few experiments now going on. It remains to be seen whether Congress and the FCC, which favors broad deregulation of telecommunications, will try to preempt state authority on this issue.

Another tough issue that Washington and the telecommunications industry will face is whether companies that offer long-distance service on the Internet should be classified as phone companies and subjected to the same fees and taxes that other long-distance firms must pay to subsidize the local phone infrastructure.

While Washington is generally opposed to taxing Internet service firms and even merchandise sales on the Internet, there is growing feeling that Internet phone service—now priced at about half regular long-distance service, but not of the same quality—is getting an unfair free ride. This will become more controversial as the quality of Internet phone service improves, and start-up firms such as IDT and Qwest Communications International take more and more market share from the likes of AT&T, MCI/Worldcom and Sprint (which will respond by going into Internet long distance themselves).

### Competition for signals

Finally, as much bandwidth as there is for everyone, there will be lots of problems with signal interference in the first few years of the wireless revolution. We got a glimpse of this in early 1998, on the debut of America's first digital-TV broadcast, from WFAA-TV in Dallas. Soon after service began, the signal began to interfere with wireless heart monitors at a Dallas hospital. Similar problems could arise with other local wireless users, including taxi dispatchers, ship radios and wireless microphones, until everyone figures out what frequency is available and adjusts accordingly. Aggrieved parties will undoubtedly ask their governments for help.

# Amazing New Appliances

All the communications systems, wired and wireless, will connect to their customers through an astounding array of new consumer electronic products—"information appliances," in the most generic description.

### Smart phones

The smart phones now on the market include all the normal features (voice mail, caller ID and so on), and soon will have a small screen for Internet access and software for maintaining a database of phone numbers, addresses and your personal calendar. Some will give you sports scores and stock quotes and handle your electronic banking, too. And all these features will soon be available in a wireless smart phone, using digital PCS technology. But the Internet access will be a little pokey and balky until more bandwidth and faster wireless modems come along.

### Hand-held computers

Sales will soar for personal digital assistants, hand-held computers that duplicate many of the features of personal computers, including Internet access, in a very small package.

Meanwhile, TVs will become more like computers and computers more like TVs. Apple is making a portable computer that plays music CDs and digital video discs (DVDs, the new high-definition replacement for videotapes) and receives regular broadcast or cable TV.

### Goodbye to picture tubes

The viewing screen on all these devices, from TVs to PCs to smart phones, won't be today's deep cathode-ray picture tube, but a flat, liquid-crystal monitor (like a laptop display) for receiving digital high-definition broadcasts with amazingly lifelike color and crispness. It might be as tiny as Sony's Watchman TV screen or the size of an entire wall. The stereophonic sound system will convey the realism of being in the middle of the action.

## Ubiquitous Electronic Spies

A major advance in the next 20 years will be the refinement of sensors—tiny cameras and microphones that will fit on a computer chip about half the size of a golf ball. "In the 1980s it was the microprocessor. In the '90s it was lasers. In the next phase of technology, it will be these sensors," says Paul Saffo of the Institute for the Future in Menlo Park, Cal.

Such devices are starting to show up in freeways on the West Coast, where it is possible to call up a Web site and see a traffic map that continuously updates the average vehicle speed at every major intersection. The information is gleaned from sensors placed at intersections and then relayed to a central computer. Over the next ten years, video cameras will be added to these sensors, making possible live pictures—even instant replay, to help investigate accidents—that can be beamed to billboards and computer systems in cars.

Someday there will be sensors all over the modern home, watching the front door, the baby's room and the kitchen. You'll be able to call up the sensor's images on the small screen of your wireless phone or hand-held computer when you're at the office or traveling. Other early applications for sensors are likely to be in retail stores, to deter shoplifting, and at restaurants, to keep track of tables to be cleared and turned over to the next diners. Sensors will also be used to provide security in apartments and offices, read meters, monitor manufacturing processes, check the stock in vending machines and inspect hazardous cargo. Tapes recorded by sensors will be played in court to settle law-suits and criminal cases.

There are still hurdles facing the widespread use of sensors—cost, for one. Privacy issues will arise, especially when sensors are used to monitor and measure the performance of workers. And, of course, there is the potential for using such video technology for illegal pur-poses, when sensors are secretly planted as bugs in offices or homes.

# CHAPTER 14

# Biotech Takes Off

T he public has been hearing about the dazzling promise of biotechnology for so long that many people—ranging from medical professionals and their patients to farmers and biotech investors—have grown impatient waiting for the social and financial payoff.

But biotech has already produced some impressive results. And it's now on the verge of achieving the critical mass of genetic research from which, over the next few years, will pour a flood of new products for health, agriculture, environmental protection and manufacturing, including new materials such as plastics from plants.

In the decades ahead, these products will provide incalculable benefits to humankind—improving diet and health, especially in the less-developed nations; conquering diseases that are terminal today; and preventing a wide range of genetically based infirmities.

As an industry, biotech will see a dizzying rush of corporate start-ups, with more researchers leaving government and university laboratories to form their own firms, backed by venture capital and public stock offerings. Pharmaceutical and agribusiness companies all over the world will acquire these small firms and combine with each other, leveraging their research and capital into enormous enterprises seeking to control patents and rush new products to market.

By 2005, genetically engineered products made in the United States alone will account for some $100 billion of sales worldwide. In human health, the arrival of biotech products will be hastened by a new law that speeds up the Food and Drug Administration's evaluation and approval process.

# Deciphering the Human Genetic Code

The basis of biotechnology is the ability to identify and understand the function of every gene in every living thing, plant or animal. In the human body, that means isolating and decoding as many as 80,000 genes, then trying to determine how they interact with each other.

This genetic sleuthing, performed by high-speed computers called genetic sequencers, goes on in government and private laboratories all over the world. The most ambitious project is the decade-old, $3 billion Human Genome Project, conducted by the National Institutes of Health and the Department of Energy. But a number of private organizations are also working on unraveling the human genetic code. In 1998, Celera Genomics, a new venture backed by Perkin-Elmer (which manufactures genetic-sequencing computers), was formed with the bold intention—overly optimistic, some say—of accelerating the deciphering of the entire human genome, completing the task by 2001, well ahead of the federal project and at a fraction of the cost.

## CONTROL OF GENETIC INFORMATION

Biotech is fast evolving into an information business, and the commercial right to sell genetic information—a form of intellectual property like a copyrighted book—is at the core of the entire industry.

It has long been clear that a biotech product—a drug or new material made from genetically altered substances—is patentable, but there has been controversy over the issuing of patents for the basic information that makes the product possible. One camp believes that all decipherings of the genetic code should be in the public domain, free to anyone to use. But to create a profit motive for research, public policy has gone in a different direction, allowing companies to patent their discoveries of particular genetic sequences, which they may license to pharmaceutical and agribusiness companies for biotech product development. Celera Genomics, for example, may take a middle ground on the commercial-rights issue, charging for the use of a few hundred of its most commercially attractive genetic sequences but allowing researchers worldwide to use some of the firm's data at no charge.

The issue of commercial rights in biotech will be hotly contested in the years ahead, with competing firms waging expensive, high-stakes battles in court over the patentable uniqueness or unpatentable similarities of thousands of genetic sequences and combinations.

# Medical Wonders

Most biotech drugs will be gene therapies, in which illnesses or disorders are treated by altering the genes within a patient's cells. A new gene may be delivered into cells to repair an inherited genetic defect, treat diseased cells directly, make the cells more sensitive to another treatment, or produce a substance the body needs. For example, diabetes patients will be implanted with a gene directing the body to produce insulin. Another approach will entail cell therapy, in which a patient's cells are fixed outside the body and then put back; this will be tried for such diseases as lymphoma, leukemia and kidney cancer.

## ATTACKING CANCERS

Of the more than 300 biotech drugs already in advanced clinical trials, about half are designed to arrest or slow the growth of cancers, including breast and skin cancers. Traditional cancer therapies resort to brute force, destroying cancer cells by surgically removing them, zapping them with radiation or poisoning them with drugs that kill the cancer cells but wreak havoc on the healthy cells, too. The new biotech cancer drugs will take a targeted approach that promises to be gentler on the body, making possible higher doses of cell-specific medicines over long periods of time.

Some biotech drugs will trick cancer cells into dying of old age, as other cells do, or switching off their cancer-causing properties. Other drugs will make cancer cells more vulnerable to medicines already available, or infect and kill cells that carry the characteristics of future cancer cells. At Baylor College of Medicine, for example, researchers are working on a new therapy for malignant brain tumors: They alter a common virus by adding an enzyme-producing gene, then inject the altered virus into the center of the brain tumor where it starts making the enzyme, thymidine kinase. When the enzyme is exposed to the drug ganciclovir, it creates a toxin that destroys cancer cells, but not healthy brain cells. In another technique, called photodynamic therapy, the patient is injected with a light-sensitive drug that accumulates in cancerous cells. After several days, doctors expose the tumor to a low-power laser for 30 minutes. This will trigger a reaction that kills the cancerous cells without burning surrounding skin.

A cancer "vaccine" being tested is believed to boost the patient's immune system to fight off new cancer cells; it won't prevent cancer, as a true vaccine does, but it should help slow its spread. At the National

:er Institute, a vaccine to boost the immune systems of gravely ill
ınoma patients is being tested. So far, the vaccine consistently
ınuuces the patient's body to create tumor-fighting white blood cells.
Eventually, genetically engineered drugs will target particular kinds of
cancer cells, focusing specifically on cancers of the brain, blood
(leukemia), liver, kidney, breast, colon, lung, skin, prostate or ovaries.

## NEW DRUGS FOR EVERY DISORDER

Also in the research pipeline are biotech vaccines for AIDS, malaria, cholera, Lyme disease, ear infections, herpes and the flu. Work on an
AIDS vaccine focuses on ways to block the entry of the HIV virus into
cells and to strengthen immune systems to fight the onset of AIDS
symptoms. For obese people, there will be gene therapies that will
speed up metabolism and curb appetites. Researchers are even working on a genetic cure for baldness.

A new protein treatment will improve vision by stimulating the
healing of retinal tissue and retarding macular degeneration, a leading cause of sight loss in older people. There will be biotech treatments for auto-immune disorders such as lupus, rheumatoid arthritis
and multiple sclerosis.

## BATTLING THE AGING PROCESS

Given the aging (and the increasing affluence) of world populations, many drug companies are focusing on biotech remedies for
afflictions of old age. For arthritis, there will be drugs to block joint
inflammation, including a gel that can be injected to replace degenerated cartilage; for osteoporosis, drugs that will combat bone loss without
cancer risks; for Parkinson's disease, a gene implant that prompts a
patient's body to make the dopamine needed by the brain. Alzheimer's
disease is proving more difficult, but there are some promising developments in slowing down the onset and severity of symptoms.

There was news in late 1997 that scientists had discovered a substance called telomere, located at the tip of chromosomes, that apparently controls the aging process in cells. They later found an enzyme
called telomerase that seems to preserve the telomere. This raises the
possibility of adding cloned telomerase to cells to reset their clocks,
extending their lives or even creating "immortal cells" that refuse to age
and deteriorate. The implications—ethical, political and economic—
are almost beyond imagination, raising the possibility of extending
human life far beyond today's normal longevity.

Biotech researchers in several countries are working on genetically engineered substances that could dramatically improve the health of people with clogged coronary arteries and reduce the need for expensive coronary bypass surgery. A German team announced in 1998 that it had achieved success with this "biobypass" method, in which genetically engineered human protein that stimulates the growth of blood vessels was injected into the heart muscles of 20 patients suffering from heart disease. Within four days, all the patients showed signs that tiny new blood vessels were sprouting around the diseased arteries, channeling blood around the blockages.

## ATTACKS ON GENETIC DISEASES

Research attention is being lavished, too, on diseases affecting the very young, especially genetic disorders that could be headed off in the womb, or even in the parents before they conceive a child. This approach will be tried against sickle-cell anemia, Tay-Sachs disease, hemophilia and several immune-system disorders. If genetic repair cannot be made in the parents, it will be attempted in the fetus, and some scientists believe the day will come when they will be able to correct genes in an embryo consisting of just eight cells.

## NEW DELIVERY METHODS, TOO

Many of the new biotech drugs will be administered not by injection but by nasal sprays and inhalers delivering a powerful vapor into the lungs. Work is under way on an inhalable flu vaccine and a drug to alleviate symptoms of common cold viruses. An inhalable insulin for diabetics is expected in three or four years, and later on, an insulin pill for those with Type 2 diabetes.

## HUMAN DRUGS FROM PLANTS AND ANIMALS

Pharmaceutical biotech is an interdisciplinary industry that brings together medicine, plant science and animal science. Whereas traditional drugs have been derived largely from chemical compounds, many biotech drugs will be derived from natural substances found in plants and animals that have been genetically altered for a desired result.

For example, researchers believe that tobacco leaves, a health villain when smoked, can be genetically modified to produce beneficial enzymes. (Young tobacco plants of a conventional sort are already known to produce a high-quality protein that can serve as a nutritious food supplement and food-thickening agent, and there is a possibility that tobacco plants can be used to make a malaria vaccine.) Inexpensive foods like bananas and potatoes, popular in nations both rich and poor, will be genetically engineered to become edible vaccines against common diseases such as acute diarrhea, cholera, malaria, hepatitis and E. coli infections.

Pharmaceutical companies are joining forces with veterinary medicine to develop genetically engineered animals that will be living drug factories, producing proteins and other substances for human health. Goats, cows, sheep and other animals will produce hemoglobin, blood-clotting factors and TPA, which dissolves clots. Cows will be genetically designed to produce milk that more closely resembles a human mother's milk, for newborn infants and people who are allergic to animal milk.

## ANIMAL ORGANS FOR HUMANS

Animals will also become a source of organs for human transplants—hearts, kidneys, livers and other parts—genetically changed to reduce rejection by the human recipient. For some people, animal organs might even be superior to human transplants. People whose livers have been destroyed by hepatitis B, for example, are not good candidates for a new human liver, because the virus hides in the body and then infects the new liver. Baboon livers, however, are resistant to hepatitis B.

There will eventually emerge an industry devoted to the creation of "designer animals," whose tissues are partly human and less prone to rejection by humans—for example, pigs whose blood vessels include human proteins, due to the injection of human genes into the pig embryo. This prospect will be ethically controversial, as animal-rights activists and others object to the raising of animals for the primary purpose of harvesting organs and tissues for the benefit of humankind.

## THE FUTURE OF GENE THERAPY

Over nearly eight years of clinical trials, gene therapy has been used on an estimated 3,000 patients with inherited genetic disorders. In these therapies, millions of copies of certain beneficial genes have been introduced into the patient's body to compensate for genes that are missing or defective. No one has been cured of a disease, but many have shown improvement, and it is likely that the effectiveness of gene therapy will greatly increase in the next few years.

A milestone in gene therapy was achieved in 1997 with the invention of artificial human chromosomes, containing sets of genes that can be inserted into human cells and that will thereafter reproduce when the cells divide. This hasn't been tried yet because, up to now, all clinical use of gene therapy has been based on the understanding that genetic modifications would affect only the patient during his or her lifetime and would not be passed on to offspring.

In fact, many advanced nations, including the United States, England and Canada, now ban "germline gene therapy," in which changes in the genes of sperm or eggs would be transmitted to a patient's descendants. The prohibitions are based on several concerns, including the possibility that errors in genetic reprogramming could cause more harm than good, as well as a feeling that people living today have no right to engineer changes in the genes of future generations. "The gene pool is not owned by anyone; it is the joint property of society," say W. French Anderson, director of the University of Southern California's gene therapy laboratory and a pioneer who supports germline therapy. In an interview with *The Washington Post,* Anderson suggested that, before manipulating the gene pool, "one needs the agreement of society."

Anderson and others believe that this agreement will evolve over the next decade, enabling the medical profession to greatly reduce the number of people carrying genes that predispose their offspring to such malfunctions as sickle-cell anemia and cystic fibrosis. Before there can be a consensus for germline gene therapy, there must be a reliable technique enabling the genetically modified human sperm cells to be tested outside the human body before being combined with an egg in a laboratory dish. In one such technique, a mouse's testes might be the intermediate vehicle for receiving and growing the new human sperm cells, which would be extracted and carefully tested before use. These therapies raise the possibility of widespread use of genetic vaccines that would immunize future generations against a wide array of inherited disorders and diseases.

### Troubling ethical issues

Gene therapies raise the prospect of elective genetic enhancement, through which individuals could introduce, boost, minimize or delete in their sperm or eggs certain genes associated with—appearing to cause a predisposition toward—a wide range of human traits. According to research to date, these traits include depression, height, optimism, obesity, leadership, aggressive behavior, physical strength, addiction to alcohol and drugs, extreme shyness or extroversion, homosexuality, and high aptitudes for sports, music and mathematics. Note the words "associated with" and "predisposition," which are important reminders that it's unlikely that any one gene, by itself, causes any particular condition. Probably it works in combination with many other genes—and is tempered by environmental conditioning.

Couples contemplating having a child could decide which of their own inherited predispositions they would like to accentuate or play down in their own children. And it's not inconceivable that, in a free market in genetically enhanced sperm or eggs, people could purchase the genetic material of famous individuals, perhaps further enhanced by gene therapies.

Politically, this will be one of the most controversial issues of the 21st century. In general, public policy will permit reasonably unfettered research and clinical experimentation in gene therapies, but will be slow to embrace the widespread use of the techniques until safeguards are in place. Policymakers are far behind the scientists on these knotty questions. Only last year, in October 1997, representatives from two federal agencies met to consider for the first time whether regulations should be placed on gene therapy for cosmetic purposes. The public appears willing to accept some genetic enhancement. Surveys in 1986 and 1992 showed that 40% to 45% of the public approved of using genetic work to increase intelligence and other traits.

### THE PROMISE OF CLONING

Cloning—creation of exact replicas of living plants and mammals—will play a crucial role in the biotech industry. While the public debate over cloning has focused on the prospect of people seeking to reproduce themselves, cloning offers enormous promise for the treatment of disease and injury by creating cells and tissue that will not be rejected by the patient's body. Cloning will be used to generate new skin for burn victims, new bones, even nerve tissue for victims of spinal-cord injury.

Dr. Steen Willadsen, a researcher whose methods were used to clone Dolly the sheep, the first successful animal cloning, predicts it's only a matter of time before a human is cloned, with or without the permission of government. Remember that every advanced medical technique now in use—from heart transplants and artificial insemination to the use of surrogate mothers to carry embryos developed in lab dishes—was once scorned and recommended for regulation or outright prohibition. Now they are broadly practiced techniques, even if still controversial.

### GENETIC TESTING

The more we learn about genes that create a predisposition toward certain human conditions, the more we will be able to predict early in life who should be especially vigilant about such conditions. Genetic testing will become a major tool in diagnosing and treating many illnesses that have a genetic origin. Tests will identify those at risk for certain diseases such as breast or colorectal cancer. Early diagnosis will lead to use of drugs to prevent or delay the onset of disease.

Today couples in the early stages of pregnancy use in-utero testing to determine whether their fetus will have Down Syndrome or other severe impairments, and many couples choose to terminate the pregnancy if the tests are positive. It is likely that widespread genetic testing will increase the rate of abortion to avoid a wider variety of real or perceived disabilities, but it's likewise possible that earlier genetic counseling will allow corrective action before pregnancy.

There seems to be a strong consensus, not likely to change for years to come, that information from genetic testing should be available only to the individual affected and not to anyone else—an employer or insurer, for example—without permission. Federal and state laws will continue to assure this confidentiality.

# Biotech's Boost to the Food Supply

The world's food supply and nutritional sources will get a big boost from biotechnology in the decades ahead. Biotech's legacy on the farm will be more environment-friendly agriculture. Producers will have more tools to combat pests, overcome difficult conditions, and squeeze more food from fewer acres and resources.

Crops will be designed with built-in resistance to diseases and pests, boosting yields worldwide. This is already being done with corn, cotton, soybeans and rapeseed (canola). Plants will also be endowed with new tolerance to drought, wetness and freezes, greatly expanding the land area where grains and vegetables can be profitably grown. Genetic engineering will also produce trees that grow faster or resist disease. Applications will range from growing better-shaped Christmas trees to developing species that can quickly reforest an area cleared by logging. Of particular importance in areas of the world where fresh water is in short supply, new plant strains will tolerate salty water. In the U.S., salinity is an increasing problem for farmers in Louisiana and other coastal areas, stunting the growth of their plants or killing entire fields.

## FUTURE FOODS

Ten or 20 years from now, we will still be eating an assortment of meats and poultry, grains and cereals, dairy products, fruits and vegetables. But many items will be genetically altered to take out old traits and add new ones. Produce will be designed to be sweeter, tastier and crunchier. Some eggs will contain no cholesterol. Beef and pork will be leaner but no less tasty.

Plants will be altered to give them more fiber or less fiber, depending on the end use. Tomatoes will have higher solid content and less water, so they won't bruise so easily on the way to market. Carrots and other produce will last longer on the shelf.

Many of these changes will make foods more convenient—easier to buy, transport, prepare and eat. Other changes will give foods more nutritional value. Products will be grown and processed to carry more vitamins, minerals and fiber, with less salt, fat and calories than ever.

## LESS RELIANCE ON PESTICIDES

Pest management will be revolutionized over the next decade. Resistance to certain herbicides will be built into some crops, making it easier for farmers to apply weed killers without harming the crop. The use of some common chemical pesticides will be eliminated or greatly reduced by genetically engineered biocontrols. Science will give agriculture an army of natural pest predators, including bacteria, fungi and pheromones (sexual-attraction substances). Researchers will create stink bugs that eat potato beetles, and citrus trees will be endowed with proteins that repel nematodes. Farmers will plant decoy bushes near their crops—bushes that are genetically imbued with pheromones that lure pests away from the money-making crops. In other cases, crops will be genetically altered to produce their own bug repellents. Genetic engineering will also focus on sterilizing agricultural pests and disease-carrying insects to reduce their populations in areas of cultivation and human habitation.

## GENETICALLY ENGINEERED ANIMALS

Such genetic tinkering won't be limited to the plant kingdom. Geneticists will create super-producing livestock that yield more meat, milk and wool. They'll also endow animals with genes that make the meat more tender, or turn out better breeding stock that resists disease or tolerates heat and cold.

Cloning of livestock embryos will allow for rapid creation of identical animals with the special qualities above. This will allow farmers to quickly ramp up production of animal-based pharmaceutical products and to improve their herds with better breeding stock.

# CHAPTER 15

# Robotics, New Materials and Energy

I f microelectronics, telecommunications and biotechnology will be the most world-changing technologies of the next century, a few others—factory automation, new materials, and new ways of generating and transmitting electricity—will be close behind. Here's a quick rundown on what's ahead in these fields.

## Automation in Industry

P roductivity on the factory floor will rise steadily as computer-integrated manufacturing, robots and new materials become commonplace. These innovations will allow manufacturing industries to resemble service businesses in the way they tailor products to specific customers. Steel making is on the cutting edge of this trend. Computerized systems allow steel companies to retool the mill to make custom orders for individual buyers without costly downtime.

Manufacturing technologies that suffered through rocky introductions in recent years will come into their own in the coming years. Robotics is a fascinating example. During the 1980s and 1990s, Japan set the pace for installing robots in factories. The U.S. lagged far behind, with only about one-seventh the number of robots per industrial worker. And some U.S. companies that experimented with robots regretted it. In many cases, however, they had installed robots without having a clear idea of what the machines could or couldn't do. General Motors poured $30 billion into factory automation and wound up with robots that would spray paint on each other or crash into objects. IBM installed an entire line of robots at a North Carolina plant only to realize too late that humans could handle the assembly tasks better and more cheaply.

257

Thankfully, manufacturers learned from these and other mistakes. Companies have come to realize that robots are best-suited for jobs that are either too dangerous or monotonous for workers or too precise for human hands, such as inserting microchips into tightly packed computer circuit boards. Today the U.S. is home to some of the most highly automated factories in the world, such as Rockwell's Allen-Bradley plant in downtown Milwaukee, where many different models of its motor controls can be made on a single assembly line, as orders come in.

The U.S. robotics industry has turned the corner, and is now gaining about 25% a year, according to Leo Reddy, president of the National Coalition for Advanced Manufacturing, who credits the change to better understanding of what robots can do. "It used to be: Buy a robot, put it in," Reddy says. "Now it's seen as a piece of an overall manufacturing system." Tony Friscia, president of AMR Research in Boston, adds that the robot isn't a "smart pill" but a tool to improve the work of people and technology.

This is still an industry in its infancy. Robots are now found in only 10% of U.S. factories, but that figure will double over the next decade. Already the U.S. is the world leader in software to program robots and in systems to integrate factory automation.

As robots and their programming are improved, these machines will be cheaper and smarter, often with sophisticated vision systems that "see" objects on conveyer belts. More-talented robots, with movements more like human limbs, will move into areas of manufacturing that have so far resisted automation, such as the cutting and sewing of cloth, leather and plastics for apparel and footwear. You'll see more robots in everyday settings, too, such as delivering mail in office buildings. Some hospitals already use automated machines to deliver pills and meals to patients. Robots mop the floors at the Central Intelligence Agency headquarters in Virginia (but they don't do windows, at least not yet). These, however, are primitive machines compared with the robots that will be developed in the next century.

### DESIGNING IN VIRTUAL REALITY

Computer-assisted design (CAD) is already old hat, and devices exist that can translate the on-screen, three-dimensional image of a new part directly into a hard-plastic prototype of the part, with all the machining (cutting, drilling and smoothing) performed by laser beams. These techniques have greatly shortened the time from design to production in factories all over the world.

But this is just the beginning of what CAD is capable of doing. We can already glimpse 21st-century manufacturing at research centers around the country. At Sandia National Laboratories, in New Mexico, designers create parts, tools and assemblies that exist only on computer screens. By attempting to move pieces around, they can tell whether the factory design will work. At Argonne National Laboratory near Chicago, computer scientists have built three-dimensional computer rooms called CAVEs—Computer Automatic Virtual Environment—that allow them to create and test different products and industrial processes. A design-repair job that takes weeks now might be completed in hours. Caterpillar used CAVEs to improve visibility for drivers of its earth-moving equipment, and FMC used them to develop oil-production platforms that can withstand the pounding of waves from ships' bows.

Virtual reality makes it easier for design teams around the world to cooperate on complex projects. It will soon be used to aid in the design of aircraft, satellite positioning, even simulating the exploration of other solar systems.

# New Materials for Every Purpose

There is no simple product today—whether made of metal, wood, glass, concrete, plastic or any other substance—that will not be made of some entirely different material 20 years from now. Modern materials science will create an endless array of new substances, often combining ceramics, metals and plastics, that will have all the properties of today's common materials.

These new substances will be products of the emerging new sciences of "computational chemistry" and "molecular nanotechnology," in which researchers working with computers can design and build new materials molecule by molecule, using an exhaustive database of the characteristics of all known substances and how they combine with each other.

Eventually, manufacturers will custom-order from chemical producers whatever new materials they need, with just the right characteristic for a certain use, be it flexibility, rigidity, resistance to heat, or corrosion, or enormous strength with minimal weight.

It would have been difficult for people 40 years ago to envision a tennis raquet made of plastic and carbon fibers, or a stovetop made of glass, or titanium golf clubs, or synthetic lumber extruded from a hot dough of hardwood sawdust and shredded polyethylene grocery bags. But all of these products now exist.

Today, it may stretch credulity to picture highway bridges made of corrosion-resistant plastic and glass materials, or the cylinder block of a car engine made of a ceramic-metal substance, or pots and pans made of plastic. But these too already exist in laboratories and will be coming to commercial use in a decade or so. (Bridges made of polymer composites are here now, in Canada, Britain, China and Japan, and researchers at the University of California, San Diego are testing the use of carbon laminates to make highway bridge columns stronger and better able to withstand earthquakes.)

## AMAZING POLYMERS

Polymers (plastics) that can conduct electricity will someday be used in lightweight, solid-state batteries without lead and electrolytic fluid. Plastics may eventually supplant silicon as the raw material of semiconductors. And "ultra-oriented" polyethylene, stronger but lighter than steel, will begin to replace steel rebar as the reinforcing rods embedded in concrete on bridge decks and highways. Super-slippery polymers will make low-friction bearings, bushings and gears. Fire-resistant plastic studs, joists and rafters will eventually find their way into the framing of houses and offices.

Airliners will have skins made of super-light plastics, rather than aluminum, and metal rivets and screws will be replaced by super-strong adhesives. The jet engines will feature ceramic-metal components capable of resisting intense heat far longer than all-metal parts. Plastics will continue to replace metal, glass and paper in virtually all packaging, reducing weight (and the energy costs of transport) and enabling more food products to go right from the store shelf to the microwave or conventional oven. While steel and aluminum will probably remain the most common materials for car bodies, the metal industries are worried enough about plastic bodies they too are developing lighter-weight car designs.

Basic materials will be changing right along with technology. The development of new materials is often a spin-off from seemingly unrelated research. For example, the new plastic materials for bridges grew out of failed efforts by defense-industry scientists to find a radar-evading "stealth" material for military jet fuselages.

Virtually all plastics today are derived from petrochemical feedstocks, which are derived from a fossil fuel of finite supply—crude oil. This could pose a supply problem in a society that is rapidly shifting to plastics from metal, glass and wood, were it not for the fact that the world's oil reserves, while finite, are vast and still largely unexploited.

## New Materials from Agriculture

Long before the world's petroleum reserves run out, biotechnology will have devised countless ways to substitute plant and animal substances for petrochemical feedstocks in the making of plastics, fuels and lubricants. Just over the horizon are new kinds of plastics that are derived from biomass (virtually any living plant) and from animal proteins and acids. The biotech industry will someday be able to synthesize a wide array of plastics from living materials.

Scientists in government, university and corporate laboratories are working every day on new industrial uses for agricultural products. Much of the research is focused on industrial uses for crops. In years ahead, the result will be a rich new source of income for farmers.

Corn with extra starch will be created to make biodegradable plastic. Other plants will produce zylanase, an enzyme used in food and paper manufacturing. Oil-laden seeds from the lesquerella plant, common in the Southwest, will be used in lubricants and cosmetics. Crambe, canola (rapeseed) and other high-erucic acid oils will be used in lubricants, nylons, electrical insulation, plastic films, transmission fluid and nonshrinking paints and coatings. The nonallergenic floss of the milkweed plant will be used as fill for clothing, pillows and comforters. Quick-growing stalks of kenaf will be used in making newsprint and tissue and as a fiberglass substitute. And quayule, abandoned as a source of natural rubber after World War II, will be revived. Its hypoallergenic qualities make it ideal for rubber gloves and medical supplies.

Many more-familiar crops will also see increased industrial usage. Already 9% of the U.S. corn crop goes to uses such as ethanol fuel, a figure that will rise. Animal and vegetable fats, such as soy oil, will feed a growing market for biodiesel fuel. Citrus oils, already widely used in cosmetics, will be used in solvents to replace petroleum distillates and chlorofluorocarbons.

Another promising area of agricultural research is the creation of profitable new products from waste. As wood becomes more expensive in the next decade, demand will grow for plywood-like boards and studs made from wheat and rice straw. Corn husks, cotton ginnings and other leftovers will be burned for energy and turned into ethanol.

## New Uses for Ceramics

Ceramics—loosely defined as any product made of a hard-baked moldable substance containing all sorts of clays, metals or glassy substances—will be ubiquitous in lots of unlikely uses in a few years.

Coming soon will be practical ceramics that are superb conductors

—near-superconductors putting up very little resistance to the flow of electricity through them. Like plastics, ceramic materials could replace silicon as the matrix for the printed circuits in semiconductors and microprocessors. Ceramics will be used to create superconducting electromagnets, and they will be extruded into tough but flexible superconducting electric power lines, saving an enormous amount of the energy now lost in long-distance power transmission.

# Energy Technology

Electricity will continue to be generated by current methods, using current fuels, for years to come, and inexpensive and plentiful fossil fuels will remain the dominant energy source for homes, industry and transportation. But great strides will be made in alternative energy sources, driven at mid century by the slowly rising cost of fossil fuels and public concern that burning hydrocarbons aggravates air pollution and may contribute to global warming.

Federal studies estimate that total renewable energy sources—which now account for less than 15% of electric-power generation in the U.S.—will double their share over the next four decades. These include solar, wind, hydroelectric, geothermal and biomass (converting plants and vegetables into alcohol).

### ELECTRICITY FROM SUN AND WIND

In the decades to come, photovoltaic solar power and wind power will become significant sources of electricity in developing nations and remote locations in the advanced nations, with high-performance batteries storing the electricity for use when the sun and wind aren't cooperating.

Photovoltaic arrays—flat panels that generate electricity directly from sunlight—have enormous potential as a supplemental local source of power for homes and offices that are connected to a conventional electric power grid. The cost of making photovoltaic cells has plummeted over the past quarter-century, and it will continue to drop, making economically feasible arrays of enormous size that could be designed into the roofs of residences and commercial buildings. Some visionaries even foresee a day when tough, flexible solar panels will be built into the surface of roadways, airport runways and the walls of office buildings, making every sun-absorbing surface in the urban landscape a cheap generator of electricity.

Wind power won't be so big a factor in power generation. There are relatively few places on earth where the wind blows hard enough for long enough each day to generate enough electricity to be worth the trouble, and the enormous number of wind turbines required would not be an aesthetic delight, either.

## ELECTRICITY FROM HYDROGEN, VIA FUEL CELLS

Fuel cells will play a big part in America's energy future, someday powering electric vehicles and providing emergency backup power to homes, offices and hospitals, as well as serving as primary power sources for residences and small businesses.

The science of fuel cells is still only hazily understood by the general public, even though they've been a part of the space program for nearly 30 years, providing on-board electricity and water to astronauts. When most people hear talk about fuel cells, they first think of batteries. Functionally, however, batteries and fuel cells have almost nothing in common. A battery simply stores electricity generated outside itself, but a fuel cell generates electricity within itself by extracting electrons from atoms of hydrogen gas. The hydrogen protons combine with oxygen to form water vapor, which is the only waste product exhausted from the fuel cell—an attractive benefit for cars and trucks in urban areas.

Virtually all the major automakers have built electric vehicles that run on hydrogen-powered fuel cells. One of the most enthusiastic boosters of fuel cells is DaimlerChrysler, whose Daimler-Benz division has built a number of city buses powered with fuel cells made by Ballard Power Systems, of Canada. Now being tested in Chicago and British Columbia, the silent, nonpolluting buses can cruise at 50 mph fully loaded with passengers.

Fuel cells need hydrogen, which can be fed to the cells directly from storage tanks in the vehicle or extracted on board the vehicle from natural gas, methanol or gasoline. Because hydrogen is a notoriously flammable gas and not broadly available now, Chrysler is developing an on-board system that would extract hydrogen from gasoline. The gasoline could also power a small internal-combustion engine used in combination with an electric motor. Decades from now, hydrogen gas could be processed by specialized atomic power plants that separate the hydrogen atoms from water, creating a virtually limitless supply of energy.

Of course, the electricity to run cars need not be generated in the car, from on-board fuel cells. It could be generated anywhere—from fossil fuels, the sun, wind, whatever—and stored in conventional batteries in the car. As materials technology improves the lightness, power and recharging speed of batteries, cruising range will reach a practical level, at least for driving around town. Someday you will be able to buy electricity at a filling station the way you do gasoline, or simply recharge in your garage each night.

Many transportation gurus are putting their bets on hybrid electric cars that will have both an electric motor (powered either from fuel cells or storage batteries) and a small gasoline engine. Some experimental designs call for the batteries to get recharged from the motion of braking or downhill coasting while the gasoline engine is in use.

## COMEBACK FOR NUCLEAR POWER?

Atomic power, popular virtually everywhere in the world except in the United States, will hold its own for worldwide power generation, accompanied by improvements in the safe, underground storage of nuclear waste—always more of a political challenge than a technical problem.

Nuclear fission, as practiced for power generation today, will not make a comeback in the United States, however, despite the fact that it has a better environmental record than burning fossil fuels and transporting crude oil on the nation's seas, and it has a better occupational-safety record than the mining of coal.

### *The holy grail of nuclear fusion*

While nuclear fission generates a small but stable portion of the world's electric power, scientists in several nations continue to pursue the intriguing possibilities of making electricity from nuclear fusion—the same process that creates the unfathomable energy of the sun (and also the power of thermonuclear explosions).

The advantages of nuclear fusion over every other known power source would be enormous. Reactors would run on a limitless source of fuel—deuterium, a hydrogen isotope derived from seawater. There would be little risk of a reactor accident releasing radiation into the environment, because the reactor would run on a tiny pellet of fuel. Finally, the waste product from normal operation would be comparably small in volume and easy to dispose of, and it would be much less radioactive than the waste of fission reactors.

Two recent breakthroughs in controlled fusion research, in England in 1991 and at Princeton University in 1993, produced impressive amounts of potential electrical power, but achieving the enormously high temperatures for fusion made both experiments net losers of energy, consuming more than was produced.

Other researchers, in such nations as Japan, India and the U.S., are intrigued by the idea that fusion can be achieved at room temperature—so-called cold fusion. Since the claimed discovery of cold fusion in the U.S. in 1989, controversy has raged over whether it really works. But a number of researchers in several different countries believe they have succeeded in creating considerably more heat energy than their experiments consumed in electricity. (Others doubt that this is cold fusion at all, but perhaps an equally mind-boggling phenomenon called zero-point energy—the removal of all heat from air). In any event, the promise of limitless power from nuclear fusion will probably remain, for practical purposes, an elusive goal for decades to come.

Meanwhile, breeder reactors—a kind of fission reactor that produces more fuel than it consumes—will remain on hold, not for technical reasons (the several that were built worked fine), but because of public distrust of atomic power in general.

## THE ULTIMATE CONSERVATION PLAY: SUPERCONDUCTIVITY

Ever since the world petroleum cartel did the world the favor of jacking up oil prices in the 1970s, global business has been on an energy-conservation binge, which has had the same effect as boosting energy production. As futurist John L. Petersen, of the Arlington Institute, puts it so simply, "the largest single source of new energy lies in the efficient use of electricity and heat."

This trend will accelerate in the decades ahead, boosted by a variety of technologies in auto and appliance design, building materials, and most of all, the transmission of electricity through supply lines, motors and electronic components.

The conducting of electricity with virtually no resistance has long been thought to be achievable only at temperatures approaching absolute zero, but in recent years, it has been accomplished at considerably higher temperatures. In the early decades of the next century, it is possible that breakthroughs in room-temperature superconductivity will be achieved with new materials designed just for this task. "Over time, the need for electricity would plummet, as the internal inefficiencies of electrical equipment approached zero," writes Petersen.

# CHAPTER 16

# Outlook for Key Industries

L et's take a quick look at the near- and long-term trends affecting several enormous industries that account for much of America's total output: financial services, health care, energy, environmental services and products, agriculture and food, retailing and marketing, housing and real estate, transportation, and finally, defense and aerospace. (See discussions of computers, information technology, biotechnology, new materials and education in separate chapters.)

## The Money Business

T he next few years will see dramatic changes in the business of performing financial transactions—helping consumers and businesses to make purchases, borrow money, invest their savings, trade their national currencies for others and insure themselves against risks.

These changes will be wrought by several concurrent forces, including the technology of electronic money transfers, Internet banking and brokerage, massive corporate consolidations, and a loosening of federal and state regulation.

Credit and debit cards will be acceptable everywhere on earth and used for ever-smaller purchases. Credit cards and lines of credit will continue to be overmarketed to marginal customers who will abuse them and get into debt trouble. Bankruptcies will continue at higher levels in the U.S., and the cost of writing off bad debts will keep credit-card interest rates in the high teens.

Banks will keep pushing debit cards, but well-heeled customers will still prefer the interest-free "float" of charge cards. Banks will try to force the issue by shortening the grace period. Cash and checks, which are used in an estimated 40% of all purchases, won't go away, but they will be used less and less by people of means.

The Internet will become a significant medium for all kinds of financial transactions, from home banking and instant bill paying to online trading of stocks and mutual funds. The transfer of money by electronic means (so-called e-money) will become as easy and comfortable as e-mail is to millions of correspondents today.

## FULLY GLOBAL MARKETS

In an increasingly close-knit world economy, the volume and velocity of capital movements will continue to rise at a dizzying pace. Within a decade or so, all markets—equities, commodities, currencies—will be fully computerized in all lands, following the lead of Nasdaq in the United States. Prices will be established by the instantaneous, automated matching of buyers and sellers, a process that will replace shouted bids by market specialists and traders on chaotic trading floors.

Computerized markets will never sleep, so trading will go on 24 hours a day. Intelligent-agent software will search the globe for investment opportunities and changes in interest rates for deposits and loans.

## RELENTLESS CONSOLIDATION

Eventually Congress will get around to ratifying what the market is already doing—tearing down the firewalls that, since the 1930s, have separated the ownership of companies in commercial banking, stock brokerage, investment banking and insurance.

National and international finance will be dominated by a score of enormous financial conglomerates, centered variously in the U.S., Europe and Asia, but with operations in virtually every nation. The big players will include such American powerhouses as CitiGroup, Merrill Lynch, Bank of America, Charles Schwab, American Express, GE Capital, Chase Manhattan and Fidelity, which, in a few years, will all contain affiliates that offer every kind of consumer and commercial financial service. But customers will be slow to warm to the idea of one-stop shopping, in which all their financial needs would be filled by the same firm.

## THE NEW LOOK OF BANKING

America will continue to have the most fragmented, least consolidated banking industry in the world. A decade ago the U.S. had some

14,000 separate banks, and despite a decade of active merging (including about 600 in 1997 alone), the nation still has a whopping 9,000 banks with a total of some 63,000 banking locations. Just as many experts say American retailing is over-stored, so, too, is America over-banked.

By act of Congress and with the concurrence of virtually all the states, interstate branching will accelerate over the next few years. The total number of independent banks will plummet, and the number of full-service branches will drop, too, a casualty of mergers, the proliferation of ATMs and the boom in online banking.

While the giants slug it out for the big slices of the cake, community banks, savings and loans, and nonprofit credit unions will continue to thrive on the crumbs, giving personal attention to consumers and small businesses.

Congress will allow credit unions to continue to grow beyond their original "affinity" groups of people in a common occupation. The banks will keep screaming about unfair competition, but Congress will see credit unions, serving some 70 million accounts with their low fees and loan rates, as a healthful counterweight to the megabanks.

The very low end of the business—financial service for low-income people, through finance companies, check-cashing shops, even pawnshops—will remain entrenched in a highly profitable niche.

## COMPETITION FROM NONBANK BANKS

The financial-services war taking shape is really a competition for customer relationships and assets. And the battle will be won by the institution—bank, brokerage, mutual fund company, whatever—that can convince its customers to entrust most or all of their assets to it. At stake, even more than the daily banking transactions, is the management of an estimated $11.4 trillion of personal wealth held in stocks and stock mutual funds.

No institution wants to lose any part of the customer's business because it's unable to offer a particular useful service, so everyone will keep invading everyone else's turf. There will be more mergers between banks and mutual fund management companies. Fund companies will keep moving into discount brokerage and online stock trading, charging very low trading commissions to customers who have large balances in the company's own funds.

To stem the defection of affluent customers to brokerage houses, more banks will copy the brokers by offering asset-management accounts that consolidate all funds on one statement and sweep interest and dividends into money-market funds. Big insurers such as State Farm and the

Principal Group will try to become full-fledged banks through the purchase of existing "unitary thrift charters," a process that would convert their national field forces of agents into marketers of financial services of all sorts. These thrift charters are even being pursued by long-distance phone companies seeking to become online virtual banks.

## ONE-STOP FINANCIAL SHOPPING?

Offering a wide array of services will give the diversified financial-services giants fertile opportunities for cross-marketing of unrelated products. Some customers will be interested in the convenience of a single financial statement. But many others will continue to seek the best-priced, best-performing products and services wherever they find them. And this will mean multiple financial relationships, with separate banks, brokers, fund companies and insurers.

## RISING PROFITABILITY IN FINANCIAL SERVICES

Driven by consolidation of management, back-office operations, branch closures and productivity-boosting technology, the profits of banks and other financial institutions have soared in recent years, and there is no end in sight. Earnings have gotten a big boost, too, from the low cost of capital. Banks have gathered deposits at record-low rates, while lending the money out at consumer interest rates—on credit-card debt, 100% home-equity lines of credit, car loans and personal loans—that have stayed stubbornly high. So their spreads have been very favorable, and this should continue for quite some time.

Bank consolidations have clearly been anticompetitive and anti-consumer, as evidenced by the fact that the banks' noninterest income—from fees on everything from checking accounts to using human tellers—now accounts for a record one-third of industry profits. And fees tend to be higher at megabanks than at small community banks.

It has been customary for customers to pay a small fee, typically $1 or so, to use an ATM not operated by their own bank, and most people have found this to be a reasonable charge for the enormous convenience of getting cash anywhere in the world at any hour of the day. But now, with ATMs proliferating at retail sites—in ballparks and arenas, late-night convenience stores, gambling casinos and grocery stores—those local operators are tacking on their own stiff surcharges, sometimes as much as $5 per use. Not surprisingly, consumers will wise up and forgo this expensive convenience.

A consumer backlash will develop against rising fees, and competition by low-fee online banking will slow the fee rise, too. Smaller banks will begin to publicize these fee differences in their marketing, and eventually there will be some new price competition among big banks, as merger activity slows. In the meantime, probably the only way for consumers to benefit from the merger mania and banking profit boom is by becoming shareholders in their own banks.

## ELECTRONIC BILL PAYING AND VIRTUAL BANKS

The spread of Internet use will bring amazing changes to the way people handle their money. So will the advent of smart cards that can be coded and recharged with any amount of cash value, spendable only by a user who knows the right access codes.

Electronic bill paying, around for a decade or so, has not caught on yet with most people because it has been slow, not highly reliable and not accepted by many vendors. But this will change with the embracing by banks of a few standard, easy-to-use software programs, such as the banking industry's Integrion and MSFDC, a venture of Microsoft and First Data Corp., the world's largest processor of credit card billings. These programs enable people to do their home banking at the bank's own Web site, and the software owners will collect a small fee for facilitating each transaction.

There will be growth in so-called virtual banks—institutions that operate only on the Internet, with no physical branches, ATMs or human tellers and lending officers. In exchange for low fees made possible by their very low overhead, they will encourage their customers to go almost totally electronic—automatic deposit of paychecks and 401(k) contributions, electronic bill paying of all vendors, and so on. For cash, their customers will use other banks' ATMs, or the virtual banks will download cash to a smart-card recharger attached to the customer's home PC.

Smart cards will be accepted by card-reading devices almost everywhere—at convenience stores, parking meters, highway toll booths, subway turnstiles and school cafeterias. They're already in heavy use on college campuses, so young adults are getting the hang of them.

## FINANCIAL SERVICES AS INTERNET COMMODITIES

The Net will turn virtually every kind of financial service into a commodity that can be comparison-shopped by bargain hunters looking for low price, suitable features and the convenience (if they wish) of not dealing with human sales people. In short, financial Web sites will depersonalize some of the most intensely personal sales and service relationships in commerce today, such as insurance sales, mortgage applications and financial planning and investment counsel.

Many people already shop for term life insurance through toll-free telephone quote services, which now operate on the Web as well. (The physical exam for the policy can't be done on the Web—yet.) Eventually every kind of insurance will be available on the Web. A growing number of home buyers will compare the prices and features of mortgages on the Web, too, making applications and submitting verifying information electronically.

Online stock trading will explode in popularity, putting a lot of pressure on both full-service and discount brokers to reduce their commissions or institute higher fees for truly personal investment counsel—or both. Many customers, especially affluent older investors, will still value the personal touch and be willing to pay for it, not through commissions but by a percentage of their assets under management.

Computerized financial planning on the Web, while not as good as a customized plan, will be deemed adequate and well-priced by many families. They will submit information online, with confidentiality ensured by encryption, about their finances, their family circumstances, their needs and aspirations (date of planned retirement, for example). In response, financial-planning software will produce a plan mixing insurance, investments and estate-planning ideas.

# Delivering Health Care

The American health care system—which is both the best and most costly in the world—will continue to be run by private enterprise, but with increasing government oversight. Due to federal budget constraints, no universal national health system will be enacted in the next decade. But Congress and the states will push ahead with the recent "children's health initiative" under medicaid, the biggest expansion of federal health care in 30 years.

The ranks of the uninsured will swell beyond today's more than 40 million, as more small employers drop health insurance due to high costs. The plight of the uninsured will get worse before it gets better. Hospitals, finding it harder to pass the cost of uncompensated care on to other payers of health care such as government and employers, will be less willing to take on "charity" cases, except in true emergencies.

### SOARING TOTAL COSTS, DESPITE CONTAINMENT

The U.S. now spends more than $1 trillion a year on health care—more than 15% of gross domestic product (GDP), the highest portion in the world. In the next decade this share will rise toward

20%, with total health care costs growing at more than twice the rate of inflation and general economic growth.

Why will this happen, considering the boom in managed care and the possibility that costs per patient visit or per procedure may flatten or actually decline? Because an aging population consumes much more health care than a younger population. And because as dazzling, expensive medical breakthroughs—biotech drugs, gene therapies and surgical techniques—make it possible for previously fatal or debilitating conditions to be treated, patients will demand the best possible treatment. And because there will be no end to the practice of defensive medicine (with extensive overtesting) to ward off lawsuits.

In short, more people will live longer, more-productive lives, but the cost to society of medical miracles will be staggering. They will be borne by all Americans, through their taxes and employer health care costs that are embedded in the prices of all goods and services.

## RATIONING LIES AHEAD

The notion of what *should* be covered by health insurance policies will expand, as it has for the past 30 years. Insurance companies and employers will be under great pressure, and sometimes legal obligations, to pay for treatment they consider experimental, ineffective or optional. In some cases they'll be pushed to pay for care that isn't life saving but affects patients' self-esteem and quality of life, such as cosmetic surgery to repair minor birth defects, or drugs and surgery to cure impotence and infertility.

Despite the demand from patients to enjoy every imaginable medical enhancement of their lives, it will not be possible for society to afford them all. So there will be rationing of exotic medical procedures, especially for senior citizens. Without such rationing, the already high percentage of the U.S. health bill that is devoted to people in the last years of their lives will rise even more. This would deprive children and young adults of their "rightful" share of the health care dollar. Health care rationing will be one of the most controversial political issues of the next two decades, potentially pitting electorally potent baby-boomers (and their parents) against less-numerous younger Americans.

There will be a boom in every kind of delivery system that tries to contain costs—managed care, preventive-medicine programs, outpatient surgical clinics, telemedicine, home health care. Alternative medicine—herbal drugs, controlled-diet therapy, chiropractic, yoga, acupuncture—will continue to grow, often used combined with traditional medicine.

## THE GOVERNMENT'S ROLE IN HEALTH CARE

Managed-care organizations and for-profit hospital groups won't have as free a rein in management and pricing as they've had in recent years, and their profit margins will shrink substantially, even as their total profits rise. They will come under greater government regulation, with new rules relating to quality of care, appeal of benefit denials, minimum hospital stays for various surgeries, and so on. Government will review the outcome of treatment of thousands of patients, then issue report cards that measure the quality of the care and the effectiveness of competing procedures. These studies will seek to find the most-effective (and cost-effective) treatments and make them universal.

Washington will eventually require that all medicare and medicaid participants get their care through managed-care plans. What's more, in a bold act of privatization, Uncle Sam will probably turn to managed-care companies to take over some or all of the administration of these big programs, in an attempt to operate them more efficiently and—ideally—with less fraud.

As miracle drugs become a bigger part of health costs, prescriptions will someday be bought under medicare coverage. Medicare reimbursement caps on pharmaceuticals will be a kind of *de facto* price controls—just what the industry has long feared. One of the most controversial issues will be the issuance of patents on genetic material. Some nations, especially less-developed ones, will refuse to honor patents for drugs derived from genetic material found in their native plants and animals.

## NONSTOP CONSOLIDATION

There will be consolidation and downsizing in virtually every facet of health care, including hospitals, health insurers, pharmaceutical companies and equipment manufacturers. Today more than half of the world's medicine sales are generated by just ten enormous pharmaceutical firms, and there is even more consolidation ahead.

One-third of today's hospitals will close within ten years, as more patients are treated in outpatient clinics or at home. The only new hospitals to be built will replace aging facilities or provide care in a fast-growing metro area that is underserved. Hospitals will become places where patients go only for emergencies, critical care, complicated procedures and tests. More terminally ill patients will await death in the familiar setting of their homes, supported by home health care and hospices.

Hospitals in the same region will cease to offer so many overlapping specialties and expensive technologies. Many will move from offering a full range of services to focusing on just one specialty that is most profitable. Some will become heart centers, others cancer clinics. Still others will reinvent themselves as rehabilitation facilities.

Some hospitals will join together with local doctors to form health care organizations that will compete with the insurance companies. These new networks will negotiate directly with employers, cutting out the insurance middleman. There may be smaller networks in niche fields, such as plastic surgery or obstetrics and gynecology. The result will be more competition and slightly slower price increases than would occur without the hospital-doctor teams.

With the population of older people about to grow rapidly, many more nursing homes and hospices will be needed by 2020. Long-term-care insurance will grow in popularity for the upper-middle-income market—those with too much income and too many assets for medic-aid coverage but not enough wealth to fund nursing homes themselves. More and more states will aggressively recover medicaid expenses after death, from the estates of deceased.

Even manufacturers will get involved in patient care. Under "disease management" programs, pharmaceutical companies will contract to provide all the drugs for an entire group of patients, such as those with ulcers. But this will be controversial, due to concerns that cost could play a bigger role in the contractor selection decision than the effectiveness of the company's drugs.

## CHANGING LABOR MARKETS

There will be a surplus of doctors in some specialties and in some suburban areas, although shortages will persist in rural areas and inner cities. Managed-care networks will try to control costs by contracting with fewer doctors. In addition, physicians' time will be spread over more patients and more duties will be handled by lower-salaried physician assistants, nurses and technicians—a practice known as "offloading." Registered nurses will treat many patients with routine problems, licensed practical nurses will take over jobs formerly handled by RNs, and office assistants will perform tasks once left to the LPN.

## THE EMPLOYER'S DILEMMA

Some small employers will drop health insurance as its costs rise more steeply over the next several years. And employers will try to shift more of the cost of health care to their employees. But most employers won't cut back significantly. With labor markets generally tighter than they have been, employers will dangle good health plans as recruitment and retention carrots.

Some employers may simply give employees a choice of more take-home pay or a health plan, and a lot of younger employees—who already make up most of the uninsured—will take their chances on good health and forgo insurance. Employers will also try not to offer retiree health benefits to new hires, and they will force current retirees into managed care.

More and more small employers will pass up traditional, indemnity insurance coverage, opting to pay most costs out of pocket and relying on insurance only after costs reach a high threshold. Many employers will find that this saves them money over regular health insurance premiums, but covers them against financially catastrophic events such as a very premature baby or a heart transplant.

## NEW FOCUS ON PREVENTION

Only 1% of America's total health care bill goes toward preventive measures that can hold down health care costs later, ranging from immunizations to AIDS education. So look for more attention to prevention, including public health.

Because more than 40% of the nation's health care bill can be attributed to unhealthful and high-risk habits, more employers will insist on healthier living by members of their health-insurance plans. Wellness programs will spread, with employers paying workers to quit smoking, lose weight, exercise and take better care of their children. Agriculture will play a role in better living, too. Bolstered by genetically engineered plants and livestock, farmers will produce food lower in calories and fat and higher in essential vitamins and minerals. But the final responsibility for living better—and longer—will fall to each of us.

## HOME HEALTH CARE BOOM

Most doctors stopped making house calls years ago. Ironically, in the next several years medical care will shift back to the home, especially for elderly people.

Using laptop computers, nurses and home health aides will get doctors' orders, chart patients' progress, review medical references and show self-care videos to patients. For their part, patients who wish to remain out of the hospital will test themselves, record results and transmit them to the doctor. In addition to cutting costs, routine daily tests for things such as blood pressure and oxygen capacity might detect health problems before obvious symptoms show up.

## TELEMEDICINE

Now in its infancy, telemedicine will become routine in the next two decades, allowing doctors to diagnose and treat patients from hundreds or thousands of miles away. Doctors will view patients and read test results on two-way television screens, then discuss treatment with patients and local care providers. There will still be times when nothing will beat a visit to the doctor's office, but telemedicine promises to widely disperse medical expertise that now serves relatively few patients.

One of the great benefits of telemedicine will be its use in filling in doctor shortages in rural areas. Telemedicine will also help keep many elderly people out of nursing homes. According to one estimate, as many as 10% of the two million people in extended-care centers could live at home if their medical needs were monitored. Home-care practitioners will keep an electronic eye on these patients. Nursing homes will use telemedicine to reduce emergency-room visits.

From an economic standpoint, telemedicine will be a growing export. The Johns Hopkins Oncology Center will provide consultations and medical education to Gleneagles Hospital in Singapore. The Mayo Clinic is establishing links in Jordan and Greece. Other leading U.S. hospitals will make similar connections with foreigners who are eager to benefit from American medical expertise.

## HEALTH CARE EXPORTS

As a modest benefit offsetting the soaring cost of health care, exports of American medical equipment, drugs, information and surgery will rise substantially in the years ahead.

A more-affluent world market, especially in countries with less-advanced health care or more-restrictive, nationalized systems, will seek the finest medical treatment, and that will lead them to the finest American clinics and hospitals for such things as heart surgery, gene therapy and neonatal care. This will have a very positive effect on the U.S. balance of payments.

# The Energy Industry

Rapid economic growth and urbanization in Asia and throughout the developing world will greatly increase global demand for oil and other energy sources. This might seem like a doomsday scenario, given the uncertainty of energy supplies during the past 25 years. After all, the world has had to endure embargoes, sharp spikes in energy prices, and even a war fought in part to safeguard Middle East oil fields. If the developing world's hunger for fuel rises to Western levels, won't world supplies be strained?

Fortunately, the answer will be no. Due to rising energy efficiency, discovery of new reserves and refinement of alternative sources, energy will be abundant at reasonable prices over the next few decades.

The world will have plenty of fuel to sustain economic growth throughout the 21st century. But the choice of which fuels to use will be increasingly driven by environmental, not economic, decisions, as people become more concerned about clean air and global warming. The development of alternative fuels will be boosted more by environmental concerns than by scarcity and rising prices of fossil fuels.

## SERIOUS CONSERVATION

The world demand for energy will be constantly restrained by improvements in the efficiency of buildings, vehicles, appliances and manufacturing processes.

Conservation will be boosted by computer technology. American homes will be even better insulated, cutting heating-fuel needs by one-fourth in 20 years. Stricter energy requirements on appliances will save consumers $66 billion in utility bills by 2030. In offices, workers will be able to darken nearby windows or reduce the heat or air conditioning at their desks. Even the federal government, the nation's biggest energy waster, is under a presidential order to cut usage 30% by 2005.

There have been big improvements in the fuel efficiency of cars, under government mandate. But these gains have been slowed by the public's love affair with gas-hungry pickups and sport utility vehicles, which, being classified as trucks, fall outside of the timetables for passenger-car fuel efficiency.

## PLENTY OF FOSSIL FUELS

The world's supply of fossil fuels—petroleum, gas and coal—is by definition limited: Mother Nature isn't *making* any more of it. But humans are *finding* more of it. The world's proven reserves of oil, for example, have increased 60% in the past 12 years. In addition, better recovery techniques will allow producers to tap supplies that had been either unreachable or uneconomical. The cost of finding oil has plummeted 60% in the past ten years. Computer modeling is helping geologists locate and efficiently drain oil fields as never before. High-tech sensors and drill bits can follow the sometimes twisting trail of underground pools and find more oil. Advances in designing offshore platforms have allowed oil companies to drill in deeper ocean water.

The use of natural gas, abundant and cleaner-burning than oil or coal, will grow 1.5% a year for the next 20 years. By 2015, gas-fired electricity generation will more than double. Many cars will run on natural gas, and it will be used more widely in heating, air conditioning and appliances. Domestic supplies will be augmented by imports, especially from Canada.

Coal will continue to be a significant fuel for power generation. There will be strong worldwide demand for low-sulfur coal, but concern about global warming will make it a distant second or third choice to natural gas and even petroleum.

World prices of fossil fuels will continue to be fairly stable. While the demand for fuel will be pushed by strong economic growth in developing nations, production will keep pace and conservation techniques will limit demand.

## AMERICAN ENERGY PRODUCTION

The United States is far and away the world's leading producer of primary energy—petroleum, natural gas, coal, hydroelectric power and nuclear power.

But production of petroleum has been falling steadily for 25 years, limited by low world oil prices and environmental restrictions in the United States. A quarter-century ago, crude oil accounted for about 31% of America's total energy production, with natural gas 40%, coal about 23%, nuclear less than 2%, and all other sources less than 5%. But by 1996, crude oil's share had fallen to only 20% and natural gas was down to 32%. The big gainers were coal (up to one-third of America's energy production) and nuclear (rising to about 10%).

In 1993, crude petroleum imports exceeded U.S. production for the first time, and the gap has widened since. Imports will probably satisfy well over half of U.S. petroleum needs for years, because production will continue strong in other nations, with new supplies coming into the market in Asia, Russia, South America and other nations.

This increasing dependency on foreign oil would be a national-security problem—with vulnerability to cartel embargoes and wartime disruptions—were it not for the fact that American imports are widely dispersed among many nations. All the nations of the Mideast together account for barely 20% of imports, half their share before the Gulf War, and they are virtually equaled by imports from Venezuela, which is America's largest single supplier of oil.

Increasing shares of American oil imports are coming in from such non-OPEC nations as Canada, Mexico and the United Kingdom.

The nations of the OPEC cartel today produce only one-third of the world's oil production, undercutting their power to restrict production and jack up prices, as they did in 1973 and 1979.

## NUCLEAR ENERGY IN ECLIPSE—FOR NOW

The number of operating nuclear-power plants peaked at 111 in 1990 and has declined slightly since then, as a few older units have been taken out of service. The decommissioning of nearly 50 aging plants will not be matched by the construction of new ones for another decade or so, despite the availability of smaller, safer designs. This is due to continuing American antagonism toward nuclear power, despite nuclear's excellent environmental record. However, American atomic-power technology and equipment will continue to be avidly sought by nations where nuclear energy is a mainstay of electricity generation.

After climbing through the '70s and '80s, nuclear's share of American electricity production has flattened out at about 22%—compared with shares of about 13% in Russia, 16% in Canada, 33% in Japan, 45% in Switzerland, 77% in France and 84% in Lithuania. Nuclear's share will probably drift downward for another decade, until atomic power's reputation is rehabilitated by growing concern over global warming from fossil-fuel-burning power plants.

Cutting back on greenhouse emissions will give nuclear energy a new lease on life. New generations of reactors will provide plenty of energy with virtually no atmospheric emissions, and eventually the public will become comfortable with the safe storing of radioactive waste in government-supervised underground facilities such as the one being developed in Nevada.

## ALTERNATIVE ENERGY SOURCES

In the past 25 years, the share of America's total energy production accounted for by alternative fuel sources—hydro, geothermal, solar, and wind—has been stuck at just a little over 5%, with the vast majority of the share coming from hydroelectric dams. Hydropower—once a darling of the environmental movement for its clean-air benefits, but now a villain for its disruption of river flows, land habitat and fish spawning—will increase only slightly in the U.S. Other countries, including Canada and China, will push ahead with big, controversial dam projects.

Wind energy will come down in price due to better turbine technology, but it will remain a limited source of power due to its low output and intermittent nature. As the cost of photoelectric cells plummets and efficiency rises, solar arrays mounted on buildings will become significant supplemental generating sources for homes, offices, schools and vehicles.

## ALCOHOL AS A FUEL

In another decade or so, ethanol—alcohol distilled from fermented plants and biomass—will become a significant motor-vehicle fuel, burned in modified gasoline engines that can handle fuels containing as much as 85% alcohol blended with 15% gasoline. The high-alcohol fuels, which will be produced for about the same price as a gallon of gasoline (but without today's corn alcohol subsidy) will catch on not for economic reasons, but to cope with ever-tightening clean-air standards in urban areas.

Today about 12% of the gasoline sold in the U.S. contains a 10% dose of corn ethanol, which burns fine in regular car engines. Motorist demand for this blend is stimulated by a $600 million federal-tax subsidy at the pump.

Over the coming years, corn—a valuable global food product that is energy-intensive to grow—will be supplanted by other kinds of biomass for making alcohol, including rice straw, the waste from sugar cane refining, fast-growing trees such as willows and poplars, and switch grass, a tall, fast-growing, perennial prairie grass that needs little water. Using new microbial fermentation processes from the biotech industry, the biomass alcohol industry will become a significant contributor to the American energy mix. At the same time, it will be contributing to a reduction in "greenhouse" gas emissions from motor vehicles, estimated to account for one-third of America's total emissions of such gases.

## DEREGULATION AND GLOBALIZATION

The biggest change ahead for American energy and its customers is the deregulation of the electric-power industry.

Over the next couple of years, utilities that have been fully integrated, regulated monopolies—generating power and selling it to captive customers in a specified service area, at government-set prices—will be given new freedoms. They will be free to decide which part of the business they wish to be in—generating, or transmission, or local distribution and service, or some combination of these. They will be free to sell their power to residential and commercial customers anywhere in the nation, competing on price. Some will diversify into other service businesses, such as cable TV, telephone service and Internet access, using new technologies for transmitting digital data over electric power lines coming into homes and offices.

Electricity prices will fall for large industrial users in the Northeast, Midwest and California, who will now be able to shun high-priced local power and bargain for better rates from distant power generators in the South and Rocky Mountain states, where coal and hydropower are inexpensive local energy sources. But most homeowners will see only modest cuts in their power rates, and they will be dismayed to discover that their monthly electric bill will resemble a phone bill—full of separate charges for different services, such as the power itself, the cross-country transmission, and the use of the local utility's wires that carry the electricity into the home. In some states and cities, local officials will invite many far-away power companies to bid for their citizens' residential business and then authorize just a handful to provide competing service.

Some states will be generous with utilities in letting them continue to bill customers for their billions of dollars of "stranded costs"—past investments in power plants, especially very expensive nuclear generators —while others will limit such recovery and force utilities to write down those costs as losses. The number of firms in the electric-power business will sharply shrink in the decade ahead, with only the largest and most efficient surviving.

Giant U.S.-based utilities such as Enron, Southern and AES will keep moving aggressively into world markets, buying and operating formerly government-run utilities and building new, efficient power plants. Enron, for example, is developing new overseas power and pipeline projects with an estimated value of $20 billion. Southern, America's biggest electricity producer, owns and operates generating plants in such nations as China, the Philippines, Germany and the United Kingdom.

## MILLIONS OF ELECTRIC CARS

The electricity business will get a real shot in the arm from the government-mandated creation of an electric-auto industry to reduce the emissions of pollutants from vehicle exhausts. Someday the owners of cars and trucks equipped with fast-charging batteries will buy electricity from metered plug-in power dispensers wherever they rest on the highway or city streets—at truck stops and fast-food restaurants, shopping center parking lots, or the parking garages of office buildings and hotels. While battery-operated electric vehicles eliminate pollution emanating from them, generating the electricity on which they run— most likely from a fossil fuel—causes some degree of pollution in a distant, probably rural locale. (But this would not be the case with an electric motor running off a fuel cell powered by natural gas or gasoline.)

# The Environment Business

In the coming years, living, working and manufacturing in the "green"—environmentally conscious—style will spawn an industry of enormous size and variety. The industry will include many disparate activities that overlap with many other fields: making equipment for capturing and processing industrial wastes; developing non-polluting electric vehicles; recycling paper, plastics and metals into other uses; creating packaging that is lighter, thinner, more recyclable, and uses less energy in transportation; desalinating seawater; designing and making appliances, planes, cars and climate-control systems that use less energy; neutralizing hazardous waste, oil spills and sewage, often with new biotech products; substituting enviro-friendly products for polluting materials; and supporting ecotourism to exotic, unspoiled places.

The environmental business is so big and far-reaching that it almost defies aggregation. For example, by the year 2000, the U.S. will have spent $1 *trillion* on water cleanup since the passage of the Clean Water Act in 1972, and there is no end in sight.

Americans will support increasing the amount of money spent on safeguarding the environment, but they will also demand results. They won't accept tax increases or other costs if the benefit is small or hard to prove. They will increasingly favor economic incentives rather than laws to force industry to clean up. And looking back on the success of clean-air and clean-water laws, Americans will demand action against big environmental threats abroad before paying a steep price for marginal improvements at home.

The U.S. Senate will not endorse any international treaties imposing environmental restrictions on America that threaten the nation's and world's economic growth. The developed world certainly won't go cold turkey in its reduction of fossil-fuel use, no matter how dire the predictions of global warming. Forcing an immediate conversion to other energy sources would be both impossible and financially staggering, so transitions will be gradual.

## A FULLY RECYCLABLE WORLD?

The holy grail for environmentalists is "sustainability," when waste created by humans and their machines would be rendered harmless or even beneficial. Such a world will remain just a dream, even 20 years from now, but industry will take big steps to reduce humankind's impact on the planet.

The paper industry is an interesting example. Worldwide, paper mills consume six billion trees and dump nearly one billion tons of chlorinated waste into rivers and streams each year. Facing tighter regulations in the U.S. and Europe, the paper companies have invested billions on research and recycling to dramatically reduce pollution. In the near future, in fact, this industry may build a closed-loop system in which environmentally suspect chemicals such as chlorine are no longer used or are fully recycled.

## FREE-MARKET APPROACHES

Most of the economic activity in environmental protection will be forced by government edict, such as California's mandate to develop non-polluting cars. But government will also encourage the development of pollution-control and recycling technology through tax and research subsidies.

And more and more free-market approaches will creep into environmental protection, encouraged by the federal government. The most ambitious, and controversial, program is the Environmental Protection Agency's system, begun in 1994, for issuing certificates that are bought and sold among regulated air polluters. This gives some of them the opportunity to benefit from their aggressive cleanups, while others buy permission to move more slowly.

Trade in U.S. pollution rights, especially among power utilities, is already a $1 billion-a-year business, as big as the commodity trade in some major agricultural products. Many states are getting into the credits act, too, and some people believe it could work in the international realm as well. But it's doubtful that an international market could include the compliance monitoring and enforcement that is required to make credits work.

## CORPORATE INITIATIVES

Companies that break ground with cost-effective pollution-control technology will turn an expense into a revenue generator. In fact, companies that patent such advances will join their former enemies in the environmental movement to lobby for tougher regulation, with an eye to marketing their technology.

Corporations will pay for many environmental programs. Merck & Co., the giant pharmaceutical firm, pays $1 million to Costa Rica's National Institute of Biodiversity in exchange for access to the rain forest. The company hopes to discover and patent—as the basis of new drugs—genetic materials derived from Costa Rica's plants, microbes and insects.

## ECOTOURISM

Individuals, often as tourists, will also contribute to international environmentalism. "Ecotourism" is already helping save endangered wildlife in Africa and preserve the rain forest in tiny Belize in Central America.

Several African nations are moving away from trying to protect endangered species by banning all hunting and futilely trying to catch poachers, who are typically impoverished local hunters. Instead they are enlisting the support of local communities by allowing them to manage the herds responsibly—culling weak animals, selling the byproducts, and earning money by guiding rich tourists on legal hunts.

## THE WATER BUSINESS

The handling of water—finding it, shipping it, cleaning it, recycling it, using less of it, and removing the salt from seawater—will become a vast world business in the decades ahead. Water is a very valuable commodity that is generally underpriced in the world. This underpricing is about to come to an end, as water supplies get tight, environmental concerns rise, and competition for water intensifies among residential, farm and commercial user, in such water-hungry businesses as paper making and computer-chip manufacturing.

In the U.S., water-conservation measures will become more strict, affecting lawn maintenance, gardening and water use by businesses. In parts of the U.S. and other countries, the rising cost of water will make alternatives such as desalination more practical. Polluted water will be recycled for many uses other than drinking. Advanced countries will develop two-track water systems—one pipe carrying water for drinking, cooking and washing dishes, and a second with reclaimed water for disposing waste, washing the car, and watering yards and lawns. Industrial plants will rely heavily on nonpotable water. Filtration systems will help remove salt that finds its way into aquifers. Areas that collect water for aquifers will be set aside in conservation areas or "blue fields," where nature preserves and recreation will be allowed, but not water-polluting industries.

Agriculture will remain the world's leading consumer of water. The U.S., China, India, Indonesia and Israel are all heavy irrigators. This has allowed them to become major food producers. But years of heavy water use have taken a toll in places ranging from the San Joaquin Valley of California to the Aral Sea in the former Soviet Union. The soil in such heavily irrigated areas becomes high in salt and other minerals, reducing its ability to grow crops.

Advances in technology will help farms conserve water. Biotechnology researchers will develop new drought-resistant plants. Water-saving irrigation techniques such as drip systems will spread. All of this will gradually reduce water consumption on a *unit* basis—per acre, per ton of grain—but not in total amount, since agricultural production will continue to grow. Decades from now, desalination will be effective and much cheaper than today, so water will be more plentiful. By then, hydroponics (soilless "tray" agriculture) and fish farming will provide substantial amounts of the world's food.

# Farming and Food

Humankind's ability to feed itself will be put to the sternest test yet in the next few decades, as the world's population surges to 7.5 billion by 2020, accompanied by rapid urbanization and the growth of a large middle class in the developing countries. But world farming will meet the challenge successfully.

Here are some of the trends that will dramatically reshape American and world agriculture in the early years of the 21st century: fewer, bigger, more-efficient farms; soaring world demand for high-value crops and processed foods; rising farm productivity and total production; surging global trade; declining government subsidies in all nations, following America's lead; greater volatility in agricultural prices; development of amazing new versions of current crops and livestock through biotech.

## HIGHER PRODUCTIVITY AHEAD

In this century, farm productivity has jumped ahead due to mechanization, use of chemicals and hybrid seeds, and irrigation. In the next century agriculture will make similar advances due to computer science and biotechnology—which will help reverse the long trend toward more input-intensive agriculture. More food and fiber will be grown and processed on less land, with less water, less fertilizer and fewer pesticides, allowing farmers to feed the world with less harm to the earth's air, water and land. Farms will become bigger, more efficient and more specialized, as the number of the world's farmers continues to fall.

U.S. agriculture will remain the most productive in the world. It will continue to rate at or near the top in many production and export categories. Other countries, however, will gain ground, as they acquire the know-how and technology that have revolutionized American farming. As a result, American farmers will face tough competition from world growers, both in U.S. and overseas markets.

## FEEDING THE WORLD

Given the seemingly constant news stories about starvation and famine in one part of the world or another, you might be surprised to learn that the world's farmers produce enough food to feed everyone. The existence of hunger is mostly a problem of income and distribution. Some countries are simply too undeveloped agriculturally to feed themselves or lack the money to buy food from others. At the same time, the U.S. churns out great surpluses; about one-third of all the food and fiber produced is sold to customers overseas.

Hope for the future lies in repeating the success of American farming in other parts of the world. Some of the largest countries, including Russia and China, are currently net importers of food but will take steps toward self-sufficiency in the next 15 to 20 years. World grain production will continue to grow over the next decade or two, although more slowly than in the past 35 years. Most of the growth comes from increased yields, especially in developing countries. Meat and poultry production will also rise, but so will demand from enormous new middle classes in China, India and other developing countries.

In short, the increase in food supply will keep up with global population growth. But there will still be shortages now and then caused by crop failures, governmental bungling and slow growth in personal incomes.

## PRECISION PRODUCTION

Computers, sensors and global positioning systems will instruct farmers in the best crops and seeds, livestock, chemicals, cultivation techniques and irrigation to use on each field. Satellite images will pinpoint pest infestations, wet and dry spots and soil deficiencies. Infrared thermometers will read crops' leaf temperatures and moisture. Optical sensors will detect weeds, right down to the type. Irrigation systems linked to computers will turn on and off in response to plant moisture levels. Mechanized pesticide and fertilizer applicators will vary spray rates in response to readouts from the field. More harvesting will be done by robots, working around the clock.

The same technology will be applied to livestock production.

Microchips implanted in animals will track their genetic makeup, feed rations, medications, milk output and other information. Producers will be able to treat individual animals instead of the whole herd. As a side benefit, it will be easier to trace the source of contaminated meat back to its source. Within a few years, this technology will be priced within the reach of most commercial operations.

### FEWER BUT LARGER FARMS

The number of farms and farmers in the U.S. has been shrinking for decades and will continue to do so, at least for another decade or two. Economy of scale is turning the family farm into a relic of the past. From about two million today, the number of farms will slide to 1.75 million by 2005. But the remaining farms will be larger. From about 475 acres, the average farm will grow to 530 acres by 2005. The amount of land under farming won't change; the big farms will grow at the expense of small ones, not by plowing new ground.

The growth of precision, technology-aided agriculture will intensify the trend to fewer but larger farms, typically run by big corporations, and not just in the U.S. but overseas as well. It now takes considerable capital to run a farm, plus an unprecedented degree of specialized expertise—both of which are more likely to be found on a large farm. The country's biggest 400,000 farms, less than one-fifth of the total, produce more than three-quarters of U.S. food and fiber output. In a decade, they'll account for 90% of production.

Paradoxically, a few small farms will also prosper; these will be well-run operations with the knowledge and confidence to venture into niche markets. These kinds of operators will specialize in supplying fine restaurants and the growing number of grocery stores that carry only locally grown organic foods.

In the next decade, producers and food processors will be more closely tied together through takeovers, joint ventures and contracts. The result will be more consistency and higher quality in the raw commodities supplied to processors.

Calves will be bred and raised to meet specifications set by feedlots. Poultry processors will own feed mills to raise exactly the kind of bird they want. Wheat farmers will control pasta plants. Produce growers will buy processing and packing operations.

With bigger farms and a more integrated agrifood industry, employers will need employees and consultants with more specialized training and experience. They will look for people with expertise in genetics, pest management, nutrition, marketing and waste control.

## LESS GOVERNMENT IN U.S. AND WORLD AGRICULTURE

In the spirit of budgetary restraint in 1996, America embarked on a gradual withdrawal of government price supports and production controls that had been in place since the 1930s. The effects have been many and varied, including wider swings in production, supplies and prices. Many farmers are switching almost annually from one hot crop to another; some are prospering greatly, but others, in record numbers, are fleeing the business.

By the time that fixed, diminishing transition payments end in 2002, U.S. taxpayers will be saving some $6 billion in subsidies a year, food processors will be getting generally lower prices for commodities, and American farmers will be facing the classic boom-and-bust cycles in one of the riskiest of all businesses.

As heavily as America has subsidized its farmers for decades, and protected them with trade barriers on foreign food and fiber, it's nothing compared with what most other nations still do. Eventually the taxpayers of Europe and other nations will question the wisdom of supporting overly large farm work forces, at a cost of higher-than-necessary consumer food prices. So farm subsidies will gradually decline worldwide. But farmers are politically more potent in other nations than they are in the U.S., and nations with a strong tradition of social safety nets will have to weigh the savings in farm subsidies against the higher costs of public assistance for idled farm workers.

## FARM-CITY CONFLICT

As cities and their suburbs grow—especially due to rapid urbanization in the developing countries—there will be more conflict over land and resources. Once isolated in the countryside, agricultural producers will increasingly find they have city slickers for neighbors. In the U.S., suburbanites won't like the noise, odor and dust that sometimes accompany agricultural operations. They will argue with producers over chemical spraying, livestock waste and wildlife protection, and won't be impressed with the fact that the farms were there first.

Perhaps the biggest fight—one that will also occur in other countries—will be waged over water. Agriculture has historically accounted for most water use. In some Western states, farming swallows 80% to 90% of all available water. But cities are developing a thirst for more and more water to nourish growing populations and new businesses. Some disputes will be cured by the free market—city interests will buy water rights from farmers, who will then grow fewer crops, different crops, or quit working the land altogether. In other cases, legislative bodies or the voters themselves—most of whom live in cities—will simply dictate that more water be diverted from farms. In exchange for more water, city residents will have to pay more and obey ever-tougher water-conservation requirements.

### AGRICULTURAL TRADE

Few sectors of the U.S. economy have been as concerned about free trade as agribusiness. Farm operators worry about foreign producers undercutting their prices on beef, wine, citrus fruits, tomatoes and dozens of other commodities. But world agricultural trade will blossom in the next two decades. Grain trade will increase two-thirds or more by 2020. Imports and exports of soybeans will double. Livestock trade will triple.

The U.S. will be a major beneficiary of rising trade and will remain the world's dominant seller of agricultural products. No other country can match its efficiency of production, processing and transportation of farm products. The U.S. is the world's leading exporter of feed grains, wheat, soybeans, cotton and poultry. It is second in beef, pork, rice and value-added consumer-food exports. Trade liberalization under GATT, the General Agreement on Tariffs and Trade, and NAFTA, the North American Free Trade Agreement, will consolidate America's position.

As the world reduces barriers to agricultural imports, especially in the fast-growing Asian economies, U.S. exporters will take advantage. But the spread of American-style technology and management techniques will eventually improve the ability of today's importing nations to meet more of their own food and fiber needs, and a few decades from now, this will flatten the growth of American food exports.

### THE FOOD INDUSTRY

The growing quest for good health will keep demand strong for fresh vegetables and fruits; low-fat, low-cholesterol and less-sweet foods; whole-grain and high-fiber products; and foods grown and prepared with fewer chemicals and additives.

The busy-ness of American families will support the growth of processed convenience foods available in a wide variety of portion sizes, containers and methods of heating.

The raw agricultural products in commercial foods will account for a constantly declining share of the retail price, compared with processing, packaging and marketing costs. Given strongly rising personal income and the push for convenience, a rising share of the American—and world—food budget will go for food prepared (and consumed) away from home. To compete with restaurants, grocery stores will continue to offer more-varied fully prepared meals that can be taken right home for dinner.

## GLOBALIZATION OF FOOD

The food and beverage business, like most big businesses, will be dominated by enormous multinational firms, such as Nestlé, Procter & Gamble, ConAgra, Coca-Cola, RJR Nabisco, Campbell's, Cadbury-Schweppes, and Diageo (the merger of Britain's Grand Metropolitan and Guinness). It's impossible for consumers to keep straight which company owns which brands and what nationality the company is. Nor does anyone seem to care that such thoroughly American brands as Dr Pepper and Pillsbury are owned by two British firms, Cadbury-Schweppes and Diageo, respectively.

## DINING OUT

The restaurant business will be increasingly dominated by national chains with casual dining, moderate prices, big national ad budgets and reliable (if standardized) food quality.

Just as in their shopping experiences, families and young adults will seek to combine dining with entertainment, as provided by "eatertainment" restaurants with themes such as rock concerts, sports and simulated rain forests and space travel. The trick will be maintaining repeat patronage after the novelty wears off.

# Retailing, Marketing and Media

Consolidation. Slower growth in spending on consumer merchandise. Market segmentation. A surge in direct selling, especially on the Internet. Globalization of retailers. Traditional shopping as entertainment. More appeals to ethnic groups. Small retailers competing against the big guys with service and convenience. Proliferation and fragmentation of the media outlets used by advertisers. All of this and more lies ahead for the businesses involved in how goods and services are sold in America.

The next decade will bring a shakeout in the retail industry because there are just too many stores dotting the landscape. Babyboomers, the largest group of shoppers, will have more disposable income as they reach their peak earning years. But they will save more, and their spending will be selective, with more emphasis on travel, entertainment and nicer homes.

More and more shopping will be conducted over the phone and by computer on the Web. But stores won't disappear. Shopping the old-fashioned way will survive as a form of recreation, and small retailers will emphasize personal service and convenience in their fight against the national chains. Big American retailers will aggressively target foreign consumers.

## TOO MANY STORES, TOO-BUSY LIVES

Despite recent strength in sales growth for most so-called "general merchandise and apparel stores" (including department stores), there are still some underlying problems that plague the highly competitive and fragmented retail industry.

There are about 20 square feet of retail space for every shopper in the U.S. Twenty years ago, it was just nine square feet. That's the legacy left from a store-building binge that has lasted more than a decade.

To make matters worse for retailers, this boom in store building occurred just as the "shop 'til you drop" mentality fell out of fashion. Consumers now spend half as much time in shopping malls as they did ten years ago. The diminished appeal of shopping isn't a passing phase. Nor is it tied to economic cycles. Rapid growth in merchandise spending has slowed, largely for demographic reasons. When baby-boomers were in their twenties and thirties they were marrying, setting up households, having babies—and making all the purchases that go along with those stages of life. They bought houses, furniture, appliances and all kinds of consumer electronics. Boomer women who joined the work force in record numbers spurred huge increases in women's apparel sales.

Now that most baby-boomers are in their forties and fifties, their spending habits are changing. They are taking more-lavish vacations, spending more on services and entertainment, and saving aggressively for their children's college and their own retirements. As their mid-career lives have become busier, they have less time to spend on leisurely shopping trips. As they age, they will become less interested in keeping up with the latest fashions.

Just as the coming of age of baby-boomers was a boon for retailers, their passing through and out of the prime shopping years will present a challenge for stores. The smaller size of subsequent generations virtually guarantees that U.S. retail spending will grow less strongly than capital spending by business and American exports.

## CATALOGS AND ONLINE SHOPPING

To a growing number of busy, high-income Americans, shopping isn't recreation. It is simply a way to find and buy the products they need, and they want to accomplish this in the least possible time, with the least possible effort and hassle. These people are fueling the boom in direct-response retailing (catalogs, online, etc.). Once largely limited to a few big players in clothing and general merchandise, the catalog market now includes hundreds of niche retailers in different fields—everything from pet products, gardening supplies and toys to videos, furniture, high-end jewelry and easy-living products for older Americans.

The life cycle of mail-order catalogs will continually speed up. In the future, it will take far less time to go from new idea, start-up and growth to the inevitable competition from imitators and rivals. That will make it tough on mom-and-pop operations. New catalogs will have to find narrow niches, then continually hone their product offerings and mailing lists.

Online shopping is the new frontier in direct selling, and it will see explosive growth when Internet access speeds take a giant leap forward over the next two or three years. No longer will "www" stand for "While We Wait," with frustrated shoppers cooling their heels as Web pages fill in their elaborate graphics. You will be able to advance to new pages and sites with the same speed you can turn a catalog page today, and you will be treated to several different views, and more detailed descriptions, of the merchandise for sale.

Rather than browsing among retail Web sites, you will use an online "personal shopper" to find you products of the style, size and price that meet your needs. The computer will also allow quick price comparisons, making for fierce competition among virtual retailers. Web shopping will be especially strong for brand-name products that don't differ from store to store and don't require in-person examination to check fit, ease of use or other special features. But it will also catch on for specialty shopping for unusual objects such as art, antiques and collectibles, with dealers posting lists and photos of their inventories. There will even be online auctions among bidders who have preregistered with the virtual auctioneer.

Web sites will reflect the character of the virtual retailer. Some will be bare-bones and practical, like a discount warehouse store. Others will be extravagant productions, complete with music, video entertainment, special information and other touches. This trend will parallel the effort by malls and stores to appeal to the shopper's desire for entertainment. Virtual-reality technology will eventually be called into service at Internet retail sites, enabling a shopper to try clothes on a computerized model of her own measurements to check the fit. Or, when going online to buy tickets to a game, a sports fan will be able to sample the view of the field from different seats.

The Internet will enable any retailer of any product to "go global" instantly, finding customers all over the world without having to deal with the legal and commercial red tape of establishing stores in other countries. Eventually Web retailers will have language-translation programs—written and verbal—built into their sites, enabling shoppers to browse and make purchases in their preferred language. They will pay by credit card, with computers making the currency conversions automatically. Global Internet commerce will be a boon to worldwide package-delivery services.

Most shoppers, both in stores and using direct-marketing channels, will pay by some kind of electronic payment, including credit and debit cards. Personal checks will eventually disappear in retail commerce, and cash will be little used. The scrambling and encryption of credit card numbers on the Web has already convinced most shoppers that Internet shopping is no more risky than giving their credit card to a store clerk or restaurant server.

### *Taxing online sales*

State and local governments regard sales of merchandise by online "virtual retailers" the same way they do interstate catalog sales—it deprives them of the sales tax they would get if you bought the same stuff from a store in your community. They want laws requiring all Internet retailers to collect sales tax from their shoppers and remit it to the appropriate jurisdiction. But they haven't yet succeeded in forcing catalog merchants to do this (except for in-state purchases and other state "nexus" situations where it's determined a company is doing business within that state), and they probably won't succeed in getting online merchants to collect sales taxes from all their customers, either. The general absence of sales-tax collection by Web retailers will give Internet commerce a big competitive edge over local stores, and it will deprive state and local governments of increasing amounts over time.

### SHOPPING AS ENTERTAINMENT

So what will become of regular local stores? They will still be the dominant shopping mode for most people, enabling shoppers to see, feel and touch the merchandise and, best of all, take it home with them immediately after purchase.

For many people, shopping isn't just the acquisition of goods. It's a social custom, a relaxing way to spend time with friends or by oneself. That's why catalogs and online shopping, despite their obvious advantage of convenience, won't entirely replace the mall and downtown stores. Malls, which in many areas have lost their earlier luster as fun places to meet friends and hang out, will revitalize themselves with an emphasis on entertainment, adding amusement rides, sports activities and nightclubs that lure affluent young shoppers in the evening.

The trick for retailers in the future will be attracting ever-busier men and women to spend time in their stores. This will start with store location. More stores will leave the big shopping malls for smaller strip centers in affluent or trendy neighborhoods.

Malls and stores will also offer more services. They'll want to become one-stop destinations for harried shoppers. Malls will add more health and fitness facilities, banks, medical clinics, restaurants, even day-care centers and schools. Police substations will be a common sight. Malls will also be designed differently, with more outside-facing windows and open spaces to recreate the feeling of a small town center.

Grocery stores will have parcel-delivery service windows, offer diet and cooking classes, babysitting, even casual restaurants. Department stores will operate museums and art galleries. Sporting-goods stores will offer indoor basketball or tennis courts, or a sports bar so patrons can watch the pros on television and then buy a replica jersey with their favorite player's name on it.

Department stores will try different formats, often narrowing their selection of goods. For some, that will mean focusing on luxury items. Discount chains will continue their shakeout of recent years, with a few strong national chains such as Wal-Mart and Target continuing to bloody regional discounters such as Caldor, Rose's and Bradlee's.

## PAMPERING THE CUSTOMER

Customizing merchandise for each shopper, once the domain of the finest shops, will become increasingly common due to technology and demand for better service. Modular factories with adaptable machinery will be able to churn out clothing, beauty products, bicycles and all sorts of other goods quickly for individual customers. With improved distribution systems, it won't take four weeks for delivery, either.

Convenience will be critical. An aging population will demand better service, everything from more restrooms to quick home delivery. Shoppers will insist on more knowledgeable and patient salespeople.

Stores that fail to provide service will discover that shoppers have more options than ever before.

Automated self-checkout systems now being tried in a few grocery stores will spread across the country within ten years, as did self-service gas stations a few years ago. Customers scan their own groceries as they put them in the shopping cart or at the check-out aisle, and the payment is handled by a credit or debit card. Various measures guard against shoplifting. Self-checking will someday spread to discount and clothing stores. Putting such systems in place will be expensive at first, but it will allow stores to stay open later and increase profits by lowering labor costs.

## MORE MARKET SEGMENTATION

Marketers and retailers have become much more adept at identifying and targeting narrow groups of consumers, particularly affluent ones. This trend will intensify in the next ten or 15 years, helped by high technology.

More and more of our daily purchases are recorded on computerized databases. Once gathered, this information can be sliced, analyzed and sold in many ways. It might be used to help diaper makers identify households with infants, or let a soft-drink company know who is drinking its rival's beverage. There is virtually no limit to the use of this technology. While it raises some privacy concerns, Congress is not likely to significantly restrict the compiling of consumer-preference information for mass marketing. But consumers will be given more rights to inspect information on file about themselves and to have their names deleted from marketing databases for direct mail and telephone sales.

Direct marketing by phone, mail and Internet will become much more sophisticated in the next decade. By gathering more information about each household's income and buying habits, marketers will more effectively target the most fruitful prospects and waste less money sending mail and making calls to households that aren't interested in their products.

## SELLING TO MINORITIES

Up to now, most mainline U.S. retailers haven't made much effort to target the increasingly numerous shoppers who are in racial and ethnic minority groups. That will change in the next several years, starting with a better understanding of how different minority groups differ from the overall population in their tastes and preferred ways of shopping.

For example, African-Americans at every income level, especially in the middle- and upper-middle-income brackets, tend to spend more than the general population does on upscale consumer goods such as apparel and cars, and they are attracted to the latest styles and status brands. Hispanic immigrants often stick with the brands that they know from their homeland or that they first encountered when they arrived in America. Sellers of a brand unavailable in Latin America shouldn't assume Hispanics will never buy their products, but they must figure out how to market to a large and growing group of consumers who aren't familiar with their brands. Asians, whose average household income is well above the national average, are a prime growth prospect for marketers, and several large companies have begun using a new Asian American Association to target them. The Association provides a hotline in several Asian languages and a buyer's club for its members.

Advertisers shouldn't assume that the same pitch will work for all consumers. For instance, according to Loretta Adams, president of Market Development Inc., "100% Colombian coffee" might connote high quality to most Americans, but it doesn't necessarily impress Hispanics who come from other (rival) coffee-growing nations. Three-fourths of older Hispanics prefer being addressed in Spanish, but the children of Hispanic immigrants become quickly Americanized and respond best to advertising in English.

Advertising agencies and sales departments will increase their hiring of minorities. Companies will also retain ad agencies and marketing consultants that are adept at communicating with ethnic markets, such as Chicago's Burrell Advertising, which specializes in targeting African-Americans, and San Antonio's Bromley Aguilar, with Hispanic expertise. More newspapers will print Spanish-language editions or include Spanish articles in regular English editions, as *The Washington Post* does with its soccer coverage. Shopping malls will pay more attention to holidays important to different groups, such as Kwanzaa and Hanukkah in addition to Christmas.

## GLOBAL RETAILING

Just like U.S. manufacturers, American retailers will target the growing middle class in Asia and Latin America to provide the sales growth they can't find at home.

A few icons of U.S. retailing, such as Toys "R" Us, Amway, Avon and Tupperware, have already gone global in a big way. U.S. catalog companies such as Lands' End and L.L. Bean are already selling abroad, and in coming years they'll build distribution centers overseas. Wal-Mart deals through brokers, and others will follow. Foreigners have seen American products and styles on television and in the movies. They have a huge appetite for the quality and value represented by many U.S. goods.

Retailers who study tastes and styles of different cultures will have an advantage. They'll know, for example, that Hispanics overseas like a bustling shopping atmosphere, Asians aren't very brand-loyal but do buy expensive goods, and Canadians worry less than Americans about buying foreign-made items. Venturing abroad also means decoding local laws. Japan, to cite one case, has in the past limited the number of stores a company can operate, making it hard to establish a reputation there.

## TARGETED ADVERTISING

The era of mass communications and marketing is virtually over, and the new era of specialty marketing is well under way. Media that can be used by advertisers are splintering and proliferating at a dizzying pace, each segment with its own attributes, audiences and efficiencies. This makes the selection of media a much harder process for all marketers, and it's only going to get more tricky.

You can't reach most Americans by placing ads in a few mass-circulation magazines, as was possible decades ago with *Life*, *Look*, *Saturday Evening Post* and *Time*. And you can't reach most Americans by buying commercial time on the major broadcast networks, because their share of TV viewing will keep dropping as cable channels multiply. The cost of commercial airtime on the broadcast networks hasn't yet reflected the erosion of their audiences, but it will over time as advertisers develop better ways of measuring the effectiveness of their commercials.

### Supply and demand in media costs

The cost of advertising, like all prices, is a supply-and-demand equation. Ad budgets are rising, driven by a proliferation of new products at home and abroad, and this is keeping ad rates firm in most media. There is also growing consolidation of media in the hands of a few companies, a monopolistic practice that supports ad rates.

But the sheer amount of media dependent on advertising is exploding, too, with a boom in new special-interest magazines, cable networks, radio stations and Internet Web sites. This is causing cutthroat competition for advertiser dollars and is moderating the increase in ad rates. In general, there are many more media outlets than advertisers and subscribers can support—too many magazines, too many TV channels, too many Web sites. Failures and consolidations will, over time, reduce competition and firm up ad rates.

The electronic media, especially cable TV and the Internet, will be the boom fields of the coming years, but print publishing will survive and even flourish. Newspapers and magazines will continue to be the preferred news and information (and even entertainment) outlet for the most highly educated, affluent and influential citizens—"opinion makers," in marketing jargon.

Rather than trying to compete against the electronic mass media on low price for fleeting exposures to advertising messages, the print media will charge premium ad rates that reflect the demographic quality of their audiences and the strong impact of print ads appearing in a reader's most-trusted publications.

Most print publishers of periodicals survive on a mix of revenues from subscribers and advertisers, and they will try to replicate this financial model on the Internet, by selling advertising and also charging visitors to use their editorial content on their Web pages. This will work for business information, but Web surfers are showing a strong resistance to paying subscription fees for so-called consumer information: news, weather, travel information, personal finance guidance, and so on. There are so many free Web sites, supported by advertising or funded by a company for its own promotional purposes, that it will be difficult to get Internet users into a subscription-paying habit, even for unbiased content of a very high quality.

But this may change when Web sites are able to debit an online user's charge account for tiny microfees to read content on a pay-per-read basis. In the meantime, print publishers will be careful not to give away for free, in an electronic format, the same information that their current subscribers are paying good money to read on paper.

# Housing and Construction

Real estate and construction is one of America's most important and varied industries, employing many millions of people and affecting the employment of many millions more in such allied industries as furnishings, decor, landscaping, appliances, advertising and publishing.

These are some of the trends that will affect the construction, sale and management of real property—houses, offices, factories, stores, warehouses—in the years ahead: strong demand for housing and industrial space; moderate demand for offices and retail space; bigger and better-equipped homes, with values keeping pace with inflation in most areas; tougher land-use conditions for development in metro areas; and the broadening of commercial real estate ownership through real estate investment trusts (REITs).

Real estate has always been a boom-and-bust business, prone to the overenthusiasm (and reactive pessimism) of developers, lenders, investors, builders and home buyers. These cycles won't go away, but the memories of painful oversupply and collapse in the late '80s and early '90s will smooth out the extremes for years to come.

Our forecast of moderately accelerating income growth in an environment of low inflation and moderate interest rates is highly favorable for the housing and construction industries. All real estate markets are local. The strongest ones will be those that experience the greatest population and economic growth in the decades ahead—states such as Utah, Oregon, Colorado, Nevada, Washington, Arizona, Texas, Florida, Georgia and North Carolina.

But don't forget the enormous task of revitalizing and replacing America's aging structures, which is a business whose total annual volume sometimes exceeds new construction. Given reasonable economic growth, this rejuvenation and replacement process goes on continually in every part of America, even in older cities in the Northeast and Midwest that aren't experiencing much population growth.

## MORE SUBURBAN SPRAWL, BUT URBAN VITALITY, TOO

Suburban sprawl will continue forever, due to the simple fact that land and housing are cheaper in outlying areas, and people of modest income will endure long commutes to afford a larger home.

But "neotraditional" land planning will grow in popularity. The old suburban standard of wide curvilinear streets, cul-de-sacs and large lots with deep setbacks will give way to old-fashioned grids of blocks with sidewalks, smaller lots, and houses closer to the street. Suburban developments will seek the intimacy of older small cities through new "town centers" that integrate housing, small shops and office space, and slightly reduce dependence on the car for short trips around town.

More communities will take a tougher position on the true cost of sprawl. They will impose all the costs of new physical and social infrastructure—roads, sewers, schools, libraries, police, fire protection—on developers, who in turn will try to pass them on to home buyers and tenants of commercial space. This will raise the cost of moving to distant exurbs, and it will make "in-fill" development in older urban and suburban neighborhoods relatively more attractive financially.

But at the same time, higher-density in-fill development—the environmentally positive antidote to suburban sprawl—will be fought by neighbors who decry any change in the density of their older communities. This double-bind—limits on greenfield and in-fill development—will make the development process more arduous and costly virtually everywhere in America.

Growing suburban congestion will swell the numbers of affluent homeowners rediscovering the joys of living in older urban and close-in suburban neighborhoods. Many aging baby-boomers, emptying their nests of children, will sell their large homes in the far suburbs and move back into town to enjoy shorter commutes and convenience to offices, shopping and entertainment. Homes of architectural distinction and quality construction in older neighborhoods will be sought-after as candidates for extensive remodeling.

## STRONG DEMAND FOR HOUSING

Housing demand will be steady and strong over the next 15 years, driven by population growth (especially through immigration) and gains in household formation and personal income. But when times are occasionally tough, young people will remain in their parents' homes longer, and more people will take in roommates and housemates, reducing the number of new households.

Housing affordability—the value of housing that can be purchased with a median household income—is at a quarter-century high, thanks to low interest rates, strong personal-income growth, and government programs to help middle-income buyers. That's why housing starts have been so robust the past several years and why homeownership is at a record-high level—two-thirds of all households.

Construction will remain strong for several years—well over one million single-family units (detached and townhouses) per year, plus a half million or so apartments, condos and manufactured homes. In the next decade, with the baby-boom echo coming into the market and the economy continuing strong, total housing production will approach the two-million-unit mark—a record level.

## MODERATELY RISING HOME PRICES

Home prices will appreciate more slowly in the next 15 years than they have in the last 15. House prices will rise about 3% to 4% a year, just a little above inflation. Add those numbers on top of current median prices for homes—$124,500 for a used home, $173,000 for a new one.

Homeowners will still improve their houses with an eye to boosting resale value. But they'll move less frequently. As a result of slower appreciation, homeowners will see their houses less as an investment and more as a place to live. Although ownership still enjoys tremendous tax advantages over renting, it is no longer a sure-fire investment. Gone are the days when people bought the most expensive house they could afford, leveraged themselves to the max and then waited for inflation to make them rich—at least on paper. Many of those people saw their homes lose value in the early '90s and won't forget that experience anytime soon. That's a major reason why in the mid '90s, for the first time, stockholdings eclipsed the value of home equity. Just 15 years ago, home equity was three times as great at stockholdings.

## THE DEMOGRAPHICS OF DEMAND

Today's first-time home buyers are mostly in their late twenties or early thirties—members of the small "birth dearth" cohort of the late '60s and '70s. Their meager numbers have dampened demand for starter houses, condominiums and apartments. But a countervailing force has been the enormous desire of new immigrants for homeownership, and they have been a positive force for neighborhood renewal in countless urban areas.

Forecaster Stan Duobinis of the National Association of Home Builders expects there will be a minor downturn in housing demand right after the turn of the century. But by 2005 or so, the housing market will begin feeling the impact of the "echo boom" generation— people born to baby-boomer parents in the '80s and '90s. The same boys and girls who are now causing elementary and secondary schools to burst at the seams will begin moving into apartments and houses in the next decade, improving the market for starter homes.

Upscale homes will be the strongest segment of the market. Demand for luxury homes, bought by trading-up boomers, will be boosted by the astounding wealth formation of broadly rising stock markets, corporate reorganizations and successful start-ups in high technology. Baby-boomers entering their peak earning years covet larger and more elegant homes. Most will prefer to buy new homes, and they won't be overly concerned with price.

Some baby-boomers in some areas will be hindered in their trade-up aspirations by weak prices for their present homes due to soft demand for the enormous number of starter homes built over the last 20 years. This trade-up dilemma will be most difficult in markets that experienced big price drops in the early '90s, such as New York, Washington, D.C., and Los Angeles, and have barely recovered to their previous levels.

Many builders keep trying to design new homes for the low-end and mid-price housing market, but it's tough to do without government subsidies, which will be dwindling in the years ahead. So low- and middle-income families will continue to find their housing in two places—the far fringes of metro areas or decayed urban neighborhoods where cheap housing can be remodeled.

Demand for new apartment units will remain weak for several more years. Households headed by 18- to 25-year-olds, a primary driver of apartment demand, will decline in actual numbers until at least 2003. In addition, too many units were built in the '80s, creating a glut of both rental and for-sale condominium units that remains in many metropolitan areas. The situation will improve when the "echo" babies born in the '80s begin to form their own households early in the next century.

## CATERING TO SENIORS

Today's 45- and 50-year-olds will be less interested in living in retirement communities than today's senior citizens are. The vast majority will remain in mixed-age neighborhoods after they retire, preferring to live around children and young adults rather than being surrounded exclusively by older people. They will want to stay close to health care and shopping. In one concession to age, however, older buyers will want smaller houses that are easier to keep up. Housing aimed at those 50 and up will become increasingly important and increasingly lucrative in the next two decades.

Aware of that, the National Association of Home Builders and others are busy surveying middle-aged Americans. They're finding that the huge migration of retirees to Florida and Arizona will probably slow down, as many seniors opt to stay closer to family and friends. After the children leave home and they retire, many of tomorrow's seniors will move to nearby small towns. But they'll also want the amenities of city life—nice stores, theaters and other cultural venues.

For their houses, most older buyers will want one-level living, easy-maintenance materials inside and out, good home security (locks and alarms), multiple phone lines and jacks (for voice and Internet connections), and products such as grab bars in the tub, scald-protecting faucets and hand-held showers. Two- and three-story upscale homes will often have an elevator, and some builders are already creating a shaft to accommodate an elevator later.

## VACATION HOMES AND TIMESHARES

Lots of busy baby-boomers will yearn for a place to get away from it all in the coming years. And as they enter their peak earning years, many of them will be able to do more than just yearn. They'll buy second homes at a brisk pace, driving up prices over the next couple of decades.

The strongest demand will be for warm-weather locations, such as beaches. That's especially true among the second-largest group of potential getaway buyers—people in their late fifties and sixties who plan to live at least part of the year in a second home. But homes in northern mountain and lake areas, especially near ski resorts, will be desirable, too, especially if they're in an area known for year-round recreation. Many buyers of vacation homes cut their costs by renting out the property at least part of the year.

Time sharing (not a real estate investment, but prepaid vacation lodging) will boom, especially for older Americans. The creation of time share trading networks has greatly increased the attractiveness of timeshares, enabling you to swap your week at one resort for someone else's time at another, in choice locales all over the world.

## THE CHANGING LOOK OF HOMES

American homes of the early 21st century will look similar to what exists now. There won't be a surge in geodesic domes or other exotic designs. But building materials will change. Steel framing will be used in a rising percentage of homes, from 2% now to 10% by 2010. Builders will use more plastic-and-wood composite materials in decking, railings and trim pieces. The materials will look like wood and can be painted but will cost less.

Homes will continue to get bigger. The average house in the mid '70s was about 1,400 square feet. By the mid '90s it was 2,100 square feet and by 2010 it will be closer to 2,300 square feet.

The typical detached house built in the next decade will be a bigger house on a smaller lot, with two or more stories to limit the per-house costs of land, foundation and roofing. It will feature four or five bedrooms, at least two full and two half baths, a large kitchen with lots of counter space and a walk-in pantry, nine-foot ceilings downstairs, a specially wired home office and, quite often, a three-car garage.

Upscale houses will have master bedrooms on the first floor, his-and-hers home offices, computer rooms for the kids, a entertainment rooms for large-screen TV viewing, bigger and fancier kitchens and family rooms—but smaller living rooms, dining rooms and foyers (along with some modest downsizing of outrageously large master baths of the '80s and '90s). New materials and greater efficiency will bring these features into the mid-range house as well.

Many moderately priced houses will be assembled from prefabricated sections made in factories under ideal construction conditions. So-called modular homes used to suffer from a cookie-cutter appearance. Computer drafting and new construction materials will allow them to look as distinct as site-built homes but at much lower cost. Also look for more site-poured concrete houses, using plastic foam forms with rebar and grooves for mechanical systems. They cost about 5% more than frame houses to build, but save money in insulation and heating and air-conditioning costs.

There will also be a resurgence in what used to be called mobile homes, referred to now as "manufactured housing" by those in the business. Manufactured homes will bear no resemblance to trailer houses. They'll have high roof pitches, drywall finishes, more room, bigger windows, and better siding and roofs.

Houses will incorporate advances in technology and telecommunications. Motion-detecting security systems will be standard. Cameras and closed-circuit television systems to watch entrances and sensitive areas will be common in luxury homes. Various features in the home, such as lighting and entertainment systems, will be controlled remotely. As you drive home in the evening, you'll be able to call your home's control system and turn up the heat or fill the bathtub.

## SECURITIZING OF COMMERCIAL REAL ESTATE

The biggest structural change ever to hit the commercial real estate industry has occurred in just the past few years, and it will accelerate in the decades to come. It's the shift in ownership of commercial property from wealthy individual developers and small private investment partnerships to enormous, publicly traded mutual funds called REITs—real estate investment trusts.

REITs now own an estimated 10% of all the commercial property in America, and the percentages are much larger in major urban areas where, in a decade or so, they will own most of the big buildings. Virtually every kind of commercial real estate is being bought by fast-growing REITs, including office buildings, shopping malls and strip centers, hotels, warehouses, hospitals, and the land and buildings of auto dealerships. Assets held by REITs have soared from $8 billion at the start of the '90s to more than $130 billion, and there is no end in sight.

Development and construction projects will still be locally run and lender-financed. But completed projects will be sold to REITs, which constitute a secondary market—an exit strategy for developers, who can trade their ownership stake for shares of stock in the REIT, getting instant liquidity in a business that was once notorious for its illiquidity.

REITs are shifting investment risk from a small number of big private players to a large number of public shareholders. But they aren't reducing risk, just spreading it. The same laws of supply and demand still apply. In a softer economy, or if a particular kind of asset gets overbuilt, rents and property prices will fall, and shareholders will suffer. And some REITs are paying inflated prices for assets today, making it hard to keep giving their shareholders the double-digit total returns of recent years.

But overall, by spreading the risks among millions of national and international shareholders, REITs will bring a little more stability to the commercial real estate business. Downturns in a particular region will have a less severe, debilitating effect on local investors and banks than before.

## SLOWER GROWTH FOR OFFICE SPACE

It has taken most of this decade to work down the nation's glut of office space, and while it's gone in most cities, it lingers in a few. Office construction, which fell from a high of more than $40 billion in 1985 to $15 billion in 1993 (both figures in 1992 dollars), will inch up slowly over the next ten years, but probably not surpass $30 billion a year.

Growth in office jobs will be slower than it has been in recent years. Many corporations that are huge users of space are still aggressively downsizing, particularly in white-collar jobs. In addition, tenants are learning ways to use less space, reducing the average of about 300 square feet of space per employee.

Telecommuting, long dreamed about but slow in taking off, will finally begin to gain serious ground in the next few years. With advances in computers and telecommunications, including the Internet, many workers can be just as productive at home as at the office. "Hoteling" will further crimp demand for office space. Rather than provide space that sits empty most of the time, a company leases time at fully equipped desks in a shared facility. When workers are done, they store their gear in a locker and clear out the desk for the next user. Some firms also use hoteling for the sharing of space in their own company-owned office space, managed by an in-house "concierge" who books employees into available offices.

The cost of downtown space will continue to drive more commercial tenants into the suburbs. Many companies will decide that the cachet of a downtown address just isn't worth the price, unless it is more convenient for important customers. In their quest for larger or cheaper plots, big companies will also flee close-in suburbs for the outer 'burbs.

Most job growth in the next few years will be at small and medium-size companies, further boosting growth in the suburbs and exurbs. A hot software-development company can operate just as easily in Walnut Creek, Cal., as it can in San Francisco. Or, for that matter, it can move to Jackson Hole, Wyo., or Sun Valley, Idaho, if that's where the entrepreneur-owner wants to live.

This trend of employment away from central cities and close-in suburbs will have some negative implications, especially for traffic. Mass transit handles straight-path commuting well—from suburbs into central cities—but not the intricate web pattern of cross-suburban commuting. So we'll see a nightmarish increase in car traffic over secondary roads. And it will be more and more difficult for low-income people, living in center cities, to get to and from the new service-sector jobs in the far suburbs.

With companies now closely watching their real estate costs, tenants will feel less tied to a building than ever before. They will hop across the street, across town or across the country if it makes sense to their bottom line. That means bargaining hard and demanding upgrades from building owners.

Unless they have been renovated, many older buildings—even ones built as recently as the '80s—will become "see-throughs" in a few years, with lots of empty suites. Some will be torn down; there won't be another profitable use for them. They will simply be too expensive to improve, to make layouts more efficient and to rewire for modern telecommunications. But those in good locations, with good "bones" (ceiling heights, structural solidity, and so on), will be candidates for total rehab, from facade to mechanical systems to interior walls.

## STRONG DEMAND FOR INDUSTRIAL SPACE

The future is brighter for industrial property. Expansion of trade, especially with Latin America and Canada, will increase demand for warehouse and distribution properties, and America's resurgent manufacturing will also require the construction of new factories.

Warehouse and distribution will account for about two-thirds of all demand for industrial space between now and 2010. Manufacturing will account for about a quarter, with most of the rest going for research and development facilities.

As with offices, there will be a shift of industrial space away from cities to suburbs and even rural areas, where labor is cheaper, there is less congestion, and most state and local governments are eager to clear the regulatory path for development. Regionally, New England will lag the nation in new industrial space, but expansion will be fairly uniform in other parts of the country.

## SLOWER GROWTH IN RETAIL SPACE

In general, demand for retail space will be soft for a number of years. The number of stores will shrink slightly after years of frenetic building. The fallout will be greatest in older shopping centers and in malls. Many of these developments will have trouble staying fully leased, and they will have to be constantly upgraded to remain competitive. (See the discussion of retail earlier in this chapter.)

# Transportation and Travel

Economic globalization means booming world trade in merchandise, and that will mandate a parallel boom in the movement of goods and people. So the transportation of merchandise, business travelers and tourists around the world will be a high-growth business, with fierce competition among all modes of travel. Consolidation and the resulting monopolistic tendencies will keep prices firm, but competition among big players will restrain price hikes.

## STRAINS ON ENERGY SUPPLIES AND THE ENVIRONMENT

Transportation already consumes more than 20% of the world's primary energy needs and probably creates more air pollution than manufacturing does. That's with 400 million cars on the world's roads. By 2020, with the rapid urbanization of developing countries and growth of a worldwide middle class, there will be more than one billion cars. The Federal Highway Administration forecasts that congestion on America's highways will quadruple by 2005, resulting in an enormous loss of productive time.

It will take entirely new ways of thinking about transportation to minimize environmental degradation and the risk of occasional fuel shortages. Fortunately, we're on the verge of a reinvention of transportation, made possible by advanced electronics, new materials and engineering breakthroughs.

### Cars of tomorrow

A "supercar" that would get 80 miles to the gallon will be ready for showrooms by 2004. The big U.S. automakers, the federal government and many universities are cooperating on the Partnership for a New Generation Vehicle, and all the world's major car companies are developing their own versions. The goal is a family-sized car that will triple the mileage of today's most efficient cars without sacrificing safety. Such a car could cut energy use per car in half by trimming weight, improving aerodynamics, reducing rolling resistance and probably using both a small gasoline engine and an electric motor.

A decade from now, vehicles running on clean natural gas will be common, as will electric cars fueled by storage batteries or generating their own electricity from on-board fuel cells. (See chapter 15 for a discussion of electric car-technology.)

In a few years, many cars will be equipped with navigation and collision-avoidance systems. Engines will routinely go 100,000 miles without a tune-up, and heat-resistant plastics, ceramics and composites will replace steel in many car parts, including engines.

Due to intense international competition, car prices will remain fairly flat for a number of years to come, even as their performance and durability improve.

### Smart highways

By 2010 or so, major metropolitan areas will be linked by smart highways with sensors and transmitters that will relay traffic data to drivers through a communications system in their cars. A few years later, many of these highways will also have designated lanes for hands-free driving. Computerized systems will take over control and keep cars zipping along, separated from each other by just inches. By packing cars closely together, these roads will handle higher volumes without sacrificing speed, greatly reducing rush-hour gridlock. Cars will have radar systems to see through fog and darkness, to warn of obstacles ahead and of unsafe maneuvers by drivers in other lanes.

Packing more cars on the roads safely won't alleviate the need for many more highways and wider existing roads. Rather than build new roads for peak demand during rush hours, more communities will offer incentives to encourage their big employers to use staggered work schedules, subsidize mass transit, require car pools and reduce parking. The growth of home offices and telecommuting will help, but it won't be enough in itself. In some metro areas, federal and state environmental authorities will try to mandate traffic reduction by regulation, but this will be fought in the courts.

## THE WORLDWIDE AUTO BUSINESS

Just 15 years ago, there were 42 independent auto companies around the world. The number is down to about 20, and in another five years, there will be fewer than ten. Giants such as Ford, Toyota, GM, Nissan, VW and DaimlerChrysler will be eyeing companies like BMW, Volvo, Renault, Daewoo, Mazda, Peugeot and Fiat as possible merger partners.

Meanwhile, every major world auto company will try to capture soaring global car sales by building or acquiring factories in Eastern Europe, China, Southeast Asia and Latin America. All of this will contract the auto industry to a handful of enormous players making every kind of vehicle and operating on all continents.

Even though worldwide demand for cars and trucks will be growing strongly, especially in the developing world, the auto market is still facing serious overcapacity. So, along with corporate consolidation will come a manufacturing-capacity shakeout. Less-productive, higher-cost plants in Europe, Japan and North America will be closed or combined. Overall, U.S. factories—with moderate wages and a high level of automation—will be in better shape than those of Western Europe. Compared with German production costs, South Carolina and Alabama look awfully good to BMW and Mercedes, respectively, and the same is true of the Japanese auto plants in Ohio, Kentucky, Tennessee and elsewhere in the U.S.

In 1950, when the world was still recovering from World War II, vehicles made in the United States accounted for a stunning 76% of total world motor-vehicle production. By 1960 that figure was down to 48%, and by 1970, 28%. Today American auto production accounts for about 23% of total world production. This share is likely to fall further as production surges in the less-developed nations, whose share of total production more than doubled since 1990. These figures record only the *place* of manufacture, not who is making them. U.S. multinational automakers will be contributing to, and benefiting from, the global automaking boom through their new plants in less-developed nations.

### How cars will be sold

The retail auto industry is in the early stages of a true revolution. Manufacturers are trying to sharply reduce the number of dealers that handle their cars by encouraging mergers and even by buying up some dealerships themselves. National and regional chains of auto superstores, many of them handling only late-model used cars, are beginning to compete with traditional hometown car dealerships—which, in turn, are merging with each other to better fight the national chains.

With many small dealers going out of business, the number of dealers will shrink from 22,000 to fewer than 15,000 by 2010. Many longtime dealers with locations in valuable urban and suburban settings will sell the land beneath their dealerships to real estate investment trusts and then lease them back, unlocking their equity and improving liquidity for estate planning.

Auto megastores will stress fixed prices, convenience and service. Each new model will be stocked in different colors and feature packages. Consumers will do their price-comparison shopping ahead of time over the Internet or through a buyer's service, but the transaction will be through a local dealer, who will service the car. The trip to the dealer will basically be to pick up a car that's already been already chosen. And more cars will be manufactured to the buyer's specifications, with delivery in just two weeks.

For dealers, the net effect of this retailing revolution will be thinner profit margins, which are already razor thin in new-car sales and only a little better in used cars. Dealerships will try to maintain their comfortable profitability in parts, service and financing, but even these profit centers will be squeezed by nondealer competitors.

### *Navigating cars by satellite*

Global positioning—satellite navigating systems now used in ocean shipping and trucking— will be as commonplace on new cars as airbags are today. The driver will use a small, hand-held receiver to pinpoint location. That information, along with the destination, will be fed into a computer and, presto, out will pop directions. You'll be able to find the nearest bank, the nearest gas station, or the nearest Chinese carry-out. Global-positioning receivers will also be attached to airbags and will automatically call for emergency help in case of accident.

Global positioning is about a $2 billion to $3 billion industry, but it could reach $30 billion by 2005. In addition to cars, it will be used on pleasure boats, by emergency vehicles, even by backpackers.

### EVER-FASTER TRAINS

Inter-city train travel in the U.S. will get a lift from European and Asian bullet-train technology, with speeds of over 160 mph slashing travel time along the Northeast corridor from Boston to Washington, from New York to Chicago, along the Pacific Coast, and someday across Texas and Florida. And looking further ahead, new kinds of trains will use frictionless magnetic levitation; the repulsion of a magnetic field will keep their wheels a fraction of an inch above the rails as they whoosh along.

The major roadblock for high-speed rail might be financial rather than technological. It will cost $2 billion to make the necessary track improvements in the Northeast alone. But train advocates say that doing nothing would be *more* costly, in congestion and lost time, so work is proceeding now.

Freight trains will continue to be the workhorses of interstate transportation for bulk commodities and heavy equipment, and they will increasingly tie together with all other modes of freight transportation—trucking, river barges and ocean shipping—for seamless intermodal transport of containerized cargoes.

## MORE COMPETITION IN MAKING AIRPLANES

The merger mania that has hit every area of business will sweep over the aviation business, from manufacturers to carriers. The combination of Boeing and McDonnell Douglas will keep the United States dominant in world manufacturing for years to come. But a revitalized Airbus, the European consortium, is coming on strong, moving from a 30% share of world aircraft orders a few years ago to a recent 45%, aiming for a once-inconceivable goal of 50% share.

Both Boeing and Airbus are embarking on ambitious plans to make planes faster and for substantially less cost, and the competition will be fierce. With price and quality about the same between competitors, orders will often go to the maker most likely to deliver the products on schedule. Airbus will eventually have to do without the governmental subsidies that Boeing says it still receives but Airbus denies getting.

With air travel booming and most of the world's commercial airlines highly profitable, global demand has exploded for all sizes of jetliners, from small, fuel-efficient 100-seaters to wide bodies with nearly 400 seats, for transoceanic travel. Airbus is working on a 555-seat superjumbo jet for the Asian market, but recent economic woes on that continent will dampen the expected demand for several years. Within a decade or two, Boeing and Airbus will probably be joined by new airline manufacturers, perhaps involving joint ventures among several Asian nations.

### *Consolidation in airlines*

While U.S. airline deregulation has been a success—stimulating an enormous increase in travel with only moderate increases in fares—the government will cast a suspicious eye on proposed domestic mergers and joint-marketing agreements.

That's because one goal of deregulation—entry by new carriers—has proven elusive. The big carriers have a lock on gates and slots at major airports, and it's almost impossible to build new airports, due to citizen opposition in metro areas. So consolidation among domestic carriers would almost certainly be anticompetitive.

However, there will be more international mergers, joint operating agreements and cross-selling arrangements among carriers in different countries, as the airlines of every nation seek landing rights and travel market-share. Of the several cross-national marketing ventures made so far, one of the most successful appears to be the Star Alliance among United Airlines, Lufthansa, Scandinavian Airlines, Air Canada and Thai International Airways. Lufthansa credited the alliance with its hefty 20% increase in trans-Atlantic passengers in 1997.

While brand-new airports will be rare in the U.S., smaller airports on the fringes of sprawling metro areas will be expanded and modernized, becoming popular, lower-fare alternatives for short regional flights. For example, more travelers going to the Boston area will shun high-fare Logan airport in favor of airports in Providence, R.I., and Manchester, N.H. Former military airfields, such as Stewart AFB north of New York City or Pease AFB in Portsmouth, N.H., will be increasingly busy with commercial cargo and passenger traffic.

### New kinds of air traffic control

The Federal Aviation Administration is developing a system, using global-positioning technology, to guide the takeoff, routing and landing of planes.

Such a system could replace ground-based air-traffic control, which has been in use since the '40s. A related development, called "free flight," will allow pilots to choose their routes, altitudes and speeds, cutting travel time. Controllers will intervene only if one plane's route conflicts with another's.

### Supersonic travel ahead

Supersonic air travel never really took off after the introduction of the European Concorde SST, for a variety of reasons: The plane is small and cramped, it guzzles expensive fuel, and it isn't allowed to fly across North America at supersonic speeds.

But superfast air travel is too enticing to remain on the shelf. Boeing/McDonnell-Douglas and Rockwell International have been working with Russia's Tupolev Design Bureau on an upgraded version of an SST that could make supersonic travel viable by 2015.

SSTs will continue to be controversial for the environmental impact of their noise (breaking the sound barrier) and their engine emissions. And some airline-industry executives oppose a new SST, fearing it would siphon off lucrative business and first-class travelers. But their voices will be drowned out by those of a growing army of trans-Pacific business travelers, says Joel Johnson, vice-president for international trade at the Aerospace Industries Association. Executives will willingly pay a lot more to get across the Pacific in four to six hours instead of 12 or 13.

Further into the new century, long-distance airliners will resemble hybrids of rockets and jet airliners, hurtling into space to traverse the Pacific and Atlantic Oceans (and continents too) in just a few hours.

## TOURISM, HOTELS AND CRUISES

The world tourism industry will flourish in the coming years of rising personal incomes all over the world, and the United States will get a big share of this income. It is already the second most-visited nation (behind France) and a strong number one in money spent by international visitors, accounting for more than 15% of the world's total tourism budget. As one of America's biggest service exports, international travel to the U.S., for business and pleasure creates a trade surplus that has risen from $5 billion in 1989 to more than $20 billion.

Strong tourism by both Americans and foreigners has made for boom times in hotels, resorts, cruise lines, amusement parks and national and state parks. The American lodging industry, often afflicted by boom-and-bust cycles, has bounced back from its severely overbuilt condition in the early 1990s to enjoy high occupancy and strong room rates. But by 1998 there were once again signs of overbuilding in the luxury segment of the hotel market.

Cruises, whose U.S. passengers have more than tripled since 1980, will experience a broadening appeal not just to affluent older tourists, but to younger Americans, too, especially "cruises to nowhere" on enormous floating-hotel cruise liners with nonstop entertainment. There will also be strong growth in specialty cruises to environmentally interesting wilderness areas and archeological and historical sites.

In foreign travel by Americans, the high-growth areas will be destinations in Asia, Africa, Latin America and Eastern Europe that have been little-visited in recent decades due to political restrictions, safety risks, and lack of tourism facilities. The most-natural, least-developed areas will have the greatest cachet, and envirotourism will be especially hot.

Travel agents will see their commissions being squeezed by travel vendors, especially airlines and by Internet agencies. Travel agencies will undergo the same consolidation that will occur in other parts of the transportation and travel industries. Many agents will move toward charging their clients a fee for making arrangements, rather than relying solely on commissions paid to them by vendors.

# Defense and Aerospace

A decade ago, on the verge of the Cold War's conclusion, there were several dozen independent American corporations that were major players in supplying the Pentagon, and America's allies, with armaments and military systems of all sorts. These companies employed nearly four million in 1987.

What a difference a decade, and the end of the U.S.-Soviet military rivalry, has made. Today, after painful downsizing and consolidations, the defense industry has just three enormous defense contractors—Boeing, Lockheed Martin and Raytheon—that together will account for about two-thirds of all federal military procurement spending in the years ahead. Total employment in the private defense industry has been cut in half.

Total defense spending will remain relatively flat, consuming about 15% of the federal budget and only 3% of GDP, the lowest levels since before World War II. But while employment and base operations will get the big squeeze, military procurement will rise over the next few years to the range of $60 billion to $70 billion a year. That's because national security is deemed to be highly dependent on having the most advanced weapons—planes, ships, missiles—rather than enormous numbers of personnel in uniform.

The greatest growth will be in sales to foreign governments, which, in a strong world economy and very unstable geopolitical climate, will be able and very willing to acquire American-made armaments of all sorts. The U.S. is far and away the world's leading arms supplier, with sales twice those of any other nation. American military exports, which contributed strongly to the U.S. balance of payments, amounted to some $11.5 billion in 1997, 23% higher than in 1996.

## WATCHING FOR COST PADDING

With so much consolidation and vertical integration in defense contracting, the Pentagon will be watching closely for signs of anticompetitive practices, not just because of extra cost to the taxpayers, but because of the threat to innovation and creativity from a reduced supplier list.

The Defense Department will try to make sure that plenty of outside parts suppliers get a piece of big contracts. Indeed, "spreading it around" to as many contractors and states as possible will be in the interests of the giant prime contractors, because that will build and sustain political support for major, long-term procurement contracts.

The Pentagon will try, wherever possible, to hold down procurement costs (and past public criticism of exorbitantly priced toilet seats and bolts) by buying commercially available, dual-use technologies and products. That means many more high-tech U.S. firms will be eligible to be defense contractors. The goal is to blend the creativity and market-driven competitiveness of civilian commercial industries with the unique technologies and systems integration abilities of the traditional U.S. defense contractors.

## NEW MILITARY TOOLS

Many new weapons systems will be developed in the next 20 years, and old systems will be upgraded to extend their useful lives. There will be new fighter jets for the Air Force, Navy and Marines (in some cases, the same plane for all services), the V-22 tilt-rotor plane that takes off and lands vertically like a helicopter, a new generation of nuclear submarines, the Aegis guided missile destroyer, and surveillance by space-based infrared systems and unmanned aircraft.

The U.S. will stretch its lead in high-tech military communications systems—"command, control and communications," in Pentagon parlance. While such systems will give U.S. commanders unprecedented advantages in the field, they will have to guard against information warfare—that is, sabotage of communications by an opponent.

Even more futuristic designs are on the drawing boards. Engineers at Lockheed Martin are making designs for a pilotless, remote-control fighter jet that could be launched from a submarine and land on an aircraft carrier. Whether such a design ever becomes practical, other types of pilotless aircraft certainly will. They would be smaller and cheaper than manned aircraft, and could be used on dangerous missions without risking a pilot's life. Unlike cruise missiles, pilotless planes could bomb several targets, not just one. Among the systems to be upgraded with new electronics or other features are tanks, the Bradley fighting vehicle, the B-1B bomber, F-14 jet and the AV-8B Harrier aircraft.

Much of the procurement dollar in the coming decade will go into aircraft, including Lockheed Martin's new attack aircraft, the F-22, and the all-services Joint Strike Fighter (which will be made by the winner of bidding between Boeing and Lockheed Martin). Both new aircraft will utilize radar-evading "stealth" technology.

While developing new weaponry for the Pentagon, the U.S. defense industry will continue to sell its current equipment to the rest of the world, contributing strongly to the U.S. balance of payments. For example, while the Pentagon isn't buying many new F-16s from Lockheed Martin, the company is still selling them like hotcakes to foreign governments, as evidenced by a 1998 contract from the United Arab Emirates for as many as 80 of the planes over the next several years. In this competition and others around the world, foreign buyers had a choice between an American fighter and such competing planes as the French Rafale and the Eurofighter, a new product from a consortium of European defense firms.

## A Shield Against Enemy Missiles

The most hotly debated new defense project in the next 15 years will be an anti-missile system. Almost $40 billion has already been spent on research for such missile shields, and much more will be spent in the future. The anti-missile system was dismissed as science-fiction a few years ago, but there will be a sea change in public and political sentiment toward such a project as the threat of missile attack by an outlaw nation grows.

The initial system probably will consist of a mix of ground-based missile interceptors connected to space-based sensor devices to detect an attack. Eventually there will be a network of space-based weapons to shoot down missiles before they reach the U.S. This will be an undertaking of unprecedented complexity, with no guarantee that it could really work. Over several years of testing various designs of interceptor "kill vehicles," the successful hit rate has run only about 33%.

## Industrializing Outer Space

The often dreamed-about commercialization of space will become a reality during the next century. Even though the space age is only four decades old, we have grown accustomed to using satellites for communications and weather forecasting. In the coming decades we'll take much bolder steps into space, including tourism and the first manufacturing facilities. Some scientists even envision capturing brighter solar power on the moon and beaming it down to earth.

These developments won't happen overnight. The cost of building and launching rockets must come down dramatically. With government subsidies remaining flat or declining, aerospace companies will have to become more efficient to attract needed private capital. Investors will await further technological advances from work done aboard orbiting space stations.

The resources and know-how to commercialize space will come from partnerships of government agencies, such as NASA, and private interests. Entrepreneurs already see the potential of space to improve medicine, biotechnology, agriculture and manufacturing, and they are prodding NASA and its contractors to speed up their work.

## COMMERCIAL SATELLITES

The next ten years will bring a boom in commercial-satellite launches—possibly 1,700 more satellites worth an estimated total of $121 billion. Most will be communications satellites, serving all areas of the globe and allowing for expanded use of cellular phones and other new devices. Some will be an advanced form of weather satellites, better able to predict solar storms, which can damage power grids on earth. By 2010, many of the Pentagon's eyes in the sky will need replacing, providing more business for the satellite industry. Civilian companies will play a large role in developing next-generation satellites for the military. The growth of global positioning systems to help guide cars, trucks and ships will also increase demand.

A byproduct of this huge increase in satellites will be something of a traffic jam in earth's orbit. Increasingly, "rules of the road" will spread to space so that satellites don't crash into each other. And don't worry about an old clunker falling out of the sky. Most of the big communications satellites are in geostationary orbit—meaning they float high above one spot on the earth—and when they die, they are simply boosted farther out into space.

### *Growing international competition*

The building of satellites will continue to be a U.S.-led industry for at least the next several years. Hughes, Loral and Lockheed Martin account for about 90% of the world market, but they will face tough foreign competition in the building of next-generation laser satellites, which will be capable of transmitting up to 10,000 times as much information as the old models.

Investors are eager to jump on board the satellite boom. More than $40 billion in financing has been approved for launches, despite the huge risks in this emerging field. The French company Ariane commands about 70% of the launch business, but U.S. companies such as International Launch Services, a unit of Lockheed Martin, and Boeing/McDonnell Douglas will cut into the French lead. Companies in Japan and China will also break off a piece of the launch business. The same missile technology that China acquires from American firms for its satellite-launching industry will also improve the reliability of its nuclear missile program—a classic example of potential conflict between commercial and security interests.

*New ways of launching satellites*

Today satellites are launched with the same multistage, single-use rockets that have put things into space since the beginning of space exploration.

Now researchers and private firms are experimenting with a new concept in satellite launches—a reusable launch vehicle that also holds some promise for passenger space travel. One such concept, the Astroliner from Kelly Space & Technology, Inc., would be towed behind a conventional jet cargo plane to about 40,000 feet, then fly by its own small rocket engines to about 400,000 feet, from which altitude it would launch its satellite payload into orbit. It would glide back to earth, landing with conventional aircraft jet engines, and be ready for another use after a few weeks of service and refueling. Kelly believes the cost would be considerably less than conventional high-thrust rocket launches, and some significant potential customers, including Motorola, are very interested in testing the technology. And technology such as the Kelly Astroliner could be the key to intercontinental passenger travel in space, like a long-dreamed-of "Orient Express" rocket plane that would fly from New York to Tokyo in just a few hours.

## THE AMBITIOUS NEW SPACE STATION

The most ambitious, costly and long-anticipated space project ever—an enormous space station for scientific experiments—is scheduled for completion by the end of 2003. Scientists and engineers from 16 nations, including the U.S., Russia and France, are building the manned space station under the leadership of NASA and prime contractor Boeing.

It will be launched piece by piece—in 70 or so separate launches. The space station will weigh about one million pounds and be the length of a football field, with living and working space equivalent to two Boeing 747 jumbo jets. It will hold several labs, some run by the U.S., others by Russia, and one each by the Europeans and Japanese. The U.S. will pay three-fourths of the construction costs, now estimated to total some $24 billion by completion, with major contributions by such partners as Japan, Canada and several European nations.

At first, work on the space station will focus on increasing human endurance in space and assessing the vehicle as a steppingstone to interplanetary travel. Later, the focus will shift to space-based research into manufacturing. Work on the space station will have one big advantage over work on earth: lack of gravity. Without the pull of earth's weight, scientists hope, manufacturing processes may yield new metals, plastics and composites, and purer compounds. Researchers may also learn more about basic biological processes, leading to improved medicines.

The space-station project has many critics in Congress, who believe that its ballooning budget has deprived other space exploration and research projects of money that could be spent more productively. But there is no realistic chance the station will be abandoned, after so much investment and with such high hopes for its utility in scientific experiments. Meanwhile, NASA's smaller and less expensive space shuttles will continue their science experiments in space.

## SPACE EXPLORATION

There has always been a noncommercial angle to space exploration: the dream of escaping earth's grip, seeing worlds that earlier generations could only imagine. NASA's long-term plans include increasing knowledge of the nature of life, exploring and settling the solar system, and making space travel routine. Manned space shots to Mars—even colonizing the red planet—are a more distant goal. But by 2020, such an otherworldly step will be seen as within reach.

The search for life beyond earth will intensify. Many space authorities, such as Dr. Jerry Gray, believe it's unlikely that life exists anywhere else in our solar system or others nearby. But many consider the odds good that there is life in some other far-flung places.

By 2010, scientists hope to build something called the Terrestrial Planet Finder, an array of telescopes with infrared sensors to detect radiated heat from planets circling other stars. Discovery of more planets would certainly increase interest in exploring them, but that will be a job for centuries beyond the 21st.

# CHAPTER 17

# The Future
# Shape of Business

T ruly fundamental changes in the structure and management of business—such as the creation of the modern corporation in the 1920s and multinationals in the '50s and '60s—were once pretty rare. Now they're coming along once a decade or even more frequently. Some are short-lived fads driven by a hot new management concept or external market condition, such as the conglomerate craze of the '70s or leveraged buyouts in the '80s. But a change of great and enduring impact is now taking shape in the global economy: the creation of immense *transnational* corporations, born of megamergers between giant *multinational* corporations.

Other significant shifts, already evident, will accelerate and have an enormous bearing on how your business will be conducted in the decades ahead. These include:

• perpetual restructuring of corporations, unrelated to how the business is doing;

• "rolling up" of geographically dispersed small and medium-size businesses in a given field;

• demise of large, closely held corporations;

• securitizing of every kind of asset;

• homogenizing of world standards in production and management styles;

• a backlash against overly complex and unreliable technology;

• commercialization of every kind of activity in America;

• growing diversity in corporate leadership, and the rise of the itinerant executive;

• geographic dispersal of corporate headquarters, creating new business power centers; and

• rise of immensely rich charitable foundations and nonprofit organizations as a force in business.

# New Business Structures

A decade ago, drastic corporate reorganization—downsizing, combining divisions, closing or selling some—was done only in crisis. Now it's a constant way of life at most successful companies. Companies unapologetically announce large layoffs even when profits are strong. They restructure as a preventive rather than remedial measure.

Companies will constantly reassess what they do well and what they're not suited to do. Itinerant corporate leaders, not wedded nostalgically to the original mission of the firm, won't hesitate to throw weak divisions overboard and move the company into promising new fields.

Companies famous for a certain line of products will abandon their original mission altogether, as in Monsanto's departure from chemicals to focus on biotech drugs (even before its unsuccessful 1998 merger plan with American Home Products) or Westinghouse's exit from power-plant equipment to become solely a broadcasting company. The divested divisions will often perform better under new owners who are more committed to and savvy about those fields.

Perpetual reorganizing and downsizing will tend to weaken employee loyalty. And employees will respond with similar self-interest, keeping their eyes open for better opportunities and moving more often from job to job.

### THE IMPERATIVE OF BIGNESS

By midyear, the megamerger mania of 1998 had already seen seven of the ten largest mergers in world history, with a value of nearly $800 billion, closing in on the record $916 billion of mergers the previous year.

Merger activity will not continue at this pace indefinitely, due to occasional stock-market slumps, recessions and growing government scrutiny of mergers. But the general trend toward bigness in world enterprise will quicken and spread to all continents in the years ahead. It will be driven by many forces, including the need to raise capital for global expansion, pressure from mergers among competitors, corporate egos, and the lure of quick money to be made (by executives, investment bankers and attorneys) simply from doing the deals.

Quite simply, big companies are better able to marshall the capital for research and development in new products and services, build national and global brand identity, cut through the din of competitors' marketing and advertising expenditures, and convince distributors, retailers and other intermediaries to carry their products.

The merger mania has revived a once-moribund antitrust policy in the U.S., while also stimulating spirited debate among government and academic economists as to what role, if any, government should play in promoting business competition and consumer protection from monopolistic behavior. In general, bigness itself will not be penalized by government, but anticompetitive practices by businesses of any size will trigger a sharp regulatory response. (For a fuller discussion of future antitrust policy, see chapter 5.)

## ASCENDANT TRANSNATIONALS

International megamergers will boom, creating behemoths quite different from the traditional multinational corporation. Recent examples include Daimler-Benz and Chrysler, Bertelsmann and Random House, Britain's Pearson PLC and the educational division of Viacom's Simon & Schuster, Sweden's Pharmacia and America's Upjohn, and Germany's Siemens and Westinghouse power-generating operations.

Transnational merger-and-acquisition activity involving publicly traded U.S. companies was strong in the '80s, hitting a peak of about $175 billion in 1990. It slowed in the soft world economy of the early '90s, then skyrocketed to more than $400 billion in 1997 (nearly half of all U.S. merger activity last year). And an even higher total was expected for 1998.

Two things distinguish a transnational from a multinational corporation: how it grows big, and how it operates as it grows. In the original American model of the multinational, epitomized by IBM in the '50s through '70s, a company grew organically by extending its own products and brands into distant markets, first by export and then by establishing factories overseas. The company retained a strong identification with the nation where it was founded, and most products were branded with the corporate name. Acquisitions of existing companies were relatively rare, and when they occurred, the identity of the acquired firm was submerged in the parent's. Overseas operations often were led by executives transplanted from headquarters in the home country.

A transnational corporation, by contrast, is created from the combining of corporations that are already giant multinationals with enormous power in their existing markets. Powerful brands are maintained and extended into new lands. Product lines maintain their own distinct identity, but the leadership (drawn equally from the merged firms) creates a new corporate culture that spreads throughout the enterprise. Overseas operations are staffed with local talent who are given strong operational authority. Transnationals of tomorrow will be true global businesses that will, over time, lose their identification with any particular country.

Transnational mergers will invite the scrutiny of antitrust officials in each affected nation, complicating approvals and forcing the arduous evolution of a global consensus on what constitutes anticompetitive size, structure and behavior in business.

### CONSTANT 'ROLLING UP' OF MEDIUM-SIZED FIRMS

All these imperatives toward bigness will propel the combination of smaller firms into much larger ones, in the U.S. and throughout the world, so they have a fighting chance against the biggest firms.

With enormous ad budgets behind them, national products will continue to gain market share over local and regional products. Because of their power to buy cheaply in quantity, national chains—whether general-merchandise discounters, grocers, home and hardware stores, restaurants, movie theaters, or auto service centers—will enjoy an increasing advantage over purely local firms.

Small, local firms will compete by finding something—anything—that they can do for their customers that the big guys can't. But even then, smaller firms will be at a distinct disadvantage in attracting capital. Lenders and venture-capital investors know that it takes as much time and effort to do due diligence on a small deal as a big one, so they'll avoid the small ones.

Given all that, there will be constant "rolling up" of small firms (often closely held) into new public companies in previously unconsolidated industries, as has happened already in newspapers, banking, auto dealerships, commercial printing, radio stations, funeral homes, real estate, office-supply companies, telemarketing, home-cleaning services, subscription fulfillment, temporary employment, movie theaters and countless other fields.

The result will be more large, publicly traded companies dominating many lines of business. The market leaders will prosper, but so will many of the much smaller firms that stay out of the way of the elephants' feet as they do battle for the number-one spot. The smaller firms can fill niche markets, often creating new products more innovatively and faster than the big guys can—and then positioning themselves to be bought out. Success will go to the top one or two firms and the nimble little competitors, but the medium-size firms will get stepped on or passed by.

## GROWTH BY ACQUISITION

The most ambitious (and impatient) companies will choose to expand through mergers and acquisitions rather than gradual internal growth. The "not invented here" syndrome will continue to fade, as companies look with admiration on what their colleagues and competitors have already accomplished. Better to buy it than try to replicate it, so long as the price is not exorbitant.

### *Goodbye to conglomerates*

The days of the conglomerate of disparate, unrelated companies are over. The idea made conceptual sense—unrelated lines of business serving as countercyclical balances to each other, with some doing well while others were in a down period—but in practice, it was hard to manage, and many ended up as a collection of mediocre near-contenders in many fields.

Some firms will continue to give this a try, as the Bronfman family's Seagram beverage corporation seems to be doing with its forays into the entertainment business. But the dominant trend will be the divestiture of unrelated businesses, such as Sunoco and Mobil getting out of real estate development; DuPont divesting itself of Conoco to concentrate on chemicals, new materials and biotech; and H&R Block leaving the online business, selling its once-dominant CompuServe subsidiary to focus on tax-preparation services and software, and other personal-finance software.

### *Less vertical integration*

Likewise, the days of the vertically integrated company are numbered. No longer will most successful companies manufacture every component themselves or acquire their key suppliers to operate as subsidiaries. They will instead buy more from the outside, developing close relationships with independent vendors.

Vendors and suppliers, nervous about their relationships with big customers, will seek to tie themselves more closely to their customers, working with them on developing new products and manufacturing techniques and cutting costs. Vendors will become true partners. Some will actually manufacture on the customer's site, but will maintain their commercial separateness.

## MORE JOINT VENTURES

The merger and acquisition boom will be accompanied by a surge in joint ventures, both domestic and international. Joint ventures will take many forms, from joint launch of new manufactured products and services to co-branding and cross-marketing. Joint ventures will be a popular way for prospective partners to get to know each other, sometimes leading to mergers later on.

Joint ventures will enable corporations to share costs and engineering expertise in bold new undertakings of great complexity and expense. Motorola and Lucent, for example, will conduct joint research on new kinds of semiconductors that convert analog signals to digital signals in phones, modems and other devices. Ford announced in late 1997 it would invest $420 million in a joint venture with Daimler-Benz (now DaimlerChrysler) to develop and manufacture, by 2004, as many as 100,000 electric cars powered by fuel cells designed by Canada's Ballard Power Systems, a fuel cell pioneer. And the following year Ford entered into an alliance with Mobil to work on higher-efficiency diesel engines, fuel-cell technology and using natural gas a motor fuel.

## QUESTIONABLE PROFITABILITY OF MEGAMERGERS

Creating higher value from mergers and acquisitions is no easy slam-dunk. Sometimes the acquiring company can't figure out how to integrate the acquired firm into its corporate culture and marketing plan. Sometimes it is difficult to make revenue grow after the initial kick of cost cutting is finished. Sometimes the acquired company, which once showed entrepreneurial zeal as an independent, gets bogged down in the bigness of the parent firm. The record is replete with examples of acquisitions that didn't work out well, including AT&T's purchase of NCR computers, Dow Jones's acquisition of the Telerate financial-data system, Union Pacific's merger with Southern Pacific, and Quaker Oats' buy-out of Snapple fruit beverages.

Even in mergers that are not beset with severe financial and managerial crises, there is the thorny issue of whether the deal was financially advantageous for the shareholders. When a company is bought with the stock of a high-flying acquirer, there is a tendency not to look as closely at the price. The merger and acquisition boom of the '90s has been fueled by appreciating shares of stock in a soaring stock market, just as the restructuring boom of the '80s was fueled by junk bonds. The cash portion of merger and acquisition transactions in early 1998 was running at a record-low 13%, down from 42% in 1994. When stock markets cool off from time to time, so will the total volume of merger and acquisition activity and the portion of the price that is financed with stock.

In the superheated, stock-heavy merger and acquisition market of 1998-1999, some acquisitions took place at levels that represented, based on the acquired firm's previous year's earnings, a return of less than 10% on shareholder equity—much less than the acquirer or its shareholders could probably earn by passively investing in broad stock indexes. Such prices require enormous earnings growth to justify, and the growth must come from hard-won cost cutting, revenue hikes or both.

Some of the hot megamergers, driven by corporate ego as much as market sense, will turn out to have been overpriced deals. It may have been smarter for management just to buy back shares of its own company (although high stock prices make that questionable, too), use higher amounts of cash to drive harder bargains, or simply sit on cash for acquisitions later, when market corrections will make stock prices more attractive.

### A push from investment bankers

Many future corporate restructurings—mergers and divestitures—will be stimulated not by clearheaded strategic planning within the corporation but by the hunger of investment bankers for deals to do—any deals. Investment bankers live off transactional activity, and they make money whether or not their deals pan out in the long run.

Here's an example of hyperfrenetic merger-and-acquisition activity, which although hypothetical is a type actually seen today: An investment-banking house finds a closely held company in a hot field, takes it public in an initial public offering (IPO), merges it into a larger company in a stock swap, then convinces the acquiring management to take the enlarged company private. The bankers then try to enlarge it with additional acquisitions, and take it public again with another IPO. Finally, management reassesses the structure of the firm and decides to spin off several divisions. At every step of this process, investment bankers generate enormous commissions and fees, and management gets rich off the IPOs—if the company continues to prosper at what it actually does.

### Effect of mergers on trade associations

Trade associations have traditionally existed on dues from their member corporations, and as the number of large, independent companies dwindles from consolidation, dues income will suffer. That's because, while most associations charge dues based on the member's size in revenue, the dues are typically capped for the largest members. Unless the caps are raised, the combination of two or three big companies already at the maximum dues level will deprive the association of a lot of money.

The response of most trade associations will be to try to generate proportionately less income from membership dues and more from special services to members, including conferences (with paying exhibitors and commercial sponsors), special reports and research, and sales of goods and services bought at a discount for the members' benefit.

## THE DEMISE OF BIG, CLOSELY HELD COMPANIES

The world boom ahead will see the paradox of exploding small-business entrepreneurship amid the simultaneous decline of the closely held big business.

The paradox is explained by the different life stages of a business and how its needs change with growth. More and more businesses will be formed, but a higher percentage of them will get bought out or go public earlier in their life than in years past. It will be more difficult to replicate the model of the gigantic closely held business, on the order of today's Mars, Newhouse or Cargill. Most closely held companies will be sold before they reach that size.

Closely held businesses are limited in the ways they can grow—typically with retained earnings and loans, without being able to sell shares to the public or swap appreciating stock with other public companies in mergers. And closely held businesses will continue to be at a disadvantage in recruiting top management. While they can pay competitive salaries and use a variety of bonus and profit-sharing plans as incentives, they can't match the lavish stock-option programs that attract talent to publicly traded firms.

New businesses started with venture capital will always sell out or go public fairly early, because the investors demand a prearranged timetable for the return of their capital. But even the vast majority of new firms started with personal savings and bank loans will sell out to someone else earlier than in the past. The reasons will vary—the impatience of the founder to start something new or retire with liquidity, the role the business plays in estate planning, or simply a desire on the part of owners to affiliate with a larger company in whose fold their business can grow faster and stronger, with better access to capital, technology and far-sighted management.

## THE SECURITIZING OF EVERYTHING

A parallel trend to the "going public" of America will be the securitizing of virtually every kind of asset that produces income (and even some that don't). In this process, the value of an asset, or bundle of assets—companies, buildings, packages of mortgages, credit card debt, art and antiques, sports teams—is cut into pieces for sale to the public.

This phenomenon has been driven in part by the hot stock market of the '90s, with its hunger for any kind of new securities to sell to an eager public. Securitizing an asset can be a boon to the seller, because the sale of shares to the public usually brings a higher total price than the undivided asset would fetch from a knowledgeable single buyer in a private transaction (that's the alchemy at the heart of the boom in initial public stock offerings, or IPOs).

Far and away the greatest securitizing mania in any class of assets in recent years has been the sale of commercial real estate by private investors to real estate investment trusts (REITs). But there isn't any kind of asset that can't "go public" in this way—even a pro sports franchise, as the locally owned Green Bay Packers have demonstrated. Over the years, when art and antiques markets are hot, some entrepreneurs try to sell shares in mutual funds that buy and hold rare paintings and furniture for future appreciation (but no current yield).

A particularly hot field will be the securitization of future royalty income from movies, TV shows, books and songs. Aging rock star David Bowie started a small trend when he borrowed $55 million from Prudential Insurance, which issued a private placement of ten-year, 7.9% bonds (rated A by Moody's) secured by Bowie's future royalties. And rocker Rod Stewart has done a $15.4 million private placement with Japan's Nomura Capital.

Simply securitizing an asset won't do anything to increase its intrinsic value. Whether as an undivided whole or in slivers of stock, it will rise and fall on its performance and the laws of supply and demand. But securitizing assets has some advantages for the liquidity of markets. It will soften the pain of collapsing asset values and defaults by spreading the losses, in small amounts, over millions of shareholders.

# Globalization

The quickening pace of globalization will lead to unprecedented standardization and homogenization in world markets. For example, Ford chairman Alex Trotman put a stop to the company's practice of using entirely different parts in its basically similar Escort cars, depending on whether they were being built in America, Europe or Asia. Uniform, or at least compatible, world standards will evolve in engineering, manufacturing, commercial law, management techniques, accounting, lending and underwriting methods, advertising, etc. The metric system will become universal in world production and commerce, even if the Americans and British cling to their quaint weights and measures in daily life at home.

No longer will various large nations have their own different telecommunications protocols for TV and telephones. Technical standards for entire industries will be set by groups of scientists and engineers from all of the world's leading transnational corporations. There will be competing technologies, of course, as with the old Beta and VHS videotape standards, the Japanese analog high definition TV standards and the new U.S.-developed digital standard, or more recently, competing standards in Internet access over phones and cable-TV systems. But interconnectivity and interchangeability will be the keys in telecommunications and many other fields, so dominant standards will emerge faster, and the also-rans will fall by the wayside sooner.

Standards set in the most advanced nations, especially the United States, will be dominant. But if any major player sets a standard different from others (for example, a tougher environmental standard, or a product-quality benchmark, as the European Union is beginning to impose) it will be honored by world manufacturers, so long as the more-demanding market is big enough and rich enough to justify the effort.

Uniformity of engineering standards should not be mistaken for standardization of all end products. Successful companies will constantly modify products and create new ones for various global markets. In Japan, for example, Coca-Cola developed a successful sweetened coffee beverage, sold in cold cans from vending machines. In India, where cows are sacred, McDonald's Big Mac is made with lamb patties.

## IMPROVING WORKPLACE STANDARDS

In a world of global journalism and vigilant watchdogs from organized labor, environmental and human-rights groups, it will be impossible for multinational companies to conduct their business in ways that violate the norms of their home countries.

Of course, it is the differences in operating costs—wages, health and safety regulations, environmental rules, and so on—that cause businesses to manufacture in one nation rather than another. The rush of European and Japanese businesses into the U.S. economy for instance, is based in part on the lower production costs they find here—including lower nominal wages and taxes, shorter vacations, and weaker unions. The same impulses lead American companies to set up shop in Asia, Latin America and Africa.

Lower (but legal) wages will still be considered an acceptable difference, but not prison labor, dangerous working conditions or child labor, even if legal under local law. Shoe-and-apparel marketer Nike, feeling the heat of broad criticism of the overseas operations of its contract manufacturers, announced in 1998 that it will impose American-level air-quality standards on all its contractors' shoe factories abroad. More important, it said it would raise the hiring age for all new overseas contract workers to 16 or 18, depending on the nature of the work.

Similar agreements will become a trend in transnational corporate management, especially with companies that (unlike Nike) actually own and manage their own plants. In this way—ironically, given the reputation of multinationals for fleeing the high standards of advanced nations—transnational corporations will become a force for improving not just the living standards of less-developed nations, but also environmental standards, working conditions and nondiscriminatory hiring practices. The appropriate comparison won't be with the standards of advanced nations but with other, locally based businesses in the developing nations.

## CONVERGING MANAGEMENT STYLES

Successful transnational corporations will find ways to meld their managers of different nationalities and cultural backgrounds into cohesive teams.

Corporate cultures and management styles will still vary from nation to nation, as well as among different companies within nations. European and Asian management models, for example, tend to be more hierarchical and formal, with a large dose of consensus building and polite respect for disagreement. The American model, on the other hand, puts a premium on independent thinking and decision making by line managers, fast decisions, and free-for-all debate, with a strong dose of office politics. The American style of promoting young star employees, without much regard for seniority, will slowly catch on all over the world—even in hierarchical Japan and South Korea.

The American model will be the dominant pattern for world business in the years ahead, leavened with some of the core values of the transnational's home culture. More and more companies will adopt plain, simple "business English" as the universal language for managerial communication in all their offices all over the world. For example, ABB—born of a Swedish and a Swiss company—has decreed that all its internal reports and memos must be written in one language, English, even by colleagues who speak one of the local languages in any of the 128 nations in which ABB does business.

## MORE LOCAL HIRES, WITH MORE AUTHORITY

It was once common in multinational corporations for the senior management of overseas operations to be expatriates from the home office, seasoned veterans who knew the corporate culture. The big decisions were made from afar. Today's preference is to hire top local talent, involve them fully in setting policy in their region and give them broad decision-making authority. "The best expatriates are about half as effective as an equally qualified national," Gary Pfeiffer, the chief financial officer of DuPont, said in a 1998 interview with *The Washington Post*. DuPont regards the United States not as its headquarters country, but as simply an operations region like Latin America, Europe or Asia. "What makes a company global is having the willingness and ability to deal in an appropriate fashion in every place in the world, and to value your employees no matter what nationality they are," Pfeiffer said.

Ahold, the Netherlands-based grocery retailer whose U.S. acquisitions (most recently, the Giant Food chain in the Mid-Atlantic region) have made it the fifth-largest grocery seller in the U.S., prides itself on having no Dutch executives based in the U.S., in an American work force of 140,000.

Rather than conceiving, designing and developing all new products in the home office and sending the specs overseas for manufacturing, companies will disperse these functions around the world. This will tap into the creative talents of local leadership and make sure that the company's products go over well in diverse markets.

## THE INTERNET AS BUSINESS TOOL

The increasing importance of the Internet in world business cannot be overestimated. It will become the dominant path for all commercial communication—both within a company and among companies. It will be key in finding new customers and suppliers, recruiting employees, soliciting bids, generating market intelligence, and many other functions.

The Net will be a great leveler of playing fields, especially for small and medium-size firms, enabling them to use direct marketing to expand to international markets in competition with vastly larger firms.

The bartering of goods and services, a growing trend in American business for dealing with excess inventory, will get a boost from the creation of enormous Internet-based clearinghouses and exchanges for merchandise of all sorts. Some are already in existence (www.irta.net and www.nate.org), and they establish standards, deposit and withdraw "trade dollars" in company accounts, and handle all the record keeping, including reporting each party's barter income to the IRS once a year. Someday barter will be an easy world-wide activity.

# Management and Marketing

More businesses will cast a skeptical eye on extravagant claims of productivity and quality enhancement from every new automation project, especially computer upgrades that increase the complexity of systems while often diminishing reliability.

Upgrades require staff retraining and often increase costs of system administration and maintenance. A new generation of corporate executives, more tech-savvy than their predecessors, will be better able to cut through the hype of consultants and systems marketers, asking tough questions and making more-independent decisions. Increasingly, they will decide not to be on the cutting edge of new technology but to let other firms be the guinea pigs.

In this "de-engineering" trend, more companies will seek reliability and ease of use, rather than exotic new features, in their new automation projects. And they will hold contractors more responsible for how new systems perform. Finally, they will sometimes opt for a more labor-intensive and human solution to a problem, rather than the high-tech option—adding more human operators instead of expanding voice mail, for instance, or using skilled machinists instead of fully robotic machine tools.

## GROWING COMMERCIALIZATION

The commercialization of life will spread relentlessly in the years ahead, injecting corporate sponsorship, advertising and influence into every area of human endeavor. This process will have many negative effects, often unnoticed, especially on the objectivity of journalistic information, academic research and professional judgment. And it will ultimately erode the effectiveness of some kinds of sponsorship by creating a jaded, skeptical public.

Every kind of organization with a captive constituency (a membership roster, magazine readership, student body, audience for a conference or concert, stadium full of fans, or group of party goers) will solicit sponsorships from businesses. And businesses will aggressively offer to pay increasing sums of money to get their name and products before the eyes and ears of those constituencies.

Linkages between Web sites, and even the sequence in which

information pops up on some search engines, will be influenced by payments from companies eager for their sites to be visited.

Business trade associations, hungry for income to supplement stagnant dues memberships, will open their activities to more sponsorship by vendors eager to sell to the members. Senior-citizen organizations will get a cut of the sales of products and services they recommend to their members, without regard to whether the stuff is the best available and well priced.

MTV, the rock-music channel, already suggests that movie producers pay it fees for prominent on-air plugging of their new films, and this practice will spread to more cable and broadcast networks. The ad-sales departments of some personal finance magazines (not including *Kiplinger's*) direct their writers and editors to appear at public investment seminars sponsored by financial-services firms that advertise in the magazines. This practice—called "merchandising"—will spread even more widely.

All these activities will grow out of a perception of mutual self-interest. Enterprises, both for-profit and nonprofit, will seek new sources of revenue, and marketers will desire new kinds of promotional projects.

The effects will be especially pronounced in education, from kindergarten to universities. To build brand awareness and loyalty early on, marketers will seek promotional tie-ins with elementary and secondary schools, sponsoring everything from sports and musical performances to science fairs, often in exchange for free merchandise that the school needs (an extension of the PC-giveaway programs so popular around the nation). Despite the resistance of school boards and principals in some areas, more and more of the educational TV programming seen in schools will be interspersed with commercials for products aimed at kids.

More corporations and trade associations will fund sponsored research at universities, often bankrolling entire institutes whose output, heavily influenced by the sponsors, will carry the prestige of the university. For example, a 1997 study of personal bankruptcy done by Georgetown University's Credit Research Center was funded by a $100,000 grant from Visa and MasterCard, which used the study to lobby Congress for tougher bankruptcy laws.

Companies will continue to pay large sums to movie producers to have their products used by actors on screen and woven seamlessly into the plot. Someday, if it hasn't happened already, companies will pay best-selling novelists to mention their products in upcoming books.

Powerful advertisers in magazines, newspapers and broadcast outlets will increasingly pressure media owners and executives—who will in turn pressure their editors and writers—for favorable journalistic treatment. Professional societies, research centers and think tanks will also solicit or accept corporate sponsorship of their scholarly work and their meetings.

About the only major institution in society that hasn't seen heavy commercialization is organized religion, but perhaps someday large churches will accept commercial sponsorship of their youth groups, Bible classes and weekend retreats.

## MARKETING WILL TRUMP PRODUCT INNOVATION

People won't always beat a path to your door to buy your better mousetrap—if they don't know it exists, can't grasp its clear advantages over similar products, or aren't able to buy it easily for an attractive price.

So increasingly, success will go to the company that can rush its products into the marketplace faster than its competitors, establishing its version as the worldwide standard, the product of choice—even if the product is not superior to a competitor's undermarketed product.

This will often favor the biggest, best-capitalized firms, but not necessarily. Sometimes the giants will be outmaneuvered by small, nimble competitors with better products. For example, AT&T stubbed its toe badly trying to break into the online service business, as did Sears and IBM, who squandered the early lead enjoyed by their Prodigy joint venture and were outmaneuvered by upstart America Online.

In all the boom fields of the future, especially consumer electronics, telecommunications and pharmaceuticals, there will be many competing products that are roughly similar in function and quality. Some will prosper and some will fall by the wayside, and the winners won't necessarily be the best products—just as the Apple operating system, generally considered superior to Microsoft's MS-DOS and Windows, failed to achieve dominance in the home and office marketplace.

## MORE PATENTS, BUT LESS PROTECTION

In an era of rapid technology transfer and constant modifications of existing products, patents will offer less protection than in the past. Patents will be legally sidestepped by relatively small changes in design and engineering, and before long, anyone can make a reasonable imitation of any product.

Protecting patents will become an increasingly difficult and contentious battle—especially in biotech—and there will be constant fights between large companies over alleged patent infringements in key products. Many cases will be settled by defendants' being allowed to continue making their products while paying court-ordered royalties to the aggrieved plaintiff.

The ease of legally sidestepping and modifying patents doesn't even address what will be the growing problem of blatant violations of copyrights and patents in the Third World—counterfeiting of software, CDs, videotapes and designer clothing, and pirating of TV signals. Even with growing publicity and enforcement, this infringement will be an increasing problem in a freewheeling global business environment, in which many poor nations feel entitled to level the playing fields with rich nations by stealing proprietary technology and products.

## CORPORATE LIABILITY WILL BE LIMITED

Legal considerations—the prevention and handling of legal challenges of all sorts, from competitors, vendors, employees, customers and the government—will be an ever-growing, daily presence in corporate life.

But notwithstanding the ongoing tobacco-liability movement, there will be a slow pendulum swing away from the long trend of holding businesses liable for anything that goes wrong while someone is using, or even abusing, their products or services. The reform will be part of a broad trend away from America's preoccupation with victimhood and toward a new ethic of individual responsibility.

This reform will also occur in the name of international competitiveness, to stabilize the rising insurance and litigation costs that threaten the profitability—even the very existence—of businesses in fields ranging from aircraft manufacturing to pharmaceuticals. Without such product-liability reform, new product development in high-risk areas of medical devices and drugs would be financially dangerous.

Aggressively fought by trial lawyer associations, new laws at both the state and federal level will limit liability to egregious cases of negligent design or manufacture, will limit the time of liability exposure, and will cap jury awards for pain and suffering, focusing instead on real monetary losses.

While business wants broad relief for enterprises of all sizes, Congress will start with help for small businesses—those with fewer than 25 employees. They will get a liability cap of, say, $250,000, and wholesalers and retailers will get some protection from being named as parties to suits involving defects in products they merely distribute and sell.

## ENVIRONMENTALISM IN EVERY DECISION

"Green" considerations will enter into more business decisions in the years ahead—everything from product design and choice of materials, to recycling of waste materials, to commuting and parking subsidies for employees, to the design of company offices and factories.

Many of the changes will be forced by governments at all levels, but more businesses will "do the right thing" not just for their image but because they can save money by using less energy and raw material. In the short run, forced compliance with environmental regulations is often an added cost; in the long run, it can save big money.

Environmental protection will play a bigger role in international business, too. Pollution doesn't obey international boundaries. Sulfur emissions from one country fall as acid rain in a neighboring country. Chemicals discharged into a river contaminate fish in another country downstream. So the world's nations are taking a more international view of controlling pollution. Fifty years ago, there were just a handful of treaties on the environment. Today there are 170, with many more on the way in the next 20 years, covering issues from carbon-dioxide pollution to sharing ocean resources.

Because of the stakes involved—fishing treaties can idle whole fleets, for example—there will always be resistance to some agreements. But cooperation will come about, sometimes forced by the threat of trade sanctions. International lending organizations will be enlisted in the effort, dangling the carrot of development funds to help countries improve their air and water.

## GROWING CLOUT BY INSTITUTIONAL INVESTORS

A larger share of America's wealth will be concentrated in institutions that invest in stocks. These institutions include corporate and union pension funds, public-employee retirement plans, charitable foundations, university endowments, and mutual fund companies managing individuals' 401(k) plans. And a few years from now, even the trustees of the social security system will be investing some of the trust fund assets in private equity markets.

These institutional investors will take an even stronger interest in the management and social policies of corporations than they do now. In deciding which stocks to own and in the voting of their shareholdings in mergers and proxy battles, they will take positions that combine their fiduciary responsibility—to make their assets grow—with a sense of responsibility to society, on environmental issues, workplace issues and behavior in the international realm.

# New-Style Executives

The business world of tomorrow will be too complex and too fast-moving for any one corporate leader—or even team of leaders at headquarters—to keep up with. Micromanagement won't work, even in fairly small companies. Executives will have to rely on the judgment and creativity of subordinates, both in their headquarters office and in branch offices around the nation and the world.

The role of senior management—including boards of directors—will be to work out the company's broad missions and goals, including deciding which lines of business to be in or get out of, for maximum growth of shareholder equity.

But the execution of the vision will require input from every level in the workplace, even (or especially) from the factory floor and the customer-service telephone bank. In many cases, the men and women who have to make the product and field customer complaints can spot a potential problem long before it surfaces publicly, so smart management will make sure their ideas are heard early on.

## THE RISE OF THE CIO

Management will become more dependent on getting timely information about what is happening anywhere—around the nation and around the world—that will affect the company's prospects. The trick will be selecting the information carefully for reliability, culling the most important information from the cacophony of news, and organizing it in succinct ways that are useful to management.

This task will fall to ever-larger staffs of corporate information specialists, headed by CIOs—chief information officers. Their skills are derived from the information-services business, augmented with an aptitude for investigative reporting and even intelligence work.

Companies will transform their corporate libraries into electronic information centers, using online services and the company's own intranet. Corporate librarians will select commercial databases for companywide site-license subscriptions, then create customized in-house databases and information services. That will also allow them to, say, give their managers all over the world a daily morning briefing on the key news and intelligence they all must share to work together effectively.

## DIVERSITY IN SENIOR MANAGEMENT

Global companies will hire and promote talented managers with no regard for their race, sex or nationality. The president of Ford,

Jacques Nasser, is a Lebanese reared in Australia. Alcoa today is headed by a Brazilian, Alain Belda, and the president and CFO of US Airways, Rakesh Gangwal, is an Indian who came to the U.S. to get an MBA and entered the airline industry with United in 1984.

Traditionally, the best way for women and minorities to get to the top was by being their own boss, and there will be a growing number of such entrepreneurs, especially in high-tech fields. But there will also be increasing numbers of women and minorities being selected by outgoing CEOs and boards of directors to lead large corporations, such as Carly Fiorina of Hewlett-Packard and Asian-American executives Andrea Jung of Avon, and Bob Nakasone of Toys "R" Us. African-Americans, in particular, are beginning to ascend to highly visible corporate leadership positions—men like Richard Parsons, president of Time Warner; Franklin Raines, the former federal budget director who is now the operating head of Fannie Mae; Thomas Jones, vice-chairman of Travelers and former operating head of TIAA-CREF; and Kenneth Chenault, president of American Express.

## THE MINORITY-EXECUTIVE ADVANTAGE

Greater diversity in leadership background will be a real plus for corporations. It's not just a matter of their looking like a socially progressive firm: Minority executives' marketing insights and their ability to communicate with, motivate and build team spirit within an increasingly diverse corporate work force will help companies prosper.

Top transnational executives will be managerial paladins of every nationality and race, going from assignment to assignment, often by lateral entry rather than by working their way through the ranks. Pharmacia & Upjohn, for example, turned to Fred Hassan, a native of Pakistan, to help downsize and revitalize the newly merged company, which was experiencing cross-cultural friction among executives of the pre-merger Swedish and American drug firms.

## ITINERANT CEOS, WITH SHORTER TOURS OF DUTY

In the years ahead, more and more senior corporate executives—indeed, the senior leadership of all kinds of institutions, from colleges to trade associations—will come from outside the organization, and often from entirely different fields, rather than rising from within.

Executives will move around much more, staying shorter periods at the helm, due to their own ambitions, burnout, or the dissatisfaction of their boards with their performance. All this mobility will keep boards very busy, and also be a boon to the executive search and recruiting business.

Promotion of veteran insiders is still the overwhelming norm at public companies, accounting for between two-thirds and four-fifths of all CEOs, as measured by various recent surveys. But the percentage of CEOs coming in from the outside has doubled in the past 20 years or so, and the trend will accelerate in the years ahead.

When a company needs a good shake-up, and boards doubt that an insider can break ranks with old colleagues to do the job boldly, the nod will go to an outsider. The prototype itinerant executive, or "portable CEO," has to be IBM's Louis V. Gerstner, Jr., who went from American Express to RJR Nabisco and arrived at a struggling IBM without any experience in computers or high tech in general. What he did have was a bold vision, guts, a clear mandate from his board, and the ability to lead the troops through wrenching change.

## EVER-RISING EXECUTIVE PAY—WHILE TIMES ARE GOOD

Years ago, the only ways to make a truly vast fortune in business were as an entrepreneur (founding a successful company) or as a financier (combining and reorganizing companies in creative ways). Senior executives—salaried managers hired by the owners to run the companies—earned generous, sometimes lavish, annual incomes, but they rarely became multimillionaires.

That changed in the '80s, with the explosive growth of performance-based executive compensation using stock options. The trend has accelerated in the '90s, with relatively young executives of high-tech firms making vast fortunes when their companies go public or merge. This has widened the traditional gulf between the pay of top executives and all other employees—from middle managers to production workers—in virtually all lines of work. One recent study of executive compensation in Silicon Valley tech firms found that top executives, whose total compensation in 1991 averaged 40 times the average production worker's pay, are now averaging 220 times that level.

Today, discussions of executive pay don't even entail concepts of what is "reasonable" or "appropriate" for one human being to earn in one year of work. Top management is assumed (questionably) to be almost solely responsible for a surge in the company's earnings and market value, and therefore entitled to a sizable chunk of that increase. That's how Michael Eisner has become a centimillionaire, helping create billions of dollars of equity for Disney shareholders.

The most breathtaking example of this phenomenon occurred in 1998, when three top executives of Computer Associates cashed in stock options (bestowed on them by the board just three years earlier) totaling $923 million, with more than half of it ($550 million) going to CA founder and CEO Charles B. Wang. This event was automatically triggered when CA's stock closed above $53 on 60 days in a 12-month period. Wang justified the largess by noting that CA shareholders had seen their equity rise by $20 billion over the past few years. (No provision was made for the return of the bonuses when the share price plummeted more than 50% later that year.)

### *American-style pay will spread worldwide*

This kind of compensation, heavily tilted toward stock options, is still largely an American thing, not common in European and Asian multinationals. But as multinationals merge into transnationals, the American model will spread and become the world norm.

Global merger partners will have a hard time at first reconciling the different pay levels of their executives. For example, when Daimler-Benz and Chrysler decided to merge in 1998, it was noted that the German firm's CEO had earned "only" about $2 million the previous year, compared with the American CEO's $16 million of salary, bonuses and stock options. Chrysler's top five executives averaged $10 million in 1997, compared with Daimler's average of $1.1 million.

The odds are good that, over time, pay will settle into a middle range that is closer to today's American level—assuming the merged units create stunning value for their shareholders (a big assumption, in some cases).

### *More up-front pay, less risk for star CEOs*

CEOs who have been with a successful public company for several years often have so much wealth tied up in stock options that they won't consider leaving for another firm unless the new employer "makes them whole." That means paying them, in advance, the equivalent of their unrealized stock options and, in some cases, what they might earn if they stayed with the first company.

In effect, that means companies trying to lure new star-caliber CEOs will have to pay signing bonuses not unlike the lavish up-front sums that pro sports teams pay to sign free-agent stars. Executive compensation for itinerant CEOs is becoming pay for *past* performance at *another* company, unrelated to their future success with their new employer. This is a perversion of the concept of executive pay based largely on *future* success that will benefit all shareholders.

### *Challenges ahead to high executive pay*

A backlash, driven by institutional shareholders and shareholder-rights organizations, will emerge against lavish executive compensation, especially when business and earnings soften. CEOs will be given less say in the composition of their own boards of directors, to lessen the inherent conflict of interest in their selecting the same people who set their pay. More-independent boards will trim the compensation of underperforming executives and force them out earlier.

In crafting bonus and stock-option packages, more boards will reward not just any increase in earnings and shareholder value, but only results that exceed broad stock averages (like the S&P 500) or, more relevant, the performance of other firms in the same field. This will reduce the likelihood that a lackluster CEO will get rich from simply being at the helm of a boat that is lifted by a rising tide.

But, as in pro sports, it will be hard to fundamentally change the "star system"—so long as a company's earnings are growing and most shareholders are so happy with *their* investment returns that the CEO's pay, rich as it is, looks like a relative bargain.

# The Geography of Business Growth

In a world of interstate branch banking, instant telecommunications and dispersal of high-tech entrepreneurship, corporations can be headquartered anywhere—and anywhere is where they will be. This trend will favor the creation of new business in places that are attractive to live in, often in less-congested areas of the West and South.

Who would have thought, 20 years ago, that a company based in Bentonville, Ark. would become the world's largest retailer, eclipsing Chicago-based Sears? Or that Jackson, Miss., would be the official home (even if operations are widely dispersed) of not one, but two, world-class telecommunication companies, WorldCom and Skytel? Or that Omaha, Neb., would become a worldwide teleservices center, anchored by credit card billing processor First Data? Or that the world's largest software company would be based in Redmond, Wash.? Or that the largest commercial bank in America would be headquartered not in New York City or Los Angeles, but in Charlotte, N.C.? (NationsBank's dynamic CEO, Hugh McColl, recognized that his merger partner, BankAmerica, had a stronger global brand name, but the nerve center of the new Bank of America empire is in ambitious Charlotte, not sophisticated San Francisco.)

The success of one business in a town will spawn many new companies in related fields, creating powerful new centers of entrepreneurship in once-unlikely places. And regions will show great resilience in recovering from setbacks. Boston's Route 128 and I-495 corridors took a terrible hit in the '80s and '90s from the collapse of the midsize computer markets (once dominated by local firms Digital Equipment, Prime, Wang and others). But now the region has bounced back with new kinds of technology, including software and biotech.

The area from Cleveland to Akron, once the center for rubber, chemicals and tires, is now the Polymer Valley, with leadership in all kinds of new plastics. The Washington, D.C. suburbs, depressed by the downsizing of the federal government and defense cutbacks in the late '80s and early '90s, have become a hotbed of telecommunications, information technology and biotech. The I-85 corridor, from southern Virginia through the Piedmont of North and South Carolina to Atlanta, is still powerful in textiles, but today its manufacturing base includes everything from pharmaceuticals to automobiles, largely due to heavy foreign investment from Europe and Japan.

Investment banking and venture capital will be more widely dispersed, too, but anchored close to the nerve centers for innovation in various high-tech industries—such as California's Silicon Valley, and software centers in the Pacific Northwest and Utah. It's no accident that one of the hottest firms in the initial public offering (IPO) and "roll-up" markets of the late '90s, competing with venerable Wall Street investment banking houses, was the young firm of Friedman, Billings and Ramsay in the Virginia suburbs of Washington, D.C., where it has close contact with fast-growing area firms in many high-tech fields.

## FIERCE COMPETITION IN ECONOMIC DEVELOPMENT

States and local governments will continue to throw lucrative incentives at major prospects for new plants and business relocations— tax abatement, job-training credits, and free infrastructure (roads, sewer and water). The incentives won't always look cost-effective in terms of the numbers of new jobs created by a particular project, as with Alabama's lavish offer to Mercedes-Benz. But attracting the right "trophy firms" will have such a galvanizing effect on the image of the region, with broad spillover benefits for other new relocations, that the incentives will be deemed a good bargain for all concerned.

States will continue to vie with each other to improve their general business climates—lower taxation, worker's comp, regulation. But increasingly, relocation decisions will be made not just on business costs—which will converge to smaller differences from the Frost Belt to the Sun Belt—but on quality-of-life issues too. Local schools, parks and recreation, transportation links, arts and culture, commuting time, attractiveness of executive neighborhoods, and other such issues.

# Growing Power of the Nonprofits

There will be heightened rivalry between for-profit and nonprofit businesses in the years ahead, as both invade each other's turf. Nonprofits will establish more quasi-commercial, tax paying operations (such as book stores and travel bureaus) to boost their revenues beyond traditional sources like membership dues, tuitions and ticket receipts.

And nonprofits will see new competition from for-profits—in education, for example. Commercial firms will come on strong at all levels, fueled by voucher plans—day care and preschools, elementary and secondary schools, and "virtual colleges" that cater to adult students with Web-based curriculum.

While many nonprofits are expanding, others will throw in the towel. In health care, many nonprofit hospitals and nursing homes will go out of business, selling their assets to for-profit firms and devoting the sale proceeds to related charitable purposes.

In the biggest battle of all, banks will continue to challenge the right of credit unions to expand beyond their original affinity group, but Congress will side with credit unions most of the time.

## HIGH TAXES AHEAD FOR NONPROFITS

For-profit businesses resent expansions by entities that pay no taxes, and they will pressure federal and state authorities to go after activities by nonprofits that seem to be unrelated to the primary mission of the organization but merely a way of generating sales. These activities include museum catalogs full of merchandise not reproduced from the museum's collections, travel sponsored by museums and colleges, and ever-larger university stores that reap licensing income. Also targeted are advertising sales in magazines published by nonprofits, and general merchandise and services sold by unions, trade associations and retiree groups to their members (and increasingly, to non-members by direct mail).

Nonprofits will concede some battles, and fight others, but will also modify their programs to make challenges less likely. Alumni cruises, for example, will institute required reading and faculty lectures. And more nonprofits will set up for-profit affiliates that will pay taxes, as the National Geographic Society has done in creating a chain of retail outlets for selling its videotapes, maps and books at shopping malls and airports.

## GROWING POWER OF CHARITABLE FOUNDATIONS

America (and the world) is in the early stages of the greatest period of capital formation and private wealth building ever seen in human history, even exceeding the creation of the immense industrial fortunes in the late 19th and early 20th centuries.

In the United States, the high taxation of wealth at death virtually assures that much of the money now being made by entrepreneurs and financiers will be given away for charitable purposes, before and at death. Already in the '90s, charitable institutions have benefited from an amazing torrent of philanthropy, and charitable giving will continue to climb at a brisk pace for years to come. Gifts to colleges, hospitals and art museums of $1 million to $5 million hardly get national attention any more, and gifts of $20 million or more are not uncommon. In the years ahead, there will be more eye-popping gifts such as the $100 million pledge in 1998 to the Cornell Medical School by financier Sanford Weil, chairman of Travelers.

As enormous as these midlife gifts will be, they will represent relatively small shares of the total net worth of dozens of donors whose personal wealth approaches a billion dollars or more. The lion's share of the wealth transfer will await the passing of the great capitalists. The staggering fortunes amassed by the likes of Warren Buffett, Ted Turner and Bill Gates (with a fortune estimated at over $100 billion in 1999), not to mention dozens of lesser-known centimillionaire moguls, will go mostly to charitable purposes ranging from population control to the funding of educational reform.

A preview of this was seen in the death of electronics pioneer David Packard in 1996. Packard, cofounder of Hewlett-Packard, owned "only" 9% of H-P at his death in 1996, but those shares, bequeathed to the David & Lucile Packard Foundation, form the bulk of an endowment worth an estimated $9 billion in early 1998.

There are some 50 American grant-making foundations with assets of $1 billion or more today, and the number will grow substantially in the years ahead. Those that happen to have core holdings in a hot stock will see their wealth grow faster than they can give the money away. The Lilly Endowment, for example, saw its wealth grow 140% in

1997 alone, on the strength of appreciation in Eli Lilly stock and other investments in the foundation portfolio.

The newest wrinkle in the foundation fabric is the growth of the so-called conversion foundation, a grant-making endowment created when a nonprofit organization liquidates by selling its assets to a for-profit company. In most states, the proceeds of the transaction must be placed in a foundation that supports activities in the same general field as the nonprofit did before the sale. In California, for example, a new foundation supporting health care was created from the sale of nonprofit hospitals, worth more than $1.5 billion, to for-profit hospital companies.

## FOUNDATIONS AS CAPITAL SOURCES FOR INNOVATION

Direct charitable giving by corporations will not increase at a brisk rate in the years ahead, due to the push for higher profits and the growing desire of many shareholders to do their own giving with highly appreciated shares of the company's stock.

Similarly, all levels of government—federal, state and local—will be under taxpayer pressure to restrain their spending for social services of all sorts, from health and housing to support of cultural programs.

But charitable foundations of immense size will step in to fill the void, becoming as powerful as government agencies and for-profit corporations in shaping tomorrow's world. Their professional staffs—not elected by voters, and answerable only to their boards of trustees—will wield vast power over public life. Rather than just making grants to whatever organizations apply for support, foundation trustees and staff will become proactive, creating richly funded programs to support special areas of concern. These could include targeted medical research, housing for the poor, public-school support, charter schools and voucher programs, contraception in the Third World, noncommercial broadcasting, private education in cities, violence-prevention programs, farmland preservation, creation of parks and wildlife refuges in sensitive environments, and promotion of entrepreneurial activity in urban areas.

# CHAPTER 18

# The Changing Way We Work

T he American way of working will change greatly over the decades ahead, driven by technology, a shift in the demographics of the labor force and new concepts of management. People will continue to work more each week, often taking work home, and the lines between office and home will become even more blurred. More people will work mostly at home or on the road, rather than going to the same office each day. Self-employment will boom. So will part-time and temporary work, especially for adult women and senior citizens. People will change jobs, and even careers, more often. Firms will be more informal and flexible in hours, job assignments, attire and collegial relationships. Although formal affirmative-action programs (such as hiring quotas) will lose ground, women and racial minorities will be more prominent in all levels of management, on their merits. Unions will continue to decline in their share of the labor force.

## THE LENGTHENING WORKWEEK

The average American works about 47 hours a week—wherever that work takes place. The extra hours seem to be coming from personal time (hobbies, reading, time with friends) rather than from time spent with the family. This trend will probably continue in a strong economy.

Because there is little or no additional cost for benefits, employers often prefer to pay an hourly premium for overtime work rather than add employees. However, because many workers will prefer more leisure time to higher earnings, forced overtime will continue to be resisted.

A growing feeling of being rushed, of not having enough leisure time, augurs well for service businesses that save time or assume the burden of mundane tasks, especially for two-career families. These include grocery delivery services, lawn care, home-cleaning and handy-man services, home delivery of restaurant meals, prepared food sales in grocery stores, and oil-change and auto-repair firms that come to your home. The busyness of life is also fueling rising sales from catalogs and Internet sites, which save shoppers time and trips to the mall in search of elusive merchandise. Call it a boom in "DDIY"—Don't Do It Yourself.

## DECLINING JOB LOYALTY

Even more than now, employers won't be reluctant to lay off unneeded workers, and workers, not surprisingly, won't hesitate to jump ship for a better position, even after just a short time on the job.

Years ago, a résumé that showed a change of employer every two years or so would raise the eyebrows of a personnel director, suggesting a "job jumper" with little loyalty to an employer. Today such a résumé is not uncommon, especially among younger workers, and if the demand is strong for the employee's talents, he or she can get away with frequent job changes. Younger workers tend not to be as patient about waiting for time and seniority to carry them up the corporate ladder. They see no reason why, regardless of their youth, if they are performing better than others, they shouldn't be promoted ahead of more-senior people. It's this impatience that will lead more and more younger executives to leave the womb of corporate America and strike out on their own.

A business that wants to keep its best employees will have to bid for their services in an increasingly tight job market, offering them better benefits, more performance-based bonuses, profit sharing or stock own-ership, more responsibility, a more flexible work schedule and—most of all—a clear sense of being appreciated for their creativity and hard work.

Changes of career will also accelerate in the years ahead. In an era of self-fulfillment, people will be less inclined to remain in a field they've never liked. The boom in adult education at universities is being fueled not just by people who seek to improve their skills in their present line of work, but also by those who want to learn a totally different kind of job. Some people won't get around to changing careers until late in life, at an age when their parents retired altogether.

## TELECOMMUTING

Fully equipped home offices—with faxes, personal computers, scanners and multiple phone lines—will become a standard feature of most middle-class homes, creating a growing boom in telecommuting. Because real estate expenses represent the second highest cost after labor for most businesses, more companies will encourage employees to work at home, especially if their work doesn't require close supervision. When they have to come to the office, these employees will not have their own office or even cubicle, but will use shared space. Such "hoteling" already occurs in some large companies, where executives who travel a lot reserve an office in their headquarters building through the corporate concierge, who arranges to have their files, phone and other needs (even photos of the spouse and kids) in place when they arrive.

Rather than create their own branch offices, businesses will contract for temporary space with firms that operate furnished and equipped office suites in prime business locations all over the nation, staffed with receptionists and secretaries for support.

Today's telecommuting, even with e-mail and phones, can create a feeling of isolation and disconnection in the distant employee, a sense of being "out of the loop." Video teleconferencing and v-mail (visual messaging) will greatly ease this concern when they become widespread in both homes and offices. In a few years, virtually all personal computers will come with a tiny camera and microphone, and employees will be able to hold real-time conversations with one or several office colleagues, through high-speed modems and phone lines or wireless transmissions.

Judgments vary on whether telecommuting from home will diminish or increase productivity. The home can be a pretty distracting place to work, unless you can filter out the interruptions of family affairs and resist the temptation to putter around the house when office work should be done. But working at home can be a productive improvement over the random socializing common in many offices.

Despite instant communication, telecommuting's popularity will be restrained by the realization that good management and the demonstration of corporate leadership—essential to career advancement—are enhanced by face-to-face interaction with colleagues, whether subordinates or superiors.

## SELF-EMPLOYMENT BOOM

There are many factors behind the self-employment boom of the past 20 years, and they won't go away: job insecurity; corporate downsizing and outsourcing; a desire to profit more directly from one's own talent; and for women and minorities, a feeling they can advance further as their own bosses than they can in a corporate environment.

Self-employment seems to be especially appealing to today's young adults, who are coming of age in a very entrepreneurial era. Graduate programs in business administration, which a decade ago tended to ignore entrepreneurship as an alternative to corporate employment, will increasingly cater to the self-employment aspirations of their students, whether just out of college or taking mid-career classes as adults.

Entrepreneurship will enjoy a further boost from the preference of many large companies to test a new market or product line not by in-house expansion but by partnering with an independent small firm. If the venture fails, the big company doesn't have to lay off its employees. While this approach is very risky to the small-business person, the upside profit potential can be very enticing.

## THE OUTSOURCING TREND

Self-employment will get a big lift from the boom in outsourcing of business services that firms once performed themselves with their own employees—everything from accounting and benefits adminis-tration to office cleaning and computer management. More compa-nies will engage almost all of their work force from "employee leasing" companies that contract with the employer to do all hiring, personnel management, payroll accounting and benefits administration, elimi-nating the need for the employer to provide these functions in-house.

As outsourcing grows, the federal government will heighten its scrutiny of relationships between large companies and a growing corps of "independent contractors," suspecting that many of these contin-gent workers are really employees forced to work without the benefit of wage-and-hour laws, fringe benefits, antidiscrimination protections and (of special interest to the IRS) without taxes being withheld on their earnings. Especially in cases where employees are laid off and then immediately hired back as "independent contractors," the government will apply an ever-tighter multipart test of true independence and will, in the end, reclassify many of them as permanent employees.

## TIGHT JOB MARKETS

Given the slower growth in the labor force that we foresee, many employers will have a hard time finding reliable help in many fields, ranging from the least-skilled jobs (fast-food servers, for example) to highly skilled positions in such fields as computer programming, health care, finance and high-tech mechanical repair.

Since the best way to deal with tight labor markets is to keep good employees, smart businesses will make sure their working environment, pay and benefits are highly competitive. For example, when a stressed-out parent asks about a more flexible work schedule, the boss will go to unusual lengths to meet his or her needs, because it's a lot cheaper to keep a good employee than to break in a new one of uncertain quality.

Elderly people will be in demand as employees, and so will people with physical disabilities—not only because the Americans with Disabilities Act requires "reasonable accommodation" of their needs, but also because employers will probably be rewarded with higher-than-typical loyalty. In the most labor-short areas, former welfare recipients with modest skills will get a closer look from employers who are willing to invest in remedial education and training to fill a need.

Employers will use ever-more resourceful methods to find the workers they need—short of just jacking up the starting pay offer. Creative employers are already attending job fairs at colleges and holding open houses to show off their work environment and tout their benefits. They advertise in metro areas where joblessness is higher than in their area. They may even give existing employees bonuses for recruiting a good new hire (provided the new employee stays at least a year).

### *Expanding employee benefits*

In a tight labor market, the range of employee benefits will continue to expand, but more companies will cap the total value, requiring workers to choose, cafeteria style, the benefits they want.

Despite the protests of promarriage forces, more companies will offer spousal benefits to unmarried domestic partners, both male-female and same-sex couples.

All newly created retirement programs will be 401(k)-type plans, with varying degrees of employer match, from almost nothing at many small businesses to a 100% match at the most progressive companies.

Small businesses will continue to be reluctant to offer health coverage independently. But more of them will team up in insurance-buying cooperatives, creating large enough groups to qualify for reasonable rates, with the employee paying most of the cost.

Employers will face the dilemma of whether to extend medical coverage for all the new, expensive drugs and procedures that their employees demand. Take fertility treatment, for example, which can be as simple as a few doses of drugs or as complex—and expensive—as artificial insemination, in vitro fertilization and embryo transplantation. More than a dozen states now mandate that employers who provide health coverage (except self-insuring employers) offer some infertility benefits, and an estimated 25% of all health care plans cover it. Coverage will spread, but employers and insurers will seek to control their costs by specifying the kind of treatment, limiting the number of tries for conception, and setting age limits on couples using the techniques.

### Help with child care

To attract and retain employees who are parents of young children, more companies will devise policies and benefits to help with the child-care challenges faced by most two-career families and single parents.

These efforts will include, at the very least, a greater tolerance of employees' bringing their children to the office when an occasional day-care problem arises. But this seemingly progressive policy often proves awkward for everyone—distracted parents trying to do their work and occupy the kids, bored children, and co-workers who can be annoyed by loud or fidgety kids. That's why more companies are offering subsidies for stopgap care on school snow days, Saturdays and evenings that employees must work late. Others are creating small, supervised on-site play and study centers, where children of various ages can come occasionally to play games, do homework or watch educational videos. Chase Manhattan bank is planning six such centers around the country.

For many companies, off-site "backup child care" is the answer, and the business of backup care is poised to boom. These are day-care facilities, located in major job centers, that contract with local companies to provide emergency child care for their employees. In Washington, D.C., for example, Lipton Corporate Child Care Centers, Inc. serves 40 local employers. It can accommodate up to 37 children each day but usually has just a dozen or fewer. Before backup child care, "people were using their secretaries to babysit children," Lipton founder Diane Dennis told *The Washington Times*. "It wasn't productive, and the companies were looking forward to not having kids in the office by the paper shredder."

It was in vogue a few years ago for employers to offer regular on-site child care. While some large corporations still do this, the trend will be toward subsidies to help employees buy child care of their choosing. Many employees will select day-care centers near their workplace, permitting lunchtime visits with the kids. And some day-care centers will use live video and two-way teleconferencing to enable parents at work to observe or even "visit" their kids during the day.

### The new contingent work force

The coming decades will see the growing importance of part-time and temporary workers—the so-called contingent work force. Like contract workers, contingent workers reduce labor costs and can be hired and fired more easily as the need arises.

There are sociological and economic reasons for the boom in contingent work. Part-time work enables parents to better balance the burdens of career and child rearing. More parents—especially working moms, but lots of dads too—will voluntarily give up full-time employment in favor of working for themselves at home or working part-time for an employer. Some employers will split a job between two workers, with each working about three days a week, or half of every day. While contingent workers often don't have the benefit packages of full-time workers, that's less of a problem if a working spouse has family coverage.

With mandatory retirement illegal today, more people will work past 65, often into their seventies, either full-time or, more typically, part-time. Given labor shortages in many fields and various parts of the country, seniors will be in high demand by employers who value their strong education and old-fashioned work ethic.

Employers will increasingly use temporary agencies as a substitute for a regular employment agency or recruiter that finds permanent hires. The reason is simple: Federal and state employment law has made it so risky to terminate an employee, even a relatively recent hire, that employers are skittish about offering anyone permanent employment, even with a probationary review period. So more firms are hiring temps even when they know the position will be permanent. If they don't like the staffer, they can get another, continually replacing temps until they find a "keeper," whom they hire away from the agency.

More small businesses will adopt a deliberate strategy of keeping their full-time, on-staff employment as low as possible, not just for the flexibility of expanding or contracting as needed, but to circumvent some employment laws (such as the Family Medical Leave Act and Americans with Disabilities Act) that kick in at some arbitrary number of employees, say 50 or 75. Taking a leaf from such enormous "virtual companies" as Nike, many small firms intend to employ just a small core of key managers—say, in marketing, finance and new-product development—and outsource virtually every other need.

While many free-market business owners see an advantage in contingency workers, some liberal economists, fearing rising unemployment (which we don't foresee), will argue for the social benefits of reducing work time through job sharing, shorter workweeks and earlier retirements.

### Less acceptance of corporate transfers

The next decade will see a continued decline in employee acceptance of mandatory, or even voluntary, transfers to new assignments within the company. This is due to the rise of the two-career family, not just to declining employee loyalty.

An employee's transfer usually means a job change for his or her spouse, too, and if the spouse can't find a job in the next city as good as the one left behind, the working couple is likely to turn down the relocation. Many couples will follow informal guidelines on whether to accept the transfer, such as "I did this for him last time, so it's his turn to make a sacrifice for my career," or "Her raise from this promotion will more than offset the hassle of the move, so I'll go along." Increasingly, a desire not to uproot the kids—from their education, their friends, their soccer team—will play a big factor in the decision.

## INDIVIDUAL EMPOWERMENT AND TEAMWORK

Jobs of the future will involve more decision making, even by line employees, and fewer specific orders from supervisors. Companies will empower their employees, especially those in customer service, to spot problems, take corrective action and do whatever is necessary to satisfy the customer on the spot, without bucking the problem to a higher authority.

Employees will increasingly be part of teams that make important decisions together. Teams will need the skills, confidence and authority to say, "That way isn't going to work, let's try this way." Of course, the flip side is that teams of employees will bear more responsibility for making the right decision—no more hiding behind the excuse that managers don't know what they're doing.

The concept of teams in the workplace, already well established, is a reaction to the rising importance of satisfying the customer in a more competitive climate. "Companies are merely running as fast as they can to keep up with demanding and unforgiving customers," says Dr. Michael Hammer, president of the Center for Reengineering Leadership. Those customers, Hammer says, want results, not just a good effort. Teams help companies respond more nimbly to changes in customer preferences. The traditional top-down structure will be too rigid to deftly handle such changes.

## MORE SCRUTINY OF EMPLOYEES

Despite privacy concerns, there will be more monitoring of employee performance, using video cameras and computer tracking of productivity in routine office tasks. Employees will be cautioned about use of the Internet for nonbusiness purposes during work and reminded that the contents of their office PC belongs, in most cases, to the employer.

Drug testing is now used by an estimated 20% of all businesses, which employ about 40% of the U.S. labor force, including nearly all of the nation's largest corporations. Testing for illegal drugs at hiring and randomly during employment will spread in virtually all industries, except for Hollywood, the pop-music business and Wall Street, where drug policy will continue to be "don't ask, don't tell."

## LESS FORMAL AFFIRMATIVE ACTION

Congress and state legislatures will limit the reach of formal affirmative-action programs—especially quotas—in the next decade, but that won't affect job opportunities for women and minorities much. Labor will be in short enough supply that employers won't reject applicants on any factors other than skill and motivation.

Affirmative action will survive mostly in the form of "outreach" and "diversity" programs to attract minority job applicants. Numerical quotas or goals will be eliminated in nearly all cases.

But governments at all levels will aggressively pursue evidence of overt discrimination against women, minorities, senior citizens and disabled people in hiring and promotion. An increasingly common method for spotting hiring bias will be sending in professional "testers"—mock applicants with comparable skills and experience but of different sexes, races and ages.

### *More women and racial minorities in management*

As the older, predominantly male generation of corporate leadership retires, women and racial minorities will ascend to senior management positions in record numbers. Their experience in being "outsiders"—real or perceived—will give them empathy with an increasingly diverse work force of subordinates and colleagues, and the resulting rapport will become a highly prized management aptitude.

In addition, women and minorities will be able to bring a fresh perspective to key management challenges, including creating and marketing products and services of special appeal to female customers and the growing ethnic markets.

At the same time, a significant number of women in management will be reluctant to make the same sacrifices—of time with family, leisure and emotional balance—that male executives have traditionally made (sometimes to their later regret) to reach the highest rungs of the corporate ladder. More than their male counterparts, executive women will seek a balance in their lives between career and family, and this—more than discrimination—will impede their achieving senior management positions in proportion to their share of the work force.

## CONTINUING DECLINE IN UNION POWER

Only 14% of the nation's wage and salary employees are union members today, continuing a long trend of declining membership. In private, nonagricultural industries, union members account for just 10% of employees. But in government at all levels, nearly 40% are union members.

The long, steady decline of union strength is probably flattening. That isn't to say unions are making a comeback. They'll never return to their 1950s heyday, when roughly one-third of all workers belonged. Unions faced with declining membership and dues revenues are acting like the beleaguered businesses they often attack: they are trimming expenses, downsizing staffs and, if all else fails, merging with other unions in similar straits. There are more than 80 member unions in the AFL-CIO, but the number will shrink to fewer than 25 over the next decade.

The greatest U.S. job growth will be in the service fields, which have been harder for unions to organize, and in high-tech manufacturing, in which young, highly educated workers—sought after in a tight labor market—don't feel a need for a union to win them higher pay. So unions' share of the private work force will stay in the doldrums. Many heavily unionized industries—steel, autos, auto parts, aerospace—will employ fewer people while accounting for the same percentage of the country's economic output. But transportation, utilities, construction and mining will remain heavily union.

To try to replenish their ranks, unions will continue to turn to government workers and entry-level service workers. And they will target new entrants to the labor market—minorities, immigrants and especially women. Labor organizers believe that women, who are more likely to be in entry-level jobs with low pay and benefits, will be a recruiting gold mine.

At the bargaining table, unions will continue to see their leverage taken away by foreign competition and the willingness of companies to withstand strikes. Congress is not likely to infringe on employers' right to hire permanent replacements for strikers in many instances. Employers find that they must keep their costs in line or lose out to competitors here and abroad. That's why they are automating, downsizing and taking on unions more boldly.

Unions will appeal to workers' lack of job security, trying to promise protection from downsizing. But unions' record of accomplishing this goal has been mixed. In the future, it will be the profitability of the employer—and not the negotiating skill of the union—that will best guarantee workers' jobs.

# CHAPTER 19

# Good Careers for Tomorrow

There is hardly any kind of work done in America—with the exception of low-skill manufacturing, clerical tasks, farming and mining—that will not see a strong demand for more labor in the next two decades. For every kind of low- to moderate-skill job that will be reduced by technology—say, telephone operators and stenographers—countless new jobs will be created in designing, making, marketing, distributing and servicing the new technology. And these jobs will tend to pay more than the jobs they replace.

Job growth will be modest in manufacturing, but there will be good demand for skilled metal workers, operators of numerically controlled machine tools and people who can master factory automation.

Job growth will be strongest in high-tech services such as biotechnology, telecommunications, computer science and financial services, as well as in health care, hospitality (hotel and restaurant management) and marketing.

There will also be a high demand for low-skill service labor, such as restaurant kitchen workers, retail stockers, lawn and house-cleaning help, hospital orderlies, and night watchmen. Even low-skill jobs will require a good work ethic and the ability to interact pleasantly with others. The lack of these aptitudes—or a background spotted with crime or drug abuse—will continue to make some unskilled youths virtually unemployable, even in labor-short markets.

In more and more high-tech fields, labor shortages will be met by higher levels of immigration, and this will slightly dampen the generally strong pay gains in fields ranging from computer programming to health care.

### *Totally new kinds of work*

Many of the hottest careers will be in jobs that barely existed just five years ago, such as "content" editors (Web-site writers and editors), webmasters, Internet advertising media buyers, forensic accountants (fraud-sniffing CPAs), cyberlibrarians, digital video editors, and bio-informatics technicians (people with skills in both biology and computer software who chart and decipher DNA code in biotechnology labs).

### *Wanted: global managers*

The globalization of business will create special opportunities for U.S. managers, engineers, technicians and professionals (such as attorneys and accountants) who are fluent in one of the world's major languages of commerce or technology—German, Russian, Japanese, Spanish or Chinese. Young people, increasingly, will strive for full bilinguality to go along with a specific skill.

### *A boost from Uncle Sam*

Increasing government regulation of the conduct of business will create boom fields in environmental science and human resources—corporate "compliance" officers who will spend their time trying to figure out new rules in hiring, job safety, sexual harassment, disabilities accommodations and health care.

### *Highly specialized jobs—and generalists, too*

Specialization will accelerate in every field from health care and accounting to education and law (where more attorneys will practice nothing but the law of health care, sports, entertainment or biotechnology patents).

Despite the trend toward specialization and high technology in job markets, there will be an undiminished demand for the broad-gauged generalist—the executive with the talent of communicating clearly in writing and speech, articulating a vision, motivating colleagues to do their best, and building cooperative teams. Men and women with these skills will always be hot commodities.

### *A premium for great salesmen*

In any field—whether financial services, real estate, even the professions—men and women who have a flair for selling (both themselves and the goods and services of their firm) will enjoy the highest average pay. These aren't "marketers" and "sales managers," but the people who excel at actually finding new customers and closing the deal.

At law firms, investment-banking houses and consulting firms, the top earners are often the "rainmakers" who bring in the big new clients, even if the tough legal and financial follow-up work is done by others.

The top-producing brokers in insurance, stocks and real estate, and the top traders in bonds and currencies, usually earn far more than their nominal bosses in senior management. Scratch the surface of any successful person—even in staid professions such as scientific research and education—and you will find the heart of a true salesman beating within.

### Demographic determinants

The need for certain kinds of labor will track closely with demographics—such as the waxing and waning demand for teachers at various levels, and health care personnel for an aging America (and more morticians 15 years from now, as the large baby-boom generation begins to die off).

### Pay still driven by supply and demand

The concept of "comparable worth"—that jobs requiring similar education and skills should be priced similarly, regardless of differing supply and demand—will not catch on. The larger the pool of people who are able to do a certain kind of work, and the greater the number of people who want to do it, the lower the pay will be, irrespective of the worker's intelligence and education. Even in fields for which there isn't a big supply of labor—say, scholars of Italian literature—pay won't be very exciting if the demand for their labor is commensurately low.

Supply and demand explains everything. Entry jobs in journalism will continue to pay very low starting salaries because there are vastly more talented, well-educated young people who want to be reporters and writers than there are job openings at newspapers, broadcast stations and magazines. And the skills required for the work can be learned on the job. Much the same is true of work in child care; it's deemed to be socially valuable work, and not everyone has the temperament to do it well, but the pay will continue to be low so long as there is a good supply of young people willing to do it.

On the other hand, pay gains will be fine in nursing, as the demand continues to be strong but increasing numbers of young adults decide on other careers. The same dynamics have contributed to hefty pay hikes for elementary and secondary teachers.

The highest starting pay for college graduates will continue to be in fields in which the demand for labor is high but the number of people who can do the work is low, due to the academic difficulty of the preparation. This accounts for the high starting pay of chemical- and electrical-engineering grads, for example.

### Higher pay for less-pleasant jobs

The only exceptions to the normal linkage between job skill and pay will be in low-status, unpleasant work or hazardous work that relatively few people want to do. That's why in many areas garbage collectors make more money than day-care workers. Long-haul trucking firms are having a hard time finding enough drivers who don't mind long stretches away from home and family or the tedium of interstate highway driving. So pay will keep rising strongly (and more companies will hire husband-and-wife driving teams).

### Working on your own

Consultants will blossom in every field, and they will do much more than just dispense their advice and mosey on to the next client. Clients will need, and demand, help with implementing the consultant's plan and seeing it through to success, which will often take several years.

Franchises will continue to be very attractive to would-be entrepreneurs who want the support of a national organization for marketing, product development and management. Growth franchises will focus on convenience services (home cleaning, medical care), specialty foods (coffee, donuts, yogurt, pretzels, bread, fruit juices, nuts) and the outsourcing of business services (office cleaning, employment services, temping, security).

The boom in self-employment and "independent contractor" status will be accompanied by an opposite trend among professionals who love their work but hate to beat the bushes for clients and patients, bill and collect fee, and manage others. So more and more attorneys and physicians will choose to work for others on a fixed salary, without seeking to become, respectively, law-firm partners or private practitioners.

### Temping as a career

A corollary of this trend will be the boom in permanent temporary work—employment by a temp agency that sends you out on assignments of varying duration, collects the pay, and remits some of it to you in wages and benefits. Temping as a career will become even more respectable than it already is. Temp agencies will employ growing numbers of high-wage executives and professionals, such as marketing managers, lawyers, scientific researchers, engineers, programmers, accountants, technical writers, graphic designers and architects. High-skill temps will go by a variety of high-tone names, such as "contract attorney" or "interim executive."

# A Sampler of Career Outlooks

A list of jobs for which demand will be strong in the years ahead would encompass almost all the kinds of work that people do in America today, so this list must of necessity be just a sample. Still, the list below will give you (or maybe your offspring) an idea of the enormous range of job opportunities in the new high-tech, service-oriented global economy.

## SCIENCE AND ENGINEERING

Scientists and engineers—and entrepreneurs, who will increasingly be scientists and engineers, too—will be the stars of the new global economy. They face a highly favorable job market, driven by rising spending on research and development and the resurgence of high-tech manufacturing, at the same time that colleges are turning out fewer engineers than a decade ago. A growing share of engineering graduates are foreign students, who—if America is lucky—will stay in the U.S. to work, rather than return to their home countries.

Biochemists and molecular biologists, for both research and manufacturing, will be in short supply in the hot biotech industry. Electrical engineers and computer-science majors will be soaked up by the exploding fields of microelectronics and telecommunications, which will also need generalists in systems integration who know something about all the allied fields in phones, computers and Internet programming.

Environmental engineering will boom because of stricter statutes regulating air and water emissions from factories. Chemical engineers will be sought after by the expanding plastics, new-materials and biotech industries. The demand for geologists and petroleum engineers won't be quite as robust, with energy prices stable and plenty of world supply.

The outlook will improve for civil engineers as the nation starts to address a backlog of infrastructure improvements, such as roads, bridges, and water and sewage systems. There was a glut of aerospace engineers and scientists after the defense spending cutbacks and industry consolidations, but demand is firming up again, with commercial space launches, aircraft design and manufacturing, and satellite telecommunications gaining strength.

Continuing education will be particularly important as employers will want workers with the latest skills in their rapidly changing industries.

## THE RED HOT INTERNET

The world of the Web will create hundreds of thousands of new kinds of jobs—people who design Web sites, maintain them, adapt editorial material from other formats, sell ads on them and fulfill online orders for merchandise.

Since the whole industry is new, everyone is more or less learning on the job. Some have come from the world of desktop publishing and graphic design, others from computer-network administration and programming (especially in the Java language of the Internet), still others from journalism. Marketers are migrating into the Internet from traditional advertising media-buying jobs.

The average age of the work force looks to be about 18, though that might just be their attire; every day is "casual Friday" in Webland. In fact, lots of brilliant teenage computer jocks and hackers are going into the Internet business right out of high school, earning excellent pay without even going to college. The pay is seductive to an 18-year-old, but those who do this will be limiting their eventual earnings by missing the broad education that college can offer them.

## GOOD FIELDS FOR SOCIAL SCIENCE AND HUMANITIES MAJORS

People with a flair for oral communication, writing and interaction with others will be in demand in a variety of growing fields, ranging from human resources, sales management and publishing to public relations, advertising and technical writing. (And of course they must be computer literate, too.)

Many employers won't care so much about what applicants studied in college as they will about the intelligence, creativity, maturity and trainability they will bring to their new career. In a fast-changing economy, relatively few people—outside the highly technical fields—will end up working in the same fields they studied in college. Most will learn a new skill through employer training. The most tranferable skills, valuable anywhere, will be flexibility and openness to new challenges.

## SLOW GROWTH FOR MIDDLE MANAGEMENT AND GENERAL OFFICE WORK

More than one million management jobs will be added by 2010, an impressive figure until you realize that the rate of growth in new management jobs will drop about 50% from that of the past dozen years. Reasons for slower growth include: the flattening of management structures for more efficiency and cost savings; productivity gains from automation in intra-office communications, accounting and analysis, enabling fewer managers to watch more projects; and consolidation of businesses in the same fields, eliminating overlapping management.

Growth will slow markedly for office support people, too—the kinds of jobs that a young man or women could once do with a high school diploma and some training in typing, filing and operating a phone switchboard. Many of these jobs are being replaced by "self-sufficiency technologies." Bosses now compose their own letters on a computer, eliminating the need for a secretary to take dictation and type the letter. They might send the letter via e-mail, meaning that no one has to address an envelope, either. Voice-mail systems reduce the need for support personnel. (And in a few years, the boss will simply dictate letters to a voice-recognition computer.)

## THE HEALTH CARE BOOM

The aging population will demand more medical services. At the same time, diagnostic and treatment equipment will need to be operated. These trends will create strong demand for family-practice doctors and geriatric specialists, internists, pharmacists, dental hygienists, nurses, physical and occupational therapists, physician assistants, emergency-care specialists and home health care aides. School systems will employ many more speech pathologists, audiologists and mental-health counselors.

There will also be strong demand for alternative health and medicine practitioners, including acupuncturists, chiropractors, osteopaths, masseurs, herbalists and yoga instructors. For general fitness, more people will seek regular exercise led by aerobics instructors, personal trainers and health club personnel.

Many health or fitness occupations can be entered with as little as a two-year certification program, while others require four years of school and, in some cases, master's degrees or doctorates.

## FINANCIAL SERVICES

Automation in financial services will reduce the demand for certain kinds of workers, such as bank tellers and back-office clerks, and middle management will be squeezed by the wave of consolidations and mergers among banks, mutual fund companies, insurers and others. The boom in discount brokerage and online stock trading will dampen the growth rate for full-service stockbrokers.

But an aging, well-heeled population will still want a lot of hand-holding from their financial counselors. So many insurance agents (who are losing business to online shopping services) and stockbrokers will transform themselves into fee-based financial planners.

The surge in entrepreneurial activity will stimulate demand for accountants and financial analysts of all sorts, though demand will be slightly offset by the combining of corporate accounting offices after mergers and acquisitions.

## MAKING PEOPLE HAPPY

An increasingly affluent society, full of retirees, will create an enormous number of jobs in fields that relate to leisure, entertainment and travel—in short, the pursuit of the good life. Some of the jobs include: hotel, restaurant, resort and club management; travel planning and tour guiding; airline operations (although automation will cut into counter labor); film and music production; golf course design, development and management; live entertainment (the classical and popular arts); and professional sports management.

## EDUCATION

Teaching is such a diverse profession that demand will vary greatly from one field to another. Some specialists will be in great demand while others will face keen competition for a smaller number of jobs.

Given the soaring number of youths defined as having learning disabilities, plus the mainstreaming of more children with physical and mental disabilities, plus tough government mandates to cater to all these educational needs, special-education teachers will be hired in record numbers over the next decade.

Secondary school teachers will be in high demand over the next decade, especially in math, science and ESL (English as a Second Language) programs. But elementary school teachers will be in oversupply, except in inner-city schools. That's because elementary school enrollment will peak in 2003 and decline slightly for several years thereafter.

Many college professors will be retiring in the next several years—people who began teaching in the 1950s and 1960s. While that will open up some jobs, the competition will be fierce. New professors are less likely to teach full-time or receive tenure. The best college opportunities will be teaching business, engineering, computer science, physical sciences, health sciences and math.

With a growing emphasis on lifelong learning, adult education will be a growth field, especially to teach computer technology and medical training. Many of these positions will be filled by full-time professionals in various fields who will moonlight at night school.

Of the nearly two million new elementary and secondary school teachers who will be needed in the next ten years, many will come into the profession through unconventional paths. Retired military officers, business executives, engineers and others will change careers in midstream, looking for a new challenge or more-fulfilling work, says Chris Pipho, executive director of the Education Commission of the States. These nontraditional teachers will freshen schools with their experiences from earlier careers and be a strong force in making schools operate more like businesses, including pay for merit instead of seniority.

## GOOD JOBS WITHOUT MUCH OR ANY COLLEGE REQUIRED

People with less than four years of college can find good jobs as nurse's aides, correctional officers, police officers, emergency workers, legal secretaries, radiology technicians, dental hygienists and restaurant managers. But increasingly, these fields will attract college grads, too.

For jobs requiring little training—and usually offering moderate pay—job growth will be strongest for medical and therapy assistants, cashiers, janitors, local delivery drivers, guards, retail sales clerks, home health aides and food servers.

### People who can fix things

There will be no shortage of work for people who are good with their hands, can read and understand technical manuals and generally have a flair for trouble-shooting and fixing machines.

From automobiles, heating and cooling systems, and computerized printing presses to medical equipment, office computer networks and home entertainment systems, the more complex the devices, the more skilled technicians will be needed who can operate, maintain and fix them. Building engineers, who oversee the equipment of complex office buildings and factories, will be masterly jacks of all trades.

Some of these technicians will have simply on-the-job training after high school, while others will have two-year associate degrees or vocational degrees in electronics from a community college. The credential will matter less than the ability to get the job done.

### The building trades

Traditionally, the highest-paid work that a person could do without higher education has been in the building trades, and that will still be the case. There will always be a strong demand for carpenters, bricklayers, concrete finishers, electricians, plumbers, heating and air-conditioning technicians, heavy-equipment operators, painters and drywall installers —trades that can be learned in apprenticeship programs of businesses and labor unions. Many of these jobs will be filled by women, whose numbers are rising in all the building trades, and by immigrants, especially from Latin America.

Bureau of Labor Statistics economists Arthur Andreassen and Jay Berman estimate that $41 billion in infrastructure construction will be undertaken over the next ten years, creating 833,000 new jobs. Despite deteriorating roads, bridges, sewer systems and the like, spending on infrastructure has been steady or declining in recent years, they note, and America is about to reverse this trend.

## FINDING YOUR NEW CAREER ON THE INTERNET

The Internet is already the medium of choice for most professional and executive job seekers and employers, and this will accelerate. Newspaper classified ads will be limited to lower-skill jobs that attract only local applicants. But the classifieds of most major dailies are also on the Internet now, so an ad run in, say, *The Washington Post*, will be seen by job hunters everywhere.

Universities, high-tech companies and trade associations already post most jobs and read the arriving résumés on the Internet. This makes sense for employers who are recruiting computer-savvy college students or filling specialized jobs for which qualified applicants may come from far away.

The Internet won't be just a résumé service. Applicants and employers can exchange a lot of information before ever meeting face to face. Already, newspaper reporters send samples of their work over the Internet, and advertising designers and graphic artists transmit their portfolios.

In the near future, interactive software will screen applicants by testing their skills. Preliminary job interviews will be conducted long distance by video conference. Freed from the expense of flying in leading candidates, large employers will cast a wider net for key jobs, talking with many more applicants. When it comes down to job finalists, however, nothing will replace the personal meeting.

# Investing for the Years Ahead

G iven the thesis of this book—that global economic growth will accelerate in a climate of low inflation, moderate interest rates, expanding world trade and steadily improving corporate earnings—it should be no surprise that we remain partial to the long-term ownership of stocks. Over long periods of time, carefully selected equities will appreciate more strongly than other kinds of assets, including bonds, cash, real estate or hard assets such as gold, art and collectibles.

Because growth will be much stronger in the less developed nations, foreign markets will generally outperform the U.S. market, but with much more volatility. U.S. equities will be a declining share of the total value of publicly traded companies in the world economy. In 1970, stocks traded on U.S. exchanges accounted for about two-thirds of worldwide market capitalizations. Today the U.S. share is less than 40%.

But rather than invest in entire national markets—even the U.S.—successful investors will cherry-pick the most dynamic multinational corporations and smaller firms, regardless of their country of origin or headquarters. Owning multinationals will be a surrogate for investing in particular countries or regions.

The stocks to own through the years ahead generally fall into two broad categories: 1) giant multinationals, U.S.- or foreign-based, with world leadership in high-growth industries like pharmaceuticals, computers and microelectronics, telecommunications, information technology, financial services, food products and entertainment; and 2) smaller firms in the same fields, some of which will soar in value and some of which will fall flat, but which, averaged as a group, will outperform the big companies.

### GREATER VOLATILITY AHEAD

With rapid movements of capital around the world, especially by large institutional investors (such as mutual funds and pension funds), volatility will increase. Nervous sell-offs will be sharp, but they will be of shorter duration. The world community is more closely linked than ever, so responses to international shocks will be quicker and better coordinated. Investors will be more confident that regional ups and downs in markets won't—in and of themselves—cause worldwide economic slumps.

After the long U.S. stock surge of the '80s and '90s, and with the Dow Jones Industrial Average in a very pricey range around 11,000, we hasten to remind investors that there will be occasional slumps in stock prices, sometimes lasting a couple of years. Some downturns will be confined to one national market, but others will affect all world markets simultaneously, if briefly. During these slumps, other forms of capital will outperform stocks, so it's important to leaven your stock holdings with some bonds and cash.

### TAKING THE LONG VIEW

Investors should stay calm in the face of turmoil and slumps, taking a long view. There is no bad time to buy stock in a good company, and the best time of all is in a bear market, when no one else wants to own it and the price is all the more attractive.

Every asset you own—including your home, investment property, art and antiques, and collectibles—changes in value every week. But you can't get an instant price quote on anything you own except your stocks, bonds and mutual funds. And you can't sell those other assets, as you can your financial assets, with a quick phone call or online order.

While liquidity is one of the most attractive things about financial assets, the ease of selling them is the biggest barrier to long-term success for the small investor. Stocks are just too easy to dump in a moment of queasiness (or when some impulse purchase catches your eye). Remember, the most successful investors are the ones who ride out the peaks and valleys of markets. Active trading is not a sign of sophistication. If it were, Warren Buffett would be a country bumpkin.

### THE IMPORTANCE OF DIVERSIFICATION

Diversification is crucial, not just by asset class but within each category, too. That means owning a variety of asset categories, such as stocks, bonds, real estate (through real estate investment trusts, REITs) and cash equivalents. And it also means owning enough different issues within each class to balance the risk of unforeseen trouble with a particular stock or bond. Every type of asset will have ups and downs in value; even cash held in the form of low-yielding insured deposits has a modest risk associated with it—the risk that a spike in inflation will cancel out your small return. Diversification is your antidote against the investor sins of overconfidence, arrogance and assumed omniscience.

The precise mix of your asset types will vary according to your age, income, tolerance for risk and other personal factors. One very conservative asset mix is the 40-40-20 portfolio, with 40% in stocks, 40% in bonds and 20% in cash equivalents such as CDs. You should find your comfort level within wider ranges, such as these: 40% to 70% stocks, 20% to 50% bonds, and 10% to 20% cash. For comparison, here's how the aggregate financial assets of American households were allocated in 1997, according to Federal Reserve data: 58% stocks and stock mutual funds, 25% bonds and bond funds, and 17% cash.

Remember to occasionally rebalance your portfolio when strong gains (or losses) in any one asset class create an unintended imbalance in the mix. Take some of the gains and spread them over the other assets to maintain the allocation you want.

# U.S. Equities

American equities have had an amazing run in the '80s and '90s, with the Dow rising fourteenfold, from 777 on Aug. 12, 1982 (near the end of the severe 1981–1982 recession), to over 11,000 in 1999. Between 1990 and the summer of 1999, the Dow more than quadrupled. This long U.S. bull market, like all such booms, has been driven by strongly rising corporate earnings, which have risen fourfold since 1982 and have doubled since 1990.

But rising business profits are only half the story. If stock prices had merely risen in lockstep with business profits, the major stock indexes would be at less than half their current levels.

The other half of the gain can be explained only by investor exuberance over excellent economic fundamentals, and the absence of good alternatives to stocks. Confident of continued low inflation, low and stable interest rates, and strong future corporate earnings, investors have shown a strong preference for U.S. equities over every other class of asset, for their retirement accounts, college savings accounts and general investment portfolios.

At the end of 1997, America's love affair with stocks had surpassed the last great romance in the late 1960s, just before the market began to fall into the long bear market of the '70s. By the end of 1997, a record-high 44% of all American households owned stocks or stock mutual funds, far surpassing the previous peak of 38% in 1968.

Household wealth held in equities nearly quadrupled in the '90s, from $3 trillion at the end of 1990 to $11.4 trillion at the end of 1997. Most significantly, the share of total household wealth held in stocks— 28%—now exceeds real estate's share by one percentage point, the same as in 1968.

## HIGHER STOCK VALUATION

Stock investors have bid up stock prices to twice their traditional valuations. Over the past five decades, price-earnings ratios (a stock's price divided by its per-share earnings for the previous 12 months) have averaged about 14. But by mid-'99, the P/E on the S&P 500 was around 35, and the Dow's was around 27. And investors no longer seem to care about dividend income from the stocks they own. They have willingly accepted declining yields on equities (barely 1.5% on the major indexes), allowing corporate managers to retain more earnings for internal growth, mergers & acquisitions or buybacks of the company's stock.

## OVERHEATED IPO MARKET

One of the most spectacular parts of the long superbull expansion has been the market in initial public offerings (IPOs), stock issued by companies just starting up or going public after a few years of operations as a closely held venture. Tempted by such successes as eBay, Amazon.com and Yahoo!, investors pumped some $66 billion into almost 1,300 IPOs in 1996 and 1997 alone.

The IPO boom, like big mergers and acquisitions funded entirely with soaring stock shares, is a sign of an overheated stock market. IPOs will cool off in the next economic slowdown, but they will continue at a very high level, given the long surge in start-ups and the preference of entrepreneurs and venture capitalists for taking their new companies public. Small investors should be careful of IPOs. The hot "concept" IPOs—such as Internet and biotech phenoms, and roll-ups in previously unconsolidated industries—tend to soar at offering to unreasonable P/E ratios and then decline substantially a few months later, as the euphoria fades and the companies have to produce real earnings. The big money in IPOs is made by the insiders who bought preoffering shares or are allocated shares simultaneously with the offering. If you're attracted to an IPO's concept and think the company will make it big eventually, keep an eye on it for a few months after the initial offering and buy in later, probably at a lower price.

## HISTORICAL AVERAGE RETURNS

The 500 large U.S. companies in the Standard & Poor's index have generated total returns (price appreciation plus dividends) averaging about 11% annually since 1926, and a little over 12% since 1946. But returns have averaged about 20% a year since 1982.

For long-term investors today, the big question is this: Which past period is the best guide to future results? The more modest five- and seven-decade averages, leavened by several long market slumps? Or the much higher average of the past 18 years, a superbull market punctuated by only three flat or declining years (1987, 1990 and 1994) and several spectacular years in a row in the '90s?

## THE U.S. OUTLOOK

We believe that future total returns on U.S. equities will comfortably match or *slightly* exceed the average returns of the past seven decades—but not by much. Yes, average returns have moved to a new higher level, but only a little higher, in no way resembling the returns of this decade. These gains will come to be regarded as historically atypical, and over time they are likely to be averaged down by the occasional flat years and bear markets that lie ahead. "Give up your fantasies of permanent 20% annual returns," advises *Newsweek* financial columnist Jane Bryant Quinn. "Being an optimist doesn't mean putting your brain on hold."

It would be prudent to expect the long-term trend to resemble the trend line since 1946—total returns averaging about 12% or possibly a point higher. But with less of the total return coming from dividends (only about 1.5%), more will be in price appreciation, averaging a little less than 11% a year on the S&P 500.

The stocks of "small-capitalization" companies (with annual sales of a few hundred million dollars, rather than billions) traded on the Nasdaq exchange and included in the Russell 2000 index will generally outperform blue chips. Because it is difficult to select and follow small companies, and difficult to own enough issues to provide security against their high volatility, they should be owned only through aggressive-growth or small-cap mutual funds—ideally, several such funds.

### *Lower growth in corporate earnings*

Why do we think the higher performance of the '90s is not sustainable over the long run? First of all, this long bull market has benefited from atypically strong earnings boosts from a broad, deep wave of U.S. restructurings and downsizings. While these trends aren't finished, the easy gains are behind us. In a fiercely competitive global economy, U.S. corporate earnings growth in the years ahead is more likely to be in the high single digits than the double digits of the past few years. That will make it hard for investors to continue justifying the high-20s P/E ratios they are now paying for U.S. blue chips. Some highly successful U.S. firms, of course, will continue to churn out double-digit increases in earnings year after year, and they will command even higher valuations.

Second, American business got a big head start on foreign competitors in the restructuring game, but now the foreign companies are catching up. That makes their equities look as attractively undervalued as U.S. stocks were in the early '80s, so more U.S. and global money will flow into foreign markets, giving price competition to U.S. equities.

### Keeping expectations realistic

Many stock investors, especially those who first came into the stock market in the '90s, have been spoiled by this bull market. Some of them have come to expect year after year of double-digit increases, and they could regard an 8% or 10% year to a disappointment—and a declining year to be a cause for alarm. Investors should shed these expectations and remember that a good year in the stock market is any year in which the total return on equities exceeds the return on alternative uses of capital, such as bonds or cash in CDs or money-market funds. Over time, quality stocks have beaten all the alternatives by wide margins and with surprisingly little risk. And this is likely to continue for decades.

The biggest force supporting stock prices today and in the foreseeable future will be the notable absence of better alternatives to equities. With inflation and interest rates behaving pretty well, bonds and cash won't be much more enticing than they are today. Their primary value will be for predictable income and as hedges against inevitable but unforeseeable bear markets in stocks.

### Staying calm through slumps

After a long, hot run in the stock market, it's easy to forget the periods when stocks declined—not just a brief, mild "correction" of 10% or so, but a real gut-wrenching plunge of about 20% or more.

There have been 15 such declines in the past half-century, and they have taken stocks down an average of 23% for an average duration of about 11 months. The two most recent slumps were also the mildest and shortest—a 16% drop over five months in 1990, and the 19%, 3-month slump in the Summer and Fall of '98. The shortest but sharpest was the three-month, 30% collapse in 1987. The deepest slide was also the longest one—a 46% decline that lasted nearly two years in 1973 and 1974 and made the '70s the worst decade for stocks since the Great Depression.

So long as the fundamentals of the economy are strong, stocks don't crash or go into a long slide just because they are deemed over-priced by a theoretical benchmark like price-earnings ratio, dividend yield, or price-to-book-value ratio. But even when the fundamentals are good, high stock valuations make a market more fragile, more vulnerable to some surprising external shock, like the specter of war (as in 1990) or a tenfold increase in the price of a key commodity like oil (as in 1973).

The most common shock that spooks a high market is a rise in interest rates, which lures investor money into bonds and also raises the cost of borrowing for consumers and businesses, thereby dampening consumer spending and corporate earnings. Significantly, rising inter-est rates have been a factor—sometimes the key factor—at the begin-ning of a dozen of the 15 bear markets since 1950.

The hardest thing for most investors is to continue investing in quality equities through long slumps. Fear and the herd mentality take over, overwhelming rational judgments about long-term stock values. (Stockbrokers joke that stocks are the only products that are harder to sell at a low price than a high one.) But the foundations of great for-tunes are laid in bear markets, by investors who buy undervalued assets that others are shunning.

Investment adviser and author Peter Lynch believes that invest-ment success has little to do with general economic conditions, since it's largely a matter of owning the stocks of companies that will outperform their peers, regardless of what the broad economy is doing. He's right. In any particular market, even the long bear market of the '70s, people who picked stocks skillfully made good money.

### *Forget about market timing*

There is no shortage of experts who will advise you when the broad stock market is about to rise or fall. But we've never been very impressed with their records of timing the peaks and valleys. It's easi-er to spot an overpriced market and get out than it is to figure out when to buy back in. So the real risk of market timing is that you won't be fully invested on the days and weeks when prices soar.

One study, at the University of Michigan, calculated that 95% of all stock gains between 1963 and 1993 occurred on just 90 trading days. Since no one can predict just when those special days will be, it's best to be fully invested (according to your asset-allocation model) and sit tight. As many a long-term investor has learned, the key to success is time *in* the market, not timing *of* the market.

You will do better at equity investing, in stocks and mutual funds, by investing fixed amounts of money on a regular basis, whether monthly or quarterly, regardless of what the market is doing at the moment. Using this technique, called dollar-cost averaging, you will tend to buy more shares at lower prices than higher prices in a generally rising market.

If you want to try market timing—against our better judgment—at least be contrarian about it. Invest more when others aren't, and vice versa. Raise cash to take advantage of bargains, not by cashing in all of what you already own, but by adjusting the amounts of your new purchases. That is, continue your regular monthly investments, but cut the amount by a third or a half when the market looks overpriced. Keep the held-back amounts in a money-market fund, building a reserve to beef up your normal monthly amount after a market dip or correction, when valuations look better.

Likewise, when you sell issues that you and your advisers believe to be fully priced, hold back some of the proceeds to be invested later in a possibly softer market. This method of modified dollar-cost averaging will work much better than precipitously cashing out of high markets or plunging into low ones at some perceived (but possibly elusive) bottom.

### *No big U.S. market slump 15 years from now*

Some forecasters predict a very strong American economy and stock market for another 15 or so years, followed by a long downturn in U.S. economic growth and stock prices—something on the order of the stock-market slump in the 1970s.

This forecast is based on several demographic assumptions, starting with the fact that the enormous baby-boom generation, in its peak earning and spending years for the next decade, will begin retiring between 2010 and 2015. As the theory goes, boomers will follow the traditional retirement pattern of cutting back on their spending and converting their stock holdings to higher-yielding, less risky assets such as bonds and CDs. This will depress U.S. consumer spending, corporate earnings and stock prices.

There are several flaws in this forecast. First, the baby boom lasted for almost two decades, from 1946 through 1964, and the younger boomers, those born in the 1960s, will still be in their fifties—peak earning and spending years—when the older boomers begin to retire. What's more, most of the boomers will continue working far longer—for love of work, out of financial necessity or because the demand for their labor will be so strong—than any previous generation. Many of them will be happily and gainfully employed well into their seventies, and this will sustain strong consumer demand for decades to come. In short, there just won't be any mass exodus of boomers from the workplace (or the stores) in the 2010–2015 period.

Second, while the next age cohort, the birth-dearth generation of the 1970s, is markedly smaller than the boomers in size, the one following them—the boomers' own children, the baby-boom echo of the '80s and '90s—is enormous. These young adults will be in their thirties, spending heavily on households and children, in the first two decades of the next century. All of this augurs well for consumer demand. And immigration will continue strong through this whole period, supporting population growth and consumer demand.

Third, not only will the boomers work longer and retire later, but when they do retire, they will probably not cash out of their enormous equity shareholdings in a precipitous way that will depress prices. The boomers are the last generation that will have substantial retirement income from traditional company-funded pension plans of the defined-benefit style. These regular payments, plus social security (yes, it will still "be there" for the boomers and their successors), will make it unnecessary for most boomers to convert their stocks to higher-yielding assets, at least not all at once. Many older Americans will remain avid stock investors well into their seventies and eighties, while gradually diminishing the equity share of their total assets.

### U.S. market is global

But the biggest flaw in the forecast of a demographically based economic and market slump beginning in ten to 15 years is that it ignores global integration. It is a nationally insular forecast that pins the fortunes of the United States economy too heavily on domestic consumer demand, and the fortunes of the U.S. stock market too heavily on the behavior of American investors. On the contrary, American businesses will be deriving a rising share of their future earnings growth from foreign consumers, through exports and overseas operations. And the prices of their shares will be supported by ever-increasing ownership of American equities by foreign investors.

In short, American demographics will be just one piece in the complex puzzle of global market values. There is no great American stock-market slump on the horizon a decade or two from now. Instead, the price of quality stock will continue to rise in the traditional sawtooth pattern—rising, flattening, or falling in step with changes in corporate earnings, inflation, interest rates and perception of value.

# Global Investing

E ven if the U.S. economy continues to be the world's largest and most successful for years to come, that doesn't mean U.S. equities will always be the best value in world stock investing. In light of the extraordinary performance of U.S. equities over the past few years, and the carnage in emerging markets in 1997-1998, global investing might seem a fad whose time is past. But it would be a mistake to abandon global investing—or not consider going into it—at just the moment in history when most of the world is poised for a long surge in growth.

The odds are good that foreign markets will outperform U.S. stocks over the next few years, and probably for a decade or more. The reason is simple, and it's no knock on the U.S. economy: Growth will be stronger overseas, and American markets are relatively expensive compared with most foreign markets.

That's why successful investors, like business managers, will think and act globally, putting a substantial portion of their stock portfolio— maybe 25% to 50%—in foreign-based stocks, whether non-U.S. multinationals or smaller companies in emerging markets.

## THE STRONG RECORD OF GLOBAL MARKETS

Despite the recent record, U.S. markets haven't significantly outperformed the rest of the world over long periods of time. As a 1998 research report from investment managers Sanford C. Bernstein & Co. pointed out, "The U.S. stock market has displayed no long-term advantage over its foreign counterparts" from 1970 through 1997. In that period, the S&P 500 had a total return averaging about 13% a year, compared with a 12.3% return for the Morgan Stanley EAFE index, consisting of shares in 1,000 foreign companies based in Europe, Australasia and the Far East.

Dividing the years since 1985 into 11 rolling three-year periods and comparing regional performances, you find that U.S. markets have

CHAPTER 20 **Investing for the Years Ahead**

been the star performer only twice in the 11 periods. Looking at performance starting in 1981, the EAFE index equaled or exceeded the S&P 500 in 14 of 16 ten-year periods, from the decade that ended in 1981 to the decade preceding 1996.

At any particular time, economic growth and corporate earnings will be advancing more strongly on one continent than another. Even with the growing integration of the world economy, one or more regions will be doing well while others are struggling, and it will be difficult to tell which are poised for their moment in the sun and which are about to go into eclipse. For example, Japan's Nikkei index (225 prominent Japanese companies) has had a really tough decade in the '90s, after a spectacular '80s, but it rose 28% in 1994, a year when U.S. markets were flat.

This is why spreading your money around the globe makes a lot of sense. "Given how the baton passes from one group to another," writes the Bernstein group, "global diversification ensures some exposure to the year's best-performing market and not too much exposure to the worst."

## CONTRARIAN GLOBAL INVESTING

We don't believe in attempting market timing in world equities any more than we do in the U.S. markets. If anything, it's even harder to do abroad, without the intimate knowledge of local economic conditions that timing requires. It makes much more sense to invest on a regular basis in whatever mix of assets you have chosen to meet your particular objectives and tolerance for risk.

But having said that, we also urge you to take a slightly contrarian approach to global investing. Look for value where others see only trouble. That frame of mind would have led you into American equities in the darkest hours of severe recession of 1981–1982, when uninformed pessimists believed the U.S. was sliding into depression. Savvy contrarians recognized that the U.S. was taking the bitter medicine that would prepare it for unparalleled global leadership in the decades ahead. And a contrarian frame of mind would have led you to lighten up on Japanese stocks in the late '80s, before their bubble burst.

## WELL-PRICED REGIONAL MARKETS

Where are today's good regional values for the long-term investor who isn't afraid to buck the crowd? Asia certainly rates a close look, despite—or because of—the economic problems that trouble the region today. Some quality Asian companies are now selling at the same prices as they did a decade ago, when they and their home economies were less than half the size they are today. Japan deserves an especially close look, as the most important economy in Asia and one that is finally undertaking the structural reforms that it put off for so long. At a time when high-quality U.S. multinational firms cost three times book value (their break-up asset value), some of Japan's most dynamic world-class corporations—such as Matsushita and Toshiba—can be bought for prices not much more than their book value.

Another mildly contrarian play for the next decade would be buying European stocks, to benefit from the increasing integration of the European economy, reduced taxes and regulation in Europe, and the adoption of American-style management by European corporations. Kevin McCarey, a Fidelity fund manager, noted in 1998 that "the European stock market has the same characteristics today that the U.S. stock market did 20 years ago, before it began its bull-market run." He believes that "European earnings are going to grow faster than in the U.S. over the next few years, and there's going to be a lot more money coming into the European stock markets than the U.S. stock market."

But as McCarey and other international money managers hasten to emphasize—very wisely—global investors shouldn't invest in a whole national or regional market, but only in carefully chosen companies that happen to be based there and trade on the nation's stock market. The trick is to identify the most successful world-class companies wherever they reside, whether in the U.S., South Korea, France, Japan, Brazil, Great Britain or Finland.

## PICKING TOP MULTINATIONALS

There are two basic ways to participate in the soaring economic growth and rising living standards that will be enjoyed by nations of Asia, Latin America, Eastern Europe, the Middle East, the former Soviet Union and Africa. The first is by investing in multinationals, which have no particular nationality anymore but are really corporate citizens of the world. The second is by investing in companies headquartered in a particular developing country and growing primarily on the growth of that economy.

Investing in multinationals is by far the safer way to invest globally, because their management will go where the growth is. They will deploy their stockholders' assets in any nation, on any continent, where they think they can get the best return. For starters, select your stocks from the 50 companies in the Morgan Stanley Multinational Index, a roster of all-star, world-class, blue-chip U.S. firms. It includes GE, Coca-Cola, Intel, Microsoft, ConAgra, AT&T, Merck, Procter & Gamble, Hewlett-Packard, Johnson & Johnson, IBM, Gillette, Medtronic, 3M, Eli Lilly, Disney, Oracle, Citicorp, Xerox, EDS, Bank of America, Cisco, Enron, Texas Instruments, McDonald's, Pfizer, American Express and many more.

But the U.S. has no lock on skilled international management and technology, so you should also look into fast-expanding foreign-based multinationals, too, such as Great Britain's Cable & Wireless, Bass PLC and British Aerospace; Sweden's Ericsson; Finland's Nokia; Canada's Nortel; Switzerland's Nestlé and Norvatis (owner of Ciba Geigy and Sandoz pharmaceuticals); the Netherlands' Unilever, Royal Ahold (grocery retailing), Philips and Aegon (insurance); and Japan's Mitsubishi, Hitachi, NEC, Bridgestone, Canon, Mitsui, Toyota, Honda and Takeda (pharmaceuticals); and Germany's Mannesmann, Siemens and DaimlerChrysler.

## SUCCESS IN EMERGING-MARKETS STOCKS

But being enormous corporations already, most of the great multinationals won't achieve the same *rates* of earnings growth that smaller companies (whether U.S. or foreign) will achieve from much smaller bases. And the multinationals will see their worldwide earnings depressed occasionally by a particularly nasty slump in a single region, such as Asia in 1998, or by a rising dollar that cuts into their export growth.

So the stocks of smaller, foreign-based companies have a place in your portfolio, too, but only if purchased through U.S. mutual funds that carefully research overseas markets and select an array of stocks to own and follow. It's hard enough for individual investors to follow the American companies whose shares they own, and it's virtually impossible for them to do the same for companies based in Brazil, Poland or the Philippines. The U.S. managers of foreign funds will watch the local economies like hawks, looking for signs of trouble and for new opportunities.

Stay away from single-country mutual funds, because an economic crisis in that one country will send your fund shares into a tailspin. That goes for single-region mutual funds, too, unless you plan to own several single-region funds for diversification. For global investing, stick to mutual funds that own shares in companies all over the developing world. For extra stability, look for funds that also include some North American, European and Japanese multinational companies.

In these so-called global and international funds, managers can move your investment dollars all over the world, loading up on companies in regions that are poised for strong growth and lightening their positions in economies that look overpriced and ripe for a sharp correction. But no manager is omniscient, so don't rule out the possibility that the fund will sometimes be caught dangerously heavy in a given nation or region when it hits choppy waters and stocks sink under global selling pressures, as happened in the Asia crisis.

# CHAPTER 21

# Postscript: The Kiplinger Record

Y our confidence in any prediction will be based, fairly or not, on the past performance of the forecaster. To help you judge the plausibility of the forecasts in this book, we want to tell you a little about how the Kiplinger organization has done on calling major economic, demographic and technological changes over the past 75 years, since first publication of *The Kiplinger Letter*.

We don't keep a scorecard or calculate a batting average on our forecasts. We've had our share of strikeouts and our share of home runs, and our faithful subscribers remind us of both.

In the discussion that follows, we'll tell you, as best we can recall and history reminds us, how our judgment related to the conventional wisdom of the times and forecasts being made by others. We make no claims of being the first or only voice to make a certain forecast; accurate forecasts, like scientific breakthroughs, often occur simultaneously to people working independently.

## 1920S: ON A SUNNY DAY, STORM CLOUDS IN THE DISTANCE

Throughout the business boom and public euphoria of the '20s, *The Kiplinger Letter* felt a duty to remind its readers of underappreciated and growing economic problems, including the long slump in the enormous agricultural sector, rising urban unemployment from factory automation, and import competition from revived European manufacturers.

In the spring of 1928, the *Letter* raised the specter of "difficult business ahead, next five years," and warned, "the (political) party which is in power between 1929 and 1933 will have more than its share of troubles and will have difficulty maintaining itself in the presidential elections of 1932."

As the stock-market mania reached dizzying heights, the *Letter* generally endorsed the judgment of such leading market observers as investment banker Paul Warburg and financial pundit Roger Babson that a major correction was coming.

A few weeks after the crash, the *Letter* surveyed its readers and detected "a spirit of caution on future commitments." These business people "may not be trimming expenses now, but they are prepared to do so" later, if necessary. "This is akin to the 'psychology of pessimism,' which many say is not warranted, but which they fear may get started anyway and do some unnecessary harm."

Five weeks after the crash, the *Letter* told its readers to expect a recession lasting well into 1930, but said "a serious depression is not on the business horizon."

## 1930S: LINGERING DEPRESSION AND APPROACHING WAR

The psychology of pessimism did, in fact, take hold with a vengeance, throughout the world. Whether this made it inevitable that a great depression would follow a great market crash, we'll never know. But it *is* known that governments all over, including in the U.S., bungled their possibly constructive role in a recovery in the first few years after the crash by imposing restrictive monetary policies and maintaining protectionist trade barriers ill-advisedly erected in the late '20s.

At the time, most people (including the staff of *The Kiplinger Letter*) didn't know that the Federal Reserve was dosing the economy with precisely the wrong monetary medicine between 1930 and 1933, by contracting the money supply an estimated 33%, as verified many years later in seminal research by economists Milton Friedman and Anna Schwartz.

In early 1936, after several years of business expansion that may or may not have been stimulated by the radical market restructurings of the New Deal, the *Letter* warned of the possibility of another contraction when New Deal spending began to trail off. In early 1937 it reiterated its forecast of a "moderate business recession." The so-called Roosevelt recession turned out to be a significant relapse for the fragile American economy, which was ultimately rescued from depression only by industrial conversion to fight World War II.

The *Letter* has always tried to alert readers to emerging technologies—sometimes still in the research-and-development stage or soon to be launched—that would have a major impact on business and society. In

1937, our list of "inventions which may make deep changes in things in the future" included: plastics, television, the "photo electric cell," "tray agriculture" (aquaculture or hydroponics), "facsimile transmission," air conditioning, the mechanical cotton picker, and synthetic cotton, wool and rubber. It noted that "social changes from new inventions never come without warning; there's always a period of advance notice. Thus planning is needed."

Beginning in the early '30s, the *Letter* warned of the likelihood of major regional wars in Europe and Asia. It repeatedly predicted—to disbelieving clients who were as isolationist as most Americans were— that the U.S. would find it virtually impossible to stay out of the European conflict.

## 1940S: PREDICTING POSTWAR BOOM THROUGH THE '50S

"War with Japan is a serious possibility...not yet a probability," the *Letter* staff wrote in the fall of 1940. One year later, the *Letter* said, "Naval war with Japan now threatens, but is merely the opener, and the major objective is Hitler."

From the beginning of America's entry into World War II, the *Letter* presumed several years of war and an Allied victory, and it began preparing its business clients for the shape of the postwar world. At the start of the war and well into it, most economists and politicians believed that an abrupt collapse of military production and employment at war's end would plunge the country and the world back into the depression. But the *Letter* sided with a minority view that held that, after a brief recession for peacetime conversion, pent-up consumer demand would explode into a high-growth expansion.

Just three weeks after Pearl Harbor, the *Letter* predicted "boom activity for years after war," and added, "Especially a boom for those industries which are cut down during war...and notably the durable goods industries." A year later, the *Letter* said the postwar boom would be fueled in part by "new products, new processes, new industries coming out of the war, or out of the stimulation which war has given to technology."

Shortly before the end of the war, the *Letter* devoted space to demographic trends that would play a powerful role in business for years to come: "West Coast will gain most heavily;" "rims of cities will expand fast...the suburban areas;" "3–4 million more marriages will occur soon after men return;" "total births per year are the highest in history and will hold at a high level for several more years."

In the last month of 1949, the *Letter* offered these forecasts for the

1950s: "Generally prosperous business; living standards higher, despite a creeping inflation; some sort of a slump by the middle 1950s, but no deep depression like the early '30s; political trend, leftward; taxes will stay high, spending will stay high…by either party."

## 1950s: Forecast of the 'Soaring Sixties'

That call turned out to be pretty good, including the one recession in the '50s, though it ended up arriving later in the decade. Over the course of the 1950s, the *Letter* took note of a surge of Japanese imports (1952), the positive effects of racial desegregation (1954), and the likelihood that "electronic office machines" (digital computers and automatic printers) would revolutionize record keeping, accounting, billing, and inventory control in countless industries, including insurance, retailing, publishing and banking (1953).

Toward the end of the decade, U.S. growth was slowing and approaching a recession, and the public mood was very gloomy. But the *Letter*, in 1957, looked out a few years and forecast a boom of unprecedented strength, accompanied by rising inflation.

The Kiplinger editors dubbed the coming decade "The Soaring Sixties," a phrase that would creep into the public vocabulary. The boom would be driven by demographics—the growing up of the enormous postwar baby-boom generation—and by new technology. Growth in the economy would run about 4% a year through most of the decade.

## 1960s: Seeds of Trouble Ahead in the '70s

The U.S. economy did grow strongly from 1961 through 1969, in the longest business-cycle expansion in U.S. history up to that time. It was fueled not just by robust consumer demand but also by accelerating government spending on social programs and the war in Southeast Asia. This "guns and butter" approach to keeping the public happy without tight monetary policy or tax hikes would lead to problems, the *Letter* warned. "We are entering a long period of inflation," we wrote in 1967. "In ten years, inflation of nearly 25%, when compounded yearly."

This inflation warning turned out to be sound but understated. The *Letter* did not foresee that the inflationary pressures of war and the Great Society programs would be exacerbated by a tenfold increase in the price of petroleum, triggered by Arab oil embargoes in 1973 and 1979. The *Letter* also didn't foresee the extent of U.S. economic stagnation, when corporate profits, employee earnings and stock prices would be battered by high inflation and surging global competition in industries such as steel and autos.

## 1970S: AMID ECONOMIC DECAY, FORECASTS OF A NEW BOOM

The '70s was a time of growing pessimism about the nation's future, and not without cause. In 1977, the *Letter* warned that America's longtime "edge in manufacturing technology is being progressively chipped away...in Germany, Japan, other industrial nations." If this trend were not reversed by a new capital-spending commitment to boost productivity, we warned, "U.S. will become less competitive" both at home and in export markets, "which will bring renewed efforts to provide more protection from imports."

But during the same period, the *Letter* frequently noted that foreign investment was beginning to flood into the U.S., in part because, as we wrote in 1978, "many U.S. firms are UNDERvalued on the stock market." In short, "America looks better abroad than it does to many at home. Maybe distance gives better perspective."

Following the theory that every excess is self-correcting, especially in so feisty and adaptive a nation as the United States, the Kiplinger staff looked for signs that America's tough problems were about to be addressed by American business. It found plenty of evidence that something important was about to happen—a spurt in U.S. manufacturing productivity and competitiveness, due in part to radical downsizing of industry but also to a burst in capital spending.

The *Letter* began to report this as-yet-unappreciated trend in 1978: "Long-term outlook is better...beginning with the early Eighties." "Productivity gains will start picking up then, rather strongly; these lines will boost productivity dramatically in the Eighties: Computers. Electronic components. Medical services. Office services. Synthetic fibers. Chemicals. Drugs. Housing. Air transportation. Improvement in these will give a boost to others, which will add up to a rise in TOTAL productivity in years just ahead."

In a book published in 1979, *The Exciting '80s*, Kiplinger editors acknowledged the deep malaise hanging over the usually upbeat American people: "They are somber, worried, unsure of their future...of the country's future." Above all, "there seems to be a nagging fear that the depression of the '30s may repeat itself." But "the conclusion of this book," we wrote, "is that the fear of a devastating bust is unwarranted. It's not going to happen." As a matter of fact, "one of the major periods of business growth in the nation's history is just ahead; it will begin in another year or two and persist through the decade of the '80s. There will be an occasional stumble here and there, intervals of uncertainty and pause. But overall, a strong business expansion is coming."

At this time some best-selling books by such authors as Harry

Browne and Douglas Casey were urging investors to continue shunning the stock market and to adopt a survivalist, "crisis investing" mentality, while awaiting worse times ahead. In this climate, Kiplinger's forecast was wildly—some said laughably—out of step with broad public sentiment and popular writings in the press.

*The Exciting '80s* forecast a U.S. GNP of $6 trillion in 1990, more than twice the 1980 figure. (The actual figure for fiscal 1990 turned out to be $6.1 trillion.) With inflation running at 13% in 1979, we predicted that the average annual rate for the 1980s would be cut in half to about 7%, with the rate trending down over the course of the decade. The actual average annual CPI increase for the '80s turned out to be a little over 5%. With the Dow Jones industrial average stagnating well under 1000 for most of the '70s, Kiplinger advised readers in 1979 to "invest now and get in early for the growth ahead."

## 1980S: FORECASTS OF U.S. GLOBAL LEADERSHIP IN THE '90S

Kiplinger's prediction of the start of a great business boom "in a year or two"—that is, by the end of 1981—was a little premature. What's more, things got a lot more grim between 1979 and the end of 1981. Before Paul Volcker's Federal Reserve Board began its all-out attack on inflation, the first year of the new decade saw the prime interest rate hit an all-time high of 21.5%. In the severe industrial recession of 1981–1982, unemployment hit the highest level in five decades, a shade under 11% in the fall of 1982. From the farm belt to the factories of the Midwest, misery abounded. Once again, there was widespread speculation in academic circles and the press that a bad recession would deepen into a true depression.

While Kiplinger editors had not anticipated the depth of this business slump, we stood by our earlier judgment that the resulting restructuring of American business would lay the groundwork for a resurgent, high-growth economy during the rest of the '80s.

We continued to be a pretty lonely voice of dissent in a wilderness of economic despair, but a few other voices (some of them sources of ours) sounded similar themes. During the 1982 recession, Herman Kahn of the Hudson Institute published a bravely contrarian thesis, *The Coming Boom*. He wrote: "A revitalized America—in terms of traditional values, of worldwide status and influence, and of citizenship and morale, as well as of economic improvement—seems to me very probable, and with sensible social and economic policies, a near certainty."

The recession came to an end that fall, the stock market took off like a skyrocket, and America embarked on what would be one of the longest expansions in any nation's history—a 15-year climb inter-rupted by only one brief, mild recession from the fall of 1990 through the spring of 1991. The U.S. had taken its bitter medicine, regained its competitive footing in world markets and emerged stronger than ever.

But many Americans in the '80s remained deeply skeptical that the country was fully recovered. They were anxious about many things: job insecurity (a permanent part of the new economic land-scape); heavy foreign investment (especially Japanese); the "twin deficits" in the federal budget and foreign trade; and the apparent omnipotence of Japan as a world competitor. Their anxiety seemed confirmed by a slowdown in economic growth that occurred in the late '80s, the savings and loan debacle, and the subsequent collapse of overheated commercial real estate markets in many large cities. Despite worldwide euphoria over the disintegration of the Soviet empire and the potential defense savings from the cessation of the Cold War, many Americans remained unsure, almost suspicious, of their growing economic power.

The concept of "America in decline" continued to hold sway in the public arena. One of the biggest-selling books of the 1980s was Ravi Batra's off-the-wall *The Great Depression of 1990* (published in 1988), which he predicted would be "the world's greatest depression," even worse than the 1930s—in short, "the worst economic crisis in history." Few serious observers agreed with Batra's forecast, but numerous high-ly respected academic analysts foresaw a long, insidious decline for America—either in absolute living standards, or simply relative to other nations, or both. The most influential proponent of this view has been the English historian and Yale professor Paul Kennedy, author of *The Rise and Fall of the Great Powers* (1988) and *Preparing for the Twenty-first Century* (1992).

The broad public assumption that Japan would soon supplant, or had already supplanted, the U.S. as the world's dominant economic power was fueled by such books as Clyde Prestowitz's *Trading Places* (1988), a badly flawed thesis that sold vastly more copies than a bril-liantly farsighted book the following year, *The Sun Also Sets*, by *Economist* editor Bill Emmott.

Kiplinger believed that America in the '80s wasn't in the early stage of a long decline, but just the opposite—the early stage of what would be a long, positive reshaping of our economy and our society. We said so in a 1986 book, *The New American Boom*, and restated the thesis three years later in *America in the Global '90s*. As journalists, we were hearing of these remarkable changes from our sources, men and women in management, in science and engineering, in education and government.

We were influenced by the opinions of many other keen observers of economics and technology, who were finding and reporting signs of remarkable changes ahead—people like George Gilder, a trenchant debunker of a peculiarly American malady he dubbed "economic hypochondria," and *Wall Street Journal* editor Robert Bartley. Julian Simon, the brilliant University of Maryland and Cato Institute economist, provided scholarly yet readable evidence of the long trend of improving world living standards. Ben Wattenberg, of the American Enterprise Institute, demolished myth after myth of alleged American decline in his informative and entertaining 1984 book *The Good News Is The Bad News Is Wrong*. A compelling look at the rise of Asia—and America's benefit from that rise—was provided by Joel Kotkin and Yoriko Kishimoto in *The Third Century (America's Resurgence in the Asian Era)*, published in 1988.

But as the '80s drew to a close, the dominant forecast for the coming decade, at least in the popular press, was pretty gloomy. To many observers, the slower growth of the late '80s foreshadowed a decade of American economic stagnation. The '80s were broadly characterized as a wild party from which Americans would awaken with a severe economic hangover that would last through most of the next decade, with low growth, declining world market share in exports, and declining domestic living standards. We disagreed, viewing the late-'80s slowdown as a normal phase of breath-catching, after which the U.S. economy would resume robust growth throughout the '90s. The United States, we believed, would continue to be the world's most influential nation in technology and economic and political leadership.

Among our 1989 forecasts in *America in the Global '90s* were GDP growth averaging 3% through the 1990s, declining interest rates, and strong growth in U.S. productivity, especially in manufacturing. We also said the federal budget deficit—then running $152 billion—would shrink and possibly disappear by the end of the '90s, due to soaring federal revenues, restrained spending and—most of all—the trick of using the surplus in social security taxes to fund current operations of government. And that's just how things had turned out by 1998.

With the Dow in the low 2000s, we told readers to expect a tripling during the '90s, finishing off at about 6000. That sounded outlandishly high to most investors, but we reminded them that this would represent merely a typical decade of price appreciation for blue-chip stocks, based on historical performance over many years. We saw no reason to expect any less in the coming decade.

Our 1989 judgment on what lay ahead for the '90s was greatly out of sync with mainstream thinking, especially as portrayed in the popular press and academic circles. Differing with the thesis of Japanese-preeminence, economist Lester Thurow, dean of the Sloan School of Business at MIT, predicted that an economically integrated Europe would pull away from the U.S. in the '90s. But the "U.S. in decline" school also got skillful rebuttals from international businessman Charles Morris, in his marvelously prescient *The Coming Global Boom* (1990), and from international affairs professor Henry Nau, in *The Myth of America's Decline* (1990). John Naisbitt and Patricia Aburdene enjoyed deserved bestseller success with their persuasively optimistic *Megatrends 2000* (1990).

## 1990s: STAYING THE COURSE TO THE YEAR 2000

These late-'80s judgments about a resurgent America didn't look very good during the first three years of the '90s. There was a brief recession in the fall of 1990 through the spring of 1991, caused primarily by a sudden collapse of consumer spending when Americans, both fascinated and worried by the coming war in the Persian Gulf, glued themselves to their televisions and abandoned shopping malls and car showrooms.

America was also trying to handle, with painful difficulty, much more fundamental readjustments. Some regions, such as New England and California, were mired not in a brief, mild recession but in a long, painful restructuring, in some areas caused by sharp cutbacks in defense and aerospace spending. Corporate downsizing continued at a brisk clip in the early '90s, deepening job insecurity and eroding the income of many laid-off middle managers who didn't earn as much in their next jobs. Unemployment rose to almost 7.5% in the spring. Despair was deepened by the specter of recessions in Japan and Europe, which many had previously viewed as being economically more vibrant than the U.S.

A *Newsweek* article in the fall of 1991 said, "Americans feel gloomy, almost desperate, about the future of the economy," and a *Washington Post* story that same week cited a poll revealing a rising tide of "pessimism and political powerlessness" in the American people.

Lugubriousness about America's future role in the world was deepened by the presidential campaign of 1992, when President George Bush, a wise but inarticulate president, failed to make the case for a strengthening America and was badly outdebated by the two best talkers in American politics, Bill Clinton and Ross Perot. Bush's challengers painted a vivid but highly inaccurate picture of America as an ailing giant, facing (unless the Republicans were turned out of office) a certain future of persistent budget deficits, sluggish productivity growth, stagnant wages and eroding competitiveness in world markets.

In fact, in the fall of 1992, all of these claimed crises were either unfounded or were well along the road to correction. After Clinton's victory, it was learned that the U.S. economy had been growing at the brisk rate of nearly 4% at the time of the election, and it would pick up steam through the following year.

The rest of the story is one you know pretty well. Led by a revitalized manufacturing sector and explosive growth in high-value services, the U.S. economy set the pace for the world, opening up more daylight on our closest competitors. Meanwhile, several of our major trading partners, especially Japan and Europe, languished in recession, seemingly unwilling to take the bitter medicine of major economic restructuring and opening of markets.

Here in America, exports boomed and the U.S. gained market share in many fields. (The trade deficit actually expanded, but with exports growing and the economy strong, the deficit became the non-issue it should usually be.) Corporate profits soared, bringing stock prices along for a wild ride upward. Job creation was awesome, especially in high-skill, high-wage jobs, and especially in small and medium-size firms. Inflation remained low. Unemployment dropped to less than 5%. Real wages continued their modest advances of the '80s. Due mostly to strong economic growth, but with a boost from tax hikes and spending restraints, the federal budget deficit shrank to virtually nothing by the end of the decade (helped greatly, by, of course, the social security "surplus").

Credit for most of this belonged to the private sector, but governments at all levels played an unusually positive (or benign) role in the process. Clinton moved to the political center on most issues, becoming a old-style Republican "balanced-budget hawk" and championing free trade. On trade and other economic issues, he worked better with the new GOP majority on the Hill than with the congressional leadership of his own party. But Washington wasn't the governmental star of the '90s. State and local governments, many of them led by GOP governors, mayors and legislators, were innovators and pathfinders, setting the pace in improving business climates with tax and regulatory reductions.

# Keep Looking Ahead

There are no perfect records in forecasting, as anyone who ever prepared an annual budget (or, with much dread, a five-year business plan) knows too well. When budgets come out just right, if often means that your errors offset each other very neatly, and the same is sometimes true of economic forecasting.

Professional forecasters can console themselves in the knowledge that the best hitters in baseball manage to hit safely in only about three out of every ten trips to the plate. But forecasters who want to continue practicing their craft had better aspire to, and achieve, a higher batting average than that. Successful forecasting means getting things right most of the time, with relatively few enormous miscalculations and more than your share of accurate calls on the big picture—the effect of economics, demographics and technology on daily life.

No one knows how the next few decades will turn out. This book contains simply our best judgments. Our forecasts are informed by our current reporting, drawing upon the wisdom of the best sources we can find. Our judgment is also informed by our staff's institutional memory—our knowledge, gained through many years of this work, of how the world handled the many enormous challenges it faced in the past.

The slogan of the Kiplinger organization, printed across the upper left corner of every *Kiplinger Letter* for many years, is the simple imperative to LOOK AHEAD. When W.M. Kiplinger founded the *Kiplinger Magazine* (now *Kiplinger's Personal Finance Magazine*) in 1947, he said its mission was to help you "peer ahead and see straight." We still feel that way. As useful as history is, you won't find the future in your rearview mirror. Future success always belongs to those who can look ahead most clearly. Success belongs to the most adaptive, flexible and creative individuals—those who can feel the winds of change shifting in a different direction, enabling them to adjust their sails and change their course.

You have our best wishes for success in making your own accommodations with the exhilarating and daunting changes that lie ahead.

# Index

foreign-owned facilities, 53-55
growth capital, 45-48
inflation, 41-42, 63-66
interest rates, 65-66, 183-184
intergovernmental relations, 125-126
investment destinations, 56
investment rate, 45
land resources, 38, 42, 199
lifestyle changes, 10-14
median age, 167
military alliances and preparedness, 204
nuclear capability, 206
overall forecast, 48
overseas business, 55-57
percent of world production, 42
productivity increase, 43-44
prosperity, 9
quality of life and human values, 161-163
recessions, 68
regional boosts, 54
reindustrialization, 60
savings, 42, 45-47
service industry weakness, 44
stocks (See Equities, U.S.)
top achiever, 70
trading partners, 52, 74-75, 93, 95, 97
world GDP, 8-9, 23
United Technologies, 55, 79
University of California, San Diego, 260
University of California at Irvine, 187
University of Chicago, 187
University of Maryland, 144, 388
University of Michigan, 195, 373
Population Studies Center, 178
University of Pennsylvania, 230
University of Phoenix, 129
University of South Carolina, 144
University of Southern California, 253
Unskilled labor, 365
Upjohn, 323, 339

Urban Institute, 132
Urbanization, 36-37, 38, 169-172
Uruguay, 95, 98
U.S. dollar, 57-59, 214
U.S. Enrichment Corporation, 207
U.S. Patent Commission, 26
U.S. Treasury, 83
US Airways, 339

**V**

Vacation homes and time-shares, 303-304
Vaccines, 12, 250, 252
Vanderbilt University, 144
Venezuela, 96-97, 279
Vietnam, 25, 55, 70, 91, 92, 182
Villaraigosa, Antonio, 189
Virginia Tech, 144
Virtual banks, 270, 271
Virtual college, 129
Virtual corporations, 3
Virtual reality, 13, 227-228, 258-259
Virtual retailers, 233, 293-294
Visa, 334
Vocational education, 63, 130-132
Voice-activated/recognition systems, 13, 227
Volcker, Paul, 386
Volkswagen, 310
Volvo, 102, 310
VW-Audi, 79

**W**

Wages, 67, 359-360
comparable worth, 359-360
growth restraints, 152
management, 155, 340-342
service sector, 63
standard of living, 149-152
Wales, 74
The Wall Street Journal, 25, 49, 70, 224, 388
Wal-Mart, 295, 297
Wang, 343
Wang, Charles B., 341
Warburg, Paul, 382
Warfare, global trends, 38-39
Warsaw Pact, 204
The Washington Post, 21, 183, 195, 238, 253, 297, 332,

366, 389
The Washington Times, 352
Water supply, 37-38, 285-286
Wattenberg, Ben, 172, 388
Weapons, 205-208, 316-317
Weather Channel, 208
WebTV, 240
Weil, Sanford, 345
Wellness programs, 276
West Europe, 7, 20, 22, 23, 26, 48, 73, 310
See also Europe; specific countries
Westinghouse, 322, 323
Whirlpool, 55
Willadsen, Steen, 254
Women
employment, 61-62, 339, 347, 355, 356
empowerment, 39-40
female-headed households, 159
income inequality, 155-156
single mothers, 151
standard of living, 145, 150-151
Workplace standards, 330-331
Workweek length, 347-348
World Bank, 7, 23, 36, 91, 99
World Competitive Yearbook, 82
World Policy Institute, 170
World Trade Organization (WTO), 20, 75, 81
WorldCom, 33, 125, 342
Worldspace, 242
Worldwatch Institute, 167
WTO. See World Trade Organization

**X**
Xerox, 60

**Y**
Yamaichi Securities, 84
Yellen, Janet, 122
Yeltsin, Boris, 104
Yemen, 100
Yen, 83
Yugoslavia, 39, 80, 206

**Z**
Zambia, 103
Zimbabwe, 103, 104